Reimagining the Bible

By Howard Schwartz

POETRY
Vessels
Gathering the Sparks
Sleepwalking Beneath the Stars

FICTION
A Blessing Over Ashes
Midrashim
The Captive Soul of the Messiah
Rooms of the Soul
Adam's Soul
The Four Who Entered Paradise

EDITOR
Imperial Messages: One Hundred Modern Parables
Voices Within the Ark: The Modern Jewish Poets
Gates to the New City: A Treasury of Modern Jewish Tales
The Dream Assembly: Tales of Rabbi Zalman Schachter-Shalomi
Elijah's Violin & Other Jewish Fairy Tales
Miriam's Tambourine: Jewish Tales from Around the World
Lilith's Cave: Jewish Tales of the Supernatural
Gabriel's Palace: Jewish Mystical Tales
First Harvest: Jewish Writing in St. Louis, 1991–1996

ESSAYS
Reimagining the Bible: The Storytelling of the Rabbis

CHILDREN'S BOOKS
The Diamond Tree
The Sabbath Lion
Next Year in Jerusalem
The Wonder Child
A Coat for the Moon

Reimagining the Bible

The Storytelling of the Rabbis

HOWARD SCHWARTZ

New York   Oxford   Oxford University Press   1998

Oxford University Press

Oxford   New York
Athens   Auckland   Bangkok   Bogota   Bombay   Buenos Aires
Calcutta   Cape Town   Dar es Salaam   Delhi   Florence   Hong Kong
Istanbul   Karachi   Kuala Lumpur   Madras   Madrid   Melbourne
Mexico City   Nairobi   Paris   Singapore   Taipei   Tokyo   Toronto   Warsaw

and associated companies in
Berlin   Ibadan

Published by Oxford University Press, Inc.
198 Madison Avenue, New York, New York 10016

Oxford is a registered trademark of Oxford University Press

Library of Congress Cataloging-in-Publication Data
Schwartz, Howard, 1945–
Reimagining the Bible : the storytelling of the rabbis / Howard Schwartz.
p. cm.
Includes bibliographical references and index.
ISBN 0-19-510499-4; 0-19-511511-2 (pbk.)
1. Aggada—History and criticism. 2. Midrash—History and criticism.
3. Jews—Folklore—History and criticism. 4. Mysticism—Judaism—History.
5. Jewish literature—History and criticisim.
I. Title.
BM516.5.S39   1998
296.1'9—dc20   96-31594

The cover illustration is a detail from *Abraham and Isaac* by Los Angeles artist John August Swanson, who
is represented by the Bergsma Gallery, Grand Rapids, MI; (616) 458–1776. Full-color reproductions of
Swanson's work are available from the National Association for Hispanic Elderly, 3325 Wilshire Blvd., Suite
800, Los Angeles, CA 90010; (213) 487-1922. Benefits go to its programs of employment of seniors and to
housing low-income seniors.

1   3   5   7   9   8   6   4   2
Printed in the United States of America
on acid-free paper

For Cynthia Read

"Turn it and turn it over again and again, for everything is in it, and contemplate it, and wax gray and grow old over it, and stir not from it, for you cannot have any better rule than this."

Mishnah Avot 5.22

"Ben Azzai was sitting and expounding Torah, and a flame was burning around him. They said to him: 'Are you perhaps engaged in the study of the Mysteries of the Chariot?' He replied: 'No, I am but finding in the Torah parallels to the Prophets, and in the Prophets parallels to the Aggadah. And the words of the Torah are joyful even as they were on the day they were given at Sinai, and they were originally given in fire, as it is said, *And the mountain burned with fire.*' " (Deut 4:11).

Leviticus Rabbah 16:4

"To be in the book . . . to be part of it. To be responsible for a word or a sentence, a stanza or chapter."

Edmond Jabes, *The Book of Questions*

Contents

Part III   Mythic Echoes

Part IV   Modern Jewish Literature
and the Ancient Models

Preface

There is an unbroken chain of tradition linking all of Jewish literature from the Bible to the present. The Bible serves as the foundation stone on which this literary edifice has been built. Yet, though every generation of Jewish literature hearkens back to this first, primary phase, each also has a distinctive character of its own, declaring its loyalty and its independence in the same breath. Instead of remaining fixed, once they were written down, the biblical myths and legends continued to evolve. As a result, there is an ongoing process of reimagining the Bible found in virtually all postbiblical Jewish texts.

Here the history of Adam and Eve is recounted after they were expelled from the Garden; Cain, with a horn growing from his forehead, is said to have been killed by his own descendants, Lamech and Tubal-Cain; Noah is said to have brought a giant with him, who sat on top of the ark; Abraham is reported to have slain Isaac after all; and Moses to have ascended all the way into heaven to receive the Torah. Thus were these biblical stories embellished, taking on a life of their own.

With a natural desire to know more about their heroes, and an overwhelming impulse to resolve all the problems in the biblical text, the ancient rabbis drew on the oral tradition they had received and cultivated it, giving birth, in the process, to a rich and vital legendary tradition. Yet it must never be forgotten that the original impulse out of which these legends were created was exegetical. Great importance was put on resolving contradictions and filling gaps in the narrative. In this way the rabbis sought to discover the nature of the light of the first day, when God said, *Let there be light*, since God did not create the sun and moon until the fourth day.

So too did they seek to learn more about the childhood of Abraham and the death of Cain, about which nothing is said in the Bible. To find these answers, the rabbis searched not only in the black letters of the revealed Torah, but in the white letters of the hidden Torah as well.

Remarkably, the desire to explicate every hidden truth in the Torah gave birth to a rich legendary tradition, revealed in fragments scattered through every period of Jewish literature. Ultimately, detailed accounts of heaven and hell emerge, creating a fantastic geography. Here the cave of Machpelah is side by side with the Garden of Eden, while the horn of the ram that Abraham sacrificed in place of Isaac will be blown by Elijah at the End of Days. What emerges is a legendary chain, linking together all of the generations. Yet how is it possible that the same rabbis who revered the Torah as the literal word of God gave themselves the astonishing freedom to change the very biblical text they hallowed?

The answer lies in the unique nature of the dual traditions of the Written Torah and the Oral Torah. The former sets down the binding covenant between God and Israel, as well as the primary myths and legends. But it is accompanied by the Oral Law, an oral tradition as ancient as the written one, which comments on, interprets, and often embellishes the original text, in the process transforming it. Both traditions were regarded as equally valid, both stemming from God at Mount Sinai. As one legend puts it, during the day God dictated the Torah to Moses, and at night He explained it to him. Thus the legendary tradition that emerges in the postbiblical literature finds its basis in this Oral Law, attributing every assertion "to Moses at Mount Sinai." This resulted in an exceptionally rich literary tradition, spanning both sacred and secular literatures, with countless links between every phase of the tradition.

This method of transformation can be identified as the midrashic method, in which the rabbis not only drew upon existing oral traditions, but actively sought out new meanings and interpretations of the sacred text. These rabbinic commentaries and legends were first collected in the Babylonian and Jerusalem Talmuds, and in the multitude of midrashic collections. Later these same legends were further transformed in the kabbalistic era and in medieval Jewish folklore. They underwent yet another phase in their development during the hasidic period, and yet another during the era of modern Jewish literature.

Thus Jewish literature is very much like an archeological dig, with every generation built on the previous one. Thus Hasidic literature is built on the Kabbalistic, and the Kabbalistic is built on the rabbinic literature of the Talmud and Midrash. And at the bedrock of all Jewish literature is the Hebrew Bible, especially the first five books of the Torah. This has created a remarkably unified tradition, despite being drawn from both sacred and secular sources, and coming from far-flung realms.

It is both that continuity and diversity that these essays seek to discuss, as well as to identify the primary genres of Jewish literature and the nature of the literary development that took place. The first section of this book, "The Ancient Models," presents the principles of the midrashic method, outlines the development of the legendary tradition, and discusses the tools developed for interpretation of these sacred texts, texts that permitted multiple interpretations, often of a contradictory nature, which were all regarded as legitimate.

The second section examines the folk tradition and considers two specific types of Jewish folktales, the fairy tale and the tale of the supernatural. So too are the negative implications of the key legend of Lilith discussed, in contrast to the positive role model offered by Eve.

The third section considers the mythic elements displayed in these works. There is an attempt to define the mythology of Judaism, as well as the legendary aspect of the Jewish mystical tradition, and the psychological implications of the primary motif of the quest that so pervades the Jewish legendary tradition.

The final section considers the influence of Rabbi Nachman of Bratslav in the formation of a modern literary tradition, discusses the role of the ancient models in the creation of a modern Jewish literature, and examines specific Jewish themes and motifs found in a variety of modern Jewish texts.

Throughout, the key principles of the midrashic method can be seen to serve each new literary generation, although the focus and intent of the authors may change considerably, especially about whether the texts created are regarded as sacred or secular. These principles make it possible to recognize how Jewish literature has followed a path established very early in the tradition, and how it has remained true to that path even as it transformed that very tradition while, at the same time, preserving it.

I would like to note the following personal acknowledgments: To my editor, Cynthia Read, for her consistent encouragement and support; to Muriel Jorgensen, for her valuable editing of the manuscript; to my wife, Tsila, for her patience over the years these essays were written; and to Dov Noy and Edna Hechal of the Israel Folktale Archives, who have done more than anyone else to keep Jewish folklore alive; and to the following, whose assistance made the completion of this book possible: Dina Abramovitch of YIVO, Jennifer Accardo, Rabbi Tsvi Blanchard, MaryBeth Branigan, Marc Bregman, Daniel Breslauer, Deborah Brodie, the late Rabbi Shlomo Carelebach, Clayton Carlson, Michael Castro, Ellen Chodosh, Robert A. Cohn, Sarah Blacher Cohen, Joseph Dan, Laya Firestone-Seghi, Ellen Frankel, Jeremy Garber, Pinhas Giller, Reuven Goldfarb, Rabbi James Stone Goodman, the late Robert Gordis, David Green, Joel Grishaver, Edna Hechal, Aron Hirt-Manheimer, Rabbi Terrence Jones, Rodger Kamenetz, the Khanem family, Leah Kramer, Arthur Kurzweil, Rabbi Yosef Landa, Charles Larson, Ellen Levine and Diana Finch of the Ellen Levine Literary Agency, the late Rabbi Zvi Magence, Daniel Matt, Donny Maseng, David Meltzer, Rabbi Abraham Ezra Millgram, the late Eugene Murrary, Gedalya Nigal,

Dov Noy, Arielle North Olson, Clarence Olson, Cynthia Ozick, the late Raphael Patai, Barbara Raznick, Steven Rowan, Linda Robbins, Barbara Rush, Marc Saperstein, the late Gershom Scholem, Peninnah Schram, Henry Schvey, Charles Schwartz, Maury Schwartz, Nathan B. Schwartz, Rabbi Zalman Schachter-Shalomi, Dan Sharon, Aliza Shenhar, Byron Sherwin, the late Morton Smith, Y. David Shulman, Ted Solotaroff, Ida Stack, Mary Ann Steiner, Steve Stern, Rabbi Jeffrey Stiffman, Michael Stone, John Swanson, Michael Swartz, Rabbi Susan Talve, Shlomo Vinner, Ruth Waxman, Rabbi Gershon Winkler, Jane Williamson, the late Yehuda Yaari, and Eli Yassif. I also wish to acknowledge the University of Missouri–St. Louis, which provided research leaves that assisted in the completion of this book.

Acknowledgments

ome of these essays, in earlier versions, were previously published in the
following journals and anthologies, to whose editors grateful acknowledgment is made:

"Reimagining the Bible" in *Response.*
"The Aggadic Tradition" in *Judaism* and in *Origins of Judaism*, Volume I,
    Part 3, edited by Jacob Neusner (New York and London: Garland Pub-
    lishing, 1990).
"Tools of Interpretation" in *Agada.*
"On Jewish Fairy Tales" in *The Melton Journal.*
"Mermaid and Siren: The Polar Roles of Lilith and Eve" in *The Sagarin
    Review.*
"Jewish Tales of the Supernatural" in *Judaism.*
"The Mythology of Judaism" in *The Seductiveness of Jewish Myth: Chal-
    lenge or Response*, edited by S. Daniel Breslauer (Albany: Suny Press:
    1997).
Part I, "The Quest for the Lost Princess" in *Judaism* and in *Opening the
    Inner Gates: New Paths in Kabbalah and Psychology*, edited by Ed-
    ward Hoffman (Boston: Shambhala: 1995), and in *The Fifty-Eighth
    Century: A Jewish Renewal Sourcebook*, edited by Shohama Harris
    Wiener (Northvale, N.J.: Jason Aronson, 1996). Part II, "The Quest
    for Jerusalem" in *Judaism.*
"Rabbi Nachman of Bratslav: Forerunner of Modern Jewish Literature" in
    Judaism.

"S. Y. Agnon, I. L. Peretz, and I. B. Singer: Modern Masters of the *Aggadah*" in *Jewish Frontier.*

"Modern Jewish Literature and the Ancient Models" in *Midstream.*

Sections of "Tales of the Great Jewish Mystics" appeared in *The Forward* ("A Trove of Jewish Mystical Tales"), *Parabola* ("Spirit Possession in Jewish Lore"), and *Tikkun* ("Tales of the Great Jewish Mystics"). The complete essay was published as The Daniel K. Kosland Memorial Lecture (San Francisco: The Congregation Emanu'el, 1997).

Some of these essays are reprinted from the following books by Howard Schwartz:

From *Gates to the New City: A Treasury of Modern Jewish Tales*:
    "Reimagining the Bible," "The Aggadic Tradition," "Rabbi Nachman of Bratslav: Forerunner of Modern Jewish Literature," "Modern Jewish Literature and the Ancient Models," "S. Y. Agnon, I. L. Peretz, and I. B. Singer: Modern Masters of the *Aggadah*," and "Tools of Interpretation." Reprinted by permission of Jason Aronson Inc.

From *Elijah's Violin & Other Jewish Fairy Tales*:
    "On Jewish Fairy Tales." Reprinted by permission of Oxford University Press.

From *Lilith's Cave: Jewish Tales of the Supernatural*:
    "Jewish Tales of the Supernatural." Reprinted by permission of Oxford University Press.

From *Gabriel's Palace: Jewish Mystical Tales*:
    "Tales of the Great Jewish Mystics." Reprinted by permission of Oxford University Press.

"The Story of Lilith and Eve" by Jakov Lind is reprinted from *The Stove* by Jakov Lind with the permission of Sheep Meadow Press. Copyright © 1983 Jakov Lind.

"The Sacred Goat" is reprinted from *Tales of the Hasidim* by Martin Buber with the permission of Schocken books. Copyright © 1947 by Schocken Books Inc.

PART I

The Ancient Models

Reimagining the Bible

There is a great paradox and mystery at the core of rabbinic literature. On the one hand the ancient rabbis, the authors of the Talmud and Midrash, firmly believed that the Torah—the first five books of the Bible— had been dictated by God to Moses on Mount Sinai, that every word and letter of the Torah—even the crowns of the letters—were meaningful, and that the Torah contained all truth. On the other hand, they did not hesitate to embellish, retell, reimagine, or even radically change the stories of the Torah. How is it possible that the rabbis, who had the greatest possible reverence for the text of the Torah, permitted themselves this kind of literary license?

The answer lies in the existence of dual sacred traditions, both of which were said to have been received by Moses at Mount Sinai. For Moses is said to have received two Torahs: the Written Torah and the Oral Torah, each inextricably linked to the other. One midrash recounts that God dictated the Torah to Moses during the day, and at night He explained it to him.[1]

Indeed, there was such an oral tradition, which was not written down until long after the destruction of the Second Temple, when it became apparent that it would otherwise be lost. That is how the two Talmuds, the Babylonian Talmud and the Jerusalem Talmud, came to be written. It is certainly true that many of the legends found in the Talmud are of ancient origin,[2] but it is also apparent that the rabbis did not limit themselves to the oral tradition they had received—they continued to add to it extensively, and in the process legends emerged that are a radical departure from the biblical text.

One good example of this kind of midrashic revision of the text is found in several late midrashim about the *Akedah*, the Binding of Isaac.[3] In the biblical account in Genesis 22, Abraham is about to slay Isaac, when, at the last minute, the angel of the Lord tells him, *Lay not thy hand upon the lad, neither do thou anything unto him* (Gen. 22:12). It is clear from the text that Isaac was not sacrificed. But these late midrashim turn to the end of Genesis 22, where *Abraham returned unto his young men* (Gen. 22:19) where there is no mention of Isaac, and, noting Isaac's absence, they offer a midrashic revision of the original tale, in which Abraham *does* sacrifice Isaac, and Isaac's soul ascends to heaven. There he is shown all of Paradise, and, in some versions, studies for three years in the heavenly Academy of Shem and Eber, where he is taught all the mysteries of the Torah. Finally, after three years in Paradise, Isaac's soul returns to this world and he comes back to life, having been resurrected:[4]

> "When the blade touched his neck, the soul of Isaac fled and departed, but when he heard God's voice from between the two angels, saying to Abraham 'Lay not thine hand upon the lad' (Gen. 22:12), his soul returned to his body, and Abraham set him free, and Isaac stood upon his feet. And Isaac knew that in this way the dead in the future will be brought to life. He spoke and said: 'Blessed art thou, O Lord, who quickens the dead.' "

This is a radical and probably Christian-influenced legend.[5] The three years Isaac's soul is said to have spent in Paradise strongly echoes the resurrection of Jesus on the third day. This and a multitude of other rabbinic legends demonstrate the extreme midrashic license the rabbis felt that they were permitted to draw upon in the name of the Oral Tradition. These legends are known as *aggadot* (singular: *aggadah*), a particular form of Jewish legend that appears in the Talmud and later biblical elaborations known as the Midrash.[6] Because the rabbis thought that the answers to all inquiries could be found in the Bible, and especially in the first five books known as the Torah,[7] the whole ethical system of the Jews depended on the interpretation of these particular texts. And, perhaps inevitably, constant meditation of these same laws and legends led the rabbis to invent resolutions to the incomplete narratives and to discover the meaning of the obscure passages that are found, in particular, in the early books of the Bible. They sought to reduce, for example, the guilt of Eve that resulted from the sin of the Fall, or to shed light on the childhood of Abraham, the patriarch who was the first to have perception that there was only one God. For clues, the rabbis searched in the details of the given text, and since there often was little to go on, the conclusions drawn in these cases tended to reflect their creators as much as they resolved the unfinished tale.

Another example of the aggadic-midrashic method concerns Enoch, about whom the Bible says only *And Enoch walked with God, and he was not, for God took him* (Gen. 5:24). This statement, in the midst of a genealogical list, distinguishes Enoch from the others, about whom it is said, "And he died." But since even the slightest variation in biblical phrasing was taken to have profound significance, extensive conclusions were drawn from the unusual statement about his death. Enoch came to be described as one of the few righteous men in the evil generation preceding the Flood, who was taken up into Paradise at God's command and taught the secrets of heaven. Then he was returned to earth, to instruct men, and finally he was taken back into heaven, where he was transformed into the fiery angel Metatron, who became the heavenly scribe, the attendant of the Throne of Glory, the prince of the treasuries of heaven, the ruler and judge of all the hosts of angels, and executor of the Divine decrees on earth — quite a promotion for a figure who appears in only a brief passage in the Bible.[8]

As the examples of Isaac and Enoch make apparent, this imaginative opening out of biblical exegesis was utilized with remarkable freedom, under the circumstances. For in these postbiblical legends we find a literature that flowered under some of the most stringent restrictions ever devised by men. After all, the purpose of many midrashim was not primarily literary; they were an attempt to substantiate a point of the Law, clarify a contradiction in the biblical text, or offer an analogy. Like Adne Sadeh — a midrashic creature who was believed to have been created before man, and who was bound to the earth by his long navel cord and thus could move no farther than it reached — the legends of the Midrash had to remain linked to the biblical verses that served as proof-texts.

In each generation it has been the practice of the Jewish people to return to the Bible for guidance in both ethical and spiritual matters. The radical changes in culture and environment that they experienced over the ages made it necessary to interpret the biblical laws so that they would be applicable to their existence. Thus the Bible, and specifically the Torah, is not only the covenant between the people of Israel and God,[9] but it is also the source of the primary myths of the culture and the bedrock for all commentary, both in the halakhic, or legal, realm, and in the aggadic, or legendary, realm. Indeed, it is not difficult to understand why all subsequent sacred texts exist in the shadow of the Holy Scriptures.

It is generally acknowledged that some of the narratives in Genesis preserve myths that can be traced back at least four thousand years, and probably more. The composition of these myths was believed to have been begun approximately three thousand years ago. Once the Scriptures were canonized, the Book was regarded as closed. Evidence gathered by biblical scholars indicates that the texts of the oldest book of the Bible, Genesis, are likely reworkings of earlier texts, with subsequent interpolations. These scriptural texts have been handed down, essentially unchanged, since the rabbinic council at Yavneh around 90 C.E., although unshaken agreement about the scope of the canon of Hebrew Scriptures was not achieved until the middle of the 2nd century C.E.

Once the canon of the Bible was closed, the creativity of the People of the Book had nowhere to turn but back to the Bible. It was firmly believed that the answers to all questions could be found there, if one only had sufficient breadth and depth of knowledge to understand: "Turn it and turn it over again and again, for everything is in it, and contemplate it, and wax gray and grow old over it, and stir not from it, for you cannot have any better rule than this." [10]

However, the need to update the meaning of the Bible extended not only to the laws it contained but also to the stories themselves. These stories retained their immediacy because subsequent generations gave themselves to projecting themselves into the biblical archetypes and reliving the myths in themselves. In this way it was possible for the *Aggadah* to become a vehicle for the personal and mythic expressions of the people that could then be absorbed into the tradition, as well as a means of permitting the religion to evolve, which it did. The premise here is that a tradition must continually expand its boundaries in order to incorporate all generations at the same time.

Since an entire theological and legal system also depended on the interpretation of these particular texts, determining the resolution of certain incomplete biblical narratives took on extraordinary importance. Thus, perhaps inevitably, constant meditation on these same myths and legends led the rabbis to invent or discover in some fashion the solution to these incomplete mysteries. These, in turn, often took up motifs that had first appeared in earlier *aggadot*. In this way the Jewish legendary tradition has reflected a remarkable continuity underlying the stylistic differences of various stages in the aggadic tradition, "forming," as Martin Buber said, "a second Bible of legends, scattered in innumerable writings, around the nucleus of Scripture." [11]

On first consideration, it is true, the Bible seems to thoroughly overshadow all subsequent Jewish literature. The Bible, and in particular the Torah, was held in such high esteem as the literal Word of God that it has been the focus for postbiblical Jewish literature, both sacred and secular, until this century, much of which presents itself simply as commentary on it. To a remarkable extent this commentary itself is regarded as sacred, since all oral commentary and much of the later written commentary claimed its source in the Oral Torah. This companion tradition holds that at the same time Moses received the Written Torah, at Mount Sinai, he also received the Oral Torah, which interpreted the written one. So central was this oral tradition considered to be that Rabbi Nehemiah is quoted as saying, "Two Torahs were given, one written and one oral." [12] This spoken commentary was not committed to writing but was transmitted by word of mouth for many centuries until Judah ha-Nasi, known as Rabbi, compiled and edited the Mishnah, the core of the Talmud, about 200 C.E. [13] For a thousand years the Oral Torah remained oral, but only well after the Babylonian exile and the destruction of the Second Temple did the rabbis agree to set down the

Oral Torah. That is how the Talmud came into being. Considering the reluctance with which the oral tradition was committed to writing, it is understandable that the rabbis had to seek out a form in which to preserve the laws and legends that constitute it. This structure was from the first an effort to record the discussions of the rabbis, in the form of what appears to be—but in fact is really not—verbatim text. Here, and in the literature that followed, there are constant reminders that the words of the speaker are in a direct line with those handed down from Sinai: "Go and tell them I have a tradition from Rabban Yohanan ben Zakkai, who heard it from his teacher, and his teacher from his teacher, and his teacher from his teacher, reaching from Moses at Mount Sinai." Indeed, this direct line to Moses is stated definitively at the beginning of *Pirke Avot:* "Moses received the Torah on Sinai, and handed it down to Joshua; Joshua to the Elders; the Elders to the Prophets; and the Prophets handed it down to the men of the Great Assembly." [14]

So much importance was placed on the Oral Law that it was soon believed that the primary work, the Torah, could not be understood without it. This raises the burning question of whether or not the rabbis were aware that they were transforming the tradition. One possible answer can be found in an important legend that might be considered a secret confession of the rabbis: [15]

When Moses ascended Mount Sinai to receive the Torah, he did not stop at the top of the mountain, but God sent down a cloud, which Moses entered, and the cloud carried him aloft, all the way into heaven. As he was ascending into Paradise, the angels saw him entering their realm, where none of the living were permitted, and they sought to throw him out. Moses became very frightened and called out to God, for he was afraid that the angels would consume him with their fiery breath. And God reached down and pulled Moses all the way up to the highest heaven, to the Throne of Glory. There Moses found himself face to face with God, and he saw that God was affixing crowns to the letters of the Torah. And Moses said to God, "What are you doing?" And God replied, "I am adding these crowns to the letters of the Torah, for in the future there will be a man born whose name will be Akiba ben Joseph, and he will interpret every crown and letter of the Torah." Moses said, "I would like to see him." And God, for whom nothing is impossible, said, "Turn around." So Moses turned around, and he found himself a thousand years in the future, seated at the back of Rabbi Akiba's classroom, and Rabbi Akiba was explaining a point of the Law. Moses listened carefully, but the truth is that he couldn't follow the discussion. Finally, a student raised his hand and said, "Rabbi Akiba, where do we know this from?" And Rabbi Akiba said, "We know this from Moses at Mount Sinai." [16]

Here Moses is sent by God to sit in the classroom of Rabbi Akiba. The fact that Akiba lived over a thousand years after Moses presents no problems in the *Aggadah*, where time is subordinate to the will of God. Moses finds Akiba's teachings difficult to follow and is astonished when Akiba quotes Moses as the source of his teaching. It seems possible to read in this legend the implicit belief that the later generations had succeeded in contributing to an understanding of the Torah, so that Moses, the predecessor, must turn to his successor, Rabbi Akiba, for a complete understanding of the law that he himself transmitted.

Indeed, there is a related rabbinic tradition that while Moses did receive all of the oral law at Mount Sinai, including all future interpretations of the Torah, he did not write all of it down, but left some of it to be discovered by the future generations.[17] This seems like a clear acknowledgment that the very essence of the rabbinic commentary on the Torah required a creative process of discovery.

In many ways, then, the postbiblical written tradition may be seen as an extension of the oral tradition: instead of regarding what had been set down in writing as fixed, later commentators regarded the tale itself as malleable, as if a single story were being retold and embellished over many generations. There can be no doubt that the acceptance of the practice by which it was possible to embellish the legends of the *Aggadah* and complete the biblical episodes derived from the nature of the oral tradition. Such a tradition must come to recognize that no matter how precisely a tale is retold, there is an inevitable and necessary process of revision that takes place each time it is repeated. Even once the tale has been perfected in some form, minor details of the narrative will continue to evolve. Since a considerable period elapsed before the legends of the oral tradition were recorded in the Talmud and the Midrash, the effects of this process cannot be underestimated. But being among the world's great storytellers, the Jews recognized that a master storyteller cannot but recast the story in his own vision and style. Just as man was made in God's image, so too do the tales a man tells necessarily bear his imprint.

With the Bible and the Talmud, then, Jewish literature is securely rooted in two thoroughly sacred texts.[18] The Talmud consists of both the core of rabbinic law, known as the *Halakhah*, and the legends of the rabbis, known as the *Aggadah*. The *Halakhah*, as codified in the Talmud, served as the basis of an elaborate structure of commentaries and codes prepared by such masters of the Middle Ages and the Renaissance as Rashi, the Tosafists, Maimonides, and Joseph Karo, forming a continuous chain linked to Sinai. Legal decisions and interpretations were also transmitted by *responsa*, rabbinic replies to questions of the law and observance. The resulting body of law constitutes the definitive authority and is still in force among traditional Jews. But in the realm of the *Aggadah*, additions and innovations continued long after the work of the Talmud was brought to a close around 500 C.E., at least until the 12th or 13th century. These later traditions have been collected in several major anthologies, the most important of which is the multivolumed Midrash Rabbah, whose midrashim came to be widely regarded as a part of the legacy of the Oral Law.

The aggadic tradition is unique in the insight it permits into the process of the evolution and embellishment of the central Jewish myths and legends. In virtually every other mythic tradition the transformation of the central narratives took place early in the culture's development, and this transformation was limited exclusively to the oral phase of the culture that preceded the written phase. Any subsequent embellishment in the written tradition of these cultures was limited to the realm of self-conscious works of art, such as the plays of Sophocles and Euripides. In contrast, the Jewish legendary tradition continued to actively develop its legends long after the original versions had already been set down in writing. This distinction constitutes one of the primary unresolved paradoxes of the Jewish religion—how, on one hand, the rabbis did not ignore even the slightest word of the Torah, not even the crown of a letter, as in the story of Moses and Akiba; yet at the same time these sacred texts were subject to the often radical revision of the aggadic tradition, which tended to approach them as if they were still oral tales and had never been set down in writing at all.

Ultimately, these seemingly polar tendencies were resolved in the creation of a remarkably reverent literature, in which every detail has been carefully weighed with respect to its implications for the primary tenets of Judaism, and especially as to the necessity of upholding the paramount tenet of monotheism. It is as if a story had been told and the ones responsible for retelling it had been given the freedom to embellish it as they pleased, within the limitations of very precise and demanding rules. These rules hold that all additions must be demonstrated to be linked to the original text (thus the need for proof-texts); that all additions must clarify and complete missing elements of the original; that they must remain true to the reverent spirit of the original; and that the tone and, to a certain extent, the style, must be consistent with the original.

The *Aggadah* of the Talmud and Midrash and the legends of the Kabbalah and of the hasidim are unique among the sacred literatures of the world, since virtually every phase in their development can be traced in each subsequent generation. And this evolution continues into secular literature in the form of the folklore of an exiled and oppressed people who also found solace in reimagining the Bible and the subsequent history of their holy men, martyrs, and great rabbis. Although the style of presentation of these folk legends tends to be less didactic and more narrative than that of the *Aggadah*, the legends themselves are cut from the same cloth.

During the process of this aggadic evolution, elements of the imagination, and ultimately of literary consciousness, worked their way into the midrashic and folk traditions with remarkable freedom. It is possible to detect an increasingly conscious attitude toward the use of literary devices, styles, and techniques. The earliest written midrashim were cast in the style of the *Halakhah*—terse and judicial in style and content. Little by little, however, the later midrashim began to break out of this epigrammatic structure and rediscover the narrative expansiveness of the Bible and the oral tradition.

Unlike the fables of Aesop, in which the moral is stated at the end of the fable, the midrashic method begins with the biblical passage that is being interpreted, using it as a springboard for the imagination. At the same time, with such intense concentration on a relatively short text, the imaginations of the rabbis were inspired to complete the often unfinished tales of the Torah. As generation followed generation, a larger picture became apparent from the *Aggadah*, a vision in which image was linked to image, theme to theme, metaphor to metaphor, until finally legend was linked to legend in a way that suggested the possibility of an unbroken bridge of legends built across the gaps in the biblical narratives and chronology. What ultimately was being created was a kind of megamyth of all creation—even of the time prior to existence—through all of time until the End of Days.

Linking together the disparate legends is the central symbol of the Jewish tradition, the Torah itself. It is a symbol not only of what it contains—the essential sum of all Jewish law and lore—but also a symbol personified in many ways, which is received anew by every generation, like an eternal flame handed down from father to son. The Torah is also directly equated with the Tree of Life, so much so that the passage from Proverbs stating that *It is a Tree of Life to those who cling to it* (Prov. 3:18) became inextricably identified with the Torah.

That biblical figures in the *Aggadah* had become a model for all of Jewish history, into which the Jewish people projected the experiences of their varied history, was recognized by Louis Ginzberg in his seven-volume masterpiece, *The Legends of the Jews*.[19] Ginzberg gathered together a great many of the midrashim and wove them into a continuous narrative of their own, following the order of the Torah. In so doing he accomplished for our generation what was the unspoken goal of the aggadic tradition from the first: to write the Book of the Book, a distorted mirror image of the original that reflects its biblical source and yet is also a separate creation in itself. Indeed, there were earlier attempts to collect the existing legendary texts in anthologies dating from late antiquity, such as *The Book of Jubilees, Sefer ha-Yashar, Pirke de Rabbi Eliezer,* and *The Chronicles of Jerahmeel.* But Ginzberg's opus must be recognized as a midrashic epic of unparalleled magnitude.

The primary purpose of the aggadic tradition, then, was to transmit and reinterpret the past for each successive generation. This purpose has at its root a love for the past and a desire to carry it into the future, to keep it alive. The biblical tale, once told, was found to be true for all generations; it was open to reinterpretation as well as retelling in each generation. The Jews have long been a wandering people, collecting tales that transform their own experiences into a common tradition. This is, by definition, what tradition is—receiving and transmitting anew what has been received. In many ways this legendary literature not only is a peculiar kind of scriptural commentary, but also considers the past from the perspective of the future, searching for oracles that have since been fulfilled and for clues that will help provide safe passage into the future.

Thus in retelling and rewriting these tales, the rabbis responsible for the midrashim were like jewelers who polished an immense and many-faceted jewel. Each generation turned its gaze to a new facet of the jewel, whose facets are infinite. Still, they were always certain that it was but a single jewel they saw, whose essential structure was eternal and unchanging.

The Aggadic Tradition

I

The continuity of Jewish literature extends across the entire period from the biblical era to the present, unbroken. The legends of the Bible are the foundation on which this tradition has been built, each generation upon the preceding one. The books of the Apocrypha and Pseudepigrapha[1] are modeled on the books of the Hebrew Bible, from which they were excluded, and purport to be contemporary accounts of biblical accounts of biblical events, although they were written afterward. The legends of rabbinic literature, known as the *Aggadah*, assume a biblical context within which they elaborate on unfinished aspects of the biblical narratives, such as the evil intentions of the builders of the Tower of Babel, the childhood of Abraham, or how King David evaded the Angel of Death. Since these episodes are not reported in the Bible, the aggadists sought out these solutions themselves, working on the assumption that the missing information is implicit in the biblical narrative. According to tradition, these elaborations belong to the Oral, or Unwritten, Torah, which was transmitted on Mount Sinai at the same time as the Written Torah and is regarded as being part of the legacy that Moses received during forty days and nights. But, as will become apparent, they are, primarily, the creations of the longing and imagination of succeeding generations, each of which contributed to these Jewish myths, so that they subsequently continued to evolve. The form and style of the legends of the early rabbinic literature serve as models for the legends of the late rabbinic literature and the Kabbalah, which also emerge out of a context of biblical commentary.[2] As a result, a pattern was estab-

lished in which subsequent genres of post-talmudic literature tend toward
a generally exegetical model. This remained the case until the appearance
of later midrashim, such as those found in *Pirke de Rabbi Eliezer* (8th century) and *Sefer ha-Yashar* (16th century), which utilize a narrative mode
more like that of the Bible while incorporating material derived largely
from prior rabbinic collections, such as the Talmud and a multitude of
midrashic texts.

The exegetical form of the Midrash does somewhat inhibit the narrative
freedom of the aggadic tradition it relates, replacing this freedom with a
unique structure capable of assimilating a wide range of material, from matters of interpretation to imaginative reports about immense jewels seen at
sea.[3] This form permits, as well, the distinctive voices of individual rabbis
to emerge. Yet whatever narrative inhibitions are inherent in the aggadic
format, they are ultimately set free in the folklore that flourished in the
Middle Ages and was the first secular Jewish literature. Here the form of
the folktales was blended with the perspective, but not the style, of the
legends of the Talmud and Midrash, choosing instead a flowing style like
that of a storyteller. This folklore style is also far freer and less self-conscious
and, of course, less polished than the biblical model, which often reads as
if engraved in stone.

The legends and styles of all of these previous periods—the biblical,
aggadic, kabbalistic, folkloric, and hasidic—are utilized as models by modern Jewish authors such as S. Y. Agnon, M. J. Berditchevsky, I. L. Peretz,
and I. B. Singer. These authors, and many other modern Jewish writers,
have discovered new ways to embellish and utilize the old myths, which
seem to retain their primal power no matter how many times they are
retold. Often these authors draw on a modern stylistic and intellectual
perspective while doing this, which in itself brings the legends into a
new dimension. The result is a literature that is as much a product of the
aggadic tradition as are the legends of the Midrash and the myths of the
Kabbalah. For while these modern authors utilize these traditional forms
and genres in markedly individual ways, the essential vision of the *Aggadah*
remains unchanged, and in general they retain a tone that is essentially
reverent.

With some notable exceptions, the process of the evolution of a myth or
legend continues each time it is retold. There is even evidence of this evolutionary process taking place at the earliest stages of Jewish literature, involving myths and legends of Genesis.

In most cultures the transition from an oral to a written tradition was a
dramatic change that tended to regard the written material, after only a
few generations, as sacred and eternal in its written form. The inevitability
of the evolution of myth, which is presumed in an oral tradition, was replaced with a belief in the permanence of the written form. Such a belief
also characterized the Jewish attitude toward the books of the Bible. Yet,
paradoxically, the oral ethic that enabled mythic transformations to take

place was also retained. This apparent contradiction was resolved by the recognition of two separate but related traditions: the written and the unwritten. While the text of the Written Torah was fixed, that of the Oral Torah was not. It was this conscious retention of the oral dimension, then, that distinguished the Jewish religious and literary traditions from others and was responsible for creating a situation in which it remained possible for the central myths to continue evolving even after they had been written down.

Eventually, some of the oral traditions were preserved in writing, usually when they were in danger of otherwise being lost, or to prevent the formation of competing sects, each claiming that the Law as they had received it was the authentic version. As a result, it is possible to follow this mythic evolution in texts, although much scholarly debate continues as to their precise dating.[4] A representative example of the kind of evolution that takes place between the biblical source and its aggadic retelling is the legend of the City of Luz. There are four passing references to Luz in the Bible, but it is the first one that supplies its attributes as a place unique in the world—one of the Gates of Heavens—for it was there that Jacob had the dream of the ladder that reached into heaven with angels ascending and descending on it (Gen. 28:12). The remaining biblical references to Luz do not shed additional light on the nature of the city. But, in the Talmud, Luz is linked to a myth of a city of immortals:

> It has been taught: That is the Luz against which Sennacherib marched without disturbing it, against which Nebuchadnezzar marched without destroying it, and even the Angel of Death has no permission to pass through it. But when the old there become tired of life, they go outside the wall to die.

The Talmud also includes a legend about two men that King Solomon sent to the city of Luz to escape the Angel of Death:

> One morning, as King Solomon awoke, he heard a chirping outside his window. He sat up in bed and listened carefully, for he knew the language of the birds, and he overheard them say that the Angel of Death had been sent to take the lives of two of his closest advisers. King Solomon was startled by this unexpected news, and he summoned the two doomed men. And when they stood before him, he revealed what he had learned of their fate.
>
> The two were terrified, and they begged King Solomon to help them. Solomon told them that their only hope was to find their way to the city of Luz. For it was well known that the Angel of Death was forbidden to enter there. Therefore the inhabitants of Luz were immortal—as long as they remained within the walls of the charmed city. Very few knew the secret of how to reach that city, but King Solomon was one of those who did.
>
> So it was that King Solomon revealed the secret to the two frightened men, and they departed at once. They whipped their camels across the hot

desert all day, and at nightfall they finally saw the walls of that fabled city. Immortality was almost within reach and they rode as fast as they could to the city gates.

But when they arrived they saw, to their horror, the Angel of Death waiting for them. "How did you know to look for us here?" they asked. The angel replied: "This is where I was told to meet you."[5]

No further embellishment of this legend of a city in which the inhabitants remain immortal is found in the Talmud; further development appears in Genesis Rabbah. First the biblical passage about Jacob's dream (Gen. 28:19) is quoted in the context of an exegetical discussion, creating a link between the Luz of Jacob and the talmudic account of the city spared the Angel of Death. Then the legend is taken one step further:

Rabbi Abba bar Kahana said: "Why was it called Luz?—Because whoever entered it blossomed forth into meritorious acts and good deeds like a *luz* (nut tree)." The Rabbis said: "As the nut has no mouth (opening), so no man could discover the entrance to the town." Rabbi Simon said: "A nut tree stood at the entrance to the city." Rabbi Lezar ben Merom said in the name of Rabbi Phinehas ben Mama: "A nut tree stood at the entrance of a cave; this tree was hollow, and through it one entered the cave and through the cave the city."[6]

Note how Rabbi Lezar embellishes a detail newly added to the tale by Rabbi Simon. Taking the name of the town as a nut tree (an almond tree, the literal meaning of *luz*), he postulates it as the symbol of the city and places it at the entrance. While it is possible, of course, that this embellishment was part of an earlier tradition that Rabbi Simon was merely recalling, it appears equally possible that the description of the nut tree at the gates of the city is an example of the kind of mythic elaboration of which we have been speaking. Certainly the further development presented by Rabbi Lezar, quoting Rabbi Phinehas, takes this motif one step further, embellishing the role of the nut tree: "This tree was hollow, and through it one entered the cave and through the cave the city."

Regrettably, this attractive and enticing motif of a city of immortals, almost fairy tale in nature, was not developed any further until the late medieval period, where it is the subject of several folktales about a quest to the city of Luz.[7] However, the notion of a boundary that the Angel of Death cannot cross does appear in the Zohar (II:151a), referring to the Land of Israel as a whole rather than to the city of Luz: "It is the Destroying Angel who brings death to all people, except those who die in the Holy Land, to whom death comes by the Angel of Mercy, who holds sway there." This gradual and meandering kind of development is characteristic of the aggadic tradition, whose evolution is not, in this respect, unlike that of living creatures—what has been termed "organic thinking." At the same time, this makes reading the *Aggadah* a treasure hunt in which these kinds of gems lie scattered everywhere in the rich midrashic literature.

II

Drawing on the Oral Law that Moses was said to have received at Mount Sinai along with the Torah, the ancient rabbis evolved a system of reading between the lines of the Torah to discover the answer to all of their unanswered questions. The system they evolved enabled them to fill in the gaps in the biblical narrative, as well as to resolve apparent contradictions in the text.

For example, on the first day of Creation, God said, *Let there be light, and there was light* (Gen. 1:3). But it was not until the fourth day of Creation that God created the sun, the moon, and the stars (Gen. 1:16). So what was the light of the first day? The rabbis were quick to recognize this apparent contradiction, and set out to resolve it. In this case, they concluded that the light of the first day was a *different* light than that of the fourth day. They identified it as a holy light, a sacred light, a primordial light, which pervaded the whole world. The midrash tells us that in this light it was possible for Adam to see not only to the ends of the earth, but to the ends of the universe.[8]

What was the clue that led the rabbis to conclude that the light of the first day was different than that of the fourth day? It can be found in Isaiah 30:26, where Isaiah appears to be speaking about the transformations that will take place in the messianic era: *the light of the moon shall be as the light of the sun, and the light of the sun shall be sevenfold, as the light of the seven days.* Here Isaiah clearly distinguishes between the normal light of the sun and the light of the seven days of creation, identifying the light of the latter as "sevenfold" that of the former. This might be seen as a kind of biblical midrash, which sets the stage for the rabbis to conclude that the light of the first day was a different kind of light, a primordial light more powerful than the sun. This, then, solves the problem. Or does it? As in many such cases, the rabbinic solution solves the immediate problem at hand, but in the process raises many new questions. What, for example, was the source of the light? And what happened to it? After all, we can no longer see to the ends of the universe — even with the aid of the most powerful instruments.

Again, rabbinic ingenuity comes into play. As for the source of the primordial light, some say that it was cast from the light of God's prayershawl when God wrapped himself in a *tallit* of light.[9] This is linked to the verse in Psalms, *Who coverest Thyself with light as with a garment* (Ps. 104:2). Others say that it was cast from the robe of the *Shekhinah.* All versions seem to agree that this sacred light originated in Paradise.

As for the ultimate fate of the primordial light, there is a friendly rabbinic debate, which continued for two thousand years. The rabbis of the Talmud concluded that after Adam and Eve ate the forbidden fruit, God withdrew the light and brought it back into Paradise to save it for the righteous in the world to come.[10] Thus, its loss was one of the consequences of the sin of Adam and Eve, along with the other punishments, which included being expelled from the Garden of Eden and becoming mortal (Gen. 3:16–19). But in the 18th century the Baal Shem Tov suggested another fate for the primordial light. He said that God hid it away in the words of the Torah, where it is known as the hidden light of the Torah. Building on the Baal Shem Tov's identification of this light with the hidden light of the Torah, Rabbi Nachman of Bratslav specifically links the stories of the Torah with the legend of the primordial light:

> Every story has something that is concealed. What is concealed is the hidden light. The Book of Genesis says that God created light on the first day, the sun on the fourth. What light existed before the sun? The tradition says this was spiritual light, and God hid it for future use. Where was it hidden? In the stories of the Torah.[11]

Then Rabbi Nachman suggests that when a person delves deeply enough into the meaning of the Torah, he will at last reach a place where the hidden light shines forth in a moment of revelation.

This, then, resolves the problem of the light of the first day, and it might have been the end of the discussion, but it was not. Rabbinic legend goes on to tell us that before God completely withdrew the primordial light from the world, he saved a bit of it inside a jewel, and he gave this jewel to Adam and Eve when he expelled them from the Garden of Eden. They took this jewel with them, and the light that shone from within it reminded them of all that they had lost.

The history of this jewel, known as the *Tzohar*, is as fantastic as that of the primordial light itself, and it, too, grows out of a problem in the text of the Torah. In this case, the problem takes the form of the word *"Tzohar,"* which is found in the instructions God gave to Noah when he directed him to build the ark. Here God tells Noah to put the *Tzohar* in the ark (Gen. 6:16). Because the word *Tzohar* only appears in the Bible once, it has proven very difficult to define. This is quickly apparent if one examines a variety of biblical translations. *Tzohar* is sometimes translated as a light, sometimes as a window, sometimes as a dome: *A light shalt thou make to the ark,*[12] *A window shalt thou make to the ark,*[13] *Make a skylight for the ark.*[14] Clearly, it was intended to refer to some source of light, and, indeed, it is associated with the word *"Tzoharyim,"* meaning "noon." *Midrash Tan-huma* reinterprets the biblical verse to mean, "Place jewels and precious stones in the ark, that they may give you light as bright as noon."[15] Rashi notes that "some say this *Tzohar* was a window; others say it was a precious stone that gave light to them." It is this latter meaning that grew into the long legend that identified the *Tzohar* as a jewel containing a remnant of the primordial light, which God gave to Adam and Eve. Thus, we see that the midrashic explanation of the origin of this divine jewel depends on the resolution of *two* problems in the biblical text—that concerning the fate of the light of the first day and that concerning the meaning of the term "*Tzohar.*"

Once the glowing jewel of the *Tzohar* had entered Jewish legend, it became the basis of what might be called a "chain midrash." This is a midrash that uses some kind of sacred object to link together several biblical generations. Other examples include the Book of Raziel—containing the history of future generations—which the angel Raziel is said to have given to Adam, and the garments of Adam and Eve, which were said to have been passed down to Cain, Nimrod, and Esau.

In the case of the *Tzohar*, it is said that the glowing jewel was handed down by Adam and Eve to their son Seth, and that it subsequently reached Enoch, Methuselah, Lamech, and, of course, Noah. So when God told Noah, *Put the Tzohar in the ark*, Noah knew exactly what He meant, and thus Noah hung the *Tzohar* from a beam in the ark, where it illuminated the ark: "During the whole twelve months that Noah was in the ark he did not require the light of the sun by day or the light of the moon at night, but he had a polished gem which he hung up: when it was dim he knew that it was day, and when it shone he knew that it was night.[16]

Rabbinic legend also records, in typically scattered fashion, how the sacred jewel reached Abraham, Isaac, Jacob, and Joseph. The Talmud tells us that "Abraham wore a glowing stone around his neck, which he used as an astrolabe, and whosoever was sick and peered into that stone was healed."[17] This account offers one version of the ultimate fate of the *Tzohar:* "When Abraham passed away from the world, the Holy One, blessed be He, hung it on the wheel of the sun." But other versions of the legend insist that the precious jewel continued to be handed down. A reference to the *Tzohar* is perceived when Joseph's servant finds his cup in Benjamin's saddlebags and says, *Is this not the cup in which my lord drinketh, and whereby indeed he divineth?* (Gen. 44:5). The explanation is that Joseph discovered that if he put the *Tzohar* in that cup and peered into it, he could divine the future as well as interpret dreams. That is how he was able to interpret the dreams of the butler and the baker, and then the dreams of Pharaoh. Before his death, Joseph had the *Tzohar* placed in his coffin, which was later found by Moses, with the help of Serah bat Asher. Moses recovered the jewel from the coffin and hung it inside the Tabernacle of the Ark, where it became the first *Ner Tamid.*[18] Later, the jewel was said to have been hung in the Temple, where it remained until the Temple was destroyed. Even then the *Tzohar* does not disappear from Jewish folklore, but appears again and again in the most unexpected places, as a regular motif.

The process by which the rabbis transformed contradictions in the biblical text into mythic narratives is a fascinating one. Certainly, the mythic impulse behind it cannot be doubted. The following is a retelling of the myth of the light of the first day. It draws on a variety of rabbinic sources and brings them together into a single narrative:

> On the first day of creation, God wrapped Himself in a garment of light, and the radiance of His majesty illuminated the world. That was the light of the first day, a primordial light, distinct from the light of the fourth day, when God created the sun, the moon, and the stars. In that light Adam was able to see from one end of the universe to the other.
>
> That sacred light pervaded the world until the very moment that Adam and Eve tasted the forbidden fruit. Then the first thing they lost was that precious light, for that was one of the punishments of the Fall. Without it, the world grew dark around them, for the sun shone like a candle in comparison. Never again did they see the world in the splendor of that light, and that was the most painful punishment of all.
>
> As for the fate of the primordial light, some say that God brought it back into Paradise, where it awaits the righteous in the world to come. Others say that God hid that light in the Torah, in the mysteries hidden there, waiting to be discovered. And when it is, the hidden light of the Torah will be revealed, in all its splendor. So too is it said that God hid a small bit of that light inside a glowing stone and gave it to Adam and Eve when they were expelled from the Garden, as a reminder of all that they had lost.
>
> At the End of Days, when the footsteps of the Messiah will be heard in the world, that sacred light will be restored. Then everyone will see for himself the true glory of God's creation.[19]

III

To further illustrate the process by which midrashim evolve and develop, accruing and incorporating new material and variants, the tradition concerning the death of Cain serves as an excellent example. Since the biblical narrative of Cain is unfinished, the rabbis were left to resolve the story in both a moral and a literary sense. Using the tradition of the Oral Law as their justification, and supporting their interpretations with biblical prooftexts, the rabbis embellished the tale of Cain and Abel in many respects. They filled in the sketchy details of the births of the two brothers,[20] the mystery of the origin of their wives,[21] the conflict between the two,[22] the murder of Abel by Cain,[23] the burial of Abel,[24] and the punishment and ultimate fate of Cain. It is the final aspect of the legend that is the particular focus of this discussion.

The end of the biblical narrative about Cain describes his punishment by God and concludes by attributing to Cain the founding of the first city.[25]

After Cain has been cursed to become *a ceaseless wanderer on earth* (Gen. 4:12), he protests the severity of the sentence and has it modified (Gen. 4:13–15).

Of particular interest to the rabbis was the nature of the sign by which God had marked Cain, to signify and protect him in his wanderings. One of the earliest midrashim speculating on this sign appears in Genesis Rabbah 22:

> *And the Lord put a mark on Cain* (Gen. 4:15). Rabbi Judah said: "He caused the orb of the sun to shine on his account." Said Rabbi Nehemiah to him: "He caused the orb of sun to shine! Rather, He afflicted him with leprosy." Rab said: "He gave him a dog." Abba Jose said: "He made a horn grow out of his head." Rabbi Levi said in the name of Rabbi Shimon ben Lakish: "He suspended his punishment in abeyance until the Flood came and swept him away."

Of these five alternative accounts[26] of the nature of the mark of Cain, the version that became best known was that of the horn, which was said to be located on his forehead. The reason for this should be apparent—the horn signified Cain's essentially savage nature and thus identified him as a wild beast among men. Although it was not apparent at first, this horn was to play an essential role in the most widely accepted account of the death of Cain, which first appears in *Midrash Tanhuma*, as follows:

> Lamech was Cain's grandson of the seventh generation, and blind. When Lamech went hunting his son would guide him, holding his hand, and tell him when he saw a beast. Thereupon Lamech would draw his bow and kill it. Once he saw a horn between two mountains. "I see an animal's horns!" he exclaimed, and Lamech shot and killed it. But when they went to take it, the child cried out, "It is my grandfather, Cain!" In grief Lamech beat his hands together; accidentally he dealt his child a blow to the head that killed him.[27]

This account soon became the best known version of how Cain died, although variants of the legend existed. There was, for example, the one proposed originally by Rabbi Shimon ben Lakish, wherein Cain was seen to have found his death along with the other victims of the Flood. But this punishment was unsatisfying in that it did not single out Cain. The rabbis strongly felt that a decisive punishment for him was called for, to set a precedent for future murderers.

Another version of Cain's death appears in the apocryphal *Book of Jubilees* (4:31). Here Cain is said to have been killed when his house fell on him. Just as he had killed Abel with a stone, so was he killed by the stones of the house that collapsed on him.

Midrash Tanhuma proposes that, at the time of his punishment, Cain's final destiny was in being transformed into the Angel of Death and remaining such until he was killed at the hands of Lamech, at which time "Lamech became transformed into the Angel of Death, thus fulfilling the prophecy," *If Cain shall be avenged sevenfold, truly Lamech shall be avenged seventy and sevenfold* (Gen. 4:24).[28] It seems likely that this version combines two separate explanations. In one of these, Cain's punishment must have consisted of his being transformed into the Angel of Death and as such is a powerful origin legend to explain how this terrible angel came into being.[29] The second legend concerns Cain's fatal encounter with his descendant Lamech in the seventh generation.[30]

The first principle of supporting a midrashic interpretation is to link it to a biblical source. Since there is no description of the death of Cain in the Bible, the rabbis turned to the enigmatic passage that is quoted in part in the previous midrash. It reads in full as follows:

> And Lamech said unto his wives:
> Adah and Tzila, hear my voice;
> Ye wives of Lamech, hearken unto my speech; For I have a slain a man for wounding me,
> And a young man for bruising me; If Cain shall be avenged sevenfold, Truly Lamech seventy and sevenfold.
>
> (Gen. 4:23–24)

In *Midrash Tanhuma* this passage is seen both as foretelling Lamech's metamorphosis into the Angel of Death, and Cain's death at the hands of Lamech. But most other commentaries focus on the latter explanation linked to the curse of Cain (Gen. 4:1–15). In this reading, *"I have slain a man for wounding me"* refers to Cain, who has wounded Lamech by being the ancestor responsible for the curse that hangs over his descendants, and *"a young man for bruising me"* refers to Lamech's son, Tubal-Cain, who has bruised his father by making him responsible for the death of Cain. Admittedly, this reading seems forced, but this kind of literary license is characteristic of the aggadic tradition. In addition, the midrashic rule requiring a proof-text to support a claim makes it the only possible passage to provide the necessary biblical link.

This popular explanation of the death of Cain ingeniously utilizes two existing traditions associated with Cain—the passage concerning Lamech and the midrash asserting that Cain's sign was a horn. The enigmatic biblical passage about Lamech provides the framework for the narrative of the death of Cain, as well as the conclusion of the tale. The horn is the motif around which the whole tale turns. Together the two fragments provide the necessary link to tradition that gives the midrash its authentic ring. In addition, this version of Cain's death is satisfying in a number of other respects.

First of all, this midrash brings the tale of Cain to a conclusion, which was of no small importance to the rabbis, who had a strong sense that every tale should have a beginning, a middle, and an ending. In its biblical form the story of Cain was simply incomplete. At the same time, by extending the story seven generations, the principle was established of carrying the biblical story into the future, where the biblical archetype can occur in a new form that still permits recognition of the old. Such a system made possible identification with a biblical patriarch or king, and, at the same time, offered an opportunity to incorporate personal dreams and fantasies into the *Aggadah.*

Next, this midrash provides a unique and appropriate death for Cain, especially fitting in that his slayer is his own descendant. This is a kind of poetic (or, perhaps, midrashic) justice, since Cain slew his own brother. Note, however, that neither Lamech nor his son, Tubal-Cain, can be held responsible for Cain's death, since Lamech was blind and Tubal-Cain only a child who mistook his ancestor for an animal—which, in essence, Cain was. It is a case of perfect justice: Cain receives his due from his own offspring, but they are innocent of any crime, though they have in this way repaid Cain for making them accursed, and in this coincidence can be seen, of course, the hand of God. Also, note the presence of Cain's name in that of the descendant who assists in killing him, hinting that Cain, in a sense, killed himself.

Finally, this midrash aptly sets the precedent that a killer should be slain for his crime, and it does not succumb to the alternative interpretation that Cain repented and his repentance was accepted, on the grounds that there had been no previous murder for him to realize the import of his action.[31] This reading also supports the biblical injunction that the punishment for murder be death,[32] and avoids setting the precedent that exceptions to this rule be permitted.

It is not surprising, then, that this version of the death of Cain, which became the predominant one, served the needs of the rabbis and accurately reflected their views of the need for, and the manner of, justice and retribution. All subsequent versions of this midrash, such as the following version from *Sefer ha-Yashar,* merely embellish aspects of this midrash and present the details in an improved narrative form, but do not change it in any essential way:

And Lamech was old and advanced in years, and his eyes were dim so that he could not see, and Tubal-Cain, his son, was leading him one day while they were walking in the field, when Cain, the son of Adam, advanced toward them. Then Lamech was very old and could not see much, and Tubal-Cain his son was very young. And Tubal-Cain told his father to draw his bow, and with the arrows he smote Cain, who was yet far off, and he slew him, for he appeared to them to be an animal. And the arrows entered Cain's body although he was distant from them, and he fell to the ground and died. And the Lord requited Cain's evil according to his wickedness, which He had done to his brother Abel, according to the word of the Lord which he had spoken. And it came to pass that when Cain had died, Lamech and Tubal-Cain went to see the animal they had slain, and they saw, and behold Cain their grandfather was fallen dead upon the earth. And Lamech was very much grieved at having done this, and in clapping his hands he struck his son and caused his death.[33]

Thus it can be seen that this midrash of Cain's death solves two problems at the same time: it explicates a difficult passage about Lamech, and at the same time it solves the narrative and moral problem of the ultimate fate of Cain. And despite its intentional usage of existing sources, the Midrash still manages to be an original creation. It is in this spirit that the midrashic tradition inspired subsequent sacred literatures, especially those of the kabbalistic and hasidic, and has been carried into the present in the writings of S. Y. Agnon, I. L. Peretz, and I. B. Singer and contemporary authors such as Cynthia Ozick, Moacyr Scliar, Steve Stern, and others.

IV

Using this midrashic method the rabbis were thus able to provide an appropriate death for Cain, the first murderer, as well as to describe what the childhood of Abraham was like—information that is missing in the text of the Torah. And using this method they were able to create a full identity for a figure whose name appears only twice in the Torah—in two lists. Nothing else is said about her. Yet the rabbis were able to bring her to life and make her play an essential role in many key biblical episodes. It was she who, knowing the sign, identified Moses as the Redeemer; she who helped Moses search for the coffin of Joseph; she who crossed the Red Sea, and later reported on what the walls of the Red Sea looked like. This figure, Serah bat Asher, about whom next to nothing is said in the Torah, comes to life in the Talmud and the Midrash and becomes one of the favorite figures of the rabbis, whom they draw into the narrative as often as possible. How they did this is an object lesson in the midrashic method.

The story of Serah bat Asher, who, according to the midrash, lived longer than anyone else, even Methuselah, begins with a name in the list in the passage describing Jacob's journey into Egypt: *Jacob and all his offspring with him came to Egypt. He brought with him to Egypt his sons and grandsons, his daughters and granddaughters—all his offspring* (Gen. 46:6–7). Among the sixty-nine who accompanied Jacob into Egypt were, as recounted in Genesis 46:17: *Asher's sons: Imnah, Ishvi, and Beriah, and their sister Serah.* Serah might have remained merely a name in this list if not for a curious parallel. For in another list, in Numbers 26:46, that of the census taken by Moses in the wilderness, the name Serah bat Asher appears again: *The name of Asher's daughter was Serah.*

Now what are we to make of the fact that the same name appears in two lists separated by at least two hundred years? From our perspective, it might be discounted as a coincidence. After all, Asher was a respectable name, and it is certainly possible that someone named Asher might name his daughter Serah. But from the point of view of the ancient rabbis, the fact that these two lists had this one name in common cried out for explanation. So they arrived at what was for them the logical conclusion: they were the same person.

That resolves the problem of the identity of the two Serahs, but it doesn't explain how she lived so long. However, rabbinic ingenuity found a solution for this problem as well. Using the midrashic method, the rabbis searched for the "right place." This is the place in the text that gives the necessary clue, which makes it possible to read between the lines. And in this case the clue involved another matter that is missing in the biblical narrative: how the sons of Jacob finally informed him that his beloved son, Joseph, was not dead after all.

It all goes back to the brothers' discovery that Joseph was still alive. Indeed, he was none other than the Prince of Egypt. And now that Joseph had revealed his true identity, he commanded his brothers to bring their father and the rest of the family to Egypt, for there was a famine in the land: *And you shall tell my father of all my glory in Egypt, and of all that you have seen, and you shall hasten and bring down my father hither* (Gen. 45:13). This must have presented a dilemma to Joseph's brothers, since they had cast him naked into a pit and then sold him into slavery and then told their father that he had been slain by a wild beast. Now they had to go back to their father, Jacob, a frail old man, and tell him that Joseph was alive after all.

Reading between the lines, the rabbis intuited that the brothers were filled with guilt and remorse, as well as with fear that Jacob might die of the shock when he heard the news. So they came up with the idea of letting Serah break the news to him. They asked Serah, who apparently was a child, to play the harp for Jacob and sing him a little song, with the words "Joseph is alive, Joseph is alive." Serah, of course, was glad to sing a song for her grandfather, and when Jacob realized what she was saying, he jumped up and asked, "Is it true?" And when she told him it was true, well, he blessed her with such a great blessing that she lived as long as she did![34]

In this way the midrash brought Serah to life and explained how she lived for so long. That might have been enough, if all that the rabbis wanted to do was to identify Serah and explain how Jacob learned that Joseph was alive. But the rabbis found Serah very handy to call on in several other cases as well. One of these involved the identity of the Redeemer. There was a secret sign to identify the Redeemer that God had revealed to Jacob, and that Jacob had transmitted to his sons, and that Asher, Jacob's son, had revealed to his daughter, Serah. The sign of the true redeemer is that whoever would say, in God's Name, *"I have indeed remembered"* (Ex. 3:16) is the true redeemer. Thus when Moses said these words, Serah identified him as the Redeemer.[35]

Then we arrive at what is perhaps Serah's most important role. For it was she who informed Moses where the coffin of Joseph could be found. This midrash fills in a major gap in the biblical narrative between the vow that Joseph made the sons of Israel swear on his deathbed that *you shall carry my bones from here* (Gen. 50:25) and the report that *Moses took the bones of Joseph with him* (Ex. 14:19).

Here again we have a classic example of the workings of the rabbinic imagination. On the day before they took their leave from Egypt, while the Israelis were despoiling the Egyptians, Moses searched everywhere for the coffin of Joseph, but he could not find it, for no one remembered where Joseph was buried. Returning empty-handed, Moses encountered a little old lady, who asked, "Why so downcast, Moses?" And when Moses told her why, she said: "I can lead you to the coffin of Joseph." "Who are you," Moses asked, "and how do you know where Joseph was buried?" "I'm Serah bat Asher," she replied, "and I know because I was present at the funeral of Joseph, and his iron coffin was sunk into the Nile!"

Serah then leads Moses to the very spot where the coffin was sunk. Now Moses knows where it is, but he has a new problem: how to raise a heavy coffin from the Nile. So Moses leans over the shore and says, "Joseph, Joseph, we're leaving. If you want to come with us, come now. If not, we did our best." And at that moment a miracle takes place, and the coffin of Joseph floats to the surface, and Moses is able to pick it up and bring it with him.[36]

There are many other brief appearances that Serah makes in her long life. She even shows up at the house of study of Rabbi Yohanan. Rabbi Yohanan once asked his students to describe the appearance of the walls of the Red Sea when the waters parted for the Children of Israel to cross. When none could do so, Rabbi Yohanan described them as resembling a lattice. Then, all at once, they heard a voice say: "No, it wasn't like that at all!" And when they looked up, they saw the face of a very old woman peering in the window of the house of study. "Who are you?" demanded Rabbi Yohanan. "I am Serah bat Asher," came the reply, "and I know what the walls of the Red Sea looked like, because I crossed the Red Sea, and they resembled shining mirrors." And when she finished speaking, Serah took her leave and disappeared once again.[37]

There are two legendary accounts of the ultimate fate of Serah. One reports that she met her death in a fire in a synagogue in Isfahan, Persia, in the 12th century. That synagogue was rebuilt and named after her, and it is still the holiest Jewish site in Iran, to which Persian Jews used to make pilgrimages when they were still permitted to do so. Yet there is another legend that Serah never died—that she was one of nine who were taken into heaven alive, where she now lives in a heavenly palace of her own, where she teaches the Torah.[38]

As this rich legend of Serah bat Asher makes abundantly clear, it is the latter legend that is the right one. Serah never died. She was created out of the imagination of the rabbis and she lives on in our own imaginations, a sharp-tongued female Elijah wandering the world, setting things straight.

V

Each of the postmidrashic literatures demonstrates its own pattern of receiving the tradition and, at the same time, transforming it by their own distinct vision. The kabbalistic literature views the Torah through a mystical lens, reimagining every passage according to its mystical meaning. A rich body of legends about Rabbi Shimon bar Yohai is found in the Zohar, dating from the 13th century, along with a great many mystical allegories, such as those about princesses locked in towers, and a rich mythology about the Messiah, waiting for the signal to be given that the time has come for the footsteps of the Messiah to be heard.

In the 16th century there also appeared a cycle of tales about the circle of Rabbi Isaac Luria of Safed, known as the Ari. *Shivhei ha-Ari*, the first collection of tales about the Ari, includes tales about the miraculous birth of the Ari, his teachings, and his miracles, including that of transporting a king who was asleep in his palace to a pit in a field, where he was forced to affix his seal to a proclamation protecting the Jews. There are, in addition, tales about dybbuks, demons, and legends current in his time. It is in this period that the secular and sacred literatures flow closest together. And the subsequent hasidic literature, which turned to the tales of the masters of Safed for their model, maintains, to a considerable extent, the practice of incorporating secular legends, especially when it is possible to reinterpret them in a religious dimension.

In addition to the emergence of the Zohar and other kabbalistic literature in the Middle Ages, there was also the blossoming of folklore. Stressing narrative, and open to the influences of the folklores of surrounding cultures, these folktales and fairy tales, lacking the sacred seal of the previous literatures, were forced to fend for themselves, as a new kind of oral tradition, and to wait the first serious collectors of Jewish folklore, such as S. Ansky, Y. L. Cahan, and M. J. Berditchevsky. To a considerable extent, the subjects of this folklore are identical with those of the earlier sacred literatures. There are a multitude of legends about the ten lost tribes, the miracles of the Prophet Elijah, and the births, deaths, and wonders of the greatest rabbis, heroes, holy men, and scholars. There are also many tales of the supernatural, in which demons and dybbuks play important roles.

This medieval folklore differs from the preceding sacred literatures, however, in that it is not restricted by the ethical prerogative of the talmudic and midrashic literatures, nor is it tied to proof-texts. Instead, it is attracted to the miraculous and imaginative, as well as to tales of quests and other great undertakings. A moral element is still present, but it is the kind of clear-cut moral found, for example in *Aesop's Fables*. Above all, it is not a self-conscious literature, as is that of the *Aggadah* of the Talmud and Midrash, nor is it generally concerned with the mystical (in contrast to the supernatural) dimension, as is the Kabbalah. In this respect it is not unlike the kinds of folklore that emerge naturally out of every culture, much of it borrowed from other cultures, and recast in a Jewish context.

Here are to be found complete cycles of legends about King David and King Solomon and a substantial body of tales in which Elijah appears in disguise to provide some kind of salvation. It is apparent that these folktales reflect a simpler, more fundamental grasp of religious elements. Here, too, can be found those aggadic motifs that appealed to the popular imagination, for the inclination to embellish and extend existing myths and legends was just as intense as it was in the sacred literatures. At the same time, it is apparent that the powerful influence of the Oral Law, which lends its sacred aura to the legends of the Talmud and Midrash, is considerably diminished in medieval folklore. And while one consequence of this absence of the sacred aura is a distance that enters into the narration of the tale and does not presume that the tale is necessarily true, there is, at the same time, even greater liberation of the imagination than in the earlier literatures, now that its foremost commitment is no longer primarily to the affirmation of the sacred tradition.

Unfortunately, while we can be certain that the primary sacred texts have been carefully preserved, it is apparent that a great deal of folklore, which was never written down, has been lost. In fact, considering its exclusion from the sacred tradition, it is remarkable that so much of this oral tradition has survived. Among the best collections of this literature are M. J. Berditchevsky's *Mimekor Yisrael* (The Fountain of Israel), which is available in English, and the still untranslated collection *Sefer Ma'asiyot* (The Book of Tales), edited by Mordecai ben Yehezkel.

The last major phase of Jewish literature produced before the 20th century is that of hasidism. The movement's founder, the Baal Shem Tov, gathered around him disciples, known as hasidim, with whom he shared his teachings, which emphasize the need for *kavanah*, or spiritual concentration, in prayer in particular and in every other kind of activity. As a result, the hasidim actively sought out spiritual enlightenment, attempting to perceive the presence of the Creator or the *Shekhinah*, the Divine Presence, in every situation. In this active approach to religious experience the hasidim are not unlike the Sufis or, especially, the Zen Buddhists.[39] Hasidism also emphasizes the mystical dimension, as do these other sects, and in this the hasidim should be seen as the spiritual heirs of the kabbalists, and especially of the teachings of the Ari. Above all, hasidism was a product of messianic longings and the sense that, in the Baal Shem Tov and some of the later hasidic masters, figures as great as the sages of the past had come again into the world. This belief provided a renewed sense of meaning and enabled the hasidim to bring about an extraordinary reanimation of the process of spiritual growth in Judaism. Surely the abundance of teachings and tales that was produced in a relatively short period is equal to that of any earlier period. And the possibilities of spiritual expression that they demonstrate set in motion a process that has also revived and inspired Judaism in the present century.

About fifty years after the death of the Baal Shem Tov, *Shivhei ha-Besht*, a volume of wonder tales about the founder of hasidism was published.[40] Many of these tales, which concern the birth, childhood, and later life of the Baal Shem Tov, have parallels to earlier rabbinic literature, notably to the legends of the Ari that are reported in *Shivhei ha-Ari*. The master-disciple relationship of the Baal Shem Tov and his hasidim, about whom volumes of tales were produced after their deaths, was duplicated in subsequent generations. The result is a rich literature of over three thousand texts, much of which has not yet been translated into English. These texts are a product of the sacred literatures of the Bible, Talmud, Midrash, and Kabbalah, but what is less apparent is the influential role of medieval Jewish folklore. For hasidic tales incorporate elements of the narrative similar to those found in folktales, as well as the miracles, enchantments, witches, and demons that are so familiar in folklore and fairy tales. Imposed on this archetypal substructure are figures of angels and spirits, a supernatural aspect of hasidic literature that is found in a great many tales.

In combining the sacred intentions of the *Aggadah* with the narrative freedom of the folktale, hasidism produced a body of literature that is the direct result of the previous genres, sacred and secular. If there is any one key to understanding the hasidim, it is this profound link to the ancient tradition. There was a remarkable sense of dialogue with the past, as is suggested in these words of Rabbi Nachman of Bratslav, one of the key rebbes, as the hasidic masters were called:

> Two men who live in different places, or even in different generations, may still converse. For one may raise a question, and the other who is far away in time or in space may make a comment or ask a question that answers it. So they converse, but no one knows it save the Lord, who hears and records and brings together all the words of men, as it is written: *They who serve the Lord speak to one another, and the Lord hears them and records their words in His book* (Mal. 3:16).[41]

And from the present perspective it does appear that some of the hasidic rebbes, including the Baal Shem Tov, Rabbi Levi Yitzhak of Berditchev, and Rabbi Nachman, were among the most inspired figures of Jewish history.

While less well known than the tales of the Baal Shem Tov, the subsequent hasidic literature is one of the richest of the aggadic tradition. It consists of many collections of tales, as well as a voluminous exegetical literature. Although it is obvious that the tales of the Baal Shem Tov served as the primary model for these tales of the subsequent masters, the format is flexible enough so that the individual perspectives of the various rebbes easily emerge. The effect of groups of tales about individual rebbes is that they create a kind of legendary history based on anecdote that is attractive in itself, as well as being a valuable resource for the modern Jewish writer. Much of the compelling quality of both these sources and the modern retellings derives from the fact that the rebbe is an ideal subject for an anecdote. What is apparent, above all, is that the love of legend demonstrated by the hasidim has easily transmitted itself into the creative imagination of our own time, where hasidic lore has been recognized as one of the most accessible and moving of all Jewish traditions.

In the stories of the modern Jewish authors who have utilized these aggadic legends, the source lies like a seed in the center of the fruit of the modern creation, while the modern element has, in a sense, fused with the ancient. Much of the power of this modern literature derives from the reader's experience of this fusion. Whether the starting point is a myth, legend, ritual, or even a halakhic ruling, there is inevitably a process of both preservation and transformation that takes place.

For the authors of such works there is also the opportunity to participate in the evolution of the archetypal myths that serve as the foundation of Western culture and are, as well, at the center of Judaism. For it is important to recognize, above all, that the process that is taking place is essentially mythic and that it is the fundamental, compelling quality of myth that explains the momentum of this evolution over the centuries, even to this day. It also helps explain the lasting attraction of the tradition, even to those who do not necessarily identify with its religious goals.

The aggadic tradition, then, is more than the preservation of the past, as symbolized by the coffin of Joseph, which the Israelites carried beside the Tabernacle in the wilderness. It is also more than the present, symbolized by the Ark of the Covenant, which was carried side by side in the wilderness with the coffin of Joseph. It is a continuing process of the reintegration of the past into the present. Each time this takes place, the tradition is transformed and must be reimagined. And it is this very process that keeps the tradition vital and perpetuates it. For despite the inevitability of this metamorphosis, the essential aspect of the tradition remains eternal and unchanging. This is how the Jewish people view life in this world. On one level it is a blessing that has been given, and on another it is transitional and illusory. This dual awareness exists at all times, for neither this world nor the world to come can be ignored. In contrast to the Hindu worldview, for example, which dismisses this world and seeks to escape from the cycle of rebirths, or that of the skeptics, who insist that nothing exists beyond this world, this blend of the worldly and the eternal is the essence of the Jewish vision. In aggadic terms this correspondence is the natural harmony of the earthly Jerusalem and the heavenly Jerusalem, for the one cannot exist without the other.

Tools of Interpretation

Surely this instruction which I enjoin upon you this day is not too baffling for you, nor is it beyond reach. It is not in the heavens, that you should say, "Who among us can go up to the heavens and get it for us and impart it to us, that we may observe it?" Neither is it beyond the sea, that you should say, "Who among us can cross to the other side of the sea and get it for us and impart it to us, that we may observe it?" No, the thing is very close to you, in your mouth and in your heart, to observe it.

(Deut. 30:11–14)

The Bible serves not only as the primary sacred Scriptures for the West, but as the source of our central myths. These myths have become so entwined with all aspects of our lives that they have taken on the quality of archetypal symbols. It is into these symbols that the culture as a whole projects its hopes and dreams, permitting the mythic archetypes to assert their power.

As in any system of symbols, then, it is necessary to explicate the symbolic intent. This requires a mastery of the meaning of the primary symbolism. Fortunately, the need for interpretation has long been recognized in the Jewish tradition and the act of explication held in high esteem. Many editions of the Hebrew Bible are printed with the commentaries of Rashi and others, and these commentaries have taken on the aura, over time, of the sacred texts they explicate, even though they often disagree as to the correct interpretation of the biblical text. However, the acceptance of opposing views has been recognized since the talmudic period because of the cordial relations between the schools of Hillel and Shammai, which is apparent from the following talmudic passage:

> About Hillel and Shammai: Notwithstanding the fact that one school prohibits what the other allows, that one declares unfit what the other declares fit, the disciples of the two schools have never refrained from intermarriage. Likewise, as regards levitical cleanliness and uncleanliness, where one school declared clean what the other declared unclean, nevertheless they never hesitated to help one another in the work that according to the other faction might not be considered clean.[1]

In fact, it was the act of exegesis that was held in highest esteem as the best means of understanding the sacred text at hand. And not only for the sacred Scriptures, but also for dreams: "A dream left uninterpreted is like a letter unread."[2] Before the accepted ruling on the *Halakhah*, the Law, was reached by majority opinion, polar and contradictory interpretations were offered. The following midrash amply demonstrates how conditioned the rabbis were to opposing viewpoints:

> The school of Shammai maintains that heaven was created first, while the school of Hillel holds that earth was created first. In the view of the school of Shammai this is like the case of the king who first made his throne and then made his footstool. According to the school of Hillel, this is to be compared to a king who builds a palace—after laying the foundation he builds the upper portion. Discussing this matter, Rabbi Yonatan said: "As regards creation, heaven was first; as regards completion, earth was first." Rabbi Shimon observed: "I am amazed that the fathers of the world engage in controversy over this matter, for surely both were created at the same time, like a pot and its lid."[3]

One further legend, from the Talmud, relates the remarkable circumstances in which the majority opinion of the rabbis overruled both Rabbi Eliezer ben Hyrcanos and God Himself:

> Rabbi Eliezer ben Hyrcanos was among the sages who were debating a point of the Law. All of the sages, except Rabbi Eliezer, ruled one way, and Rabbi Eliezer continued to insist that they were wrong. He used every possible argument to support it, but the others did not agree. Then he said: "Let this carob tree prove that the Law is as I state it is." The carob tree then uprooted itself and moved a distance of one hundred ells. But the other sages said: "The carob tree proves nothing."
>
> Then Rabbi Eliezer said: "Let the waters of the spring prove that I am right." Then the waters began to flow backward. But again the sages insisted that this proved nothing.

Then Rabbi Eliezer spoke again and said: "Let the walls of the house of study prove I am right." And the walls were about to collapse when Rabbi Yehoshua said to them: "If scholars are discussing a point of the Law, why should you interfere?" Thus they did not fall, in deference to Rabbi Yehoshua, but neither did they straighten out, out of respect for Rabbi Eliezer, and they are inclined to this day.

Rabbi Eliezer then said: "If the Law is as I say, let heaven prove it." Thereupon a *Bat Kol*, a heavenly voice, came forth and said: "Why do you quarrel with Rabbi Eliezer, whose opinion should prevail everywhere?"

Then Rabbi Yehoshua stood up and said: "*The Law is not in heaven*" (Deut. 30:12). "What does this mean?" asked Rabbi Yermiyahu. "It means that since the Torah was given to us on Mount Sinai, we no longer require a heavenly voice to reach a decision, since it is written in the Torah: *Follow after the majority* (Ex. 23:2)."

Later Rabbi Nathan encountered Elijah and asked him how the ruling was accepted on high. And Elijah said: "At this the Holy One, blessed be He, smiled and said, 'My children have overruled me!' "[4]

From this example it is apparent that the rabbis regarded the very act of explication of the Torah as a Divine injunction and their decisions so inviolate that not even God could overrule them. The necessity for this interpretation goes back to the original existence of both a written and an oral law, the oral intended to explicate the written. Thus the need for commentary was regarded as a necessity from the very giving of the Torah on Mount Sinai, and we find it said in the Talmud concerning commentary: "Prior to the time of Solomon, the Torah was like a basket without handles, but when Solomon came he affixed the necessary handles."[5]

It is also of interest to note that while the ruling on a law was always observed and quoted in all decisions related to it, the opposing viewpoints were not deleted from the Talmud and thus are not disregarded. The existence of these rabbinic debates assisted immeasurably in the creation of an atmosphere in which a variety of interpretations became possible.[6]

The oldest and most elementary method of scriptural exegesis consisted of locating one passage in the Bible to explicate another. From this method evolved more intricate techniques for a close reading of the text, including the seven rules, or *middot*, of Hillel, which were later expanded to thirteen *middot* by Rabbi Ishmael. These rules were primarily formulated to reach an understanding of the *Halakhah*, and were intended to assist in the establishment of general principles that could be deduced from the text. Their primary focus is on the *peshat*, or literal meaning, but some of them are couched in general enough terms that they are able to serve as justification for less literal readings as well. Later Rabbi Eliezer ben Jose, a disciple of Rabbi Akiba, formulated thirty-two rules for aggadic exegesis.[7]

In addition to rules of exegesis there were also other techniques for extracting meaning from a text. Four particularly common techniques, which gained their widest acceptance during the kabbalistic period (13th–17th centuries C.E.), are *gematria, notarikon, temurah,* and *tzeruf.* In *gematria* the numerical value of the letters is added up, and words with identical totals are assumed to be related. By this technique, for example, the ladder Jacob saw reaching into heaven could be related to Mount Sinai, since the numerical total of *sullam* (ladder) is 130, the same as that of Sinai. After all, both the ladder and the Torah, received on Mount Sinai, connect earth and heaven, each in its own way. *Notarikon* takes the letters of a word as the initial letters of an acrostic. By this method the first word of the Torah, *Bereshit* ("in the beginning"), for example, can be said to represent in Hebrew the phrase, "In the beginning God saw that Israel would accept the Torah." By the same technique the same word can allude to the phrase, "He created the sky, the earth, the heavens, the sea, and the abyss." *Temurah* substitutes one letter for another, and *tzeruf* rearranges a word to make it into another—thus, an anagram. These methods tend to encourage a kind of free association but also lend themselves to manipulation by those intent on confirming a particular reading of the text.

One valuable medium for the preservation of early biblical exegesis was the translations of the Bible into Aramaic known as the Targumim. In these translations, interpretations were incorporated into the texts, expanding and clarifying the narrative. In this way the Targumim, particularly those edited in Palestine, prefigure the later midrashic collections, such as *Pirke de Rabbi Eliezer, Sefer ha-Yashar,* and *Sefer ha-Zikhronot (The Chronicles of Jerahmeel),* which gather aggadic interpretations from various sources and weave them into a continuous narrative. Needless to say, many of these interpretations altered the meaning of the original text. The Targum on the story of the Tower of Babel, for example, makes overt the challenge to the Divinity that is only implicit in the biblical text; the nonitalicized words are the addition of the Targum:

> *And they said, "Come, Let us build us a city, and a tower whose top* comes up to *heaven, and let us make us* an idol on the top of it and let us put a sword in its hand, and it will make formations for battle before Him, before we are scattered over the face of the earth."* [8]

From a very early period, interpretations of an allegorical nature also emerged as an accepted, albeit controversial, method of explication. One of the earliest allegorical interpretations appears in Hosea 12:5, with the suggestion that Jacob's struggle with the angel may have been a struggle in prayer rather than a physical contest. A further illustration is the interpretation of Jeremiah's prophecy (29:10) that the exile would end after seventy years, which appears in the Book of Daniel (9:2 and 9:24). Here the prophecy is interpreted to mean seventy weeks of years, to give hope for redemption from the Greek rule of that period.

Additional allegorical readings appear in the apocryphal text, The Wisdom of Solomon,[9] where Jacob's ladder is viewed as a symbol of Divine Providence; and in the writings of Josephus, who interprets the Tabernacle allegorically, equating, for example, the Holy of Holies with the heavens.

But among early allegorists, the master was Philo of Alexandria. Philo constructed an entire system of biblical interpretation based on allegory, in which every finite detail is seen as an allegory of some higher truth. Ironically, Philo's writings had very little direct impact on later Jewish tradition, but furnished a foundation stone to Christianity; his approach to interpreting the Old Testament was used as a prophecy for the New Testament. Philo's failure to influence the Jewish tradition is due to the implications of his approach, which appears to sacrifice the literal meaning for an allegorical one, reducing the patriarchs to mere abstractions. Philo interprets, for example, God's command to Abraham to *Depart thy land, and from thy kindred, and from thy Father's house* (Gen. 12:1) to mean, "By Abraham's country the body, and by his kindred the outward senses, and by his father's house uttered speech."[10]

It might appear that the rejection of Philo's extreme approach would have brought about a general rejection of the allegorical method, but this was not the case. Rather, it was a rejection, for a time, of Philo's highly abstract, all-encompassing metaphysical interpretation and its apparent denial of the literal meaning of the text (although Philo himself defended the literal meaning, while remaining vague on the subject of how it related to the allegorical one). It was not until the kabbalistic period that such thoroughly abstract allegories came to flourish and found acceptance in the tradition.

On what grounds, then, was allegory retained as a tool of interpretation by the talmudic sages? It was retained primarily as a means to explain some passages of the Scriptures that were difficult to interpret in any other way. Allegorical interpretations were necessary, for example, to explain anthropomorphic expressions such as "the hand of God," so as to sustain the conception of God as an incorporeal Being. At the same time, their intense belief in the Torah as the repository of all truth led the rabbis to assume that a literal interpretation of a passage from the Torah could not fully exhaust its meaning. Allegorical interpretations made it possible for some passages, in particular, to express more profound meanings than those conveyed by the literal reading.

Since the sages, and Rabbi Akiba in particular, saw it as their duty to explicate each and every word of the Torah, even what might seem to be insignificant, they were forced to come to grips with passages that did not lend themselves to any apparent interpretation. We read in Genesis, for example, that *Abram and Nabor took to themselves wives, the name of Abram's wife being Sarah and that of Nabor's wife Milcah, the daughter of Haran the father of Milcah and Iscah* (Gen. 11:27–29). There is no further mention of Iscah, and the rabbis were at a loss as to how to identify her. This dilemma was solved in the talmudic period by Rabbi Isaac, who observed: "Iscah was Sarah, and why was she called Iscah? Because she foresaw the future by divine inspiration."[11] With no other evidence to go on, Rabbi Isaac turns to the root of "Iscah," *sakhah*, which means "to see, gaze, or prognosticate." (This interpretation was later quoted by Rashi, commenting on Gen. 11:29.) From this Rabbi Isaac draws his clearly allegorical explanation, in which Iscah represents that pole of Sarah's personality that functioned as a seer. For tradition has it that Abraham was a great soothsayer but that Sarah was even greater. Normally Sarah was the devoted wife of Abraham, but when she served as a vessel of the Divine Word she touched on another aspect of her personality and thus could be identified by another name. In this way does Rabbi Isaac solve the mystery of Iscah's identity while incorporating the tradition of Sarah's prophetic abilities. Iscah, then, is an extension of Sarah's personality beyond its normal bounds, which in a mythological system is inevitably identified as a separate individual.

That the role of allegory was recognized as an accepted method in which to garb teachings is apparent from the following parable, which defines the ties between body and soul:

> Antoninus said to Rabbi (Judah ha-Nasi): "The body and the soul can both free themselves from judgment. Thus, the body can plead, 'The soul has sinned, the proof being that from the day it left me I have lay like a dumb stone in the grave,' while the soul can say, 'The body has sinned, the proof being that from the day I departed from it I have flown about in the air like a bird and have remained sinless.'" Rabbi replied: "I will tell you a parable. To what may this be compared? To a human king who owned a beautiful orchard that contained splendid figs. Now, he appointed two watchmen therein, one lame and the other blind. One day the lame one said to the blind, 'I see beautiful figs in the orchard. Come and take me upon your shoulder, that we may obtain and eat them.' So the blind one carried the lame one, and they picked the figs and ate them. Some time later the owner of the orchard came and inquired of them: 'Where are those beautiful figs?' The lame one replied: 'Have I feet to walk with?' And the blind one replied: 'Have I eyes to see with?' What did the king do then? He placed the lame upon the blind and judged them together. So will the Holy One, blessed be He, bring the soul and the body together, and judge them as one, as it is written, *He shall call to the heavens from above, and to the earth, that He may judge His people* (Ps. 50:4). *He shall call to the heavens from above*—this refers to the soul; *and to the earth, that He may judge his people*—to the body."[12]

The principle of allegorizing an entire book of the Bible was established by Rabbi Akiba's defense of the inclusion of the Song of Songs in the sacred canon, for even as late as the 2nd century C.E. there was a debate among the rabbis about whether or not the Song of Songs should be included in the Bible. Rabbi Akiba declares in the Mishnah that "All the Scriptures are holy, but the Song of Songs is the Holy of Holies."[13] The Holy of Holies was the most sacred part of the Temple, where the Ark of the Covenant was kept. This metaphor aptly conveys Rabbi Akiba's awe for this remarkable text. But there was resistance to this poem on the grounds that its imagery is highly erotic and that it does not concern itself at all with the Divinity. It was only after Akiba's suggestion that the Song of Songs could be read as an allegory of the love between God and Israel (rather than as that between a man and a woman) that opposition to its inclusion was finally quelled.[14] Thus, by interpreting it in an allegorical fashion, Rabbi Akiba provided a whole new perspective for how to regard the Songs of Songs and succeeded in finding a way to include it in the Canon. Nor is Rabbi Akiba's reading the only Jewish allegorical interpretation. It is interesting to note that in Jewish mysticism, dating from the 13th century, the divine wedding allegorized in the Song of Songs is not between God and Israel, but between God and His Bride, the *Shekhinah;* thus between the masculine and feminine aspects of God. At this point the technique of allegorical interpretation of Scripture was fully established, and statements in support of it began to appear: "Let not the allegoric method appear to you as slight, for by means of the allegorical method one may sometimes get to the true meaning of the scriptural words."[15] Nevertheless, the rabbis continued to resist a great many of the interpretations of the allegorists, fearing that the method might be used against Judaism by the followers of a religion such as Christianity. And, indeed, the methods and interpretation of Philo, in particular, were extensively drawn upon by Christian commentators. The rabbis' reservations about allegory remained a point of contention throughout the talmudic and midrashic periods, and allegory did not receive full sanction as a primary approach to the interpretation of the Torah until the kabbalistic era. At that time allegory was codified as one level of interpretation in the system identified by the acronym PaRDeS.[16] This exegetical approach was of the greatest value in perpetuating the expectation that any passage of the Torah is subject to multiple levels of meaning.

PaRDes is an acronym for four levels of understanding: *peshat, remez, drash,* and *sod.*[17] *Peshat* is the literal level. *Remez* is the first hint of another level of meaning; in literary terms it is the use of metaphor. *Drash* stands for midrash, when the interpretation takes the form of a legend, or, in literary terms, of allegory, which itself is simply an extended metaphor. Above all, *drash* refers to a method of exegesis practiced by the talmudic sages and their disciples and successors. This method involves deriving the essential meaning from a scriptural source by examining both its explicit and implicit meaning. In many cases a passage is explicated by a legend, or a midrash. These legends are frequently intended to be understood as allegories. It is in this way that allegory can be identified as one of the dimensions of *drash.* *Sod* is the level of mystery, of the mystical, of Kabbalah. Its literary meaning must remain inseparable from its religious meaning: entry into the realm of the transcendent. The existence of the level of *sod* is also a reminder that the metaphor is a kind of veil and that ultimate truth transcends it and must remain imageless and unknown, like the remotest aspect of God, known in Kabbalah as *Ein Sof.*

Applying the terms of *Pardes* retrospectively to the Song of Songs, it is apparent that when the poem is viewed as depicting the love between a man and a woman, it is being viewed from the literal level of *peshat*, whereas when it is seen as an expression of love between God and Israel, as in Rabbi Akiba's interpretation, it is being viewed from the third level, *drash*, allegory. In this and many other cases the second level of *Pardes*, *remez*, is actually more of a transitional phase, wherein the reader first recognizes the use of simile, metaphor, or allusion. It is not unlike recognizing the connotation of a word rather than the denotation. When the entire metaphor has been revealed, as in Akiba's interpretation, it achieves the level of *drash*. The fourth level, *sod*, was added during the kabbalistic era. This fourth level was sufficient reason for Moshe de Leon to adopt the system of *Pardes*, since it codified the kabbalistic vision of the Zohar as an integral part of the Jewish system of explication. Such a system of interpretation offered assurance for the continued existence of contrary interpretations of the same text, which could simply be seen as signifying differing levels of meaning. Furthermore, a system that posits four simultaneous levels of understanding, from the most concrete to the most abstract, is well suited to develop a rich literary tradition whose works can be approached, no matter how obscure they may appear.

The choice of the word *Pardes* as the acronym for this system derives from its use in the talmudic legend in Hagigah 14b about the four sages who entered *Pardes*. This is without a doubt one of the key legends in all of Jewish literature, and in the context of this legend the term *Pardes* added to its literal meaning of "orchard" the aura of mystical contemplation and even of the ascent of the soul into Paradise.[18]

While the system of *Pardes* was primarily designed to explicate the Torah, it is also applicable to all literature, sacred as well as secular, and can serve as a highly sophisticated tool of interpretation. It is a technique especially useful, both in its religious and literary dimensions, for coming to terms with the kinds of Jewish tales found throughout postbiblical Jewish literature. Some, of course, are intended to be understood quite literally. But most touch on all four levels at the same time and, as such, are far richer than may be apparent on first reading.[19]

Consider, for example, S. Y. Agnon's "Fable of the Goat." This tale, which exists as a folktale in several variants, concerns a goat that leads its owner through an enchanted cave to the Holy Land. On the level of *peshat* the story can be seen simply as an embellishment of the folktale on which it is based. From this perspective, the enchantment of the cave can be seen as a common motif in folk and fairy tales. But if the reader notes in the separation of father and son a hint of the predicament of those who emigrated to Israel and those who stayed behind, then the direction of the allegory can be discerned. At this point the reading has passed beyond the level of *remez* and reached that of *drash*—an allegory of the separation of the generations. It should not be difficult for readers to achieve this understanding of the story, but few will succeed in reaching into the realm of *sod*, where the tale must be internalized. From this perspective the cave comes to symbolize the path within the self that leads one to emerge from the exile of self-alienation to discover the Promised Land within. Such self-realization is the true goal of kabbalistic literature, as it was the true goal of the alchemists whom the world regarded as being concerned with the transmutation of lead into gold and whose true calling, that of transmuting the leaden soul into the golden one, was concealed.

Another illustration is provided by the tale of I. L. Peretz entitled "The Hermit and the Bear." Here a kabbalist who has gone off to the wilderness to wake the soul of the world, attempts to tame a bear, representing the forces of evil, using his mystical powers. This is a story that refuses to be read only on the literal level. It suggests that the methods of the hermit in moving the river, in seeking to wake the world-soul, and in taming the bear are the esoteric techniques of the kabbalist, who can concentrate great powers to achieve an end. These are the powers called upon by Rabbi Judah Loew in the legend-cycle of the Golem, the man of clay who comes to life in the folk legend that prefigures the Frankenstein myth of our own time.

These implications in Peretz's tale are intended to direct the reader beyond the first, literal level of *Pardes*, to the second, *remez*, where the struggle can be viewed in its abstract form as a classic confrontation of good and evil. This reading, in turn, leads to the logical allegorical meaning, in which the struggle of the hermit and the bear can be seen as the eternal conflict between the flesh and the spirit in everyone. This reading reaches the level of *drash*. But to achieve an understanding at the level of *sod* would require insight into the quest of the hermit to awaken the soul of the world, which is sleeping. Such insight would require not necessarily the ability to wake this soul, but at least the ability to recognize the existence of the soul that sleeps and of the possibility of every person, working independently or together, to wake that sleeping soul within himself. Peretz also makes it quite clear that devoting one's energy solely to taming the bear, that is, our unbridled desires, will not serve the quest of trying to awaken the world-soul, for, as he writes, "The hermit who now sleeps together with the bear will not wake the soul of the world." And asleep, how can the hermit continue his quest?

This story, then, despite its folktale exterior and its jaunty manner, has at its core a truth that Peretz has clothed in allegory for the same purpose that the kabbalists invented similar allegories. Whether the reader lifts the veils hiding that truth depends on his or her ability to reach these higher levels of comprehension. But for those capable of reaching that far, this truth glows at the center of Peretz's tale.

Thus this exegetical method is concerned not only with demarking particular levels of interpretation, but also with the natural process of arriving at a full understanding of these profound tales. This begins, naturally, with their link to the literal and familiar, and leads us, step by step, to the transcendental. Like the ascent into Paradise that was the goal of the *Merkavah* mystics, the goal of the reader should be a spiritual ascent. These tales, then, are not mere entertainment or embellishment of familiar themes, but attempts to construct around a kernel of truth a labyrinth in which some readers will wander without ever penetrating to the core and in which others will quickly find their way.

PART II

The Folk Tradition

On Jewish Fairy Tales

Tales of magic and wonder can be found in every phase of Jewish literature, both sacred and secular.[1] The sacred texts include the Bible, as
well as rabbinic, kabbalistic, and hasidic literature. The secular texts include
the Pseudepigrapha, the writings of the texts of medieval Jewish folklore,
modern enthnological tales, as well as modern Jewish literature. Among the
postbiblical *aggadot* (legends) of rabbinic lore and the *ma'asiyot* (tales) of
Jewish folklore are to be found a number of stories that can readily be
identified as traditional fairy tales. Some of these are the universal type of
fairy tale set in an enchanted land and populated with a variety of human
and supernatural beings, both good and evil, and are Jewish solely by virtue
of their source. But many others, perhaps half of the existing body of Jewish
fairy tales, have fused some specific aspects of Jewish life and tradition with
the archetypal fairy-tale framework. For the fairy-tale version of the world as
a stage on which good and evil struggle is fully compatible with the Jewish
view of the essential condition of this world, where faith in God can defeat
the evil impulse, known as the *Yetzer Hara*.

The fairy tale is an ancient genre, filled with marvels and enchantments,
and typically concerned with kings and queens ready to give up half their
kingdoms if they could only have a child of their own; with princes who set
out on quests to waken sleeping princesses; and with witches who are prepared, at the slightest offense, to throw a fly in the ointment. Above all, the
hero must overcome obstacles in order to prove himself and win his reward.
And when all is said and done, good always triumphs over evil, and the
prince and princess live happily ever after.

Yet despite the apparent simplicity and even childlike qualities of the fairy tale, much of its power derives from the timeless fantasies and human concerns it embodies, which we perceive primarily on an unconscious level when we read it, and which explain its primal and compelling power. This suggests why the fairy tale is found in virtually every culture, providing a medium of expression for the archetypes of the unconscious, embodied in such beings as witches, sorcerers, and enchanted princesses. For if fairy tales served merely as an outlet for the need to imagine ourselves as royalty, their spell would soon be broken, but instead these tales retain a remarkable power all our lives, not only when we are children. For just as the outer garments of Jewish ritual signify something much greater to observant Jews than mere custom, so too does the seemingly safe and familiar format of the fairy tale encompass some of the most elemental drives and emotions.

The pioneering work of Antti Aarne and Stith Thompson in this field, especially in *The Types of the Folk-Tale*, has demonstrated convincingly the parallel themes and patterns of fairy tales and other kinds of folktales found throughout the world. Fairy tales from a wide range of Jewish sources and periods substantiate the thesis of Aarne and Thompson. There are even Jewish variants of such well-known fairy tales as "Snow White," "Sleeping Beauty," "Cinderella," "Rapunzel," and "The Golden Bird,"[2] but at the same time they contain many unique qualities as a result of their origin. Especially those fairy tales that concern Jewish legendary figures have brought with them the customs and settings of the milieu from which they have emerged and are valuable bearers of the tradition.

That fairy-tale elements can be found at the earliest stages of Jewish literature is demonstrated by the biblical Book of Esther, in which a queen, Esther, struggles with Haman, an evil minister of King Ahasuerus, who is trying to destroy her people, the Jews. The minister's plot is foiled by a wise old man, Mordecai, who is Esther's kinsman. Whatever the historical basis for this account, it has been cast in the mold of a fairy tale, for all of the characteristics are present except for the intervention of the supernatural, and there is even a happy ending. In fact, it is possible to recognize in the Book of Esther the direction taken by later Jewish fairy tales, especially those of the medieval period, which combine the universal fairy-tale format with a distinctly Jewish context.

Indeed, other biblical episodes have fairy-tale overtones. Imagine a fairy tale about a garden in which two enchanted trees grow, one linked to Life and one to Death. There is also a speaking snake in the garden, who seethes with envy over the man who lives there with a beautiful woman. Sound familiar? The biblical account of the Garden of Eden has all of these folk elements and many others. So too can various kinds of folktale types and motifs be found in other biblical narratives, as when Moses threw down his staff, which became a serpent, or when he struck the rock from which water poured forth.

Fairy-tale qualities can be found as well in the account of David and Goliath—the young shepherd boy David slaying the giant Goliath against all the odds. That this episode was indeed regarded as a fairy tale is made apparent by the tale of David and the giant Ishbi-benob, brother of Goliath, which is found in the Talmud, the most sacred Jewish text after the Bible.[3] In this tale, "King David and the Giant," Ishbi-benob behaves exactly as do bellicose giants in fairy tales, attempting to crush King David beneath his olive press while his evil mother, Orpah, throws her spindle at Abishai, King David's general. Here the latent fairy-tale elements in the story of David and Goliath are made overt; whereas in the biblical tale it is David's skill and cunning that save him, here it is the supernatural power of the Name of God (known as the Tetragrammaton) that performs the magic of suspending David in the air so that he does not land on the giant's spear, making this much more of a fairy tale than its biblical forerunner. The use of Divine intervention is characteristic of the Jewish fairy tale in general, where it replaces the usual devices of enchantment. Thus what other fairy tales attribute to magical causes, the Jewish vision interprets as a demonstration of the power and beneficence of God. King Solomon's primary magical device, for example, is his ring, on which is engraved the Name of God. Magical rings of enchanted origin are often found in fairy tales, but the power of Solomon's ring derives explicitly from God's Name: thus Benaiah, Solomon's general, need only hold up Solomon's ring and cry out, "The Name of your Master is upon you!" and Asmodeus, king of the demons, is rendered powerless.[4]

These are all authentic folk or fairy-tale themes, along with others, such as the story of Noah's ark, the talking ass in Baalam, the whale that swallows Jonah, and Daniel in the lion's den. Still, such folk and fairy-tale elements do not play a prominent role in the Bible, and it is only in the Talmud that the first clear-cut Jewish fairy tales are to be found. This is largely due to the more prominent role of fantasy in the talmudic legends, which make liberal use of poetic license. Yet as with virtually all of the *aggadot*, the fairy tales that are found in the Talmud and the Midrash have as their starting point an attempt to resolve a question raised in the biblical text. The workings of this process are especially apparent in "King Solomon and Asmodeus."[5] The premise of this well-known talmudic tale is an explanation of how King Solomon managed to construct the stone altar of the Temple *with neither hammer nor axe nor any tool of iron heard in the house while it was being built* (1 Kings 6:7). Since there was no known way to accomplish this, a magical creature, the Shamir, was invented, as it were, that could cut through anything, and King Solomon sends his trusted general Benaiah on a quest to capture Asmodeus, king of the demons, who knows where the Shamir can be found, and then to obtain it from the hoopoe bird that has possession of it.

All in all there are no more than a dozen fairy tales to be found in the Talmud, including "The Witches of Ashkelon,"[6] "King David and the Giant,"[7] "King Solomon and Asmodeus,"[8] and "The Beggar King."[9] The first of these concerns historical figures, as do the tales about King David and King Solomon. It may well be that "The Witches of Ashkelon" is, in fact, based on a historical event: the hanging of eighty witches in the city of Ashkelon. Fabulous as the tale itself seems, in which the witches are deceived when their captors disguise themselves as would-be suitors wishing to dance with them, the Talmud also reports the fury of the relatives of the witches following their execution.[10] And thus this tale offers an instance in which it is possible to follow the evolution of a historical event into a tale of the fantastic, whereas most legends have long since succeeded in discarding the historical kernel that brought them into being.

In a tale such as "King Solomon and Asmodeus" the distinction between legend and fairy tale has become substantially blurred. Legends are typically based upon historical persons, places, or events and usually possess some degree of realism, but while it seems certain that King Solomon as well as his general, Benaiah, were historical figures, the quest described here is clearly drawn from the realm of fantasy. Such an approach is typical of most aggadic legends, which are free of most of the constraints of verisimilitude, including the portrayal of time. Yet because of the legendary intention that inspired them, the tales of the Talmud and the Midrash remain a unique form, functioning as legendary tales and tales of the fantastic at the same time. And on occasion the rule of fantasy fully dominates the tale, bringing it into the realm of the tale of enchantment. That such fairy-tale elements are present in "King Solomon and Asmodeus" is readily apparent, enabling it to function as a *drash* (biblical exegesis) explaining how the injunction that *thou shalt lift up no iron tool upon the altar of the Lord* (Deut. 27:5) was fulfilled, as well as a tale of enchantment concerned with a quest, the defeat and capture of the king of demons, the use of a magical ring to subdue him, and the discovery of a creature that can cut through the hardest stone. It is in this very tale, then, that the fusion of the uniquely Jewish aggadic tale and the universal fairy tale can be seen to take place. And it is worth noting that such hybrid creation is unusual—while most myths, legends, and folktales are colored, to a considerable extent, with the customs and setting of the culture from which they emerge, this usually is not the case with fairy tales, which exist in a timeless and spatially elastic world.

In the Talmud "King Solomon and Asmodeus" is followed by a companion tale in which Asmodeus revenges himself by outsmarting King Solomon, the wisest of all men. In this tale, "The Beggar King,"[11] Solomon's fall from glory is so complete he is reduced to being a wandering beggar, regarded as a madman when he insists he is a king. This tale exists as a brief coda at the end of "King Solomon and Asmodeus," but a considerable number of variants stemming from the Middle Ages are to be found, which expand on the wanderings of Solomon. This process of embellishment of an earlier narrative is characteristic of Jewish folklore in general and demonstrates the manner in which the earlier tale was received as a story worthy of further development rather than as a fixed work that had to be retold in exactly the same way. Naturally, much of this narrative freedom derives from the nature of folklore, which belongs primarily to the people and generally remains an oral rather than a written tradition. Although this is true of the folklore of most of the people of the world, the exceptional continuity of the Jewish tradition makes it possible to trace the evolution of many tales from their earliest written versions, preserved in sacred texts, through various retellings in later periods. And the existence of such variants inevitably gives birth to additional tales, as related versions draw on the abundant possibilities of combination and variation.

Whereas the biblical King Solomon is portrayed as a great ruler and a man of surpassing wisdom, the legendary Solomon has been transformed into a sorcerer without peer, versed in all aspects of magic, including the knowledge of the languages of the birds and other animals, and able to call upon the demons and even the winds to serve his will. At the same time, the ambivalence about Solomon found in the Bible emerges in many of the folktales about him. On the one hand there is still admiration for his prowess and grandeur, but this is qualified by a recognition of his excessive pride. Such a portrayal of Solomon also reflects a hesitant attitude toward the realms of magic and the supernatural, for Jewish legend is filled with tales of those less wise and fortunate than Solomon who were destroyed by engaging in the occult.

This theme of chastisement is also found in the midrashic tale "The Mysterious Palace"[12] when Solomon is riding his flying carpet. Filled with a sense of his own greatness, he is suddenly reminded of how fragile is the covenant that permits him to glide through the air, which God can withdraw as though it were the wind. The succeeding episode, concerning the palace of the eagles, teaches Solomon something of the lessons of eternity, not unlike those taught Ozymandias in Shelley's poem of the same title. The whole tale has a strong echo of a talmudic legend in which Solomon tries to enter the gates of the Sanctuary of the Temple, only to be rebuffed when the gates refuse to open, for he is not permitted to enter on his own merits, but only on those of his father, King David.[13]

"The Princess in the Tower," a midrashic variant of "Rapunzel," demonstrates that even King Solomon, the wisest of mortals, could not outfox fate. Solomon attempts to circumvent the prophecy that his daughter will marry a poor man by isolating her in a tower on a remote island. But a giant eagle ends up carrying her destined bridegroom to the roof of the tower. This tale confirms the talmudic dictum that "Forty days before the formation of a child a voice goes forth out of Heaven to announce that this one will marry that one."[14] And not even King Solomon can deprive a person of his or her destined match. A similar moral is found in a legend about two men Solomon attempts to assist in escaping the Angel of Death. In one version Solomon pronounces the Divine Name and suspends the men in the air, where, it turns out, the Angel of Death has been ordered to seize them; in another version he sends them to the city of Luz, which the Angel of Death is forbidden to enter, but the Angel still seizes them, at the gate of the city.[15]

As these parallel legends demonstrate, the same motifs are found through-out the Jewish legendary tradition, in which sacred legends and secular folklore, including fairy tales, are in many ways cut from the same cloth, and well-defined distinctions between them are often not possible.

This legendary city of Luz reappears in a medieval tale of the same title, which offers an opportunity to observe the evolution of a legend from its origin in the Bible through its development in the Talmud and Midrash until its crowning expression as a medieval folktale. There are four brief references to the city of Luz in the Bible. The first of these, that of Jacob's dream, identifies the city as one of the Gates of Heaven:

> And Jacob awaked out of his sleep, and he said, "Surely the Lord is in this place; and I knew it not." And he was afraid, and said, "How full of awe is this place! This is none other than the House of God, and this is the Gate of Heaven." . . . And he called the name of that place Beth-el, but the name of the city was Luz at first.
>
> (Gen. 28:16–17, 19)

But it is the Talmud that identifies Luz for the first time as a city of immortals:[16]

> It has been taught: "That is the Luz against which Sennacherib marched without disturbing it, and even the Angel of Death has no permission to pass through it. But when the old there become tired of life they go outside the wall and then die."

By the Middle Ages this city of immortals had grown into a legendary place and the storytellers' art lay primarily in telling of the quest to reach it.[17]

The most prolific period of Jewish folklore comes in the Middle Ages. It is in this period that the fairy tale first emerges as a prominent form of Jewish folklore. This abundance of folklore was brought about by the inde-pendent evolution of talmudic and midrashic motifs among the people, who were especially attracted to tales that demonstrated the greatness of the Jewish kings and prophets of the past. At a time when rabbinic formulations had become more allegorical and esoteric, especially as manifested in the kabbalistic literature, the common folk were drawn to tales with pro-nounced elements of fantasy and clear-cut morals. The fairy tales that are found in this medieval folklore demonstrate a considerable evolution in the genre, creating a form which in many ways is a hybrid, weaving the features of the typical folktale into the fabric of the fairy tale. For example, the hero in these tales is often a common Jew, but the characteristic link to royalty is usually retained by the presence of a king or queen (or prince or princess) of the opposite sex. In "The Princess with Golden Hair,"[18] the Jew Yohanan is sent out on a mission to locate the princess whose strand of golden hair has been dropped by a bird at the feet of the king, and the tale ends with the fairy-tale marriage of Yohanan and the princess and his ascension to the throne. Another example is found in "The Flight of the Eagle,"[19] in which the Jewish youth Shlomo becomes the beloved and then the husband of the daughter of the king of Spain. And in "The Demon Princess," a Jew even ends up wedded to the daughter of Asmodeus.

These medieval fairy tales also typically retain the moral basis of Judaism. A vow made to one's father is sacred, and Yohanan, in "The Princess with Golden Hair," honors it until he is left impoverished. When he has demonstrated his faithfulness, he is rewarded by the giant scorpion he has raised, and eventually he not only completes the quest to find his princess but even becomes king, a proper reward, the tale implies, for honoring a vow. It is interesting to note that in a version of this tale found in *The Maaseh Book*, which dates from six hundred years later, the scorpion has become a frog and the principal figure a rabbi. But for the most part the story remains the same, another striking example of the continuity of Jewish tradition.

As Yohanan's fidelity makes him deserving of his great reward, so does the violation of such a vow unleash the punishments that overwhelm the man in "The Demon Princess."[20] This tale, which is also known as "The Tale of a Jerusalemite," has been ascribed to Abraham, the son of Moses Maimonides, who lived at the beginning of the 13th century in Egypt. The Jew who breaks his vow to his father is portrayed as deceitful and manipulative, and he makes other vows he has no intention of keeping to the daughter of Asmodeus. The man provokes the wrath of the king of demons and his daughter, which is not tempered with mercy.

This rare occasion of a fairy tale that does not have a happy ending indicates the extent to which the form has evolved. The notion of the kiss of death, with which the demon princess takes the life of the man who has betrayed her, is echoed in a talmudic legend that describes the death of Moses as having come from the Kiss of the *Shekhinah*, the Divine Presence and Bride of God.[21] In this context it signifies a mystical union at the moment of death, whereas the man kissed by the demon princess simply has his breath snatched away. For those familiar with the talmudic legend, of course, its echo in the fairy tale is readily apparent and enriches the resonance of the tale.

Of particular interest in "The Demon Princess" is the description of the religious life in the kingdom of the demons, which seems parallel, in every respect, to that of a devout Jew of the Middle Ages. This is not intended as mockery, for the *Yenne Velt*, the world in which demons and other spirits live, was believed to be a mirror image, somewhat distorted, of the world in which we live.

It is worth noting that the characterization of Asmodeus found in this tale is consistent with that in "King Solomon and Asmodeus" and "The

Beggar King." Asmodeus is a characteristically Jewish demon who, like his nemesis, King Solomon, is one of the most popular figures in Jewish folklore. Spending part of his time in Paradise, where he studies in the Heavenly Academy, Asmodeus does not fit the mold of the typical demon of fairy tales—he performs good deeds, such as setting a blind man on the proper path, as well as mischievous ones. Further aspects of his character are found in the tales "Partnership with Asmodeus" and "The Magic Flute of Asmodeus."[22] In the former, Asmodeus saves a man from suicide—again performing a *mitzvah*, or good deed—and proposes a partnership that brings the man great benefit until he proves to be an ingrate. Then Asmodeus turns on him, as does the demon princess on her dishonest husband, and puts him in grave danger. Or again, Asmodeus appears as a grateful father who rewards the shepherd in "The Magic Flute of Asmodeus" for saving his son and gives him every magical gift he requests. And it should be noted that even when Asmodeus is responsible for Solomon's fall from glory in "The Beggar King," it is for the purpose of teaching the king an important lesson. On the one hand Asmodeus is a worthy adversary, with some of the subtlety of Goethe's Mephistopheles. On the other hand Asmodeus plays a positive role in God's design, for His agency is seen ultimately in every event, whether good or bad.

By the late Middle Ages, the primary Jewish sorcerer is not King Solomon, but Rabbi Adam, who, like Solomon, is master of many mysteries. Rabbi Adam is perhaps best known for his role as the transmitter of the fabled Book of Mysteries to the Baal Shem Tov in hasidic legend, but there also exist several independent medieval tales about him, including "The King's Dream,"[23] "The Magic Mirror of Rabbi Adam,"[24] and "The Enchanted Journey."[25] In "The King's Dream" Rabbi Adam casts a spell that causes an evil king to dream that he awakens at the bottom of a pit in another kingdom, where he is arrested and put to three tests, with his life at stake. Each time Rabbi Adam comes to his rescue, so that the king finds himself greatly in his debt, and when he awakens from his nightmare and finds himself back in his palace, he is more than willing to cancel the evil decree that prompted Rabbi Adam to take action in the first place. In "The Magic Mirror of Rabbi Adam" the wonder-working rabbi uses a magic mirror to save a Jew from being a victim of black magic. And in "The Enchanted Journey" Rabbi Adam casts a spell on a king that causes him to believe that he sails to the kingdom of his enemy, where he is hidden and protected by Jews, until he himself becomes a Jew. When he emerges from the spell, he is far more sympathetic to the plight of the Jews, and cancels an evil spell against them.

In each case Rabbi Adam comes to the assistance of his fellow Jews either by interceding with an evil king or by aiding a Jew in danger. It is not difficult to recognize in these tales the deep frustrations, feelings of impotence, and sense of isolation experienced by Jews in the medieval period, and to see how the fantasy mechanisms of the fairy tale operate. For it is out of the people's longing to be independent and secure that such tales emerged, and this is true of the tales from the Middle East and those from Eastern Europe, the lives of both the Sephardic (Middle Eastern) and Ashkenazic (Eastern European) Jews being equally difficult. The tales about Rabbi Adam also served as models for some of the legends of Rabbi Judah Loew of Prague, the creator of the Golem. In both sets of tales the role of the Jewish hero is taken over by the *tzaddik*, the righteous man who owes his powers to his knowledge of the Torah and his trust in God.

The next important source for Jewish fairy tales, after the Middle Ages, is in the hasidic era of the 18th and 19th centuries in Eastern Europe. While the hasidic masters, including the Baal Shem Tov, founder of Hasidism, had been the subject of a rich body of miracle tales, there are relatively few fairy tales, perhaps because the hasidim identified their rabbis with the patriarchs and ancient sages rather than with the more fanciful heroes of fairy tales. However, there is a treasury of such fairy tales attributed to Rabbi Nachman of Bratslav, who lived in the 19th century. In the last four years of his life Rabbi Nachman, who was the great-grandson of the Baal Shem Tov, undertook to tell tales to his hasidim as a method of transmitting his teachings. Among the tales of Rabbi Nachman that seem, on the surface, to be conventional fairy tales are "The Lost Princess,"[26] "The Prince Who Was Made of Precious Gems,"[27] "The Water Palace,"[28] and "The Pirate Princess."[29] And while they certainly are authentic fairy tales, they are, at the same time, complex allegories frequently linked to myths concerning the *Shekhinah* and the Messiah. In the tales of Rabbi Nachman the *ma'aseh*, the traditional Jewish tale, and the universal fairy tale fully merge and become inseparable.

A story such as "The Lost Princess," for example, appears to be a typical tale of the quest for an imprisoned princess, but, according to Rabbi Nachman's scribe, Rabbi Nathan of Nemirov, it is actually an allegory about the exile of the *Shekhinah*, the Divine Presence, which becomes identified as a mythically independent feminine being during the kabbalistic period. According to kabbalistic myth, the *Shekhinah* went into exile at the time of the destruction of the Temple in Jerusalem. The loyal minister who searches for her in this tale may be seen to represent the Messiah, who has been sent to bring her out of exile, since tradition holds that she will be freed only when the Messiah has come. Or the minister may be seen as a *tzaddik*, a righteous one, as the most elect among the hasidic rabbis were called, who obeys the command of the King, the Divinity, to search for the lost *Shekhinah* so as to make it possible for the messianic era to begin. Or the minister might be seen as the people of Israel as a whole, who share the responsibility for bringing the Messiah. For those familiar with these kabbalistic myths, as Nachman's hasidim were, the symbolism in his stories conveyed profound secrets, including, it is hinted, the means to hasten the messianic era.

This does not mean, however, that Rabbi Nachman's tales must be read allegorically to be appreciated. The tales have great power in themselves, for Nachman's figures, events, and images are, at once, so primary and so subtle that they evoke the numinous quality of the inner world. Furthermore, his allegorical intentions brilliantly exploit the fairy-tale form as a pure and spontaneous expression of unconscious states. So too does the kabbalistic concept of the *Shekhinah* naturally link up with the Jungian concept of the anima, the feminine aspect of the psyche of every man. The identification of the *Shekhinah* with the imprisoned princess works in very much the same way the figure of the evil stepmother in fairy tales serves as a mask for our own mothers, permitting the child an expression of fear or anger that might otherwise be repressed. Rabbi Nachman was thus especially remarkable because he recognized the vital symbolism in fairy tales, saw its link to the mystical imagery in the Kabbalah, and discovered a way to fuse the two.

From the perspective of the tradition of Jewish literature, then, it is possible to see how Rabbi Nachman's innovations represent a continuation of the development beginning with the *aggadot* of the Talmud and Midrash. For in these rabbinic legends there is a remarkably complete identification with the primary biblical figures, such as Abraham, Jacob, and Moses, which made the legends modes of personal expression as well as of biblical exegesis. The rabbis not only freely provided missing episodes from the biblical narrative, such as that of Abraham's childhood, but also attributed to the patriarchs dreams of their own, such as an apocryphal dream Abraham is said to have had about a cedar and a palm tree, which warned him of the coming danger in Egypt.[30] Such projections have always been the basis of fairy tales, in which the primary characters are often left unnamed, identified only as a king or queen, a prince or princess, thus inviting identification with the listener or reader of the tale. Beginning with the kabbalistic period of Jewish literature, the kinds of projections that were common for biblical figures came to include more abstract concepts, such as the *Shekhinah* and the Messiah. So for Rabbi Nachman the lost princess, or soul, in each of us must be sought after, for each of us must seek to accomplish the personal restoration and redemption that the Messiah represents on a cosmic scale. By linking these abstractions with the more concrete characters of the traditional fairy tale, Rabbi Nachman was making this process of spiritual projection a much simpler matter to envision.

Virtually all of the sources discussed so far have come down to us in written form. Nonetheless, all of them first existed as oral tales, which, except for the tales of Rabbi Nachman, were handed down for centuries before they were finally recorded. However, because of the low status of Jewish folklore among the rabbis, who were the primary keepers of the tradition, these secular tales were not scrupulously preserved, as were the sacred texts of the Talmud, Midrash, and Kabbalah. As a result, a great many tales were lost and will almost certainly never be recovered. At the same time, many tales continued to be retold, and thus have been preserved orally, especially in isolated areas such as Yemen, into the present century.

Among the early Jewish scholars who sought to preserve this oral tradition were S. Ansky, the Yiddish dramatist and author of *The Dybbuk,* and
Y. L. Cahan, who collected Jewish folk songs as well as folktales. Ansky and
Cahan went out into the countryside and wrote down the tales as they were
told to them. Some of these tales had already been preserved in an earlier
written form, but the majority had not. Often these tales were the purest
kinds of fairy tales, left unrecorded simply because they did not seem to
bear a religious moral. But there were also examples of the fused Jewish
folktale and universal fairy tale that emerged in its most complete form in
the Middle Ages. Among the tales collected by Y. L. Cahan and recorded
in Yiddish are "The Imprisoned Princess"[31] and "The Exiled Princess."[32]
"The Imprisoned Princess" can readily be seen as a variant of the theme
found in Rabbi Nachman's "The Lost Princess," while "The Exiled Princess" is a Jewish variant of "Cinderella."

More recently, the most important development in Jewish folklore is taking place in Israel, as might be expected, where oral tales are being collected from Jews representing virtually every Jewish ethnic community. This
good work is being accomplished by the Israel Folktale Archives (IFA),
which was founded forty years ago by Professor Dov Noy of the Hebrew
University. To date the IFA has collected twenty thousand tales from oral
sources. Collectors of the IFA work under considerable pressure because of
the likely extinction of most of the oral traditions that still survive, as a
result of the rapid transition from languages such as Yiddish and Arabic to
Hebrew among the Jewish immigrants to Israel. Thus the tales that are
known only in the old languages are dying out. Faced with this situation,
the IFA has rushed to collect as much material as possible before it is too
late. So far, the collectors have admirably succeeded in their task, and
among the tales they have collected are many fairy tales, including Sephardic tales from Egypt, Morocco, Greece, India, Yemen, Kurdistan, Persia
(Iran), and Libya, as well as Ashkenazic tales from Eastern Europe.

One unusual format for the preservation of folk material, including fairy
tales, is the ballad. Ballads were especially popular in Sephardic communities, such as those found in Greece, Turkey, and Morocco, and there are
also Yiddish folk songs that have preserved similar material. In many cases
the Judeo-Spanish ballads contain the only existing versions of the tales on
which they were based. The fairy tale in a ballad format usually has been
condensed to include only the primary episodes of the tale. But since fairy
tales are in many ways predictable, it is not difficult to imagine the details
suggested by the ballad's narrative. An example of a fairy tale reconstructed
from such a source is "The Nightingale and the Dove,"[33] which comes
from Salonika. This is a fairy tale of transformation, where each time the
evil queen kills the lovers, they are reborn in another form, as fish, birds,
and ultimately bushes that twine together.

While most of the fairy tales that have been preserved in the sacred
literature of the Talmud and Midrash and the later medieval folklore are

either specifically Jewish in content, or else parables and teaching stories that have been transmitted for their allegorical intent, the universal fairy tale without overt Jewish elements also flourished during all of these periods. Some of the tales are very old indeed, but since they existed solely in the oral tradition, it is almost impossible to estimate their dates of origin. And while the outer garment of the tales cannot be identified as Jewish, there can be no doubt that the themes of many of these tales are parallel to the concerns of the more overtly Jewish ones. As with the identifiably Jewish fairy tales, the primary themes concern quests and imprisoned princesses.

What is it about these two themes that make them so compelling? The parallels of the theme of the imprisoned princess to the kabbalistic myth of the exile of the *Shekhinah* have already been observed. The theme of the quest is often taken up in the midrashic literature, depicting, for example, the search for the legendary Book of Raziel, given to Adam by the angel Raziel, as well as the search for the Temple vessels, preserved from destruction by Jeremiah when the Romans overran the Temple in Jerusalem. And in his myth of the Shattering of the Vessels and the Gathering of the Sparks, the 16th-century kabbalist Rabbi Isaac Luria, the Ari, develops a method of restoration, or *tikkun*, which works very much like a quest. According to this kabbalistic myth, God sent out vessels filled with a primordial light (which itself is the subject of many midrashim), but these vessels unexpectedly shattered, scattering sparks of light throughout the world. The role of the Jew, according to the Ari, is to raise these scattered sparks from where they have fallen and to eventually restore the world to its pristine state. So it is that the Jew has been brought into this world, in the Lurianic view, to complete such a personal quest, and therefore he has a stake in the ultimate destiny of this world and the next.

That the standard fairy-tale quest can take on religious significance is amply demonstrated in "The Princess and the Slave."[35] Here the slave Samuel seeks Moses in an endless wilderness, suggesting the wandering of the Israelites in the time of the Exodus. As a result of the successful completion of his quest, Samuel discovers the secret of eternal youth, which in symbolic terms can be seen to represent eternal life in the World to Come. Likewise, the quest for Elijah's violin in the story of the same title is of a religious nature.[36] For the successful completion of the king's quest enables the violin's imprisoned melodies, emblematic of the Jewish spirit, to be set free.

Among the characteristics these fairy tales and the midrashic literature have in common is their timelessness. That Samuel succeeds in his quest to find Moses in "The Princess and the Slave" indicates that this fairy tale is set in a timeless world indeed. In the midrashic tradition Moses is often viewed as an immortal figure, largely because his death is not recorded in the biblical narrative. So too does the appearance of Elijah in a multitude of postbiblical tales attest to the tradition that Elijah appears in each generation to assist those Jews with the greatest need. This tradition derives from

Elijah's miraculous ascension into heaven in a chariot of fire. Yet while most of these stories concern the miraculous, very few are fairy tales in the traditional sense. "Elijah's Violin," however, is an exception, and the violin itself can be seen as a symbol for the positive attributes of the legendary Elijah as well as a magical device exactly like those found so often in fairy tales—a Jewish equivalent of Aladdin's lamp.

The characteristic Jewish fairy tale, then, can best be seen as a fusion of the Jewish sacred legend or the Jewish secular folktale with the universal fairy tale, conditioned by the biblical and postbiblical tradition in which Divine Providence takes the place of magical devices and resolutions and the moral element is preeminent. The result is a powerful medium for the reaffirmation of Jewish faith and longing, sustained over one hundred generations. The archetypal and eternal nature of the fairy tale thus becomes particularly appropriate as an expression of continuity with the past, in which all the Jewish generations merge and mysteriously enter a single, timeless present.

Mermaid and Siren

The Polar Roles of Lilith and Eve

*W*hen Rabbi Elimelech of Lizensk was still a young man, he spent all day in the house of study, and at night he walked home through the forest, always taking the same path. One night, as he was walking home, he saw a light glowing in the distance. Curious to know what it was, he left the path and followed the light. Before long he saw that it was coming from a cottage, one that he had never before seen in the forest. As he came closer, he peered into the window, and there he saw a woman with long, dark hair, who was wearing a very thin nightgown.

As soon as he saw her, Reb Elimelech knew that he did not belong there, and he turned to go. Just then the door to the cottage opened, and the woman called out: "Reb Melech, wait! Please, come in." So Reb Elimelech went in. Then the woman closed the door and stood before him and said: "Reb Melech, I have seen you pass through the forest many times, and I have often hoped you would visit me. You know, I bathed in the spring today, and I am clean. The sin would be slight, but the pleasure would be abundant." And she dropped her gown.

Reb Elimelech stared at her and struggled with himself, as did Jacob with the angel. At last he wrenched out the word "No!" At that instant the woman vanished, and the cottage disappeared, and Reb Elimelech found himself standing alone in the forest. And there were glowworms at his feet.

The woman in this tale[1] is not identified, but everyone among the hasidim who heard it knew exactly who she was—Lilith, or one of the daughters of Lilith. So vivid was the presence of Lilith in their lives that she became the projection of their sexual fantasies and fears.

Lilith, as in this tale, is usually portrayed as having black hair. In fact she is characterized this way in the Talmud, in Eruv 100b. She is brazen from the first, calling Reb Elimelech not by his full name, Elimelech, but by his familiar name, Melech. This conveniently lets her avoid pronouncing Eli, "my God," which, as a demoness, she is forbidden to do. The fact that her hair is long indicates that she is unmarried, while having bathed in the spring informs him that she has purified herself in a *mikveh*. She is appealing to his knowledge of the Law when she tells him that the sin will be slight and the pleasure abundant. According to Deut. 22:22, *If a man be found lying with a married woman, then they shall both die.* However, the expected parallel about a married man lying with an unmarried woman is missing, and, according to rabbinic principles of interpretation, what is not stated is not a law. Therefore, the sin is slight, since the law does not identify it as adultery. It is a sin, but not a mortal one.[2]

Thus Lilith comes equipped with many weapons. She does not only use the power of lust, which is her greatest power, but also appeals to his intelligence, in the knowledge that if she could defeat one of the best ones, the others would fall like dominoes. Rabbi Elimelech escapes, but only after a considerable struggle. The glowworms at the end indicate that Lilith has lost her power over him and Lilith has been revealed in her true form, that of a worm. Or, if this story is read as a hasidic sexual fantasy, that the fantasy has reached its climax.

The fact that the tale is attributed to Reb Elimelech of Lizensk indicates that Lilith was brazen enough to approach even the holiest of men. Indeed, this was her intention. For if she could corrupt the best ones, the others would be sure to follow. Reb Elimelech resists, but barely. The power of the *Yetzer Hara*, the Evil Inclination, affects everyone on this earth, even rebbes. (There is also a compensating force, the *Yetzer Tov*, the Good Inclination. But, as might be expected, there is much more heard of the *Yetzer Hara* in Jewish lore than there is of the *Yetzer Tov*.)

The power of the Evil Impulse is demonstrated, for example, in the story of the angels Shemhazai and Azazel, who, according to the Midrash, were the Sons of God who descended to earth from heaven, as recounted in Genesis, chapter 6. Observing the evil ways of men, they rebuked God for creating man in the first place. The Holy One replied: "If you lived on earth, you too would be subject to the *Yetzer Hara*." "Not us!" said the angels. "Let us demonstrate our righteousness." So God let them descend to earth, and no sooner did they arrive than they were overcome with lust for the daughters of men, and indulged themselves on an epic scale.[3]

Even two of the most revered sages, Rabbi Akiba and Rabbi Meir, are the subject of sexual parables in the Talmud. In one Rabbi Akiba saw a naked woman in a tree and was so inflamed by her that he tore off his clothes and started to climb up the tree. When he was halfway there, the naked woman turned into Satan, who said: "Were it not said in Heaven to respect Rabbi Akiba and his teachings, your life would be as nought!"[4]

Immediately following in the Talmud is a parallel legend about Rabbi Meir, about whom there are more stories with a sexual dimension than any other sage. Rabbi Meir saw a naked woman on the other side of a river. There was no bridge, only a rope that had been strung between the two shores. Jumping in the water, Rabbi Meir pulled himself along on the rope, until he was halfway there, when the woman turned into Satan, saying the same thing.[5] The moral of these tales is clear: If even angels, sages, and rebbes were subject to the power of the *Yetzer Hara*, as personified in particular by the demoness Lilith, imagine how much greater its power must be over ordinary mortals. And therefore the sin of lust was seen as deserving to be forgiven.

What is the origin of this haunting legend of Lilith? It finds its source in the rabbinic commentary on the biblical passage *Male and female He created them* (Gen. 1:27). It appeared to the rabbis that this passage contradicted the sequential creation of Adam and Eve (Gen. 2:21–22). Therefore they explained it by saying that *Male and female He created them* referred to Adam's first wife, whom they named Lilith, while Eve, who was created later, was Adam's second wife. They chose the name Lilith from Isaiah 34:14, where Lilith is mentioned *(Yea, Lilith shall repose there)*, in what is believed to be a reference to a Babylonian night demoness.

Even though Lilith seems to leap fully formed out of a line in the Bible, it it just as likely that the legend was already told among the people, and that the rabbis sought out a text to attach it to. In any case, the mythological figure of Lilith almost certainly finds its origin in other cultures of the Ancient Near East. Lilith's role as a seducer of men is likely to have been based on the Babylonian night demon Lilitu, a succubus who seduces men in their sleep, while Lilith's role as a child slayer may well derive from the Babylonian demon Lamashtu. It is interesting to note that the roles of Lilitu and Lamashtu became blurred together, just as Lilith takes on the roles of both seducer and child slayer. Indeed, Lilith seems to have taken over the role of an early Jewish demoness, Obyzouth, who was also a child-destroying witch and is described in terms identical to Lilith in the 1st-century text, *The Testament of Solomon*.

Having brought a tantalizing figure such as Lilith into being, the rabbis felt compelled to convey her entire history. In this case the legend began to grow quite extensive. The first complete version of it is found in *The Alphabet of Ben Sira*, dating from the 9th century in North Africa. Here Adam and Lilith are described as having been created at the same time, although Adam's dust was taken from the four corners of the earth, while Lilith was created from slime. It is said that Adam and Lilith bickered from the first and had a final confrontation over the question of the missionary position. Adam insisted on it; Lilith refused, preferring the opposite. At last Lilith pronounced the secret Name of God, the Tetragrammaton, YHVH, which has remarkable supernatural powers, and flew out of the Garden of Eden and landed on the shore of the Red Sea.[6] There Lilith took up residence in a nearby cave and took for lovers all the demons who lived there, while Adam, left alone, complained to God that his woman had left him. God sent three angels, Senoy, Sansensoy, and Semangeloff, to command Lilith to return to her husband. She refused, and they threatened to kill one hundred of her demon offspring daily. Lilith still refused to return; she was never very maternal. Then she offered a compromise, telling the angels that she was created to strangle children, boys before the eighth day and girls before the twentieth. But if a woman would carry an amulet with the words "Out Lilith!" on it, along with the names of the angels, she would leave that woman and her children alone.

It is here that the legend takes a strange turn. What is really occurring is that another legend is being fused to the first. Indeed, is likely that the entire identity of another demoness had been gathered into that of Lilith. In all likelihood, we can identify this demoness as Obyzouth, who is invoked by King Solomon in the 1st-century text *The Testament of Solomon*.[7] The king commands her to describe herself, and Obyzouth tells how she seeks to strangle children. Furthermore, she reveals that she can be thwarted by the angel Raphael and by women who give birth who write her name on an amulet, for then she will flee from them to the other world. This legend of Obyzouth has virtually all of the key elements of the Lilith legend. What appears to be taking place is that the demoness Lilith, who up to this point had been concerned with issues of independence and sexuality, here takes on a new aspect from Obyzouth, that of the child-destroying witch, by a process that we might call mythic absorption. Why did this happen? Probably because Lilith became such a dominant mythic figure that she absorbed the roles of the lesser-known demoness. This likely occurred very early, between the 1st and 3rd centuries, and Lilith has played a powerful dual role ever since in Jewish folklore and superstition.

So it is that Lilith is regarded both as a child-destroying witch and as the incarnation of lust. In her role as a witch, Lilith's actions provided an explanation for the terrible plague of infant mortality. Use of amulets against Lilith was widespread and is still considered necessary in some very traditional Jewish circles. Only a generation ago grandmothers often tied red ribbons on a child's bed. These ribbons symbolically represented the amulet against Lilith and served the same purpose.

According to the best-known beliefs, Lilith or one in league with her would murder an infant outright or would substitute a puppy or kitten for the human child. The human child stolen by the demons was raised to serve as a bride or groom to one of the demons. There are also said to be demonic doubles. According to this folk belief, when a human is about to wed, the demons will try to trick them into marrying the demonic double of his or her betrothed. And as soon as the wedding vows are pronounced, that person has been lost to the forces of evil.

A typical folktale about Lilith as a child-destroying witch concerns the Watch Night. This was the night before the *Brit*, or circumcision, was to take place. In one such tale of Eastern European origin, an innkeeper had seen six infant sons, all of whom had been born healthy, die on the night before the *Brit*. At last the famous miracle worker, Rabbi Yoel Baal Shem (not the Baal Shem Tov who is the founder of Hasidism—but another Master of the Name who lived in the 16th century) agreed to help the man. He remained in the inn for a month prior to the birth, making amulets for the mother and child, drawing a charcoal circle around the wall, and hanging other magical objects around the house.

On the Watch Night the rabbi had twenty Jews remain awake all night, studying. He filled the room with hundreds of candles and had them all lit, and he barred the door and the chimney as well. Nevertheless, at midnight a black cat managed to steal into the house. She grew larger and larger and tried to break into the room where the mother and child lay. Rabbi Yoel stood before the door and fought the cat with a metal-tipped cane. The cat tried to attack him, and sparks flew from its claws. Everyone was terrified.

Finally Rabbi Yoel knocked out one of the cat's eyes and then chased it out of the house. The next day the *Brit* was celebrated, and everyone came except for the midwife. When Rabbi Yoel inquired about her, he learned that she had become blind in one eye. That is how he confirmed that it was that very midwife who had been responsible for the death of the infants. She was in league with Lilith and had murdered all the children. Soon afterward the midwife confessed and died. She was buried outside the cemetery fence, and for years afterward her ghost could be seen haunting the fields and forests nearby.[8]

Strangely enough, at the same time that Lilith was being blamed for the scourge of infant mortality, she was also playing a major role as the incarnation of lust. Here she haunts men in their dreams and imaginations. It was believed that every time a man had a sexual dream or fantasy, he had intercourse with Lilith, and the product of this intercourse were mutant demons, half human and half demon, who were spurned by humans and by demons alike. There is, for example, a famous 17th-century folktale from the ethical text *Kav ha-Yashar*.[9] This story, "The Cellar," tells of a goldsmith from the city of Posen in Germany who was wed to the demoness Lilith, who lived in his cellar where he had his workshop.

He continues to visit his demon wife every day, while keeping her existence secret from his family. Little by little he yields control of himself, lusting after her day and night. Once it happens that he even gets up in the middle of the Seder, when the words *And they went down into Egypt* are read, and goes down to his demon wife. His real wife follows after him, afraid that he is ill. She peers through the keyhole when he returns to the workshop, and is amazed to see that the workshop has been transformed into a palatial chamber, while he lies naked in the arms of his demon lover. Maintaining control of herself, she then returns to the Seder and reveals nothing to the rest of the family. But the next day she comes to the rabbi and tells him everything.

The rabbi confronts the man with his sin and he confesses. Then the rabbi gives him an amulet to protect himself against Lilith, and he uses it to free himself of her. But before she will release him, Lilith demands that the cellar be bequeathed to her and their demon offspring for all time, and the man makes a vow to this effect. He escapes her powers all the rest of his life, but as he lies on his deathbed, his demon children swarm around him, invisible to his human family, crying out his name.

After his death the house becomes known as being haunted. Eventually it is sold, and the new owner has a workman break open the door to the cellar, which had been nailed shut. The workman is found dead on the threshold. Rabbi Yoel comes to investigate—the same Rabbi Yoel Baal Shem as in the tale of the midwife in league with Lilith—and when he confirms that the cellar is infested with demons, he orders a rabbinic court, a *Beit Din*, to be convened to determine if they have a legitimate right to the house. The court rules against them, on the grounds that the demons transgressed the boundaries of the cellar, and they are expelled to the wilderness.

Because the demons are living in the cellar, this story seems to cry out for a psychological interpretation. The presence of Lilith in the cellar there seems a symbolic confirmation that the cellar represents the unconscious. From a Jungian perspective, Lilith represents the dark side of the unconscious, what Siegmund Hurwitz calls "the dark feminine."[10] The polar opposite of this figure is the *Shekhinah*, the bride of light. Or, in another reading, the man might be seen as having a vivid fantasy life, with a fantasy wife. Here his fantasy is projected around the Lilith legend, which had so much power for the people, as lust and infant deaths were common facts in their lives, and both of them indicated the presence of Lilith.

This leads us to confirm, along with Bruno Bettelheim in *The Uses of Enchantment*,[11] that folktales can well be regarded as fantasies, especially certain types of tales, which seem more motivated by the desire to give form to a fantasy than to convey a moral message—although the moral dimension of the Jewish tale is always present. Therefore fairy tales and tales of the supernatural, in particular, invoke the primal imagination. So it is that a Jewish demoness became the focus for the fantasies of Jewish men and haunted the most secret corners of their lives. Certainly, of the testimony that previous generations have left us, there is little that speaks so eloquently for the most basic human impulses of hope, lust, and fear than such myths, legends, and folktales. For these are all in a sense collective fantasies, and in these stories it is possible to peer into the unfettered imagination of our forefathers throughout the generations. It is a much more intimate glimpse than we might have expected to find.

Ultimately the rich body of tales and superstitions concerning Lilith gave birth to a powerful mythic figure, who in the Middle Ages comes to be identified as the Queen of Demons. Like all mythic beings, she represents only certain poles of existence. She invokes the aspects of fear and lust. Her polar opposite, from the rabbinic perspective, is Adam's second wife, Eve, who was created from his own rib. This, the myth implies, made her more compatible with her husband. And even though she is held responsible, along with the serpent, for convincing Adam to taste the forbidden fruit, still she is forgiven by the rabbis and admired as the mother of mankind. For the rabbis had a personal relationship with the primary figures of the Bible, not only with the Patriarchs and their wives, but also with Adam and Eve as their ultimate forebears.

Indeed, in the Midrash the rabbis find a way of excusing Eve for her failings in the Garden. This interpretation turns on the observation that God told Adam not to pick the fruit of the Tree of Knowledge, while Eve reported to the serpent that God told Adam not to pick the fruit of the Tree *or even to touch it* (Gen. 3:3), lest he die. The Midrash reads between the lines here, assuming that Adam was responsible for this additional warning, telling Eve, "Don't pick the fruit of the tree. Don't even touch it!" The serpent, seeing an opening, pushes Eve against the tree. When she doesn't die, she begins to doubt the injunction.[12] Even so, she hesitates before eating the forbidden fruit, and when she does she tastes the skin first and then eats the rest of the fruit. At that moment Eve has a vision of the Angel of Death, and she runs back to Adam afraid, and has him eat of the fruit so that they will share the same fate.[13] Here the rabbis attribute jealousy to Eve at the thought that Adam might find another wife.

Both the affection and doubt about Eve that the rabbis embraced are reflected in this legend. Another rabbinic legend offers the darkest rabbinic view of Eve to be found. Here Eve is said to have conceived Cain after having had intercourse with the serpent, while Abel's father was Adam.[14] This is the rabbinic source for the legendary evil seed of Cain, which was believed to have given birth to an evil race, whom the Jews inevitably recognized as their enemies. But this betrayal is very much an exception, and despite her flaws, Eve is still generally portrayed in a positive light. After all, she was a lifelong companion for Adam. She was a good wife, a good mother. She was loyal to her husband. She stayed with him in times of trial.

Indeed, despite the importance of the wives of the Patriarchs, Eve serves as the primary positive role model for women, while Lilith is the negative one. It is something like the sea legends about mermaids and sirens. Mermaids are the good female mythic figures of the sea, half woman, half fish. They lead sailors through narrow straits and sometimes save them when they fall overboard. Sirens, on the other hand, who are half woman, half bird, sing a hypnotic song that lures sailors to their deaths on the rocks.

So it is that where Eve is dependent, Lilith is independent; where Eve is passive, Lilith is sexually demanding; where Eve is maternal, Lilith is certainly not; where Eve is a faithful and loyal wife all the days of Adam's life, Lilith abandons him. In this way they are portrayed as polar opposites, as is the nature of mythic figures, each of whom takes on specific characteristics, while actually they are the poles of a single personality. So it is that every woman has a loyal side and a disloyal side, a maternal side and a nonmaternal side, a dependent side and an independent side, a passive side and an assertive side. These characteristics are found to differing degrees in different individuals. And some individuals even swing back and forth between these extreme poles, between the Lilith and Eve sides of themselves.

Of course, the legends of Lilith and Eve are male myths in origin. The fact that Genesis recounts that the first woman was created from the man's rib, while in reality it is the female of the species who gives birth, can only be viewed as a male myth. So too is Lilith a projection of male fantasies and fears. But once the myth became as extensive as it did, the imagination of the women also engaged this mythic demonic figure. In her role as a child-strangling witch, Lilith was equally hated by women and men. But in her role as a seducer, Lilith threatened to steal a man's affection from his wife, as well as his seed. Thus, the attitude of women to Lilith was, of course, much different than that of men: women hated her; men were more ambivalent.

Professor Dov Noy of The Hebrew University, the world's leading Jewish folklorist, suggests that in certain cases it is possible to identify a folktale as having originated from a circle of men or women. Thus he speaks of "men's tales" and "women's tales."[15] The tale of Reb Melech and the woman in the forest is a man's tale, as is the tale of the cellar. Compare the male attitude toward Lilith, which mixes fear with sexual fantasy, with that of the woman in the Kurdish tale called "The Hair in the Milk," which Noy identifies as a woman's tale.

Here Lilith, flying over the house of a woman who has recently given birth, smells the mother's milk and transforms herself into a long, black hair that falls into a glass of milk. When the mother is about to drink the milk, she notices the black hair and faints. The midwife recognizes the presence of Lilith at once and pours the glass of milk, hair and all, into a jug, and closes it tightly. Shaking the jug, the midwife hears the pleas of Lilith from within and extracts a vow from her not only to spare the woman and her child, but also to serve them for three years and protect them from other evil forces. This Lilith does, for once she takes an oath, she is compelled to carry it out.[16]

Note that the portrait of Lilith in this story is quite different from that found in the male myths. For the truth is that Lilith holds far more power over men than she does over women. Perhaps this is because men are ambivalent toward Lilith, seeing her on the one hand as something forbidden and tempting, while on the other hand sharing the terror of her destructive ability. For women Lilith is primarily the child-destroying witch they fear and loathe more than anything else. And unlike the men, they are willing to struggle against her, here defeating her.

What is the link between the two disparate roles of Lilith? Why has one demoness come to play this dual role as seducer and child-destroying witch? Clearly the connection between the sexual act and pregnancy is at the root of this unlikely pairing of mythic characteristics. Just as the sexual act is inevitably linked to the creation of a child from the rabbinic perspective, so Lilith attempts to divert the holy purpose of intercourse, both by provoking the spilling of seed, and, if that fails, by attacking the infant directly. Thus Lilith's role is a destructive one in both instances, although this is not as apparent in the first case as in the second.

Why, then, is Lilith so filled with hatred toward human offspring? Rabbinic legend tells us that she is jealous of Eve, and, above all, she resents the fact that the offspring of Adam and Eve and their descendants are human, while hers are only demons, and thus—both as seducer and as a witch—she seeks her revenge.

With this in mind, it does seem strange that some Jewish feminists have selected Lilith as their role model. They have even named *Lilith Magazine* after her. Lilith was selected because of her independence, in general, and her sexual independence, in particular. At the same time, her demonic qualities were ignored.

The question is: can one be selective in identifying with some aspects of a myth and not another? The answer, in my view, is no. In its formative stage, a split preceded the creation of the myth. Certain identifying characteristics were isolated and became the essence of a mythic being, in this case Lilith, the Queen of Demons. The myth itself consists of a constellation of archetypes, which together form the mythic figure, whether a god, as in the Egyptian, Greek, Canaanite, and Babylonian myths, or angels and demons and other supernatural beings in Jewish lore. To identify with such a mythic being results in absorbing *all* of its characteristics, some consciously, the rest unconsciously. Having rejected Eve as a role model, some Jewish feminists have turned to her polar opposite, Lilith. But in setting up Lilith as a role model, they are denying the negative and even destructive side of the myth. In fact, they cannot escape either the Lilith or the Eve side of themselves. Rather, they must come to terms with both.

The key here is the concept of polarity. The two poles that Eve and Lilith represent are equally powerful, and by the very nature of polarity, they are also in general balance, where sometimes one and sometimes the other dominates. For each side, knowledge of the existence of the other pole is essential.

At this time we can reconsider the meaning of the myth of Lilith in the eyes of its creators, the rabbis. We observe that it first emerges as a myth of male/female struggle, in which neither side is willing to compromise. Lilith abandons Adam, and ever since she has sought her revenge by seducing him over and over again, making him couple with the forces of evil. This drains not only his seed, but his soul, and makes it more difficult, sometimes impossible, to attain holiness. Therefore Lilith is viewed as the agent of Satan, as in the talmudic tales of Rabbi Akiba and Rabbi Meir. And both Lilith and Satan are mythic representations of the *Yetzer Hara*, the Evil Inclination.

Given the rabbinic perspective, with its strict moral view of the world, it was inevitable that polar role models such as Lilith and Eve would be created. Indeed, if Lilith had not sprung fully formed from one problem in the biblical text, surely she would have emerged from another. Her existence was as essential for the rabbis as was that of Eve.

It seems fair to ask if there are similar polar myths, like this one of Lilith and Eve, that apply to men. Perhaps the closest parallel can be found in the three cases of brothers caught up in intense rivalry found in the Bible: Cain and Abel, Isaac and Ishmael, and Jacob and Esau. Of these three pairs, perhaps that of Jacob and Esau comes closest to the kind of polarity we find in the case of Lilith and Eve. While it would not be accurate to say that Jacob's characteristics are parallel to those of Eve, or that Esau's are parallel to Lilith, there are similarities. After all, Jacob and Esau are twins, and even in the Bible they are portrayed as polar opposites—Jacob as fair-skinned, Esau as ruddy; Jacob as one who loved to study, Esau as one who loved to hunt; Jacob as complex and even tricky, Esau as simple and direct. And in the Midrash their roles are further transformed and presented in starkly contrasting terms, where all of Jacob's actions, even the questionable ones, are justified, while Esau is portrayed as Jacob's evil and deadly enemy, symbolic of all of the enemies of Israel. Thus is Jacob offered as the positive role model, and Esau as the deeply negative one.

The danger of such role models is that they put a straitjacket on a person's emotions. In the past, if a woman permitted herself to experience the forbidden passions of Lilith, especially those of a sexual nature, she was in danger of becoming a kind of Lilith herself in the eyes of the community. Now that the community is not as judgmental, this danger is not as acute. Still, other dangers lurk, especially those of an unconscious nature. Some kind of integration of these polar myths seems much preferable. Indeed, the myths of Lilith and Eve cry out for recognition of their polar nature within a single woman, as do the myths of Jacob and Esau in every man. Every woman is likely to experience the full range of emotions, including those attributed to Eve and those of Lilith. And every man is likely to experience the light and dark sides symbolized by Jacob and Esau. To deny one side or the other is to deny the wholeness of the self.

The Jewish author Jakov Lind, a survivor of the Holocaust and the author of *Soul of Wood*, wrote a parable about reuniting these mythic sides of woman into a single being. It is called "The Story of Lilith and Eve:" [17]

> Before God created Eve, the legend tells us, he created Lilith, but Lilith left Adam, as she could never agree with him, in smaller and larger matters, while Eve became Adam's true wife, that is, a woman who is always in agreement with her man. Lilith left, but not for good. The legend tells us she returns to haunt Adam as lust.

> Once upon a time there was a man who was haunted by Lilith. The demon had disguised herself in the clothes of an ordinary, simple, agreeable woman and came to visit Adam when he was alone.

"Why are you on your own?" Lilith asked. "Where is your woman, the one who came to replace me?"

"She is out in the country, she went to visit relatives, and she will return soon. She will not be pleased to find you here, for she fears you."

"Why should my sister be afraid of me?" asked Lilith. "I am as simple in my heart as she is. I am as good and kind as she is. I love my parents and I love my children, the same as she. But I don't think as she does, our difference is hidden in the mind, not in our bodies."

"I believe you," said Adam, "and I love you, but I need a peaceful life."

"Have it your way," said Lilith, "have your peaceful life. I am just your other woman, and I will not leave you, but will love you as I always did."

Adam looked into her eyes and said no more. Her eyes were like doors wide open into a world he had almost forgotten, and he stepped inside.

They were in each other's arms and mouths when Eve returned. Lilith and Adam are united, she thought. Stay with me, sister. I will bring food to your bed. She brought food and drink to the bed for them and retired to a far corner of the house, where she crouched at the stove to keep herself warm and went into a trance. She left her own body and entered the body of Lilith and thus she embraced and kissed Adam and felt his love for her as she had never known it before.

"But I am your Eve," said Lilith. "Why do you love me so passionately? You never loved me with such passion before."

Adam laughed and said: "You will leave with dawn and I will not see you for a long time. If I am passionate it is because our happiness is but short."

"How can you say that?" said Lilith. "I will be here tomorrow and the day after and so for the rest of your life. Why do you love me so passionately? Do you think I am the one I seem? I am Eve speaking through my sister's mouth."

"You are joking," laughed Adam. "I know you will leave at the dawn and will not be back for quite some time."

Lilith, who was Eve now, kissed him and said: "I wish this were so, but alas I cannot leave you. I will stay with you, because you are full of fire for this other woman whose body I have now taken over. Look at me carefully and tell me whether you don't see that I am your wife Eve?"

"Eve sits in the far corner of the house," said Adam. But when he looked he could not see her there. What he saw were the flames from the stove.

In this brief tale Jakov Lind brings together the separate but closely related myths of Lilith and Eve. In this retelling, Lilith and Eve must ultimately be recognized as poles of the same personality rather than as separate individuals. What Lind has done, in fact, is to repair the original split, wherein Eve symbolized all positive qualities and Lilith all negative ones. Thus the reuniting of Lilith and Eve into one in this tale is clearly a call to wholeness, to reintegrate the aspects of the self that have split away into separate myths. And this reintegration, which is a form of healing, applies to men as well as to women. Surely the more we are able to integrate all sides of our personality into a coherent whole, the more conscious we will be our true nature. And the more conscious we are, the more self-knowledge we will have. And the more self-knowledge, the more likely that we will survive, and perhaps even flourish.

Jewish myths have a tendency to evolve, as did the Lilith myth in adding the characteristics of the demoness Obyzouth. So it is certainly legitimate for Jakov Lind to imagine that Lilith and Eve, ancient enemies for so long, eventually find peaceful coexistence. Lind has recognized that the polar myths of Lilith and Eve are best understood as coexisting in same person. And from this perspective the collective nature of the myths themselves offers valuable clues to the mysteries of the parts of the self. When viewed this way, these ancient myths can be appreciated not only as fantasies or compelling stories, but also as maps of the essential states of the self they portray so well.

SIX

Jewish Tales of the Supernatural

O ne day a boy playing hide-and-seek sees a finger in the hollow trunk of a tree. Assuming he has found his friend, he puts a ring on the finger and pronounces the marriage vows, all in jest, but subsequently finds himself wed to a demoness. She, in turn, kills each of his human wives, until one of them finds a way to appease her—sharing her husband with the demoness for one hour every day.[1]

This nightmare marriage is recounted in a 16th-century Yiddish folktale, "The Demon in the Tree." Like most Jewish tales of the supernatural, it addresses one of the most crucial turning points in a person's life. Times of stress, such as birth, marriage, and death, inevitably become the focus of rituals, superstitions, and folklore, and the Jewish tradition is no exception. Indeed, the vast majority of legends and folktales that draw upon the supernatural take place at one of these turning points, or on such critical occasions as *Bar Mitzvah*, Yom Kippur, or other days of observance, including the Sabbath.

It was the supernatural that provided an explanation for all kinds of events, especially misfortunes. Surrounded by a myriad of dangers, opposed by both human and demonic enemies, the Jews turned to faith and superstition for an understanding of the world. Thus a stillborn child could be interpreted as evidence of the destructive powers of the demoness Lilith, or a sudden death as the punishment of vengeful spirits. These explanations, in turn, eventually became embodied as tales that were often retold in both the written and oral traditions. These include tales about wandering spirits, marriage with demons, possession by dybbuks, ghostly visitations, vampires, werewolves, speaking heads, corpses brought to life with the power of the

Name of God, and every kind of supernatural adversary. These fantasies and nightmares, where danger is often overcome in a supernatural fashion, helped the oppressed Jews to find an outlet for their fears. For it is well-known that hearing or reading even the most frightening tales can bring about a catharsis and release from fear. These folk explanations no longer have a primary place in our vision of the world, of course, but they still invoke and explore the dark side of the human psyche that is as evident today as it was in the time of our ancestors.

The role of the supernatural in Jewish life and lore is one of fascinating contradictions. On the one hand, there is the clear biblical injunction against supernatural practices:

> There shall not be found among you any one that maketh his son or daughter to pass through the fire, one that useth divination, a soothsayer, or an enchanter, or a sorcerer, or a charmer, or one that consulteth a ghost or a familiar spirit, or a necromancer. For whosoever doeth these things is an abomination unto the Lord (Deut. 18:10–12).

On the other hand, even in the biblical account of King Saul and the witch of Endor (1 Sam. 28), this injunction is ignored, as Saul has the witch invoke the spirit of the prophet Samuel. Likewise, sorcery is resorted to on a great many occasions in rabbinic literature, sorcery not only by wizards and witches, but even by some of the most respected rabbis. On one occasion Rabbi Joshua ben Hananiah performs a magical invocation. He scatters flax seeds on a table, waters them so that they instantly take root and grow, then reaches into them to pull out the head of a witch who has cast a damaging spell.[2] In another tale from the Talmud, Rabbi Yannai diverts a witch who attempts to turn him into an ass, and transforms her into this beast instead.[3] These and many other examples clearly reveal the rabbinic ambivalence about the injunction against sorcery and lead to hairsplitting attempts to define what kind of sorcery is acceptable and what kind is forbidden. The conclusion the rabbis reach distinguishes between sorcerers who work through demons and those who work by pure enchantment. Thus, according to the talmudic sage Abbaye, "If one actually performs magic, he is stoned; if he merely creates an illusion, he is exempt."[4] Although this distinction itself may seem to be an illusion, in many cases it accurately defines the difference between the sorcery of the rabbis and that performed by those who invoked the forces of darkness.

In practice, as well, the differences between sacred magic and sorcery are apparent. Although the black magic of the wizards is destructive in intent, that of the rabbis is protective—drawing magic circles that guard against any evil onslaught; using the power of the Tetragrammaton, the ineffable Name of God, to bring the dead to life; or exorcising dybbuks, spirits of the dead who take possession of the living. But on occasion, when sufficiently provoked, the wrath of the rabbis is terrible to behold: in his anger at witches who have kidnapped and mutilated the body of a Jew, Rabbi Hayim Vital turns them into black dogs in "The House of Witches"; Rabbi Shalem Shabazi causes three stories of a building to sink into the ground at his command in "Rabbi Shabazi and the Cruel Governor"; and in "The Cause of the Plague," Rabbi Judah Loew discovers that an evil sorcerer is responsible for a plague among the Jews, and turns the sorcerer's own destructive spell against him, causing the sorcerer to burst into flames.

Powers such as those possessed by these rabbis must be kept in check, for such great power holds the danger of being abused. This theme is found in several striking tales, especially that of Rabbi Joseph della Reina, who first tries to force the coming of the Messiah by capturing Asmodeus, King of Demons, and his queen, Lilith, in "Helen of Troy." Joseph della Reina succeeds in capturing them but falls prey to their deception, is defeated, and afterward becomes a mad wizard, tutored by Lilith in the ways of black magic. Another tale, "The Homunculus of Maimonides," portrays the great philosopher and theologian as a sorcerer intent on creating an immortal being of unlimited powers. This has all the earmarks of a folk expression of the attitudes toward Maimonides found in the anti-Maimonidian controversy, in which the opponents of Maimonides portrayed him in the most negative terms. Both tales contain implicit warnings against messianic aspirations, and both emerge from periods dominated by such longings, with attendant false messiahs, especially Shabbatai Zevi in the 17th century.[5]

But most tales show a great reluctance on the part of the rabbis to invoke these supernatural powers, and it is only impending disaster that forces them to do so. The young Baal Shem Tov is forced to confront a werewolf to protect young children in "The Werewolf," and other rabbis are brought into magical combat with various demons—to save a kidnapped bride-to-be, for example, as in "The Bride of Demons," or to compel demons who have taken possession of a house to appear before a rabbinic court, as in "The Cellar." Thus these tales, which flourished in the Middle Ages, are an outgrowth in every respect of the biblical, rabbinic, and folk traditions that preceded them. Jewish tales with supernatural themes are derived from such biblical motifs as the speaking serpent in Eden, or Saul and the witch of Endor—and from virtually every phase of postbiblical Jewish literature, sacred and secular, written and oral. The written sources for these tales include the Apocrypha, the Pseudepigrapha, the Talmud, the Midrash, medieval Jewish folklore, and hasidic texts. Some variants and additional tales can be found among those collected orally from various Jewish ethnic sources, including those published in this century in Yiddish by Y. L. Cahan and Immanuel Olsvanger, as well as the tales collected, primarily in Hebrew, by the Israel Folktale Archives.[6] Nor does the tradition end there, for these same legends have been selected by some of the most important modern Jewish authors, such as I. L. Peretz, S. Ansky, S. Y. Agnon, Isaac Bashevis Singer, Bernard Malamud, and Cynthia Ozick, who have used traditional tales as the basis of short stories, novels, dramas, and poetry.

As might be expected, the imprint of the biblical sources can be recognized in many of these supernatural tales. For example, the Binding of Isaac by Abraham at Mount Moriah is echoed in "The Devil's Fire," where a rabbi struggles to persuade the people in a Persian city that the practice of human sacrifice is wrong. The rabbi witnesses the abhorrent practice himself and later learns that the reason the people are so willing to leap into the flames is because they believe they will soon return. This appears to be true, but when the rabbi investigates he discovers that the Devil has disguised himself as the one who comes back, perpetuating the illusion that the fire is harmless. With great difficulty, the rabbi finally manages to enlighten the people.

It is generally recognized that one primary purpose of the story of the binding of Isaac was to announce in clear terms that all human sacrifice for Jews had come to an end, to be replaced by animal sacrifice. And animal sacrifice essentially came to an end after the destruction of the Temple. The rabbi in this tale, then, can be seen as attempting to blot out the practice of human sacrifice among pagans. At the same time the story is cast in the form of a tale of terror.

Another biblical theme, that of Joseph cast into the pit, is echoed in the tale "The Chronicle of Ephraim." Here an evil wizard causes a Jewish family to be cast into a pit to die. The mother gives birth there, and when the wizard learns this he offers to free them in exchange for the child, and with no other choice the family relinquishes their son to him. He raises the boy as his own, attempting to hide the boy's Jewish heritage from him. This theme is also echoed in midrashic literature, in the tale of Moses being cast into a pit, where he survives for ten years, secretly assisted by Zipporah, whom he eventually marries.[7] In each of these cases the one cast into the pit has an extraordinary nature—Joseph, most beloved of his father and mother; Moses, the Redeemer; and the boy Ephraim, who is born casting an aura of light, as was said of Noah. Thus does the biblical episode of Joseph in the pit become an archetype for a stage in the experience of those destined for greatness—the dark pit symbolizing danger in which they miraculously survive.

In some cases it is possible to trace the evolution of a single legend from its biblical inception to its recounting in the Talmud, and from there to the version found in the Midrash and then retold in the Middle Ages in medieval folklore and echoed as well in some hasidic tales. The Jewish literary tradition is unique in this, for in no other culture is it possible to trace such a detailed and extensive evolution of legends in written form throughout the ages.

Among the legends with biblical origins and rabbinic and folk elaborations, none had a greater influence than that of Lilith, who plays a dual role as a child-destroying witch and as the incarnation of lust. The Lilith legend served as the basis of a substantial body of demonic tales in medieval Jewish folklore and later hasidic sources. These tales draw on the characterization of Lilith found in earlier rabbinic texts, but have more imaginative freedom. This process of embellishment has a pronounced tendency to bring together as many previous themes and motifs as possible, yet at the same time the new tale takes on a life of its own.

In this fashion the archetype of Lilith became imprinted on Jewish folk-lore, and she reappears with a multitude of names, among them Obyzouth, Naamah, Agrat bat Mahalath, and the Queen of Sheba, in early apocryphal, talmudic, and midrashic sources, as well as in medieval folklore and the later hasidic tales. So too does Lilith play an important role in kabbalistic texts, one that is essentially mythic in nature.[8] The talmudic and midrashic texts, of course, had the seal of rabbinic authority, while the apocryphal texts did not. Nevertheless, the latter had a strong influence on the development of Jewish lore.

Of the apocryphal texts, there are two, *The Book of Tobit* in the Apocry-pha and *The Testament of Solomon* in the Pseudepigrapha, that greatly in-fluenced the subsequent direction of demonology in Jewish folklore.[9] *The Book of Tobit*, dating from around 2 B.C.E., recounts the tale of Sarah, whose husbands all mysteriously die on their wedding nights. Finally Tobias is able to expel the evil demon Asmodeus who, it turns out, had killed each and every husband. This key legend prefigures both the subsequent career of Asmodeus as the King of Demons and the pattern of a multitude of dybbuk tales, in which the evil spirit must be exorcised. *The Testament of Solomon*, surviving in a Greek text that is estimated to have been written between the 1st and 4th centuries C.E., serves as an early compendium of demons, who appear to King Solomon in succession at his invocation, and is the earliest text to cast King Solomon in the role of sorcerer, which be-came the primary model for him in subsequent Jewish lore. Among the demons compelled to appear is Obyzouth, who has all the witchlike charac-teristics of Lilith and is probably the precursor of Lilith, as the mythic iden-tity of Obyzouth likely fused into that of the more famous demoness.

Sometime during the early Middle Ages the legend of Lilith, the domi-nant female demon, merged with the legend of Asmodeus, the King of Demons, and she became identified as his queen. Asmodeus was already a famous folk character because of the striking legends about him in the Talmud. One recounts his capture by King Solomon during the time the Temple was being built, and another describes how Asmodeus overpowered Solomon and threw him a great distance, turning him into a beggar king, and usurped his throne.[10] In retrospect the merging of the legends of Lilith and Asmodeus was inevitable, given their prominence.

The folk process invariably embellishes folktales that capture the folk imagination. Thus the richly expressive legend of Lilith, which grew out of a single line of Genesis, gave birth to a myriad of legends postulating the existence of another world, by some accounts existing side by side with this one, as close as the other side of the mirror; by others, in its own place, the *Yenne Velt*, Yiddish for "the Other World." In either case the demons were believed to reproduce and proliferate endlessly, creating difficulties at every turn: causing wine to turn into vinegar, fire to go out, men to be impotent, women to be unable to give birth. And of course it was Lilith who was blamed every time an infant's life was lost. Thus the presence of Lilith and her cohorts was very real, and she served as a symbol of all that was enticing and destructive.

Thus the legend of Lilith gave birth to an elaborate Jewish demonology. One theme in particular, that of marriage with demons, evolved out of the legend of Lilith the seductress.[11] In these tales the demoness is not usually identified as Lilith, but nonetheless demonstrates all of her characteristics. One brief tale from *Midrash Tanhuma*, dating from around the 8th century, sets the pattern for many later tales and also sets an important precedent in asserting that intercourse with demons does not constitute prostitution or adultery:

> On Yom Kippur, the Day of Atonement, a demon in the shape of a woman came to a pious man and seduced him and made love to him. Afterward the man was very sorry, until Elijah the Prophet came to him and asked him why he was so upset. And he told him all the things that had happened to him. And Elijah said: "You are free from sin, for she was a demon." After that the man reported this to his rabbi, who said: "Surely this judgment is true, for Elijah would never have come to a guilty man."[12]

The first and most important variant of this brief tale is *Ma'aseh Yerushalmi* (The Tale of a Jerusalemite), dating from the 12th century.[13] Here a man is forced to marry the daughter of Asmodeus, the King of Demons, in order to save his own life. He is eventually permitted to return to his human family for one year, but when he refuses to return to his demon wife she comes to his city and challenges him before a *Beit Din*, a rabbinic court. Here the rabbis take her side, commanding him either to return with her or to pay the immense sum called for in their wedding contract, and when he still refuses she gives him one last kiss—the kiss of death. *Ma'aseh Yerushalmi* contains most of the essential elements of the later variants: the forced or accidental marriage of a man to a demoness; an attempt to be freed from the unwanted vows; and a decision reached by a rabbinic court.

This theme of marriage with demons was most popular in the 16th century, both in Eastern Europe and Palestine. In *Maaseh Nissim*,[14] an important Yiddish collection of stories set in the city of Worms, there is the tale of "The Queen of Sheba." In this story a demoness by this name appears in a poor innkeeper's storeroom and seduces him both with her charms and with bags of silver coins. Another variant of this theme is "The Demon in the Tree," where a boy accidentally puts a wedding ring on a demoness, only to have her haunt him after he tries to marry. There also is a third variant from Palestine in the same century, from *Shivhei ha-Ari*, the tales about Rabbi Isaac Luria of Safed. In this tale, "The Finger," three young men out for a walk one evening find something that looks like a finger sticking out of the earth. One of them jokingly slips his ring onto it and pronounces the marriage vows. At that instant, without realizing it, he weds himself to a corpse, one who had not known her "hour of joy" while alive and is not about to let it go now. The existence of such close variants from places so distant seems to confirm a substantial exchange of lore between Europe and the Holy Land during that period, especially in the cosmopolitan environment of Safed.

One of the most recent variants of this tale, "The Other Side," dates from 19th-century Eastern Europe. Here an unsuspecting man is lured to the kingdom of the demons, not far from his own city, and step by step falls under the power of the demons, who finally wed him to one of their own, then dissolve the illusion, leaving him broken and mute. And it is only after the rabbinic court commands the demons to appear and rules against them that the man is freed from their curse.

All of the previous tales on the theme of marriage with demons concern a man married to a demoness. There are, however, a few tales in which a woman is wed to a demon, usually by deceit or by force. In one such story, "The Bride of Demons," from 18th-century Germany, Lilith lures a young girl into coming home with her, imprisoning her in order to force her to wed one of her demon sons. Only by great effort is she freed by her human betrothed—who risks his life for her without ever having met her.

Perhaps the most interesting of these variants is one from 19th-century Prague, in which a young woman, Haminah, follows her lover into the sea, prepared to end her life, only to discover that he is the demon ruler of the river, who makes her his bride in "The Underwater Palace." This tale combines two basic tale types into one. One of these is that of marriage with demons, and the other concerns a midwife who is brought to the kingdom of the demons.[15] Here the midwife motif is found in the subplot about the aunt of the girl, whose name is Shifra, and who, as a midwife, is brought to the underwater palace to deliver the child of the girl and her demon husband.[16] Such tales, involving a midwife needed to deliver a child or a *mohel* required to perform the circumcision, are found in both European and Middle Eastern sources. These stories emphasize the parallels between the lives of humans and those of demons, for the *Yenne Velt* is a distorted mirror image of this world. The older, written versions of this tale almost all concern a *mohel* who is led to *Gehenna*, and the more recent oral versions are almost all about a midwife who is taken to the land of the demons.[17] The fact that two such separate tale types have been combined here demonstrates how the folk process constantly remakes old themes in new ways, and thus keeps the tale alive in the retelling.

In one tale in which this theme of marriage with demons is found, it is possible to glimpse the historical and psychological kernel underlying it. In the tale, "The Demon of the Waters," collected in the 1930s from a Ukrainian immigrant in Israel, the stairway to a *mikveh*, a ritual bath, collapses, throwing a woman into the river, where she is carried away, while her demonic double emerges from the waters, taking her place, and proceeds to behave in a violent and abusive manner. It is a wise shepherd who recognizes that the demon of the waters is not really the wife.[18] Yet despite the traditional folk structure of this tale, it is not difficult to read between the lines to discern the human tragedy of madness. And the specific naming of the characters, the place, and the customs gives the strong impression that an actual incident lies behind it, not merely a fantasy.

This, then, reveals a great deal about the workings of the folk process. One very old legend splits off into several sublegends, gives birth to a multitude of variants, and is embellished and retold for many centuries in new versions that are themselves embellished and retold until they bear little resemblance to the original. For it is clear that despite their age and familiarity, these supernatural themes retained great power for those who told them. And much of this power came from the fact that these stories embody universal fears and fantasies: Lilith is a projection of the negative fears and desires of the rabbis who created her. For if Lilith served no other purpose than to resolve the contradiction in the biblical text, such an extensive legend, with so many ramifications, would never have come into being.

Demons are not the only supernatural beings found in Jewish lore. There are also angels, spirits, and other kinds of imaginary creatures, such as vampires, werewolves, goblins, and ghosts. Sometimes the spirit of one who is dead takes possession of a living being. This spirit is called a dybbuk, and from the 16th century on, accounts of possessions by dybbuks multiplied with alarming frequency. These are not folktales in the usual sense, because almost all of the literally hundreds of accounts of such possessions insist that the event actually occurred and give all kinds of specific details about those involved. The pattern in these tales is almost always the same: the dybbuk, the spirit of one dead, takes possession of its victim. Eventually the matter is brought to the attention of a rabbi, who interrogates the dybbuk and eventually casts it out, usually through the little finger or toe of the victim.

This pattern is found in "The Widow of Safed," a tale in *Shivhei ha-Ari* about how a widow living in Safed was possessed, and how Rabbi Hayim Vital, at the behest of Rabbi Isaac Luria, succeeded in exorcising the dybbuk.[19] This tale emerged in the 16th century, at around the same time as the major compendium of Yiddish folktales, *The Maaseh Book*, appeared in Eastern Europe, in which one of the earliest dybbuk tales can also be found.[20] It is these tales in *Shivhei ha-Ari* and *The Maaseh Book* that set the pattern for virtually all subsequent dybbuk tales.[21]

Sometimes the dybbuk finds a surreptitious way of entering the person, such as in the tale of "The Fishhead" in *Shivhei ha-Ari*, about a dybbuk who enters a fish: when a young woman eats the head of the fish, the dybbuk is able to take possession of her. In other cases a demon is able to approach a person because he or she said, "Go to the Devil," as in "The Bride of Demons." Likewise, "The Lost Princess," the first tale told by Rabbi Nachman of Bratslav, the great hasidic storyteller, begins with just such a curse, causing the princess to be taken over into the realms of evil, requiring an epic quest in order to set her free.[22]

Most often the spirit is able to enter its victim because of a lack of faith, such as not believing in the parting of the Red Sea, or because the text of the *mezzuzah* on the doors of the house is flawed or missing. Once the dybbuk finds a foothold, through one weakness or another, it inevitably takes possession. And only a ritual exorcism, such as that portrayed in the last act of S. Y. Ansky's drama, *The Dybbuk*,[23] can succeed in expelling it. These tales served as a warning, of course, against permitting the forces of evil to gain such a foothold, and the fact that they are presented as accounts rather than tales shows how deeply such cases of possession were believed to be authentic.

A Persian tale, "The Soul of Avyatar," from an unpublished manuscript of 16th-century origin, describes how the soul of the sinner Avyatar entered a horse and transformed it into a beast with great powers. This in itself is not uncommon, for dybbuks are often said to take possession of animals, especially a dog or a cow. What is more unusual is that the soul of Avyatar gives the horse great destructive powers, while other possessed animals are shortly driven to madness. Such possession usually involves a wandering spirit, that is, a dybbuk, although there are exceptions in which demons or other evil beings take possession instead.[24] One such unusual account is "The Exorcism of Witches from a Boy's Body," from 19th-century Eastern Europe, in which four witches take possession of a young boy at the same time. But as in the other cases of dybbuks, it is the power of God that compels the witches to depart, just as the various dybbuks are unable to oppose it.

S. Ansky's play, *The Dybbuk*, is the best known and most often performed Yiddish drama and is considered a classic. In recent years there have been two major works of fiction devoted to the theme of the dybbuk. These are *The Dance of Genghis Cohen* by Romain Gary and *The Dyke and the Dybbuk* by Ellen Galford. In *The Dance of Genghis Cohen* the dybbuk of a Jew killed in a concentration camp comes back to possess the officer who gave the order for his execution and turns the officer's life into a living hell. In the wonderful satire, *The Dyke and the Dybbuk*, a dybbuk by the name of Kokos possesses a highly independent woman taxi driver, of lesbian leanings, Rainbow Rosenbloom. It turns out that a sorcerer put a curse on Rainbow's ancestor, ten generations back, that their daughters would be possessed by a dybbuk until the 33rd generation. Both books work within the general dybbuk motif, but each takes its own liberties. While most dybbuks are described as coming from evil people, the Jew Cohen who possesses the Nazi is seeking revenge. This is a new turn in the dybbuk tradition. Likewise, the dybbuk Kokos serves as the first-person narrator of *The Dyke and the Dybbuk* and emerges as a sympathetic figure, which is not the case with the traditional dybbuk tale.

Underlying many of these tales is the Jewish concept of sin and its punishment. The punishments of *Gehenna* are recounted in "The Door to Gehenna," where a wife disregards a warning not to open a door. The moment she does she is pulled into *Gehenna*, Jewish Hell, where she is later found by her husband's steward. While many others are being openly tortured, her torture is more subtle and terrible: she is surrounded with gold and luxury on all sides, but everything is burning hot. This tale, as well as "The Devil's Fire," previously discussed, was recounted not only to convey the narrative, but also as a warning of what awaited sinners deserving the punishments of *Gehenna*.

In fact, the only sinners denied the punishment and expiation that *Gehenna* offers are those wandering spirits refused entrance there in the first place because their crimes are too terrible to forgive. These wretched figures are said to be chased for ages by vengeful angels bearing fiery whips. Because the punished soul cannot bear its suffering, it seeks refuge in the body of a living person or animal, thus becoming a dybbuk.

In addition to the uniquely Jewish tale types, such as those about dybbuks and Jewish demons, virtually all of the traditional types of supernatural tales are found in Jewish lore. This includes not only the expected tales about witches and wizards, but also tales about werewolves, ghosts, vampires, and even dragons. Naturally much of this material was taken in from the surrounding cultures in which the Jews found themselves and is strongly molded by its source, but in many cases the tales are recast in a Jewish context.

There is, for example, a well-known werewolf tale about the Baal Shem Tov, founder of Hasidism, when he was a boy. In this tale, "The Werewolf," found in *Shivhei ha-Besht*, the singing of the children that the young Baal Shem leads to school is so pure that Satan is threatened by it. Satan then sends an evil soul to take possession of an already wicked woodcutter, making him into an evil sorcerer who later transforms himself into a werewolf and attacks the children. The boy Israel ultimately defeats the werewolf, the very incarnation of evil, in the process showing evidence of his own great powers, which he kept hidden until the age of thirty-six, after which he revealed himself and took up the mantle of leadership. This story thus combines the theme of possession by a dybbuk with that of the popular theme of the werewolf, creating, as it were, a Jewish werewolf story.

Another of the most basic types of supernatural tales is the ghost story, describing encounters with spirits of the dead. In Jewish lore the role of the ghost, per se, is a little different, because spirits are most often encountered as dybbuks after they have taken possession of the body of a living person. There are, however, more conventional ghost stories. The most famous ghost of all is, of course, that of the Prophet Samuel, called forth by the witch of Endor for King Saul. Many of the characteristics of the ghost of Samuel, such as his anger at being brought back to this world, became the model for subsequent ghost tales.[25]

Ghost stories are also found in the Talmud. Rarely, however, do these ghosts haunt those who encounter them; instead, they are only reluctantly drawn into the world of the living. One such tale reports the dialogue between two spirits who are overheard whispering in the graveyard.[26] Still another describes how the corpse of Rabbi Eliezer ben Shimon remains perfectly preserved for ten years after his death and how his voice comes forth from the attic to reply to the questions asked of him.[27] This suggests in an allegorical manner how subsequent Jewish generations turned to the ancient sages for guidance, and even though they were dead, they still replied to the questions put to them. This, of course, was possible by consulting the ancient texts, especially the Talmud, where the opinions of the sages are still very much alive.

Ghosts also populate the oppressive world portrayed in *Sefer Hasidim*,[28] attributed to Rabbi Judah the Pious, from Germany in the late 12th or early 13th century. One such tale reports a vision of a man who fell asleep in the synagogue. He awoke at midnight and saw many spirits wearing prayer shawls, including two men who were still alive. Those two died a few days afterward, and that was why he saw their spirits already among the dead.[29]

The finest example of a Jewish folktale about ghosts is "The Dead Fiancee," where the ghost of a man's former fiancee appears to him and seems in every way to be alive. This man had wronged her many years before by marrying another when he was betrothed to her. This sin in turn caused the man to be without children, and his rabbi tells him that the only way to annul her curse is to find her and beg for her forgiveness. After great effort the man finds her. But only later does he learn that she has been dead for the past ten years and that he has met with her ghost. Her return is characteristic of many ghost tales in which a spirit returns to resolve an unfinished matter of great importance.

Far less frequent, but still to be found, are tales of vampires, which, while hardly a dominant theme in Jewish lore, appear in one of the oldest texts, *The Testament of Solomon*. Here a vampire demon sucks the blood of the child of the chief builder of the Temple until King Solomon finds a way to stop him. (This may represent a kind of folk representation of child abuse.) As to why the vampire motif is not more commonly found in Jewish lore, it seems likely that it has been replaced by the evil doings of Lilith and her daughters, who strangle their victims rather than drain the life out of them. Lilith, after all, has several characteristics in common with the vampire: she can transform herself into an animal, usually a cat, and she makes diabolical attempts to do harm, often first deceiving her victims into believing she is either harmless or irresistible. In "The Other Side," for example, a demoness first appears to a man as a modest and lovely young lady, and in "The Kiss of Death" the daughter of Asmodeus snatches the breath of the man who has betrayed her, in a way strongly reminiscent of the fatal kiss of the vampire.[30]

Just as the ghost of Samuel serves as the earliest archetype of the ghost in Jewish literature, so does the witch of Endor serve as the archetype of the witch. Several tales about witches are found in the Talmud, including that of the eighty witches defeated by Rabbi Shimon ben Sheetah in Ashkelon.[31] Another talmudic tale is "The Rabbi and the Witch." In this and other talmudic tales the witch conceals her true identity, but the observant rabbi sees through her. This also occurs in a talmudic tale where a rabbi recognizes that another rabbi's daughters are witches when he sees them stirring the broth with their hands.[32] And witches continue to populate Jewish folklore, especially in medieval texts such as *Sefer Hasidim*, where a witch casts a spell that puts a knife in a demon's heart in one tale and turns herself into a black cat in order to give the Evil Eye to a Jew in another.[33] Tales about witches are even found in hasidic lore. Just as the young Baal Shem Tov defeats a werewolf, so too does he defeat a powerful witch in one tale and a wizard in another.[34]

Tales of the rabbi-sorcerer are, perhaps, the most commonly found among all these tale types. Moses serves as a magician in several biblical episodes, including the contest with the Egyptian magicians in Pharaoh's court. This may indeed be the true model for the subsequent tales of such contests and magical combats. But it is King Solomon, not Moses, who is the prototype of the Jewish sorcerer. Solomon's exploits are a genre in themselves in Jewish lore, and only Elijah the Prophet is the hero of more tales. Solomon's mastery over the forces of the supernatural was complete. He drew on the power of his magic ring, on which God's Name was engraved, and ultimately on the power of God. Solomon, however, was a king, and a model was needed for the rabbi-sorcerer. Several rabbis demonstrate supernatural powers in the Talmud, among them Rabbis Shimon bar Yohai, Joshua ben Hananiah, Yannai, and Eliezer ben Hyrcanos. But none of these could be described as a sorcerer.

Most medieval tales involving a Jewish sorcerer include a confrontation between the Jewish sorcerer and an evil sorcerer, who often serves as a viceroy to an emperor or king and whose primary purpose is to bring harm to the Jews. Among the medieval models for rabbi-sorcerer are Rabbi Samuel the Pious of Regensburg and his son, Rabbi Judah the Pious, whose miracles are recounted in *The Maaseh Book*.[35] There is also the legendary Rabbi Adam, who has vast kabbalistic powers at his command. He is the subject of several tales in which he draws upon supernatural objects, such as a magic lamp or mirror, in order to protect Jews from impending disaster.[36]

In addition to Rabbi Adam, one other medieval rabbi in particular is portrayed in Jewish legend as having possessed great supernatural powers. This is Rabbi Judah Loew of Prague, who used his supernatural knowledge to protect the Jews from dangers arising out of the blood libel accusation, when Jews were accused of killing gentiles in order to use their blood in preparing matzoh for Passover—an accusation that occurred frequently and unfairly in the Middle Ages, often leading to terrible pogroms. Rabbi Loew himself is famous for the creation of the creature known as the Golem, a manmade man, created out of clay and brought to life with various magical incantations. This creature, according to the legend, protected the Jews of Prague from various dangers, especially that of the blood libel, with its disastrous consequences.[37]

Although the Golem cycle is the most famous of the legends of Rabbi Loew, there are many other tales in which Rabbi Loew exhibits his magical prowess, such as "Summoning the Patriarchs," in which Rabbi Loew invokes the spirits of the biblical patriarchs at the bidding of the emperor, who wishes to be initiated into the secrets of the Kabbalah. So similar are the characterizations of Rabbi Adam and Rabbi Loew that one of the tales about Rabbi Loew is identical to one that is told about Rabbi Adam: how he created a palace out of magic and invited the king to a banquet there. The source about Rabbi Adam is the older of the two and is a vivid illustration of how Rabbi Adam became the model for subsequent Jewish sorcerers.[38]

Hasidic legend, as recounted in *Shivhei ha-Besht*, the first collection of tales about the Baal Shem Tov, has Rabbi Adam identify the Baal Shem Tov as his successor while the Baal Shem Tov was still a boy.[39] Many of the tales of the Baal Shem Tov cast him in the role of sorcerer. But although he, like Rabbi Adam, is heir to a tradition of kabbalistic magic, the power of the Baal Shem Tov seems to derive more from his faith and less from kabbalistic formulas and invocations. In virtually all of these tales, even if a rabbi does not serve as the hero, the evil of the wizard is eventually uncovered and a way is found to stop him.[40] Sometimes the one who defeats him is his own pupil. One of these, "The Wizard's Apprentice," is found in an oral version collected by Y. L. Cahan in Eastern Europe. This reworks the theme of the sorcerer's apprentice, famous in world folklore, which was especially prominent in Eastern Europe.

One indication of a tale's popularity is the number of variants in which it is found, and "The Wizard's Apprentice" is found in at least half a dozen. In one oral version, collected in Eastern Europe, an evil wizard offers a son to a childless couple if they will leave the child with the wizard for one year. The desperate father makes the bargain but fails to deliver the child when promised. The wizard then kidnaps the boy and raises him as his apprentice. When the time has passed, the father comes to take the boy back, but the wizard turns the boy into a bird and forces the father to agree to a test: if the father wins, the boy will be returned; if not, the boy will remain with the wizard for good. With the aid of the boy, the father succeeds in freeing him, but the furious wizard pursues the boy in the form of various animals. Yet each time he tries to kill him, the boy, who has learned his lessons well, transforms himself into something that escapes the wizard's clutches.

In the realm of folklore there are, of course, no boundaries. The Jews drew upon the folklores of the surrounding peoples, and the folklore of the Jews made its way into the traditions of other peoples. But even the Jewish tales with universal themes, such as those about demons, vampires, werewolves, or ghosts, almost always take on a Jewish coloration, even if the tales do not have a Jewish context. In these tales, then, the people found an expression for their fantasies as well as their primal fears, and the act of telling them was in itself an affirmation of faith and of the Jewish folk tradition. Above and beyond this, the inherent power of the tale is left to speak for itself.

PART III

Mythic Echoes

The Mythology of Judaism

*T*he Baal Shem Tov was once praying with his hasidim. That day he prayed longer than usual, and the others finished before him. At first they waited for him, but before long they lost patience, and one by one they left.

Later the Baal Shem Tov came to them and said: "While I was praying, I ascended the ladder of your prayers all the way into Paradise. As I ascended, I heard a song of indescribable beauty. At last I reached the palace of the Messiah, in the highest heavens, known as the Bird's Nest. The Messiah was standing by his window, peering out at a tree of great beauty that grew outside. I followed his gaze and saw that his eyes were fixed on a golden dove, whose nest was in the top branches of that tree. That is when I realized that the song prevading all of Paradise was coming from that golden dove. And I understood that the Messiah could not bear to be without that dove and its song for as much as a moment. Then it occurred to me that if I could capture the dove, and bring it back to this world, the Messiah would be sure to follow.

"So I ascended higher, until I was within arm's reach of the golden dove. But just as I reached for it, the ladder of prayers collapsed."

In this hasidic tale, "The Ladder of Prayers," the Baal Shem Tov ascends into Paradise on a Divine quest to capture the golden dove of the Messiah, certain that this will cause the Messiah to follow, initiating the messianic era known as End of Days.[1] The failure of the Baal Shem Tov's hasidim to provide the support needed for this great endeavor, as symbolized by the collapse of the ladder of prayers, causes them to lose the opportunity to bring the Messiah. That makes this one more tale about why the Messiah has not come. Dozens of other such tales record lost opportunities to bring the messianic era, or attempts to force the Messiah's hand, and hasten the End of Days.

This tale, and virtually the entire body of rabbinic, kabbalistic, folk, and hasidic lore, exists in a mythological framework. The ladder of prayers the Baal Shem Tov ascends was surely inspired by the heavenly ladder in Jacob's dream. He climbs this ladder of prayers into Paradise, a mythological realm with its own order, its own geography, its own history, and its own inhabitants, not only God and the angels, but the Bride of God and the Messiah as well. It is understood that the Messiah is waiting for the sign to be given that the time has come for the messianic era. At the same time, Jewish mysticism contains the secret of how to hasten the coming of the Messiah, secrets that the Baal Shem Tov has at his command.

In addition, this tale draws on a rich tradition of tales about heavenly ascent, from the ascent of Elijah in a fiery chariot to the famous tale of the four who entered Paradise. Indeed, "The Ladder of Prayers," a hasidic tale of 18th-century origin, is a direct descendant of the legend of the four sages, which dates from the 2nd century. As did the four sages, the Baal Shem Tov ascends to heaven because he seeks greater knowledge of the Divine realm, and that is where he believes it can be found.

It is apparent at once that this tale, and a majority of all Jewish tales, exists purely by virtue of this extensive and intertwined body of Jewish myth. And, indeed, there is a profound mythical stratum of Judaism, which is beginning to be recognized. The earliest myths we know of are found in the Bible, but prebiblical myths surely existed, drawn from Near Eastern mythology. This earlier mythology seems to have fueled the continuing evolution of Jewish myths as new ones arose to fill the void created by the loss of the old. These myths involve not only God, but also God's Bride, the *Shekhinah*, and like the Greek myths of Zeus and Hera, they sometimes converge and sometimes diverge and often give birth to additional myths. So too are there other mythical figures, including that of the Messiah, along with angels, demons, spirits, and fabulous creatures of the air and sea, such as the Ziz, a giant mythical bird, or Leviathan, a monstrous sea creature.

The sources for these myths include the Bible and the translations of the Bible, the Jewish apocryphal and pseudepigraphical works—especially the *Hekhalot* texts describing heavenly journeys—the rabbinic texts of the Talmud and Midrash, the kabbalistic literature, medieval Jewish folklore, and hasidic texts. Some mythic material can also be found among the tales collected by Jewish ethnologists. It is the nature of this literature that its sources are widely scattered, but, once gathered, myths of remarkable coherence emerge.

The primary biblical myths are found in the stories of Creation, of the Garden of Eden, the Tower of Babel, the sons of God and the daughters of men, the great Flood, the covenant with Abraham, the parting of the Red

Sea, the Exodus, and the Giving of the Torah. So too is there the vision of Ezekiel, which is the basis of one major branch of Jewish mysticism, *Ma'aseh Merkavah*, The Mysteries of the Chariot. (Creation is the basis of the other branch, *Ma'aseh Bereshit*, concerning the Mysteries of Creation.) And these are only the major biblical myths. There are others that grow out of key episodes such as the death of Enoch: *And Enoch walked with God, and he was not, for God took him* (Gen. 5:24); or Isaiah's vision of the Throne of God, which begins *I saw the Lord sitting upon a high and lofty throne and the train of His robe filled the Temple* (Isa. 6:1).

Even texts that did not appear to be mythological, like the Song of Songs, are reinterpreted this way. In Rabbi Akiba's reading of the Song of Songs, it is not an erotic love poem, but an allegory of God's love for Israel. Here allegory paves the way for a more mythological relationship.

In some later texts the relationship between God and Israel is directly identified as a marriage. One of these is a hymn for Shavuot written by Israel Najara that takes the form of a *ketubah*, or wedding contract, between God and Israel.[2] This liturgical poem, which is found in the Sephardic prayerbook for Shavuot, is based on the verses *And I will betroth thee unto Me in lovingkindness, and in compassion. And I will betroth thee unto Me in faithfulness; and thou shalt know the Lord* (Hos. 2:21–22), and *I will make a new covenant with the house of Israel* (Jer. 31:31). The text of this *ketubah*, read on Shavuot, describes the Giving of the Torah at Mount Sinai as the wedding between God and Israel, as follows:

> Friday, the sixth of *Sivan*, the day appointed by the Lord for the revelation of the Torah to His beloved people, the Invisible One came forth from Sinai. The Bridegroom, Ruler of rulers, Prince of princes, said unto the pious and virtuous maiden, Israel, who had won His favor above all others: "Many days wilt thou be Mine and I will be thy Redeemer. Be thou My mate according to the law of Moses and Israel, and I will honor, support and maintain thee, and be thy shelter and refuge in everlasting mercy. And I will set aside for thee the life-giving Torah, by which thou and thy children will live in health and tranquillity. This Covenant shall be valid and established forever and ever." Thus an eternal Covenant, binding them forever, has been established between them, and the Bridegroom and the bride have given their oaths to carry it out. May the Bridegroom rejoice with the bride whom he has taken as His lot, and may the bride rejoice with the Husband of her youth.

Here the use of allegory is readily apparent, with God representing the groom and Israel the bride. Although daring, the allegorical nature of this text is never in doubt, for the personification of Israel is clearly a metaphor. But other kabbalistic texts describing a union between God and the *Shekhinah* are harder to dismiss as mere allegories, especially those that attribute a mythic independence to the figure of the *Shekhinah*. The figure/ground nature of these texts, where myth and allegory often reverse roles, is apparent. So too is it intentional. For as long as the rabbis were able to present mythic material that could also be understood in allegorical terms, they were spared the danger of undermining monotheism, the central pillar of Judaism. In this way Jewish mythology was able to exist and even thrive, but within a monotheistic framework.

At this point it might be appropriate to define our use of *myth* in terms of Jewish tradition. *Myths* refer to a people's stories about origins, deities, ancestors, and heroes. These are precisely what the Torah recounts for the Jewish people. Within a culture, myth also serves as the Divine charter, and this is certainly the case in Judaism, where the Torah serves both as a chronicle and covenant. Furthermore, myth and ritual are traditionally linked in an integral and mutual fashion, and this is certainly true in Judaism, where they are inextricably bound. All of these primary aspects of mythology find expression in Jewish tradition. So too have individual myths exercised great power over Jewish life. Even to this day Jews relive the Exodus at Passover and receive the Torah anew on Shavuot. Nor, in some Jewish circles, has the longing for the Messiah subsided.

There are two primary objections to the use of the term "mythology" in relationship to Judaism. The first is that the term suggests a constellation of gods rather than a single, all-encompassing, omnipotent God. From the perspective of Jewish theology, where the central principle is monotheism, it seems impossible for there to be a Jewish mythology. However, just as supernatural practices, such as using divination or consulting a soothsayer, were commonly performed despite the biblical injunction against them, so an extensive Jewish mythology evolved, especially in mystical circles, where it was believed possible to preserve a monotheistic perspective while simultaneously employing a mythological one. Here it is understood that all mythological figures, especially the *Shekhinah*, were ultimately aspects of the Godhead, despite their apparent mythological independence. Indeed, it sometimes seems as if all of Jewish myth (and perhaps all of existence) was the epic fantasy of one Divine being, or a kind of Divine illusion, similar to the Hindu concept of *maya*. For what sometimes appears to have mythic independence can also be understood as an emanation of the Godhead. Here the Divine emanations take the form of the ten *Sefirot*, as symbolized by the kabbalistic Tree of Life. But the *Sefirot* also serve as an antidote to mythology, as they are entirely conveyed through allegory and symbolism and may have been created to contain the unbridled mythic impulse released in Jewish mysticism, as well as to define its underlying archetypal structure. Certainly, this system of Divine emanations is as complex and comprehensive as that of the Jungian theory of archetypes. And while the essence of myth is archetype, it is much harder, if not impossible, to mythologize a system as abstract as the *Sefirot*. Yet underlying these abstractions are the living forces of myth.

The second objection to the use of "mythology" in terms of Jewish tradition is that it implies that the beliefs under consideration are not true. Even the mere identification of a culture's beliefs as mythological indicates that they are being viewed from a distance rather than from the perspective of a believer. That is why, with a few exceptions, there has been such great reluctance to identify any of the biblical narratives as myths or to bring the tools of mythological inquiry to bear on Judaism or Christianity. While it is true that the study of these religions from a mythological perspective does imply the distance of critical inquiry, it does not mean that the traditions being examined are therefore implied to be false. Mythological studies are now commonly linked with psychological ones, and scholars such as C. G. Jung, Joseph Campbell, and Erich Neumann have demonstrated how it is possible to recognize psychological truths underlying mythic traditions. Myth itself is the collective projection of a people, or, as Joseph Campbell has put it, myth is a people's collective dream. In the case of Judaism, many generations of rabbis received and transmitted the sacred myths and traditions, sometimes radically transforming them in the process, as well as imparting their own human and mythic imprint.

The body of these myths, multiplied over the generations, is substantial. The heavenly pantheon is as extensive as that of the Greeks, but with a host of angels playing a role equivalent to the Greek gods. Thus, instead of Poseidon, there is the angel Rahab, who likewise rules the sea. Or just as Hermes is the Divine messenger, so this role in Jewish mythology is played by the angel Raziel. Yet, despite strong parallels with other mythic systems, Jewish mythology is in many ways unique. The primary difference is that instead of consisting of a constellation of many gods, it is dominated by the presence of an all-powerful God who, seated on a throne in Paradise, has ultimate control over all events in heaven as well as on earth. That being said, God often seems to delegate this power to other figures, such as the angel Metatron, who was once Enoch, and is said to be the heavenly scribe, the attendant of the Throne of Glory, the prince of the treasuries of heaven, the ruler and judge of all the hosts of angels, and the executor of the Divine decrees on earth. Of course, the more God's power is delegated in this fashion, the greater the mythic pantheon.

Over time, as the number of supernatural figures in this pantheon increased and interacted, an abundance of mythological narratives emerged. These stories describe events such as the transformation of Enoch into the angel Metatron, the Giving of the Torah, the separation of God's Bride from her Spouse, the chain of events that has so far prevented the coming of the Messiah, and the attempts of Satan to gain inroads into the world of men. They also map out the realms of heaven and hell in great detail. By a process of accretion, these mythic realms were embellished and further defined, giving birth to additional narratives. In this way Jewish mythology has evolved into an extensive, interconnected—and often contradictory— mythic tradition.

At the heart of Judaism there is one universal, all-consuming myth, which contains within it all the other major myths. This is the myth of

God's covenant with Israel. Since this one megamyth serves as a framework for all the others, and since it finds its basis in monotheism, Judaism can be said to be a "monotheistic mythology." Such a conception best describes Jewish myth, which is its own unique kind of mythology. Its most distinctive characteristic is that all mythical Divine figures can ultimately be viewed as an emanation of the Godhead and thus can be contained within a monotheistic structure.

I have identified what I perceive to be the ten major myths contained within the framework of the fundamental myth of God's covenant with Israel. All of these myths find their source and point of reference in this fundamental myth, but each has evolved into a fully developed mythic constellation. These are: (1) Myths of God and the Bride of God, (2) Myths of Creation, (3) Myths of Heaven, (4) Myths of Hell, (5) Myths of the Holy Book, (6) Myths of the Holy Time, (7) Myths of the Holy People, (8) Myths of the Holy Land, (9) Myths of Exile, and (10) Myths of the Messiah.

These ten myths contain at least four hundred submyths that are found in widely scattered sources. These submyths can be viewed independently, or, when taken as a whole, they define the overall pattern of the larger myth. In almost every case there is evidence of mythic evolution, with fragmentary myths of biblical or talmudic origin transformed into far more extensive mythic narratives, especially in the kabbalistic era, which represents the culmination of this process.

By way of example, the category of Myths of Creation includes myths of prior worlds, of how God consulted the Torah to create the world, of the seven days of Creation, the rabbinic notion of the primordial light created on the first day, when God said "Let there be light," and other myths of the sun and moon and stars, as well as myths of cosmology and cosmogony, myths of sacred waters, including the upper waters and lower waters, the waters of eternal life, and the kingdom of the deep, and the late Lurianic myths of Adam Kadmon and of the Shattering of the Vessels and the Gathering of the Sparks. All of these Creation myths find their origin in the account of Creation in Genesis and embellish some aspect of it.

One of the most remarkable aspects of Jewish mythology is that it continued to flourish long past the periods in which it took its final form in other cultures. In most cultures the development of myth occurs during an early period, long before being written down, and once committed to writing, the mythic narrative generally remains fixed. But Jewish tradition has not followed this pattern. One reason for this is the existence of the Oral Law, which encouraged this kind of mythic embellishment. Of all the factors that permit the mythic impulse in Judaism to express itself, this is the most important. Judaism is unique in that it recognizes both a written and an oral tradition. The Written Law is, of course, the Torah, and the Oral Law is the oral commentary linked to it. As one midrash puts it, God gave the Torah to Moses during the day, and at night He explained it to him.[3] And whenever a question arises as to the authority of a statement out of the Oral Law, it is ultimately attributed to Moses at Mount Sinai.

Drawing on this extensive oral tradition, which reached back for a thousand years, the rabbis proceeded to reimagine the Bible, and in the process substantially developed its mythic elements. This makes it possible to witness the actual evolution of Jewish myths. Early myths, primarily those found in the Bible, were embellished in the oral tradition and later recorded in the rabbinic texts. These rabbinic myths were themselves transformed in the kabbalistic and hasidic periods. The most fertile period of Jewish myth took place between the 13th and 17th centuries. This is a remarkably late period in human history for such extensive mythic development. It is then that the major myths of the nature of God and of His Bride took form, along with further myths of Creation and of the Messiah. But in every case these kabbalistic myths are rooted in earlier sources and undergo a process of evolution until they achieve full expression. It is important to note that the mythic transformation that takes place between the early periods of Jewish myth and their later evolution is considerable, almost constituting a new set of myths based on the old ones.

While the varied periods of Jewish religion are characterized by their own predominant myths, there is a continuity among them that is reflected in the rabbinic axiom that "there is no earlier or later in the Torah."[4] Commenting on this statement, Rabbi Shlomo be-rabbi Yitzhak ha-Levi adds: "That is to say, every part of it is both first and last like a sphere . . . and where it ends, there it begins, for behold it is like a circle or a sphere."[5] This principle is certainly reflected in the midrashic method of drawing on one episode in the Bible, such as the childhood of Moses, to fill in a narrative gap in another, such as the missing childhood of Abraham. This results in a distinctly myth-making process, which contributes in no small part to the ongoing mythic evolution.

Because of the considerable differences between these various phases, it is difficult to speak of a single or definitive Jewish mythology. Yet it is also clear that the seeds of all the major myths are found in the earlier texts, where they are often the subject of a profound evolutionary process, a dialectic that alternates between the tendency to mythologize Judaism with an inclination to resist such mythological impulses.

The continuity of style and mode that links the legends of the Talmud and Midrash is largely preserved in the kabbalistic period. But because of the kabbalistic imperative to perceive the Scriptures from a mystical perspective, changes in the meaning of concepts and legends are common and are often of a radical nature. Perhaps no Jewish myth undergoes as radical a transformation as does that of the *Shekhinah*.

In its earliest usage in the Talmud, "*Shekhinah*" refers to God's Divine Presence, thus the presence or indwelling of God in this world. This personification of God's presence was linked, in particular, to the sense of holiness experienced on the Sabbath. At this time no attempt was made to suggest that the *Shekhinah* was in any way independent of God, or to imply that the term referred to a feminine aspect of the Deity. Instead, the term implied the nearness of God, as in this homily of Rabbi Akiba: "When a man and wife are worthy, the *Shekhinah* dwells in their midst; if they are unworthy, fire consumes them."[6]

Yet some rabbinic legends set the stage for the ultimate transformation of the *Shekhinah* into an independent being, in passages such as this from the *Mekilta de-Rabbi Ishmael:*

> Whenever Israel went into exile, the *Shekhinah*, as it were, was with them. When they were exiled to Babylon, the *Shekhinah* was with them; when they were exiled to Elam, the *Shekhinah* was with them, as it is said, *And I will set My throne in Elam* (Jer. 49:38).[7]

In this context the presence of the *Shekhinah* is intended to affirm that God remained true to Israel and accompanied them wherever they went. In time, however, the term *"Shekhinah"* came to be identified with the feminine aspect of the Divinity and came to acquire mythic independence. Myths emerge in the kabbalistic and hasidic literature that portray the *Shekhinah* as the Bride of God and the Sabbath Queen, personifying her as an independent mythic figure. Indeed, there are several other mythic identities linked to the *Shekhinah*, who is sometimes also portrayed as a princess, a bride, an old woman in mourning, a dove, a lily, a rose, a hind, a jewel, a well, and the moon. These multiple facets of the *Shekhinah* suggest that as a mythic figure, the *Shekhinah* has absorbed many types of feminine roles that are incarnated as several different goddesses in other traditions.

In the Zohar we find a reworking of the rabbinic legend about the *Shekhinah* accompanying the children of Israel into exile that demonstrates how far this mythic process has evolved:

> When the Sanctuary was destroyed and the Temple was burnt and the people driven into exile, the *Shekhinah* left her home in order to accompany them into captivity. Before leaving, however, she took one last look at her House and the Holy of Holies, and the places where the priests and the Levites used to perform their worship. . . . So in the days to come, when the Holy One, blessed be He, will remember his people, the community of Israel, the *Shekhinah* will return from exile first and proceed to her House, as the holy Temple will be rebuilt first.[8]

The presence of the *Shekhinah* among the exiled Israelites is also vividly portrayed in the following passage from the Zohar:[9]

> When Israel were journeying in the wilderness, the *Shekhinah* went in front of them, and they followed her guidance. The *Shekhinah* was accompanied

by all the clouds of glory, and when she journeyed the Israelites took up their march. And when the *Shekhinah* ascended, the cloud also ascended on high, so that all men looked up and asked: *Who is this that cometh out of the wilderness like pillars of smoke* (S.S. 3:6). For the cloud of the *Shekhinah* looked like smoke because the fire which Abraham and his son Isaac kindled clung to it and never left it, and by reason of that fire it ascended both as cloud and smoke; but for all that it was perfumed, with the cloud of Abraham on the right and with the cloud of Isaac on the left.

This last passage not only affirms the presence of the *Shekhinah* among the Israelites during the wandering in the wilderness, the archetypal exile, but it also links the *Shekhinah* to the patriarchs Abraham and Isaac. The intention clearly is to project the concept of the *Shekhinah* as a mother figure to all of Israel back into the biblical text. Certainly the identification of the *Shekhinah* with the Cloud of Glory, described in Exodus, which guided the Israelites during the day, succeeds in doing just this, and the description of the cloud of smoke creates as well a connection to the sacrifice of the ram on Mount Moriah. The final image, of the clouds of Abraham and Isaac, is pure mythology, where the patriarchs exist as archetypes. The effect is to create a sense of the timelessness of Jewish history, in which the essence of all past events clings to the present like the smoke of the sacrifice to the Cloud of Glory.[10]

Indeed, there are a series of myths about the *Shekhinah* found in the Zohar, several of which are focused, like the previous passage, on the exile of the *Shekhinah*. Perhaps the most important of these is the following, in which it becomes clear that the *Shekhinah* has achieved mythic independence:

When the Temple was still standing, Israel would perform their rites, and bring offerings and sacrifices. And the *Shekhinah* rested upon them in the Temple, like a mother hovering over her children, and all faces were resplendent with light, so that there was blessing both above and below. . . . When the Temple was destroyed the *Shekhinah* came and went up to all those places where she used to dwell at first, and she would weep for her home and for Israel, who had gone into exile, and for all the righteous and the pious ones who used to be there and had perished. . . . At that time the Holy One, blessed be He, questioned the *Shekhinah*, and said to her, "What ails you now, that you have gone up entirely to the roofs?" . . . And she said to Him: "My children are in exile, and the Temple is burnt, so why should I remain here?" . . . Now the Temple is destroyed and the *Shekhinah* is with Israel in exile . . . and there is no joy to be found, above or below.[11]

While many of the myths promulgated in the Zohar are couched in allegorical terms, this passage is clearly mythological in its intent. The dialogue unmistakably resembles that between a husband and wife at odds.

The tension between them is apparent in the words of the Holy One: "What ails you now?" and in the Bride's reply: "My children are in exile, and the Temple is burnt, so why should I remain here?" From this dialogue it is apparent that the confrontation takes place between two mythic figures, and it is at this point that it becomes clear that the *Shekhinah* has achieved mythic independence.

With this kabbalistic initiation, then, the presence of the *Shekhinah* is fully injected into the tradition. It prepares the way for a series of visions and encounters with the *Shekhinah* in subsequent literature that are associated, in particular, with the *Kotel*, the Western Wall of the Temple, also known as the Wailing Wall.[12]

In these kabbalistic and post-kabbalistic legends it is apparent that, at least from a mythological point of view, the *Shekhinah* has become an independent entity. Nevertheless, the *Shekhinah* was regarded at the same time as being an extension or aspect of the Divinity, which was, of course, necessary in order to uphold the essential concept of monotheism. True initiates of the Kabbalah were not disturbed by these apparent contradictions, but, for others, the danger of viewing the *Shekhinah* as a separate deity was recognized, and that explains why the study of the kabbalistic texts was not permitted until a man had reached his fortieth year and was married. Only such a person was felt to be grounded enough in the tradition not to be overwhelmed by the kabbalistic mysteries, while younger, more vulnerable men might well be led astray.

Nor does the evolution of the myth of the *Shekhinah* end in the kabbalistic period. The implications of the exile of the *Shekhinah* were expanded in the 16th century by Rabbi Isaac Luria, as explained below. And in the 19th century Rabbi Nachman of Bratslav told the tale, "The Lost Princess," which hints at an identification of the *Shekhinah* with Jung's concept of the anima. This implicit link between *Shekhinah* and anima is made explicit in the story, "The Palace of Pearls,"[13] by Penina Villenchik.

One other subtle identity of the *Shekhinah* is suggested in the talmudic tradition of every Jew receiving a *neshamah yeterah*, a second soul, on the Sabbath: "Rabbi Shimon ben Lakish said: 'On the eve of the Sabbath the Holy One, blessed be He, gives man an extra soul, and at the close of the Sabbath He withdraws it from him.' "[14] This extra soul is believed to depart after *Havdalah*, the ritual of separation performed at the end of the Sabbath. This second soul functions as a kind of *ibbur*, literally "an impregnation," which is the spirit of a holy figure that fuses with the soul of a living person, bringing greater faith and wisdom. But in this case it is a Divine soul that fuses with the souls of Jews on the Sabbath. It is not difficult to identify this second soul with the presence of the *Shekhinah*, the Divine Presence, who is also the Sabbath Queen. Certainly, the arrival and departure of the Sabbath Queen and that of this mysterious second soul are simultaneous. Identifying the second soul with the *Shekhinah* is a way of acknowledging the sacredness of the Sabbath both from within and without.

Thus we find, especially in the Zohar, a cycle of myths linked to the *Shekhinah*. Some of these portray the unity of God and His Bride, while others concern their separation. The key myth, as noted, is that of the exile of the *Shekhinah*, for at the time the Bride goes into exile, the mythic figure of the *Shekhinah* becomes largely independent of the Divinity and takes on a separate mythic identity.

Note that the myth of the exile of the *Shekhinah* is a two-part myth. In the first stage the Bride of God goes into exile at the time of the destruction of the Temple, while in the second stage the *Shekhinah*, identified as the *Sefirah Malkhut*, is reunited with the male aspect of God, identified by *Sefirah Tiferet*. This reunion, which is described in the Zohar as a marriage,[15] is brought about through the activities of Israel in fulfilling requirements of the *mitzvot*, and through the intensity, or *kavanah*, of prayers. When this reunification becomes permanent, the exile of the *Shekhinah* will come to an end. This development is linked to the coming of the Messiah, in that one of the consequences of the messianic era is that the Temple in Jerusalem, which was the *Shekhinah's* home in this world, will be rebuilt. Since the *Shekhinah* went into exile because of its destruction, the rebuilding of the Temple would surely represent the end of her exile. In this way the myths of the *Shekhinah* and the Messiah became linked.

Contributing to the long life of Jewish myths such as that of the *Shekhinah* are the associated rituals. The most important ritual linked to the myth of the *Shekhinah* is that known as *Kabbalat Shabbat*, recreated by Rabbi Isaac Luria in the 16th century. Here the worshipers go out into the fields just before sunset on the eve of the Sabbath and welcome the Sabbath Queen. The Ari found the basis for this ritual in the Talmud, where it is recounted that Rabbi Hanina would put on his robes and stand at sunset on the eve of the Sabbath and say, "Come, let us go out to greet the Sabbath Queen."[16] Of course, by the time the Ari formalized this ritual, the concept of the Sabbath Queen had evolved into an independent mythic figure, and the ritual itself becomes a kind of goddess worship, but, within a monotheistic structure.

According to Walter F. Otto, "Myth demands ritual."[17] This is the central premise of the Myth and Ritual school of mythological studies, which probably has more advocates than any other. Certainly, the close relationship between Jewish myth and ritual more than fulfills the requirements of this approach, and therefore it can be said that Jewish myth possesses both of the primary elements of a mythic system: myth and ritual.

As in other traditions, Jewish myth and ritual reaffirm and validate each other, for as long as they remain linked, the ritual keeps the myth alive. But as soon as the ritual falls into disuse, the myth loses its primary purposes: linking the past and the present through the acting out of the ritual. Without the ritual, the myth is no more than a story, albeit a powerful and compelling one. For observant Jews, the stories that accompany Jewish rituals have retained the status of absolute truth, which is how a myth appears in the eyes of a believer. Indeed, the key test in our time for whether one holds Orthodox views is whether one believes that God dictated the Torah to Moses at Mount Sinai. For without this belief, the seal of truth that binds the Torah and makes every detail fraught with infinite meaning would be called into question. Thus, for believers, the ultimate truth of the Torah is self-evident and beyond any doubt. This is the essential condition for a mythic system to flourish. However, even for those in our time for whom Jewish myth no longer represents the primary way of viewing the universe, the myths themselves retain their inherent power. Like all myths they are not arbitrary creations, but projections from the deepest levels of the self. From this perspective, the myths can be read as psychic maps, archetypes of the collective Jewish unconscious.

At the same time, much of the evolution of Jewish mythology seems to have had a distinctly conscious element. So too does it diverge from the anonymous nature of most mythology in that it is possible to pinpoint the authors of mythic transformation, especially Moshe de Leon, the primary author of the Zohar, and the Ari, who was not only a great rabbi, but a great myth-maker as well.

Drawing on the form and method of rabbinic commentary found in the midrashim, Moshe de Leon created a mystical commentary on the Torah that itself became the primary mystical Jewish text. It is in the Zohar that the key myths about the exile of the *Shekhinah* emerge, along with many others. The mythic daring found in this text was considered so extreme that it was forbidden to study the Zohar or other kabbalistic texts unless a man was forty years old and married. These barriers were erected to guard against the mythological impact of the Zohar and other mystical texts and to limit access to those best suited to interpret them allegorically. The great fear underlying these restrictions is that the text would be misread in a way that would undermine belief in the principle of monotheism. At the same time, for the select few who gained entrance to these mystical texts, there was the opportunity to achieve a profound level of mystical knowledge and spiritual attainment.

Among those mystics for whom the Zohar became a text as sacred as the Torah was the Ari. He was said to have purchased a manuscript of the Zohar from a wanderer, and this event was the turning point in his life. Not only did the Ari devote the rest of his brief life to mystical contemplation and study, but he modeled himself and his disciples on the portrayal of Rabbi Shimon bar Yohai, the hero of the Zohar, and his circle. This pattern of master and disciples became, in turn, the model for the Baal Shem Tov and subsequent hasidic rabbis and their hasidim.

It was the genius of the Ari to have such a deep understanding of Judaism that he was able to create the myth of the Shattering of the Vessels, the last major myth to enter Jewish tradition. This is the most cosmological of the Jewish Creation myths. Its central phases concern the mysteries of Creation: How God had to contract Himself in order to make space for the

Creation of the world, in a process known as *tzimtzum*. How God then sent forth vessels of primordial light that somehow split apart, scattering the sparks of holy light all over the world, but especially in the Holy Land. And how gathering these sparks can restore the broken vessels and return the world to its primordial condition.

This myth of the Ari is essentially an original myth drawn from Gnostic themes, yet at the same time it is a remarkable commentary on *Ma'aseh Bereshit,* has discernible links to the system of the *Sefirot,* and also links two other primary Jewish myths, those of the Creation and of the Messiah. For the broken vessels initiated the cosmic Fall, and the restoration of the vessels will initiate a messianic era that will resurrect the dead, rebuild the Temple in Jerusalem, and restore the world to its primordial state. Thus this combined myth serves as a framework for all of Jewish history.

The Ari's myth is stunning in its simplicity, originality, and essential integrity. Yet, a close examination of the components of the myth reveals that they each have analogs in some key episode of the Torah, as well as in gnostic, apocryphal, and merkavah sources. The first phase of the myth, *tzimtzum,* describing the Contraction of God, likely finds its biblical inspiration in the cloud that fills the Tent of Meeting in Exodus 40:34–35: *Then a cloud covered the tent of the congregation, and the glory of the Lord filled the tabernacle. And Moses was not able to enter into the tent of the congregation, because the cloud abode thereon, and the glory of the Lord filled the tabernacle.* This passage demonstrates that God's presence occupies space. Therefore, it leads to the conclusion, as postulated by *tzimtzum,* that it was necessary for God to contract His presence in order to make space in which to create the world. According to the kabbalistic concept of *tzimtzum,* God withdrew His Presence from the center, by contracting outward to leave a place empty of His presence in which He could create the world. So the world is created in the middle of God, but in a place vacated of His presence.

The concept of *tzimtzum* can also be seen as a reply to the verse *Do not I fill heaven and earth? says the Lord* (Jer. 23:24). This verse is reinforced by the talmudic dictim, "God is the place of the world, but the world is not the place of God" (Gen. Rab. 68:9). Such a Divine contraction is directly suggested in the Midrash Rabbah, where it is stated that "This same Glory, that was so vast, compressed itself so as to appear to be speaking from above the ark-cover between the two cherubim" (Num. Rab. 14:22). Indeed, the kabbalistic concept of *tzimtzum* may well have its specific origin in this passage.

The shattering of the vessels finds its biblical parallel in Moses throwing down the first tablets of the Law, which shatter (Ex. 32:19): *And it came to pass, as soon as he came nigh unto the camp, that he saw the calf, and the dancing, and Moses' anger waxed hot, and he cast the tables out of his hands, and broke them beneath the mount.* Yet there is also another possible biblical source for the image of scattered sparks, deriving from Ezekiel 10:2,

where coals of fire from the altar are scattered by some angelic figure, identified as *the man clothed with linen* (Ez. 9:11), over the city of Jerusalem:
*Fill thine hand with coals of fire from between the cherubims, and scatter
them over the city.* Finally, there is a potent talmudic aphorism that may
have served as inspiration for the Ari: "The words of the Torah have many
meanings. Sparks fly in different directions. Each word may catch a different spark." (B. Kid. 30b). As for the gathering of the sparks, this aspect of
the Ari's myth seems likely to have been inspired by the gathering of the
manna by the Israelites in the wilderness (Ex. 16:21): *And they gathered it
every morning, every man according to his eating.*

Note that each of these primary biblical analogs finds its origin in the
account of the wandering in the desert in Exodus. This also suggests that
the myth of the Ari can also be regarded as a mystical commentary of the
book of Exodus. These three passages delineate the three primary figures in
the drama of the Exodus, that of God, Moses, and the people of Israel. It is
God whose presence in the Tent of Meeting makes it impossible for Moses
to enter. It is Moses who breaks the tablets of the Law, after seeing the
golden calf (Ex. 32:19). And rabbinic legends, such as in *Avot de Rabbi
Natan* 2:11, speak of the letters that flew from the stone tablets before Moses
shattered them, just as the sparks are scattered everywhere in the Ari's myth.
At the same time, the image of sparks itself may have been suggested by
Isaiah 50:11: *Behold, all of you kindle a fire and surround yourselves with the
sparks. Therefore you are only walking in the light of your own fire and in
the sparks that you have kindled.* This passage also conveys much of the
beauty and mystery associated with the myth of the Ari. Finally, the falling
of the manna represents God's explicit love of Israel, as it constitutes a
miracle, especially as it is characterized in the Midrash, where it is told that
each person tasted the food they loved the best in the manna. Likewise, the
sparks that are scattered are divine, and the act of gathering them fulfills a
person's destiny, since, according to the Ari, God is said to have created the
Jewish people for the explicit purpose of gathering the sparks.

The deepest mystery of all among the students of the Ari concerns the
true reason for the Shattering of the Vessels. The most important consequences of it, however, are apparent: it shifts the responsibility for the fallen
state of existence from man to God, and it also sets the stage for the final
phase of the myth, that of the Gathering the Sparks. Here the scattered
sparks are sought out and gathered in the belief that when enough have
been raised up, the broken vessels will be restored and the world returned
to its prelapsarian state. The Ari identified this gathering of the sparks with
fulfilling the *mitzvot*, the Divine commandments, which endowed these
ritual requirements with a Divine purpose. This myth also gives a positive
explanation to the problem of Jewish exile, especially after the expulsion of
the Jews from Spain in 1492. While there is currently a scholarly debate
about the extent of the impact of the expulsion in the mystical theories of
the Ari, this event, which took place only thirty years before his birth, can-

not be ignored. For the myth of the Ari proposes that there was a Divine purpose behind the exiles that have haunted Jewish history, and that the Jews are the chosen people in the sense that they were created to search for and raise up the scattered sparks.

This myth, in its apparent simplicity, conveyed kabbalistic principles in a way that could be readily understood. As a result, it was taken up by the Jewish community at large, breaking the grip on the mystical tradition that had been the domain of a select circle of rabbis since ancient times. This myth spoke to the people, turning the curse of exile into a blessing. It gave meaning to their wandering in the Diaspora, for the scattered sparks had to be found and raised up wherever they were hidden. And it held out hope for a messianic era that could be brought closer by acts of human piety.

The most essential feature of the Ari's myth is its two-part nature, for God's contraction should be seen as a preparatory step that made the shattering of the vessels possible. Here it is understood from the first that the complete myth requires both parts; it is not possible to consider one without the other. The first part of this cosmological myth is destructive, the second part creative. The archetypal pattern is that of shattering and restoration. But instead of shifting the blame for the Fall to Adam and Eve, here it can be directly linked to God, Who, after all, is the ultimate creator and therefore responsible for any flaws in Creation.

Note the remarkable parallels between the Ari's Creation myth and that of the exile of the *Shekhinah*. Both are two-part; both involve separation and reunion, exile and return; both attribute to the prayers of Israel the power to accomplish the necessary *tikkun* or repair. Indeed, it is possible to view the myth of the Ari as a mystical restatement of the exile of the *Shekhinah*.

Thus the kabbalists did as the rabbis had before them: they received one myth and transformed it into another, which more closely mirrored their view of the world. For them this meant resurrecting the lost goddess, but doing so in a context that appeared to preserve the monotheistic basis of Judaism. So it is that the myths about God, the Bride of God, and the Messiah converge, diverge, and ultimately come together in the messianic vision of the End of Days. For when all of the holy sparks have been liberated, the Messiah will come, the Temple will be restored, and God's Bride will come out of exile, restoring the Godhead to wholeness. In this convergence we can finally see in perspective the ultimate Jewish myth, that of the long-standing covenant between God and Israel, in all its mythic permutations.

Tales of the Great Jewish Mystics

*T*he writings of mystical circles are almost always accompanied by tales recounting the mystical experiences of the key religious figures. This is true of the tales about Zen and Sufi masters, as well as those of Jewish and Christian mystics such as Rabbi Isaac Luria and St. John of the Cross. Some kind of direct experience or revelation of the Divine is often found in these tales. So too do they define the range of mystical experience. At the same time, such tales bring with them the power of the story, making them far more accessible than most mystical texts.[1]

One of the most famous Jewish mystical tales tells of four sages who somehow entered Paradise. One lost his life there; another lost his mind; the third became an apostate. Only Rabbi Akiba "ascended and descended in peace."[2] Generations of rabbis have debated what caused the downfall of the three sages and have used the story of "The Four Who Entered Paradise" as a warning tale about the dangers of mystical contemplation. Nevertheless, there was also an ancient Jewish sect that created texts describing such heavenly journeys in great detail. These writings, known as *Hekhalot* texts, seem to have served as guidebooks for ascent, much as *The Tibetan Book of the Dead* was intended to guide the soul of one who journeyed from this world to the next. Thus the story of the four who entered Paradise served a key role from the perspective of both those who understood it as a warning tale and those who saw it as a model for ascent.

This account of the four sages, of talmudic origin, represents a kind of tale, based on a mystical theme, that constitutes a genre of its own. And like fairy tales, tales of the supernatural, parables, and fables, these mystical tales are found in every phase of Jewish literature.

This unexpectedly rich tradition of Jewish mystical tales abounds in post-biblical sources, not only in sacred texts but in secular ones as well. These sacred texts include kabbalistic and hasidic sources, where such tales are most likely to be found, as well as the earlier pseudepigraphal and rabbinic texts, whereas the secular texts are drawn from a remarkable body of mystical folktales in medieval Jewish folklore and in oral tales collected in this century.

These mystical tales constitute the legendary dimension of the Jewish mystical tradition. They accompany and in many ways complement a body of complex mystical teachings that can be broadly defined as kabbalistic, when that term is used to refer to an esoteric mystical tradition that has its origins in the biblical accounts of Creation and the vision of Ezekiel[3] and is found in every subsequent phase of sacred Jewish literature.[4]

These tales include a wide range of mystical experiences, virtually all presented as true accounts, not only of mystical union but of visions, dreams, soul travel, encounters with angels and demons, possession by both good and evil spirits, miracles, and experiences out of body and out of time. Yet, despite these disparate themes, virtually all of them have in common some kind of revelation or interaction with the Divine realm and as such can be properly defined as mystical, for the imprint of the Divine is deeply reflected in these tales.

Just as the account of the four sages who entered Paradise serves as the model for mystical tales of heavenly ascent, so the models for most of the primary types of mystical tales can be found in the Talmud. The primary repositories of rabbinic legend are the two Talmuds, finally edited or "redacted" in Babylon and in the Land of Israel in about the 5th century, and the vast midrashic literature, which was produced well into the Middle Ages, up until at least the 12th century. These include tales about mystical visions, visions of God, Divine miracles, and attempts to hasten the coming of the Messiah.

Indeed, virtually all of the major mystical themes are found in the early rabbinic tales. However, the tales, as they have been preserved, tend to be concise. There is little of the narrative embellishment found in later tales, especially those of folk origin. In many cases, including that of the four who entered Paradise, the tales are fragmentary, and only the bare bones of what was clearly a more extensive tradition have survived. For example, the legend of the four who entered Paradise and the accompanying legends in tractate Hagigah of the Talmud resemble fragments of a *Hekhalot* text, some of which were contemporaneous with the Talmud.

So too is the influence of these early rabbinic tales on the subsequent literary tradition immense. Indeed, many kabbalistic and hasidic tales seem to seek out rabbinic models intentionally in order to draw a parallel between the earlier rabbis and those of their own era.

There are several early kabbalistic works, in addition to the *Hekhalot* texts, such as *Sefer Yetzirah* and *Sefer Bahir*, that clearly demonstrate a developing mystical consciousness in Judaism. But it is not until the appearance of the Zohar, the central text of Jewish mysticism, in the 13th century, that the kabbalistic era begins. This period, which is usually dated between the 13th and 17th centuries, encompasses the writing of the Zohar in the 13th century and the emergence of the teachings and tales of the Ari and the other sages of Safed in the 16th century, as well as the school of Rabbi Shalom Sharabi in Jerusalem and the messianic movement of the false messiah Shabbatai Zevi in the 17th century. It should be noted, however, that there were Jewish mystics in the 12th century whose teachings may well have influenced the Zohar, and the Hasidic movement of the 18th and 19th centuries was deeply influenced by kabbalistic teachings.

Some of the most important mystical tales emerged out of this kabbalistic period. The Zohar itself is one of the richest sources of both mythic and legendary material. It contains many anecdotes about the talmudic sage Rabbi Shimon bar Yohai, known by the acronym Rashbi, who lived in the 2nd century and who is reputed to have been the author of the Zohar. However, as Gershom Scholem and other scholars have documented, the actual author was almost certainly Moshe de Leon, who lived in Guadalajara, Spain, in the 13th century. De Leon presented the text of the Zohar as a manuscript he had found.[5] But until the work of modern scholars cast doubt on de Leon's claim of discovery, it was considered authentic, and the Zohar was soon identified as a sacred text. Even today many observant Jews continue to assert that Rabbi Shimon bar Yohai is the true author of the Zohar, rejecting the scholarship in the same way that they reject any suggestion that God did not literally dictate the Torah to Moses at Mount Sinai. But for scholar and believer alike, the Zohar remains the central text of the Kabbalah.

Because of their influence on the subsequent development of the mystical tale, the tales found in the classic kabbalistic texts, especially the Zohar, and certain key legends, such as that about Joseph della Reina, who sought to force the coming of the Messiah, as well as the tales about the Ari, constitute the core of Jewish mystical tales. At the same time, these tales are largely a continuation of the earlier rabbinic traditions, just as the Zohar presents itself as the mystical account of the life and teachings of a talmudic sage, Rabbi Shimon bar Yohai. Thus it is important to distinguish the term "mystical" from the narrower term "kabbalistic." In a general sense, Kabbalah refers to the entire field of Jewish mysticism. But in a more technical sense, it refers specifically to the period between the 13th and 17th centuries.

The kabbalistic era concludes with the trauma of the messianic movement of Shabbatai Zevi in the 17th century.[6] Since kabbalistic concepts were the underpinning of the teachings of Shabbatai Zevi, his apostasy resulted in renewed efforts to limit access to the kabbalistic texts and to keep the entire study esoteric.

During the hasidic period, beginning in the 18th century, the mystical tale reemerged and achieved a flowering that dwarfs all other periods, including the kabbalistic. Here are found an abundance of tales about the hasidic rabbis resembling those of the Zen and Sufi masters. Certain rabbis, in particular, such as the Baal Shem Tov, Reb Pinhas of Koretz, Reb Elimelech of Lizensk, and Reb Nachman of Bratslav, demonstrate great mystical powers. But evidence of these powers is also found in tales linked with many other hasidic rabbis, such as Reb Levi Yitzhak of Berditchev, Reb Eizek of Kallo, or the Maid of Ludomir, one of the only women recognized as a rebbe.[7] While each of these masters follows his or her own path, it is apparent that the models of the master in these tales are drawn from the legends of Rabbi Shimon bar Yohai, Rabbi Isaac Luria, and the Baal Shem Tov.

Although the Jewish mystical tale is primarily found in sacred texts, there are also secular expressions of these mystical tales in collections of medieval Jewish folklore and among the rich treasury of oral tales collected by ethnologists from both Eastern European and Middle Eastern Jewish communities. These tales are primarily collected in two archives: the YIVO archives of Eastern European folklore, originally of Vilna, now of New York, and the Israel Folktale Archives (IFA) in Haifa, which has collected tales of virtually every Jewish ethnic community in the world.

The majority of these mystical tales are about key Jewish masters. Certain patriarchs, prophets, and rabbis were depicted as drawing on knowledge of the Divine realm to fulfill some kind of mystical purpose. Some were described as seeking personal enlightenment, others knowledge of the Divine mysteries; some as seeking to have heaven intercede to protect the Jewish community from one danger or another; still others as seeking to hasten the coming of the Messiah. Thus these masters function as shamans, going into trances, communing with angels and spirits of the dead, confronting evil spirits, and, in general, demonstrating their mastery of all the spiritual and physical realms.

The stories about these mystical masters often form cycles of tales. There are major cycles involving biblical figures such as Enoch, Moses, and Elijah; talmudic sages such as Rabbi Akiba, Rabbi Shimon bar Yohai, and Rabbi Ishmael the High Priest; medieval figures such as Judah the Pious, Rabbi Isaac Luria, and Rabbi Judah Loew; and, among hasidic masters, the Baal Shem Tov, in particular, as well as many others. In addition, there are mystical tales about many other rabbis and hidden saints. Each of the scattered Jewish communities had their own legends. Even related stories about their disciples, such as those about Rabbi Hayim Vital, the primary disciple of Rabbi Isaac Luria, often constitute a story cycle of their own.

These tale cycles often begin with legendary accounts of the lives of these masters, from their miraculous births to the legends surrounding their deaths, as well as sporadic reports of their spirits returning after death. This pattern of return from the beyond first takes form in the many legends about the reappearance of the Prophet Elijah in this world, often disguised as a wandering beggar.[8] In the majority of Jewish folktales, Elijah draws upon his miraculous powers to assist Jews in need. But his role changes when he studies with mystics such as Rabbi Shimon bar Yohai and the Ari. He does not conceal his identity from them. Rather, he reveals mysteries of heaven, serving as a kind of heavenly master, the model for all the living masters who follow.

The first of the talmudic sages whose spirit returns after death is Rabbi Shimon bar Yohai, known as Rashbi, who spent thirteen years hiding from the Romans in a cave, where he was reputed to have written the Zohar, the primary text of Jewish mysticism.[9] So powerful is Bar Yohai's soul that there are many accounts of him appearing in the world long after his death. In one such story, "The Dancing of the Ari," he appears at the Lag ba-Omer celebration of Rabbi Isaac Luria and dances with him. In another he returns in a dream, as in this early midrashic tale:

> One of the disciples of Rabbi Shimon bar Yohai forgot what he had learned and went weeping to the cemetery. After this Rashbi appeared to him in a dream and said: "When you throw three pebbles at me I will come to you." The disciple went to a dream interpreter, who told him to repeat each lesson three times and Rabbi Shimon would come to him, and he would no longer forget what he had studied. This turned out to be true. Every time he repeated the lesson three times, Rabbi Shimon came to him and his memory was restored.[10]

This midrashic tale is the forerunner of the idea of an *ibbur*, literally "an impregnation."[11] This is a little-known form of spirit possession in Judaism in which the soul of an ancestor or a master enters the soul of a living person in order to comfort or instruct him. This is in contrast to possession by a dybbuk, in which the soul of one who has died takes possession of one of the living and must be exorcised. Thus this brief tale of Rabbi Shimon bar Yohai heralds a specific type of Jewish mystical tale, little known, focused on possession by *ibur*.

Most students of Jewish folklore and mysticism are familiar with the concept of possession by a dybbuk. S. Ansky's famous drama *The Dybbuk* portrays such a possession, and the final act of the play is based on an actual rabbinic exorcism ceremony. This is a negative form of possession, but there is also this little-known positive form of metempsychosis in which a living sage is possessed by the spirit of an *ibbur*. The presence of an *ibbur* was regarded as a exceptional blessing by Jewish mystics, especially those of Safed in the 16th century, while the same mystics strove greatly to exorcise dybbuks from those who were possessed by them.

Just as there are tales in which the possession of a dybbuk is portrayed, so too are there tales about possession by an *ibur*. However, there are far more dybbuk tales, as such possession was often the explanation for madness, and the exorcism served as the cure, one that often worked. These dybbuk tales, virtually all of which are presented as true accounts, always follow the same pattern. An evil spirit, pursued by avenging angels, enters into various objects and beings, such as a rock, a flower, a dog, a cow, or a person. The person begins to behave strangely, with the spirit speaking in a voice of its own. A rabbi is called in, who determines that a dybbuk has taken possession. The rabbi then compels the dybbuk to recount the story of his sin and the history of his soul after death, until it took possession of that person. Then the rabbi exorcises the dybbuk and it is forced to depart, usually through a little finger or toe.

In one famous tale from the 16th century, "The Widow of Safed," [12] a dybbuk takes possession of a widow because she does not believe that the waters of the Red Sea truly parted. Rabbi Isaac Luria sends his disciple, Rabbi Hayim Vital, to exorcise the dybbuk. Hayim Vital questions the dybbuk, extracts its story, and exorcises it. Later it is discovered that the text inside the *mezzuzah* on the doorpost of the widow's house was flawed and therefore ineffective. Thus it was her failure of belief and the loss of the protective powers of the *mezzuzah* that made her vulnerable to the danger of possession by the dybbuk.

Considering that possession by a dybbuk is so closely linked to evil and madness, it is remarkable to discover a Jewish form of spirit possession that is regarded as positive. Yet that is indeed the case, as demonstrated by the tales about possession by an *ibbur*. Unlike that of a dybbuk, however, this kind of possession is temporary and is linked to a sacred object, such as a holy book or phylacteries, known as *tefillin*. Whenever the living sage opens that book or puts on the *tefillin*, the spirit of the *ibbur* fuses with his own.

In one such tale, "A Kiss from the Master," [13] a rich man, who cannot read the Aramaic in which the Zohar is written, is possessed by the *ibbur* of Shimon bar Yohai and discovers that he can both read and fully comprehend the difficult text by simply opening the book. Note that the possession by the spirit of Rabbi Shimon bar Yohai only takes place when the man opens the Zohar, the book so closely identified with Shimon bar Yohai. And the possession only lasts as long as the book is open. But during that time the spirit of Shimon bar Yohai fuses with his own. This tale was collected orally in the city of Safed in modern-day Israel, demonstrating that even to this day the tradition about the *ibbur* is still recounted there. It is interesting to note that this oral tale is clearly a variant of the earlier tale about Shimon bar Yohai from Ecclesiastes Rabbah, in which Bar Yohai came to the student after he had repeated his lesson three times. Since the two tales are separated by more than a thousand years, it shows how the oral tradition in Judaism still remains alive, even to this day.

Likewise, other *ibbur* tales portray such a temporary kind of possession, such as the famous tale of "The *Tefillin* of the Or ha-Hayim." Here Rabbi Hayim ben Attar, known as the Or ha-Hayim after the title of his most famous book, told his wife on his deathbed that after his death a man would come from another city and seek to purchase his *tefillin* (phylacteries). The rabbi encouraged her to sell them for a high price and to warn the purchaser that he must never allow himself to become distracted when he wore them.

Everything took place as the Or ha-Hayim had said, and when the man who had purchased the *tefillin* tried them on, he was suddenly filled with a deep sense of holiness. And when he prayed, he did so with a fervor he had never known, and his prayers ascended on high. This lasted as long as he wore the *tefillin*, but when he took them off, the holy spirit departed.

One day, while he was wearing the *tefillin*, the man was distracted by one of his servants about a business matter. And when he returned to his prayers, the holy spirit was gone—for good. Finally he took the *tefillin* to a scribe, who opened the wooden box of the *tefillin* and found that the parchment inside it was blank, for the letters had flown away, along with the soul of the Or ha-Hayim.

As this tale makes abundantly clear, the presence of an *ibbur* was regarded as a great blessing, and unlike possession by a dybbuk, there was no attempt to exorcise the *ibbur*. How did the concept of the *ibbur* originate? It may have developed from a well-known tradition about the Sabbath found in the Talmud, dating back to the 5th century, in which every Jew is said to receive an extra soul *(neshamah yeterah)* on the Sabbath. This is a holy soul that remains with a person throughout the Sabbath and only departs after the performing of the ritual of *Havdalah*, which closes the Sabbath. Among the hasidim, it was customary to delay this closing ceremony of the Sabbath for as long as possible, in order to hold on to this extra soul. This extra soul is closely linked with the figure of the *Shekhinah*, the Divine Presence who is also identified as the Sabbath Queen said to be present during every Sabbath. It seems likely that the extra soul is the manifestation of the Sabbath Queen as experienced in each person. This is also a kind of spirit possession, a precursor of the *ibbur*.

There is still another form of spirit possession found in Jewish lore, which comes even closer to the concept of the *ibbur*. This refers to the strange case of Rabbi Joseph Karo, who lived in the city of Safed in the 16th century. Rabbi Karo was the author of the *Shulhan Arukh*, the Code of Jewish Law. Even to this day, this book is the ultimate reference for decisions about matters of ritual and law. Yet, remarkably enough for one with such a finely tuned legal mind, Joseph Karo was a mystic who wrote a book recounting his possession by a spirit when he studied the Mishnah, the core text of the Talmud. He identified this spirit as a *maggid*, a heavenly teacher. On several occasions others were present when this spirit of the Mishnah spoke through him. On such occasions Rabbi Karo seemed to go into a trance, and the spirit spoke in his place, in a voice of its own. The spirit remained as long as he continued to study the Mishnah, then departed. Rabbi Karo regarded this spirit as his heavenly guide and recorded its pronouncements in *Maggid Mesharim*. Again, this kind of possession, while not that of the spirit of a human being, is very closely linked to the concept of the *ibur*.

There are also *ibbur* tales told among the hasidim of Eastern Europe. One of the most intriguing concerns the hasidic rabbi Zevi Hirsch of Zhiadchov, who was said to have been possessed by the *ibbur* of Rabbi Isaac Luria of Safed, one of the greatest mystical rabbis, who lived in the 16th century. How this took place is recounted in the tale of "The Soul of the Ari." [14]

One winter morning Reb Zevi rose very early, when it was still very dark outside. Although no candles in the house had been lit, still a light pervaded the rooms as if it were day. Curious to know the source of this light, Reb Zevi searched until he found that it was coming from a little cupboard. There he found a precious stone as large as an egg, that glowed with a bright light from within. Reb Zevi realized that the value of that stone could not be calculated, and he hid it away.

Then he fasted from the end of one Sabbath until the beginning of the next so that heaven might inform him of what it was. And in a dream he was told that this stone had been a gift for him from heaven. If he chose to keep it, he and all of his descendants would be very wealthy. But if he chose not to keep it, then the soul of the holy Ari would become fused with his own.

Now Reb Zevi did not desire wealth, and the choice was not difficult for him to make. He asked in a dream question how he should return the precious stone, and he was told to fling it up toward heaven. This he did, and fiery sparks flew from it until nothing more could be seen.

Later one of Reb Zevi's students, who slept in the room next to his, heard a voice speaking to his master during the night. He knew that no one else was with Reb Zevi, so he rose and washed his hands and stood beside the wall and listened. The voice that spoke was interpreting a passage of the Zohar, casting great light on its mysteries. The student was filled with wonder, but he dared not ask the rabbi about it.

During the next Sabbath Reb Zevi began to expound on a passage from the Zohar, and the student recognized the teachings of the mysterious voice he had heard. And when Reb Zevi finished, he said: "This is what I learned from the very mouth of the Ari."

As this tale makes abundantly clear, possession by an *ibbur* of a great master, such as the Ari, was considered even more precious than great wealth and was one of the ultimate blessings that heaven could bestow on a living sage. What this unusual kind of spirit possession provided was a greater knowledge of the mystical meaning of Torah. For only with the assistance of the spirit of a great sage could a living sage penetrate the hidden light of the Torah, which was concealed from everyone else.

Thus we find an unusual dual tradition of spirit possession in Judaism, where possession by an evil spirit, a dybbuk, required exorcism, and, at the same time, possession by the spirit of a departed sage, an *ibbur*, was regarded as the greatest possible blessing.

One of the primary characteristics of Jewish literature is that the earlier texts serve as models for the later ones. The two tales about the *ibbur* of Shimon bar Yohai demonstrate this. Certainly, in the case of the later mystical tales, it is almost always possible to find a prototype in the early rabbinic texts. In general, these later tales draw on the models of the *Aggadah*, the legendary material of the Talmud, just as the mystical commentary in the Zohar, the central text of the Kabbalah, often seems to be built on earlier midrashic commentary. The difference is that the rabbinic commentary is primarily legal or legendary, whereas that found in the Zohar is chiefly mystical. So too are the tales found in the Zohar of a mystical nature. Here, for example, Shimon bar Yohai and his disciples see signs that reveal God's intentions, speak with an angel in the form of a rock, meet saints from the Other World, ascend to the celestial Academy, and read the book that Adam was once given by an angel.

The links between the classic rabbinic tales and those of kabbalistic, hasidic, or folk origin also reveal how the later rabbis sought their personal models in the lives of the earlier sages. The primary models were the talmudic sages Rabbi Akiba, Rabbi Ishmael the High Priest, Rabbi Yohanan ben Zakkai, and Rabbi Shimon bar Yohai. Of these, the most extensive legendary tradition is that surrounding Bar Yohai. It is this legendary model, especially as found in the Zohar, that transformed Bar Yohai into the foremost archetype of Jewish mystics.

Among those who modeled themselves after Shimon bar Yohai were Rabbi Isaac Luria of Safed, the Ari, and the Baal Shem Tov, the founder of hasidism, known as "the Besht." The Ari once took his disciples to the place where Shimon bar Yohai used to meet with his disciples. He had each of them sit in the place of one of the disciples, and he himself sat in the place of Shimon bar Yohai, making the parallel between them explicit, and even hinting that he was the reincarnation of Bar Yohai in that generation.[15]

Later, this model of the master was taken up by the hasidim, beginning with the Baal Shem Tov, and is clearly reflected in the rich body of hasidic tales. Here the role of the rebbe, the hasidic master, is of primary importance, for the rebbe was believed to possess Divine knowledge and to be in communication with the world above. Certainly a major purpose of these tales was to create a legendary tradition about these rabbis, to demonstrate the level of their spiritual attainment and the extent of their mystical powers.

It is no accident that the Ari would hint that he was the reincarnation of Shimon bar Yohai, as he was the primary exponent of *Gilgul*, the mystical doctrine of the transmigration of souls. Drawing on this doctrine, it was common to assert that one rabbi was a reincarnation of another or that one rabbi had sparks of the souls of several great figures. The concept of sparks of souls derives from the tradition that 600,000 souls gathered at Mount Sinai. Later, when there were more Jews than this, whole souls were not available to everyone, and instead one person could have the sparks of several souls. Rabbi Hayim Vital, the primary disciple of the Ari, asserted several times that his soul was the soul of Rabbi Akiba, while Reb Nachman of Bratslav stated that his soul contained sparks of the souls of Moses, the Ari, and the Baal Shem Tov. And Rav Kook was reported to have said, "I am the soul of Reb Nachman," as if he were the reincarnation of Reb Nachman or that the spirit of Reb Nachman had taken possession of him in the form of an *ibbur*. Thus the sense of spiritual continuity with specific sages of the past pervades the accounts of the great Jewish mystical masters.

Among the tales the hasidim told, there are many in which a hasidic rebbe takes on the characteristics of one of the legendary sages, especially those of the talmudic era. Since the hasidim were well schooled in the Talmud, they would recognize at once the link between the ancient tale and that of their master. In this way the hasidic rebbe was elevated, in the eyes of his hasidim, to the level of the ancient sages. Eventually this focus on the master led to the doctrine of the *tzaddik*, where the master played an almost messianic role for his followers, and each group of hasidim believed that their rebbe was the *tzaddik ha-dor*, the potential Messiah of that generation.[16] And some of these rebbes, including Reb Nachman, strongly hinted to their disciples that their role was a messianic one.[17]

Each of the masters followed a different path, something that the Ari recognized when he turned away some of those who sought to be his disciples. In one instance the Ari comforted a distraught rabbi he had turned away by telling him that in this lifetime it was his destiny to study the literal meaning of the sacred texts, while the Ari's destiny was to study the mystical meaning. But in a future incarnation, they were destined to study together.[18]

So too does each of the mystical masters demonstrate his mastery in a different way. The Ari knows the history of every soul, and he knows on Yom Kippur whose name has been inscribed in the Book of Life and who is destined to die. The Baal Shem Tov can go into a trance and guide his soul to heaven in order to open a heavenly gate that is preventing the prayers of the Jews from ascending on high. When Reb Pinhas of Koretz opens a page of the Zohar, he is transformed into the Angel of the Zohar. Rabbi Naftali Katz has the power to project his image to distant places and to control events there, as does Reb Issachar Dov of Belz, who appears in a vision to Franz Kafka's friend Jiří Langer in Prague while Issachar Dov is actually in Belz.[19] The spirit of Shimon bar Yohai returns from the dead to assist those who study the Zohar, while the spirit of Reb Nachman of Bratslav guides and protects his hasidim to this day.

Perhaps the most astonishing of the powers demonstrated in these tales is the ability to cause a person to experience an illusion out of time, wherein many years seem to pass in the space of a minute. These can be described as Jewish tales of illusion, for those who experience these spells are astounded to discover that they have been living in a world of illusion. But in every case they learn an important lesson that transforms their lives.

These tales are remarkably parallel to many Indian myths, such as those concerning Vishnu, which also portray an illusory world, that of *maya*.[20]

One of the earliest examples of these illusion tales is "The Magic Flock,"[21] of midrashic origin. Here the patriarch Jacob meets another herdsman crossing the river Yabbok, and they agree to help each other forge the river with their flocks. But no matter how many flocks Jacob carries across, the number of those of the stranger's remaining continues to increase. Finally, Jacob realizes that the flocks are an illusion and that the other herdsman is some kind of sorcerer, and he wrestles with him until dawn. The sorcerer turns out to be the guardian angel of Esau, who has come to weaken Jacob before meeting Esau the next day, and the story itself is a midrashic commentary on the identity of the mysterious figure Jacob wrestled with in the biblical account (Gen. 32:23–33).

In later Jewish folklore, King Solomon experiences the powers of illusion firsthand as a beggar king.[22] This tradition is carried on by rabbis such as the medieval sorcerer Rabbi Adam,[23] as well as Reb Pinhas of Koretz and Reb Elimelech of Lizensk in stories such as "The Underground Forest"[24] and "The Young Magician."[25] In "The Underground Forest," for example, Reb Pinhas causes a student descending into a *mikveh* to enter another world, where he has a series of adventures lasting for many years, only to discover that it was all an illusion. But as a result, he learns that he is destined to wed the daughter of Reb Pinhas.

"The Tale of the Kugel"[26] is another fine example of the illusion tale. Here Rabbi Menachem Mendel I of Lubavitch demonstrates great powers of illusion, showing a man a vision of the path his life will take if he divorces his wife for not having borne a child.

In addition to drawing on these mystical powers as they are needed, these masters transmit the mysteries of the Torah to their disciples. In their hands the Torah is revealed to be a secret code about the mythic truths of the universe. When this truth is deciphered, the role of the Jews in the fabric of Creation is revealed, and it turns out to be crucial in repairing the cosmic rents that took place at the time of Creation, as well as in bringing together God and His Bride, the *Shekhinah*, who have been torn apart. According to the myth of the exile of the *Shekhinah*, at the time of the destruction of the Temple, God's Bride went into exile with her children, Israel. Somehow God and His Bride had to be brought together. The Ari provided many special prayers for this purpose, known as *yihudim*. By prefacing every *mitzvah* or commandment with these prayers, it became possible to assist in repairing the world.

From these examples it is apparent that the Jewish mystical tale emerged out of a highly charged spiritual environment, filled with mystical expectations. In this context, accounts of the miraculous became inevitable, as well as legendary embellishments. So too was this aspect enhanced by the mode of transmission. Virtually all of these tales were first circulated orally, primarily among the followers of these masters, and they were written down only after the rabbi's death. And eventually they too became a kind of sacred text.

Among the mystical themes most often found in the tales of these rabbis are those concerning the Divine Presence, the mysteries of Creation and of the Chariot, as well as mysteries of the Torah, of the Word, and of prayer. There also are tales of the power of prayer and repentance, the mystery of the Sabbath, communication with the world above, and heavenly journeys. Many of these tales recount visits to Paradise or the Garden of Eden or journeys to the Holy Land through enchanted caves. There are many accounts of wandering souls and reincarnation, of experiences beyond time and space. Other tales offer examples of kabbalistic magic, miracles about masters and hidden saints, encounters with angels and demons, and many legends about the Messiah and the World to Come.

It is common to find accounts of out-of-body experiences in these tales, as well as events that take place out of time. In the former are many accounts of the ascent of the soul, a kind of astral projection in which the soul is guided toward Paradise. Another kind of soul travel is found in the tales of those rabbis who could cast their image to distant places and affect events there. There is also a form of enchanted journey, known as *Kfitzat ha-Derekh*, "Leaping the Way," in which masters such as the Baal Shem Tov travel from one place to another by mystical means. In these stories the hooves of the horses no longer touch the ground, for the carriage is flying to its destination, much as did the *Merkavah*, the Divine Chariot in the vision of Ezekiel.

There are two primary branches of Kabbalah. One is known as Practical Kabbalah. It makes use of the powers inherent in Kabbalah through manipulation of letters and numbers and by drawing on the powers of holy names. These are usually the names of God, of which the Tetragrammaton (YHVH) is the holiest and most powerful of all. Or the names are those of angels, each of which brings with it its own unique powers. There are the archangels, Gabriel, Michael, Uriel, and Raphael, who serve as messengers of God. In addition, there are hundreds of other angels, including Raziel, the angel of secrets and mysteries; Rahab, the angel of the sea; Sandalphon, who weaves a garland of flowers out of the prayers of Israel for God to wear on the Throne of Glory; and Metatron, who was once Enoch, chief among the angels and the heavenly scribe. And these are only the best known of the angels. There are many others whose names themselves are secrets. Often these holy names are combined into keys that can unlock the gates of heaven. The purpose of drawing on these powers is usually to protect the Jewish community or the lives of individuals. Otherwise, the use of these powers is forbidden.

The other branch is that of Speculative Kabbalah, sometimes referred to as Contemplative or Theosophical Kabbalah. It is more inwardly directed, where mystical longing finds its focus in prayer and in mystical contemplation of the text of the Torah, as well as in the interaction of the ten *Sefirot*.

So intense is this contemplation that it not only includes the words of the Torah, but even regards the letters and numbers as gates of mystery, and prayers as virtual ladders of ascent, as in "The Ladder of Prayers,"[27] where the Baal Shem Tov ascends the ladder of the prayers of his hasidim all the way to the palace of the Messiah. Some of the meditative exercises practiced, such as trying to combine the names of God in prayers of unification, produce mystical effects, such as visions of the Divine Throne and the *Shekhinah*. These visions should be regarded as a Jewish kind of *unio mystica*, the unitive mystical experience, even though there does not appear to be a loss of awareness of the self. Such visions and mystical illuminations were the ultimate goal of kabbalistic contemplation.

Likewise, these stories might be regarded as a legendary portrayal of the mystical experience in its Jewish representation, demonstrating the concept of *devekut*, of cleaving to God. Certainly, many rabbis are portrayed in these tales in a state of possession that resembles mystical ecstasy. However, while reports of mystical union in which the self dissolves into the Divine are found in the writings of Abulafia and others, few such accounts are found in these mystical tales. Most of the rabbis in these tales, no matter how profound the experience or to what heights they may ascend, retain a strong sense of self-identity even at moments of ecstasy. Those who lose themselves, as was said to have happened to Ben Azzai, one of the four who entered Paradise, often lose their lives. Furthermore, one of the goals of mystical endeavors was to obtain knowledge of the Divine mysteries. Such knowledge required continued awareness in order to be able to recall every detail of the experience. For the primary focus of the Kabbalah is on a comprehensive understanding of the mystical meaning of the Torah. Thus mystical knowledge was as highly regarded as transcendental experience.

These two branches of Kabbalah, the Practical and the Speculative, are portrayed in different kinds of Jewish mystical tales. But both branches have a substantial number of tales linked to them, and a proper definition of the Jewish mystical tale must include tales drawn from both. Among the kinds of tales that demonstrate Practical Kabbalah are those drawing on kabbalistic magic, such as "Rabbi Shimon's Escape,"[28] where a rabbi uses the power of the Name to make a drawing of a ship become real and in this way escapes execution for himself and his companions.

The themes of the tales of Speculative Kabbalah, on the other hand, concern the mysteries of the Torah and the power of the word, such as several tales about the theme of flying letters, including "The Book of Flying Letters,"[29] where a disciple of Shimon bar Yohai has a vision of his master's soul ascending, followed by the flying letters that make up the book of his wisdom, which was also departing from this world. Likewise, in "The Flying Letters,"[30] the letters of a Torah scroll in one town take flight because of the evil inhabitants and fly to another town, where they land on an empty scroll a scribe is about to write.

Jewish lore holds that the sky opens at midnight on Shavuot and the glory of heaven is revealed. This kind of revelation is at the core of these stories. In each one there comes a time when the Divine realm is suddenly glimpsed, and there is a moment of revelation. At this moment, the rabbis often appear possessed or surrounded by a Divine Presence. In "The Circle of Fire,"[31] a disciple of the Baal Shem Tov sees him lying on the floor, surrounded by a fiery circle. Such a sacred fire surrounds both Rabbi Eizek of Kallo and the hidden saint who comes to visit him in "The Prayer Leader."[32] These examples highlight the difficulty of portraying mystical experience in these tales. It is generally reported by an outsider, who witnesses the effects, or an account is given afterward by the one who has undergone the experience. Both of these perspectives are found in "Unlocking the Gates of Heaven."[33] First, the Baal Shem Tov is seen in a catatonic state, with bulging eyes. Then, when the vision has ended, he reports what took place during his heavenly journey.

Once these stories were recorded, a transformation took place, and they themselves become a kind of mystical text, with several levels of meaning. Not only do they have strong mystical and legendary dimensions, but metaphorical ones as well. From this perspective, the heavenly journey can be seen as an archetypal symbol linking this world with that of the Divine. Or an encounter with an evil angel can represent an inner struggle between the forces of good and evil. Such multiple levels of meaning were not lost on the rabbis, who created a system of four levels of interpretation known by the acronym *PaRDeS*, in which all levels of meaning were regarded as equally valid. This system of interpretation recognizes the literal, symbolic, allegorical, and mystical meanings of any sacred text, especially the Torah.[34]

There also is a strong mythical dimension underlying these mystical accounts. Four kabbalistic myths, in particular, are most influential in these tales: myths of Creation, of the Divine Chariot, of the Bride of God, and of the Messiah. The first two of these myths constitute the roots of Kabbalah in the Bible, emerging as a kind of mythic commentary on Creation and the vision of Ezekiel. Virtually all kabbalistic texts and tales grow out of at least one of these root myths, although other biblical episodes of a mystical nature, such as the giving of the Torah at Mount Sinai or Isaiah's vision of God seated on a heavenly throne, are also the focus of kabbalistic commentary. The kabbalistic term for the study of Creation is *Ma'aseh Bereshit*, the Work of Creation, while the term for the study of the Divine Chariot is *Ma'aseh Merkavah*, the Work of the Chariot. In this context *Work* can be understood as *Mysteries*.

The first of these primary kabbalistic myths, that of Creation, actually consists of three separate but related myths. In addition to the account of Creation found in Genesis 1:1–31, in which God created the world in six days and rested on the seventh, there are two additional kabbalistic cosmologies. One is that of the Ten *Sefirot*, often illustrated in a diagram of the kabbalistic Tree of Life, which proclaims Creation in ten primary stages of emanation. There are specific kinds of interactions between these *Sefirot*, which are known as the Thirty-two Paths. These paths represent the infinite possibilities of the interaction of the Divine, as revealed through the symbols of language. Each of the *Sefirot* is a symbol of an aspect of God, as well a stage in the emanation of Creation. The *Sefirot* function in kabbalistic texts as archetypes of the interaction of God and existence. Attached to each of the *Sefirot* are rich and varied meanings, some of which are mystical, some mythical. In the kabbalistic mythology associated with the *Sefirot*, Samael, the fallen angel, comes to represent the masculine principle of evil, whereas Lilith, the demoness, is transformed to represent the feminine. Countering Lilith is the positive feminine principle, identified with the *Shekhinah*, the Sabbath Queen and Bride of God. One important facet of the *Sefirot* is that they could be influenced by special prayers of unification, known as *yihudim*. This made potentially great powers available to those mystics who understood the secret of making these unifications effective. They held the power, for example, of bringing God and His Bride closer together, as well as the potential to unleash the End of Days, the messianic era.

It is hard to reconcile the Creation myth in Genesis with the emanations of the *Sefirot*, and in fact they are separate myths of Creation. Yet both myths are drawn upon by the Ari's creation myth of the Shattering of the Vessels and the Gathering of the Sparks. God sent forth the vessels that shattered, containing primordial light. To restore cosmic unity, these scattered sparks must be sought out and raised up so that the broken vessel can be restored and the world returned to its primordial condition. And this repair of the world, known as *tikkun*, can be accomplished by fulfilling the *mitzvot*, the Divine commandments.[35]

The links between the myth of the Ari and the system of *Sefirot* become apparent upon closer observation. Like the *Sefirot*, the Ari's myth describes a process of emanation in which the vessels of light progress from one realm of existence to another. The *Sefirot*, however, represent an ongoing process of transformation, while the Shattering of the Vessels took place at the early stages in Creation and was a cosmic catastrophe, similar in impact to the exile from Eden or the destruction of the Temple in Jerusalem. Yet because the first stage of the Ari's myth is inextricably linked to the second, that of Gathering the Sparks, it too can be regarded as an ongoing process. Thus, one way of viewing the myth of the Ari is as a reworking of the doctrine of the *Sefirot*, and some kabbalistic schools regard the Ari's teachings as a direct and detailed explication of the *Sefirot*.

This myth can also be recognized as the source behind many tales concerning the principle of *tikkun olam*, or repair of the world. Here the role of the rabbi is often that of a healer. In "Repairing Souls,"[36] Rabbi Hayim ben Attar goes into the mountains to repair the souls gathered there. In "Redemption of the Lost Souls,"[37] the famous kabbalist Shalom Sharabi seeks out lost souls among the "Sons of the Desert," as the Bedouins were known, and redeems them. Nor is this repair limited to the events of this world. After all, the Shattering of the Vessels was a cosmic catastrophe, and the heavens themselves require repair. This is the secret work of the hidden saints, such as Shimon Pilam in "The Tzaddik of the Forest"[38] or Hayim the Vinekeeper in "The Prayer Leader."[39]

The second primary myth is that of the Divine Chariot, based on the vision of Ezekiel. As with Creation, Ezekiel's vision gave birth to more than one myth. There is the myth of the Divine Chariot, which represents the mystery of the Divinity. Just as Ezekiel's vision is perplexing, so is the study of this mystery, known as *Ma'aseh Merkavah*, the Work of the Chariot, an almost impenetrable enigma. The *Merkavah* represents both God's Throne of Glory and the Divine Chariot, which are mystically regarded as one. Visions of this chariot are extremely rare in these mystical tales, but the mere act of contemplating this mystery often triggers mystical experiences, as in "Mysteries of the Chariot."[40]

Another key myth to emerge from Ezekiel's vision is that of heavenly ascent. This myth represents the longing to enter into the Divine presence, which is the ultimate goal of mystical ascent. This longing, then, consists of a yearning for personal experience of the Divine, to come into the presence of the King, to behold Him personally, rather than to remain outside the palace and hear rumors of the King. It is not necessarily a longing for mystical union in the traditional sense, where the mystic's identity dissolves into that of the Divine. Somehow the rabbis retain a sense of themselves in these visions, no matter how exalted. This, then, should be seen as a unique characteristic of Jewish mysticism. This myth of ascent finds expression both in the tale of the four sages who entered Paradise and in the many accounts of heavenly journeys found in the *Hekhalot* texts. In these texts the individual comes into the presence of God and experiences complete awe, in ways that are often overpowering. And, as these texts make clear, there is an inherent danger in these Divine visions, as well as great rewards.

The third of these kabbalistic myths is the exile of the *Shekhinah*, God's Bride. In its earliest use in the Talmud and Midrash, the term *"Shekhinah"* referred to God's presence in the world. Later kabbalistic myth turned the *Shekhinah* into a separate mythic being, who separated from her spouse, God, when her earthly home, the Temple in Jerusalem, was destroyed, and went into exile with her children, Israel. Furthermore, it is believed that the *Shekhinah* will remain in exile until the days of the Messiah, when the Temple will be rebuilt. This belief links the myth of the *Shekhinah* to the myth of the Messiah.

One of the earliest personifications of the *Shekhinah* is as Mother Zion, as found in this midrashic text:

When Jeremiah saw the smoke of the Temple in Jerusalem rising up, he broke down. And when he saw the stones that once were the walls of the

Temple, he said: "What road have the exiles taken? I will go and perish with them."

So Jeremiah accompanied them down the road covered with blood until they reached the river Euphrates. Then he thought to himself: "If I go on to Babylon, who will comfort those left in Jerusalem?" Therefore he took his leave of the exiles, and when they saw he was leaving, they wept, as it is written, *By the waters of Babylon, there we sat down, yea, we wept* (Ps. 137:1).

As he was returning to Jerusalem, Jeremiah lifted his eyes and saw a woman seated at the top of a mountain, dressed in black, crying in distress, in great need of comfort. So too was Jeremiah in tears, wondering who would comfort him. He approached the woman, saying, "If you are a woman, speak, but if you are a spirit, depart at once!" She said: "Do you not recognize me? I am she who has borne seven sons, whose father went into exile in a distant city by the sea. Then a messenger brought the news that my husband, the father of my children, had been slain. And on the heels of that messenger came another with the news that my house had fallen in and slain my seven sons."

Jeremiah said: "Do you deserve any more comfort than Mother Zion, who has been made into a pasture for the beasts?" And she replied: "I am Mother Zion, the mother of seven, as it is written, *She that has borne seven anguishes* (Jer. 15:9).[41]

This personification of Mother Zion eventually evolved into that of the *Shekhinah*, one of whose roles is that of the mother of Israel. The *Shekhinah* is typically portrayed as a bride in white or as a grieving woman in black, mourning over the destruction of her home, the Temple, and the scattering of her children. In "A Vision at the Wailing Wall"[42] both personifications are found, while the image of the bride is found in "A Vision of the Bride"[43] and "The Sabbath Guests."[44] The *Shekhinah* is also identified as the Sabbath Queen, a beloved figure whose presence makes the Sabbath holy. It is the Sabbath Queen that the Ari and his disciples, dressed in white, went out to meet at sunset in the hills of Safed in the ritual known as *Kabbalat Shabbat*. The Sabbath Queen is also welcomed with the famous hymn *Lekhah Dodi* every Friday evening at the beginning of the Sabbath.

The arrival of the Sabbath Queen is closely linked to the belief that every person receives an extra soul on the Sabbath. The talmudic source for this belief is in B. Betzah 16a: "Rabbi Shimon ben Lakish said: 'On the eve of the Sabbath the Holy One, blessed be He, gives man an enlarged soul and at the close of the Sabbath He withdraws it from him.'" This *neshamah yeterah* or extra soul is closely identified with the *Shekhinah*, and especially with the personification of the *Shekhinah* as the Sabbath Queen. This tradition can be considered an *ibbur* visitation in the broadest sense of the concept. Because they are loath to lose their extra soul, many hasidim put off the *Havdalah* ceremony that marks the end of the Sabbath as long as possible, sometimes until long past midnight.

The fourth and last of the primary kabbalistic myths to influence these mystical tales is the myth of the Messiah. Here, too, the myth is found in two distinct formulations, which are ultimately linked. One of these concerns a Messiah who is the son of Joseph, and the second a Messiah who is the son of David. Messiah ben Joseph, as he is known, will be a human, the *tzaddik* of his generation, who will prepare the way for Messiah ben David, who is sometimes identified as a human being and sometimes as a celestial Messiah who lives in a heavenly palace.[45]

The longing for the Messiah has been palpable throughout Jewish history. In addition to several false messiahs, such as Shabbatai Zevi, many attempts to hasten the coming of the Messiah are recorded in these tales. See, for example, "The Chains of the Messiah,"[46] about the monumental failure of Rabbi Joseph della Reina, who sought to force the coming of the Messiah by capturing Asmodeus and Lilith, the king and queen of demons. But one fatal error at the last minute caused him to lose everything. So too are there many tales about moments in time that would have been perfect opportunities to bring the Messiah but were somehow lost. In "The Journey to Jerusalem"[47] the Ari announces his plan to set out for Jerusalem at once with his disciples. Some of them agree to go unquestioningly, but others hesitate, and this causes them to lose the opportunity to bring the Messiah. In "The Sabbath Guests,"[48] Rabbi Eizek of Kallo seeks a blessing from two visiting hasidim for a mysterious couple who have come to his Sabbath table. The hasidim, scandalized by the rabbi's warmth toward the woman, refuse. Only afterward do they learn that their guests were the Messiah and the Sabbath Queen, and if the hasidim had given their blessing, the wedding would have initiated the messianic era. Accounts of these lost opportunities to bring the Messiah make up one characteristic type of these Jewish mystical tales.

Even in present-day Israel, messianic longings are widespread in the most religious circles. A few years ago there was a report that three rabbis in Jerusalem had dreamed on the same night that the coming of the Messiah was imminent. This sent a wave of messianic expectation through the community. At the same time, there are many explanations about why the Messiah has not yet come, as in this legend recently collected in Israel by the Israel Folktale Archives:

> For many generations the Messiah has sat captive, chained with golden chains before the Throne of Glory. Elijah has tried to release him many times, but he has never succeeded. So Elijah descends to earth and explains that in order to break the chains of the Messiah, he needs a magic saw whose teeth are the deeds of Israel. Every deed adds a tooth to this saw, but every sin takes one away. When there are twice as many good deeds as there are sins, then

the saw can be used. That is why it is said that the Messiah will not come until we bring him.[49]

In addition to these four primary myths, there are many other mythic concerns reflected in these tales, especially those involving journeys to heaven or hell. Many details about such mythic realms emerge here. From these a remarkably detailed knowledge of the Divine realm can be gained, as well as how to invoke its powers through the use of holy names, prayers of unification,[50] astral projection, sympathetic magic, and other mystical techniques. With these powers it becomes possible to enter into the sacred dimension where angels are often encountered and where visions of the Divine Presence, in the form of the mythic figure of the *Shekhinah*, are regarded as the ultimate revelation, as in "A Vision of the Bride."[51]

At the same time, the use of these mystical powers was reserved for exceptional situations, such as countering an evil decree against the Jewish community. These tales recount how certain rabbis are able to affect events far away by soul travel and projection of their images to distant places, where they accomplish miraculous feats. In "A Bowl of Soup,"[52] Rabbi Elimelech of Lizensk spills a bowl of soup at the Sabbath table, and later it is learned that at the same moment, as the emperor was about to sign a decree against the Jews, the bottle of ink spilled on it, and the emperor took this as a sign that the decree must not be signed.[53] Likewise, Rabbi Naftali Katz draws upon his mystical powers in "Rabbi Naftali's Trance,"[54] not only to locate a missing husband in *Gehenna*, the Jewish hell, where he is being punished, but to set up a meeting, in the presence of witnesses and avenging angels, between the husband and the wife he abandoned, in order to obtain the bill of divorce. So too are there many accounts of rabbis who use their powers to raise up the souls of the dead, who often call upon them for their help. Reb Nachman of Bratslav asked to be buried in the cemetery in the city of Uman so that he could raise up the souls of those buried there who had lost their lives in a pogrom.[55] So too, in "The Field of Souls,"[56] does a rabbi who prays in a field on Yom Kippur unknowingly free the many souls stranded there, while in "The Boy Who Blew the Shofar,"[57] a boy is called upon by the souls of the dead to set them free.

From this it can be seen that these tales are set in a world where the boundary between the living and the dead, between earth and heaven and hell, between spirit and body, is a fluid one, and the world is seen as a place populated with all kinds of spirits, including angels, demons, and spirits of the dead. The rabbis in these tales are masters of this spiritual realm. They have a remarkably complete knowledge of its workings, and possess holy names that serve as spells in calling upon angels and other spirits to do their bidding. Their goals are both spiritual and practical, their most pressing desire, of course, to hasten the coming of the Messiah.

But the mystical quests found in these tales are not limited to attempts to hasten the messianic era. Indeed, the primary quest is that for mystical knowledge, knowledge of God and the perfection of the world, which is linked to the coming of the Messiah. This quest starts by seeking the mystical meaning of the Torah and other sacred texts, where the letters of the words are as significant as their meaning, and where words that have the same numerical total are believed to be mystically linked.[58]

Thus the word is seen in these tales as a gateway to the realm of celestial mysteries. This is a natural extension of the primary rabbinic belief that the Torah, dictated by God to Moses at Mount Sinai, is the source of all truths, mysteries, and hidden meanings. The Zohar, the primary kabbalistic text, describes a celestial Torah written in black fire on white. In "The Flaming Letters,"[59] Reb Shneur Zalman creates a set of Hebrew letters that proves to be identical to the celestial model, lifting yet another veil of the celestial mystery. Even the blank portions of the page on which the words are written are regarded as being meaningful, suggesting a figure/ground[60] reversal of the text, which is seen to reveal a world of mysteries.

With the mystical experience in Judaism so remarkably focused on the page, it is not surprising that there are many tales involving the power of the word or of potent combinations of words such as incantations. Above all, there is the power of prayer. And the essence of this power derives from the intensity of the prayer, known as the *kavanah.* So too are there mystical techniques known as *yihudim* or unifications that seek celestial unity by creating an interaction among the *Sefirot,* with the ultimate goal of bringing God and His Bride closer together. These *yihudim* combine letters from different names of God in very complex mental exercises that were believed to produce profound effects in this world and the world above.[61] In addition, the *yihudim* were used to exorcise evil spirits. There are also holy names that are used to call forth angelic figures, such as the Prince of the Torah, or to open the gates of heaven. With the powers made available through these mystical methods, it became possible to enter into the sacred realm where angels are often encountered and visions take place in Paradise.

From a great many of accounts of heavenly journeys found in the pseudepigraphical texts and rabbinic lore, as well as in many a hasidic tale, a vivid portrait of heaven emerges, with a celestial Jerusalem that is the mirror image of Jerusalem on earth, except that the Temple on high still exists, while that in this world has been destroyed. And there are a multitude of secret places, treasuries, heavenly academies, and, of course, palaces of heaven, including the palace of the Messiah, known as the Bird's Nest. It is a complex, labyrinthine vision of the celestial world, which is ruled by its own laws and exists on its own terms. There is a place for every purpose in Creation, such as the *Guf,* the Treasury of Souls, from which souls are drawn,[62] or the House of Treasures, where God keeps all the things He created before the Creation of the world, including the Celestial Torah. All in all there are seven heavens, the highest of which is known as *Aravot,* and in each successive heaven the merits of the righteous who are found there increase. So too do the great sages have their own academies in heaven, where the souls of the righteous and angels gather together to hear their teachings of the Torah.

Human beings are by nature explorers, motivated by curiosity, and in many ways heaven has traditionally been considered the final frontier. Thus, from the perspective of the knowledge gathered from these heavenly journeys, the rabbis can be seen as celestial explorers. Whatever realm they entered, whether in this world or in the spiritual realm, they explored in great detail. Part of this interest, of course, comes from the belief that heaven is the location of the *Olam ha-ba*, the World to Come, where the righteous will receive their rewards. And for those generations largely deprived of material rewards, and more often than not subject to persecution, the dream of a realm in which they would be justly rewarded served as a great solace.

The first figure to be credited with journeying into heaven and exploring it was Enoch. Very little is said about Enoch in the Torah. His name appears in a genealogy linking Adam and Noah, and all that distinguishes him is the way his death is reported. For while it is said about everyone else that "he died," about Enoch it is said, *And Enoch walked with God, and he was not; for God took him* (Gen. 5:34). Even the slightest variation in biblical phrasing was taken to have profound significance; in this case extensive conclusions were drawn from the unusual statement about his death.

In three major postbiblical texts found in the Pseudepigrapha, Enoch came to be described as one of the few righteous men in the evil generation preceding the Flood. He was taken up into Paradise in a chariot at God's command and taught the secrets of the universe. Then he came back to earth to instruct men, and finally he returned to heaven, where he was transformed into the fiery angel Metatron, who became the attendant of the Throne of Glory, the prince of the treasuries of heaven, and the ruler and judge of all the hosts of angels, executor of the Divine decrees on earth and the heavenly scribe.

One of the primary purposes of the ascent of Enoch was to provide a detailed description of the rewards and punishments awaiting the righteous, as well as to map the landscape of these distant and mysterious realms. And such a map of heaven and hell does emerge from the extensive literature about Enoch.

Not only is the heavenly Paradise explored in great detail in Jewish mystical texts and tales; so too is the earthly Paradise, the Garden of Eden. In one legend, "The Gates of Eden,"[63] Alexander the Great, a popular figure in Jewish lore, comes to the gates of the Garden of Eden and is refused admittance. Instead an angel gives him an eye, which, when weighed on a scale, outweighs all his gold—until it is covered with dust. The point is that "the eye of a human being is never satisfied"—always wanting more—until death takes away all desire. In another tale, "A Crown of Shoes,"[64] the Baal

Shem Tov is transported in an instant to the Garden of Eden, where he finds angels gathering shoes that flew off the feet of those dancing on Simhat Torah. They flew off with such joy that they flew all the way to the Garden of Eden. There the Baal Shem Tov learns that an angel makes a crown out of these shoes for God to wear on the Throne of Glory, just as He wears a crown woven from the prayers of Israel. In another tale, "The Tree of Life,"[65] the Baal Shem Tov uses his great powers to transport not only himself, but also his hasidim, to the Garden of Eden. He tries to lead them to the Tree of Life, but one by one they become fascinated with some lesser mystery, and by the time the Baal Shem Tov reaches the Tree of Life, he is alone.

There also are a multitude of encounters with angels in these tales. Foremost among these is the angel Gabriel, who serves as the primary celestial guide. In "The Tzohar"[66] Gabriel assists Joseph in the pit, where his brothers had cast him, and in "Rabbi Ishmael's Ascent"[67] the angel meets Rabbi Ishmael as he ascends on high and reveals secrets that he has heard from behind the *Pargod*, the curtain that separates God from the angels. In "Gabriel's Palace,"[68] Gabriel visits the imprisoned Rabbi Meir of Rottenberg in a dream and brings him a celestial Torah to read from on the Sabbath.

But not all angels are good, as one student learns in "The Evil Angel."[69] So too does he learn how to distinguish the good ones from the evil ones: both have God's Name inscribed on their foreheads, but the letters of the name of the good angel are inscribed in white fire, while those of the evil angel burn in black.

In addition, there are beings that are neither spirit nor angel, but a combination of both. These spirits, known as *maggidim*, come into being as a result of intense study of the sacred texts, and they speak through the mouths of great sages, such as Rabbi Joseph Karo, the author of the *Shulhan Arukh*, the Code of Jewish Law. That such a respected scholar of the Law as Joseph Karo could at the same time be a mystic possessed by the spirit of the Mishnah may appear to be a great paradox. Yet in one book, *Maggid Mesharim*, he kept a diary of the knowledge he had received from this spirit, who came to him and spoke through his mouth—often in the presence of others, as recounted in "The Angel of the Mishnah."[70]

From a psychological perspective, the accounts of both the *ibbur* and the *maggid* can be seen as a kind of automatic speaking from the unconscious. It has also been suggested that parts of the Zohar, the central text of Kabbalah, were written automatically by the author, Moshe de Leon. Also, many forms of kabbalistic meditation, such as the *yihudim*, the prayers of unification, seem intended to invoke unconscious powers. This underscores one important aspect of kabbalistic study—it seems to call forth unconscious forces, which reveal themselves through symbolic language. In a very real sense, the letters of the alphabet and the ten *Sefirot* serve as gates of spiritual forces and function in ways that are quite similar to both the Platonic archetypes and C. G. Jung's concept of the archetypes of the collective unconscious.[71] Indeed, this parallel is even more striking in terms of the key feminine figure of the *Shekhinah*, the Bride of God, and Jung's concept of the anima, the symbolic feminine aspect of every man. Jungian thought requires the seeking out and uniting with the anima in order to attain psychic wholeness, which Jung calls Individuation. In the arts this figure is identified as the muse, and the artist can flourish only when he is in the presence of the muse, just as nothing is considered to be sacred that does not take place in the Divine Presence, which has been traditionally identified with the *Shekhinah*. Thus, from a Jungian perspective, one of the effects of kabbalistic study was the discovery by the kabbalists of the feminine within themselves. From this point of view, their attempts to unify God and His exiled Bride through prayers of unification can also be seen as an attempt to unite with their own anima. These mystical tales, as well, can be seen as products of this unconscious process, with a strong symbolic component and many levels of meaning. The tales of Rabbi Nachman of Bratslav, in particular, lend themselves to this kind of interpretation, where, for example, the search for the princess in his famous story "The Lost Princess" can be seen to represent a quest not only for the Bride of God, but also for the exiled anima.[72]

One further important parallel between the kabbalistic view of existence and Jungian theory concerns the understanding of evil. In the Kabbalah the world of evil is known as the *Sitra Ahra*, the Other Side. This grows out of the talmudic view that "for everything God created, He also created its counterpart."[73] All in all, the kabbalistic world is a polar one precisely in the Jungian model, where the forces of the unconscious are understood to be arranged in a polar configuration.

Just as heaven is thoroughly mapped out in the Enoch and *Hekhalot* texts, so too is the realm of evil fully explored. This world is portrayed in very different ways. There is *Gehenna*, Jewish hell, where the souls of those who sinned are punished, in ways that are as explicit as those recounted by Dante in *The Inferno*. There is also the *Sitra Ahra*, filled with evil forces and swarms of spirits, some of them poor souls who are being punished by endless wandering. It functions as a distorted mirror of existence ruled by the forces of evil. And only the rabbis who have mastered the mysteries of Kabbalah have it within their power to assist these lost souls and bring their wandering to an end, as in "The Blind Angel,"[74] where Rabbi Mordecai of Chernobyl uses the gift of a precious menorah to guide the soul of the hasid into heaven.

The existence of demons and the portrayal of evil in kabbalistic literature draw on several sources, among them popular demonological traditions, as well as the influence of magical texts such as *Sefer ha-Razim*[75] and the widespread use of magical amulets, which inevitably included magical spells. In the Zohar and other kabbalistic texts, these traditions are transformed into more abstract forces of good and evil.

Then there are other spirits who travel through the cycles of rebirth, known as *gilgul*, and are reincarnated in a variety of forms, such as a stone, a flower, or a tree, as well as in both animal and human form. Often the same soul will be forced to undergo all these transformations, as in "The Voice in the Tree."[76] More than anything else, these souls long to be freed from the chain of reincarnation to ascend on high, as happens in "The Sabbath Fish."[77]

This focus on *gilgul*, the transmigration of souls, gave the Jewish mystics a completely different perspective, in which the history of a person's soul was the primary factor in shaping his life. It is said about the Ari that he could look at a man's forehead and read his soul's history there. He could listen to the dialogue of two birds and recognize one of them as the reincarnation of Balaam. He could recognize that a black dog that continued to haunt him was the reincarnation of Joseph della Reina, who fell into evil ways after he failed to hasten the coming of the Messiah.[78] And he could even recognize a soul trapped in one stone in the wall of an ancient synagogue, as he does in "A Stone in the Wall."[79] This kind of knowledge of the history of souls was rare even among the mystical masters, but in "A Wandering Soul"[80] one of the Belz hasidim knows that he has been reborn three times: once as a sheep in Jacob's flock; once as a follower of Korah, who rebelled against Moses and was punished, along with his followers, when the earth swallowed them up; and once as himself. The concept of *gilgul* in many ways resembles that of *samsera*, the cycle of death and rebirth in Hindu thought, including the law of *karma* that is involved in the *samsera* process. Yet it has also been formed by the Jewish mystical context out of which it emerged.

As for the fate of the souls of the living, this is said to depend on the state of their soul-candles, as described in "The Cottage of Candles."[81] A person lives only as long as his soul-candle continues to burn. And it is forbidden to try to steal oil from one candle for another, as the doomed man in this story finds out. Indeed, these stories teach reverence for every kind of living being. Even trees have souls, as Reb Nachman of Bratslav discovers in "The Souls of Trees."[82]

Above all, such tales reveal the longing to communicate with the world above and the belief that such communication is possible, at least for the greatest figures. And based on the evidence of the tales, these communications took many forms, including heavenly voices, angelic messengers, omens, visits of the patriarchs and matriarchs, heavenly books, prophecy, and Divine messages such as letters sent from heaven, as well as divination by the holy spirit, known as *Ruah ha-Kodesh*. Other popular methods of divination were *Sheilat Sefer*, divining from a book. In reply to an important question, a holy book is opened at random and a passage blindly selected, which serves as the reply. "The Souls of Trees"[83] and "Divining from the Zohar"[84] contain examples of this kind of divination. And, above all, such communication with the world above took place in the form of visions or dreams. These visions might involve heavenly ascents, as in "Rabbi Ishmael's Ascent,"[85] or the *Shekhinah*, as in "A Vision at the Wailing Wall"[86] and "A Vision of the Bride."[87] In some stories, such as

"The Vision of the High Priest"[88] and "The Enchanted Island,"[89] there is even a vision of God.

Let us return to the four sages who entered Paradise. It can now be seen that this brief, enigmatic talmudic legend has multiple levels of meaning, where ascent may be understood as a visionary experience, on the one hand, and as a metaphor for mystical contemplation on the other.[90] Therefore it is important not to overlook the metaphorical dimensions of this account.

In the original talmudic legend, the four sages enter *Pardes*. This means, literally, that they entered an orchard. But because of the dire consequences of their actions, it is clear that the passage is not intended to be understood solely on the literal level. Of course, the orchard also suggests a garden, which suggests the Garden of Eden, the earthly Paradise. From this interpretation it is not far to the notion that the place they entered was Paradise, referring to the celestial Paradise. This reading is confirmed by one version of this legend that concludes that "only Rabbi Akiba ascended in peace and descended in peace" rather than that he "entered in peace and departed in peace."[91]

What, then, does the story mean? Probably that these four, among the greatest sages of all time, engaged in some kind of mystical contemplation. Observe how well this legend manages to work on two levels at the same time—the essential factor in forming an allegory. On the literal level the sages have entered an orchard. This is demonstrated when Elisha ben Abuyah cuts the shoots. On the allegorical level, there is no doubt that this talmudic legend is using *Pardes* to refer to Paradise, because some of the companion legends describe the sages in the heavenly realm.[92] But since "Paradise" itself is a metaphor for mystical contemplation, *Pardes* refers to the enticing but dangerous realms of mystical speculation and contemplation symbolized by heavenly ascent.[93]

Some such dangers are also recounted in a talmudic account of a child of exceptional understanding who read the Book of Ezekiel at his teacher's home. He comprehended the true meaning of the word *hashmal* in the passage *And I looked, and, behold, a stormy wind came out of the north, a great cloud, with a fire flashing up, so that a brightness was round about it; and out of the midst thereof as the color of electrum* (hashmal), *out of the midst of the mire* (Ezek. 1:4). At that instant a fire went forth and consumed him, like the flame that goes forth from the mouth of a furnace.[94] That is why it is written in the Mishnah: "The Mysteries of Creation should not be expounded before two persons, nor the Mysteries of the Chariot before one, unless he is a sage and has an independent understanding. For whoever ponders on four things, it would have been better for him not to have been born: What is above, what is below, what is before time, and what will come hereafter."[95]

The four sages entered into this dangerous realm of mystical contemplation, and only Rabbi Akiba emerged unharmed. What was it that they were

contemplating? It was almost certainly either *Ma'aseh Bereshit*, the mysteries of Creation, or *Ma'aseh Merkavah*, the mysteries of the Chariot. Since
the journey of the sages is understood as an ascent into Paradise, it seems
likely that they were contemplating *Ma'aseh Merkavah*, which is concerned
with ascent.

The brief account of the four who entered Paradise is clearly a barebones
summary of a more extensive legend. A few remaining fragments of this
legend are found in the same tractate of the Talmud and shed more light
on the fate of two of the three lost sages.[96] We learn that Elisha ben Abuyah
"cut the shoots," meaning that he cut his ties to his religion, after seeing
the angel Metatron sitting on a heavenly throne and concluding, "There
must be, God forbid, two powers in heaven."[97] The legend goes on to tell
us that God sent an angel to punish Metatron with sixty lashes of a flaming
whip for giving Elisha ben Abuyah this false impression. After this Elisha
becomes known as Aher, the Other, because of his subsequent apostasy.

There is also a brief legend concerning the fate of Ben Zoma, who
looked and lost his mind. He is said to have encountered his teacher, Rabbi
Joshua, who was walking with his students. This rabbi greeted Ben Zoma,
who failed to return the greeting and instead replied: "Between the upper
waters and the lower waters there are but three finger-breadths." Hearing
this the rabbi said to his students: "Ben Zoma is gone," meaning that he
had lost his mind.[98] Here Ben Zoma's statement about the upper and lower
waters seems to be linked to something he had seen during his heavenly
ascent. Referring to the Creation of the firmament, where God divided the
waters that were beneath the firmament from the waters that were above it
(Gen. 1:7), Ben Zoma seems to be expressing amazement that the upper
waters and the lower waters—symbolizing heaven and earth—are so close.[99]

As for Ben Azzai, his fate is the most uncertain. In one midrash from
Leviticus Rabbah, Rabbi Akiba tells Ben Azzai: "I heard that you sit down
and study, and flames surround you. I said, 'Ben Azzai has descended to
the Chambers of the Chariot.'"[100] Here Ben Azzai is portrayed as a great
mystic, which reinforces the tradition that he died by the kiss of the *Shekhinah*, meaning that his soul was taken directly into heaven. This tradition
contradicts that which assumes that Ben Azzai died from the shock of mystical revelations. According to this view, Ben Azzai was drawn to the mysteries
of heaven like a moth to a flame, and in this way he lost his life.

Together these legends constitute the primary account in the Talmud
and Midrash of the legend of the four sages. Over the ages they were recognized as referring to an esoteric, mystical tradition within Judaism that was
at the same time both alluring and dangerous. This tradition later became
identified as Kabbalah, and these talmudic legends about the four sages
play a central role in the creation of a mystical mythology.

On the one hand, the legend of the four sages was generally interpreted
to mean that mystical contemplation, which was regarded as synonymous
with study of either Creation or the vision of Ezekiel, was dangerous. As a

result, barriers were established, limiting the study of these subjects, as noted in the previous quotation from the Mishnah. In addition, it was required that those who studied be at least forty years old, married, and learned in the Talmud. (It goes without saying that women were forbidden to consider these subjects.) It was believed that when a man had reached this age and had a family, he was sufficiently grounded to be trusted with these dangerous subjects. Later, the prohibition against the study of *Ma'aseh Bereshit* and *Ma'aseh Merkavah* was extended to include all kabbalistic texts, which are in any case based upon one of these two primary biblical sources.

But the strictures deriving from the disaster that befell three of the four sages were not, however, the only reaction to this famous episode. For there was also the opposite reaction: their ascent into Paradise was regarded by some as a model for subsequent heavenly journeys. These sages viewed mystical contemplation, as symbolized by the heavenly journey, as the ultimate mystical objective. They are the authors of what are known as the *Hekhalot* texts, which describe in great detail journeys into Paradise. *Hekhalot* means "palaces," and this refers to the palaces of heaven. So too is this field of mystical contemplation known as *Merkavah* Mysticism, because of its focus on ascent, as symbolized by the *Merkavah*, the heavenly chariot in the vision of Ezekiel. Several of these important texts have been discovered in recent years, and they are the subject of intensive scholarly study. It is difficult to determine whether those who wrote the *Hekhalot* texts regarded the ascent as an actual bodily one, or as an ascent of the soul. But it seems more likely that it was understood as an ascent of the soul. Later accounts of heavenly journeys, such as those taken by the Baal Shem Tov, describe an ascent of the soul. And even in some of the earlier texts, such as *The Legend of the Ten Martyrs*,[101] it is clear that Rabbi Ishmael's body remains on earth while his soul ascends on high.

Sometimes these mystical ascents were said to take place in meditative states, after long fasting and prayer, and sometimes in dreams, as the soul was believed to leave the body every night and wander in the celestial realms, returning to the body shortly before waking. In any case, the *Hekhalot* texts themselves are quite explicit about the nature of each of the palaces of heaven, plus the names of the angels that stand outside their gates and what holy names must be pronounced in order to get past them. Indeed, they read as a precise map of heaven, drawing on the explorations of Enoch and recounting journeys of other sages, including Rabbi Akiba and Rabbi Ishmael, into the heavenly realms. Yet even today the true meaning and purpose of the *Hekhalot* texts—like the legend of the four sages—are elusive and open to interpretation.

Indeed, there are many theories about the meaning of this legend. It has served as a model for heavenly journeys and as a warning tale of the dangers of mysticism. To the existing theories, let us add one more: each of the four sages can be linked to one of the schools or sects of early, formative Judaism. Ben Azzai can be identified with the school that focused on the vision of Ezekiel, known as *Ma'aseh Merkavah*, or Mysteries of the Chariot. Ben Zoma can be linked to the school that studied the Mysteries of Creation, known as *Ma'aseh Bereshit*. Elisha ben Abuyah represents the Jewish Gnostics, who took a dualistic view of the Divinity. And Rabbi Akiba represents the school of Talmud Torah, emphasizing Torah study, which is the approach still followed by Orthodox Jews to this day.

We have discussed the key passages in the rabbinic texts that link each of these sages to one of these early paths of Judaism. Ben Azzai, who "looked and died," is portrayed as a consummate mystic in the midrashic texts, where he is described as being surrounded by fire.[102] It is very clear that he is actively seeking mystical illumination, and here Ben Azzai is directly linked to *Ma'aseh Merkavah*, the Mysteries of the Chariot.

Likewise, a passage in the Talmud about Ben Zoma contemplating the Mysteries of Creation clearly links him to that school.[103] Here Ben Zoma is portrayed as having been driven to madness by his contemplation of these mysteries, again directly linking him to the early Jewish sect of *Ma'aseh Bereshit*. Ben Zoma's failure to return his teacher's greeting was considered a clear sign that something was seriously wrong. Ben Zoma's subsequent explanation of proximity of the upper waters and the lower waters places his contemplation right at the beginning of Genesis, in the Creation myth that is the primary focus of those who sought to explore the Mysteries of Creation. Thus Ben Zoma's vision places him somewhere in the heavens, high enough to reach the place where the upper waters and the lower waters were separated.[104]

In another key passage Aher meets Metatron in Paradise, in which he makes the statement that "there are—God forbid—two powers in heaven," strongly implies that the heresy that turned Elisha into Aher, the Other, was Gnostic. Here Elisha has reached a level of Paradise where he has found the chief angel, Metatron, seated on a throne. Led to believe that "there was no sitting in Paradise," out of respect for God, Elisha is so disillusioned that he seems to have become a Gnostic, expressing belief in a dual divinity. The legend, however, makes it clear that Elisha is mistaken in his belief about two powers in heaven, for God then has Metatron whipped for having remained seated. This clearly demonstrates God's power over Metatron.

Thus the story of the four represents the rabbinic view that only the path of Talmud Torah is acceptable. It implicitly rejects some of the alternate paths to Enlightenment, those that turned to studies of Creation or the vision of Ezekiel as an expression of early Kabbalah, as well as the views of the early Jewish Gnostics. And, of course, Rabbi Akiba is the ultimate model of Talmud Torah and consequently is the perfect figure to represent it. Thus the brief but crucial legend of the four can be read as a defense of Talmud Torah against the three other primary paths that existed at that time.

Drawing on this interpretation, the legend of the four can also be said to provide an acknowledgment on the part of the rabbis that paths other than that of Talmud Torah did exist and that there were Jews who followed them. From our perspective, it appears that these alternate paths of Jewish mysticism were ultimately incorporated into Kabbalah and, indeed, serve as the very roots of medieval Jewish mysticism.

It is a matter of scholarly debate as to whether the legend of the four in the Talmud inspired the body of texts known as *Hekhalot* texts, or whether it itself is a fragment of an earlier, far more extensive *Hekhalot* text. Indeed, one of the *Hekhalot* texts is devoted to Rabbi Akiba's ascent into Paradise, but in this account makes the ascent on his own.[105]

This suggests yet another reading of the legend of the four: that the one legend summarizes existing mystical traditions linked to each of the four rabbis, and thus their journeys into Paradise may have been separate ones. After all, the talmudic legend does not say that the four embarked on the journey *at the same time*, only that they engaged in some kind of mystical contemplation linked to a heavenly journey *at some time*, and not necessarily all at once.

It is also possible to read the rabbinic attitude, representing Talmud Torah, toward the dangers posed by a heavenly ascent, in that only one of four of the greatest sages survived it. The other approaches, of the Mysteries of Creation and of the Chariot, are considered too risky. That of the Gnostic is beyond the pale, in the realm of the heretical. Fences are drawn around the dangers of mystical contemplation.

While mystical ascent is one method of bringing the living into contact with the heavenly realm, dreams are the most common medium by which spirits communicate with the living and by which the souls of the living are able to wander from world to world. And, of course, this tradition of dreams goes all the way back to the Bible, to the dreams associated with Jacob and Joseph. It is one more example of how the patterns established in the earliest texts, especially the Torah, are repeated in new variations in later phases of Jewish literature. No matter what their source, sacred or secular, these tales place great emphasis on the dream as a doorway to the spiritual realm, which may take the form of one of the realms of Paradise, the Garden of Eden, the Holy Land, or even an enchanted cave. In one tale, "The Handwriting of the Messiah,"[106] Rabbi Hayim Vital dreams that his master, the Ari, returns from the dead and brings him a message from the Messiah. In another, "The Sword of the Messiah,"[107] a rabbi ascends in a dream to the palace of the Messiah. And in "The Cave of Mattathias,"[108] a hasid trapped in a snowstorm lights the Hanukkah oil he has brought with him and dreams of meeting the father of the Maccabees in a cave in the Holy Land.

The distinction between sacred and secular tales in postbiblical Jewish literature is difficult to make because of the close interaction between the rabbinic circles linked to the sacred literatures and the common folk. In general, the rabbinic sources offer legends and tales as exempla, for their allegorical meaning and moral intent, without placing undo emphasis on the narrative. Beginning in the 16th century in Constantinople, however, collections of Jewish folklore were published that were not considered to be sacred texts, and the stories in these collections place considerable emphasis on narrative embellishment, while the link to the sacred text is at least once removed.

It is true that many of these folktales have their origin in one of the sacred sources, often the Talmud, whose lore is the primary source and model for all subsequent Jewish literature. But the themes that are emphasized draw from the folk elements linked to these rabbinic models—the magical powers of the Name; encounters with angels, spirits, and demons; various kinds of quests, and similar folk motifs.

To some extent, the mystical folktale—for there is such a tale type—mirrors the folk understanding of the complex kabbalistic mythology. Only certain aspects of these esoteric rabbinic theories became a part of the folk tradition. These include the great kabbalistic emphasis on the potency of the letters of the Hebrew alphabet. Thus tales focusing on letters, numbers, and holy names, especially on the Tetragrammaton, God's most sacred Name, are often found. However, the folk influence is not limited to these tale types, for some of the mystical themes are closely associated with themes of great folk popularity, such as visits to the Garden of Eden, encounters with one of the Thirty-Six Hidden Saints, or accounts of angels, demons, and wandering spirits. Certainly the fact that the mystical tale can also be found in medieval Jewish folklore, as well as in all of the sacred sources, confirms it as a primary type of Jewish tale.

Indeed, it becomes apparent that despite the fact that these tales cover a period of two thousand years, and range from Eastern Europe to the Middle East, they belong to the same genre of Jewish mystical tales. They are linked by the mystical themes they have in common, as well as by the later masters who found their models in the earlier ones. Kabbalah means tradition, and the manner of transmission of these esoteric mysteries is a chain linking one mystical master to the next, whether or not they lived at the same time. Thus the Ari considers himself to be a disciple of Rabbi Shimon bar Yohai, who lived more than a thousand years earlier. So too does the Baal Shem Tov regard the Ari as his model, while Reb Nachman of Bratslav found his model in his great-grandfather, the Baal Shem Tov. As a child, Reb Nachman spent many hours laying on the grave of the Baal Shem Tov, communing with him. So too is the chain of generations demonstrated in midrashic legends such as that of "The Tzohar," [109] which links the generations from Adam to Seth to Enoch to Methuselah to Lamech to Noah to Abraham and the other patriarchs, and so on, down through the generations. The glowing jewel of the Tzohar itself, containing the primordial light, symbolizes the Jewish mystical tradition. Just as the Tzohar has been handed down in each generation, so do the generations perpetuate this chain of tradition by transmitting the ancient and arcane secrets of the Kabbalah.

Above all, these tales serve as examples of how a mystical life can be lived. It is necessary to enter a world of signs and symbols, where everything that takes place has meaning, a world of mythic proportions in which the forces of good and evil are engaged in a continual struggle. It is a world in which the spirits of the dead are no longer invisible, nor are the angels. And a heavy responsibility hangs on the master and his disciples to repair the world in order to make it possible for God and His Bride to be brought back together, for the broken vessels to be restored, and for the Messiah to be freed from the chains that have held Him back for so long. These tales illustrate this sacred, mythical world and preserve the legends of the greatest Jewish mystics.

The Quest for the Lost Princess

Transition and Change in Jewish Lore

I

The Quest for the Lost Princess

Everyone in Israel is occupied with the search for the lost princess.
Rabbi Nathan of Nemirov

It is said that Rabbi Isaac Luria had great mystical powers. By looking at a man's forehead he could read the history of his soul. He could overhear the angels and knew the language of the birds. He could point out a stone in a wall and reveal whose soul was trapped in it. So too was he able to divine the future, and he always knew from Yom Kippur who among his disciples was destined to live or die. This knowledge he rarely disclosed, but once, when he learned there was a way to avert the decree, he made an exception. Summoning Rabbi Abraham Beruchim, he said: "Know that a heavenly voice has gone forth to announce that this will be your last year among us—unless you do what is necessary to abolish the decree."

"What must I do?" asked Rabbi Abraham.

"Know, then," said the Ari, "that your only hope is to go to the Wailing Wall in Jerusalem and there pray with all your heart before God. And if you are deemed worthy you will have a vision of the *Shekhinah*, the Divine Presence. That will mean that the decree has been averted and your name will be inscribed in the Book of Life after all."

Rabbi Abraham thanked the Ari with all his heart and left to prepare for the journey. First he shut himself in his house for three days and nights, wearing sackcloth and ashes, and fasted the whole time. Then, although he could have gone by wagon or by donkey, he chose to walk to Jerusalem. And by the time Rabbi Abraham reached Jerusalem, he felt as if he were floating, as if his soul had ascended from his body. And when he reached the Wailing Wall, the last remnant of Solomon's Temple, Rabbi Abraham had a vision there. Out of the wall came an old woman, dressed in black, deep in mourning. And Rabbi Abraham suddenly realized how deep was the grief of the *Shekhinah* over the destruction of the Temple and the scattering of her children, Israel, all over the world. And he became possessed of a grief as deep as the ocean, far greater than he had ever known. It was the grief of a mother who has lost a child; the grief of Hannah, after losing her seven sons; the grief of the Bride over the suffering of her children, scattered to every corner of the earth.

At that moment Rabbi Abraham fell to the ground in a faint, and he had a vision. In the vision he saw the *Shekhinah* once more, but this time he saw her dressed in her robe woven out of light, more magnificent than the setting sun, and her joyful countenance was revealed. Waves of light arose from her face, an aura that seemed to reach out and surround him, as if he were cradled in the arms of the Sabbath Queen. "Do not grieve so, my son Abraham," she said. "Know that my exile will come to an end, and my inheritance will not go to waste. And for you, my son, there shall be a great many blessings."

Just then Rabbi Abraham's soul returned to him from its journey on high. He awoke refreshed, as if he had shed years of grief, and he was filled with hope.

When Rabbi Abraham returned to Safed he was a new man, and when the Ari saw him, he said at once: "I can see that you have been found worthy to see the *Shekhinah*, and you can rest assured that you will live for another twenty-two years. Know that each year will be the blessing of another letter of the alphabet, for the light of the Divine Presence shines forth through every letter. And you, who have stood face-to-face with the *Shekhinah*, will recognize that light in every letter of every word."

So it was that Rabbi Abraham did live for another twenty-two years, years filled with abundance. And all who saw him recognized the aura that shone from his face, for the light of the Divine Presence always reflected from his eyes.[1]

This tale, "A Vision at the Wailing Wall," derives from the city of Safed in the 16th century. It is one of a cycle of tales about the great Jewish mystic Rabbi Isaac Luria. The Ari perceives that one of his disciples faces a midlife transition and sends him on a journey to wholeness, a quest to the Western Wall, the last remaining wall of the Temple in Jerusalem, to plead mercy from the *Shekhinah*, who is identified in the Kabbalah as the Bride of God. There Rabbi Abraham has a vision of the *Shekhinah*, in which he first sees her as an old woman who emerges from the wall "dressed in black, deep in mourning." Soon after this he faints and has a vision of the *Shekhinah* as a celestial bride.

Central to understanding this mystical tale is the concept of the *Shekhinah*. The term is first found in the Talmud, codified in the 5th century, where it refers to the Divine Presence, that is, the presence of God in the world. It is linked, in particular, to the sacred quality of the Sabbath. But by the 16th century the meaning of the term "*Shekhinah*" had evolved considerably. It came to be identified with the feminine aspect of the Divinity and took on mythic independence. Myths can be found in the Zohar and other kabbalistic texts that portray the *Shekhinah* as the Bride of God and Sabbath Queen who once made her home in the Temple in Jerusalem and later, when the Temple was destroyed, went into exile with her children, Israel. At this point the mythic figure of the *Shekhinah* becomes entirely independent of the divinity and takes on a separate identity. Nor will her exile end until the Temple has been rebuilt, which Jewish legend links with the coming of the Messiah, since the rebuilding of the Temple is said to be one of the miracles that will occur in the messianic era.

The two appearances of the *Shekhinah* that Rabbi Abraham envisions at the Wall, that of the old woman in mourning and of the bride in white, are the two primary aspects associated with her: she appears as a bride or queen or lost princess in some texts and tales and as an old woman mourning over the destruction of the Temple in others. In "A Vision at the Wailing Wall" she appears in both forms, signifying that his encounter with her is complete.

From our perspective, the *Shekhinah* can be recognized as both a mythic and archetypal feminine figure, very close to the purest vision of Jung's concept of the anima, the symbolic feminine aspect of every man. In "The Vision at the Wailing Wall" the Ari recognizes that if Rabbi Abraham continues on his present path, he is going to shortly meet his death. That is to say, his life has reached a dangerous transition, and in order to survive it, he must undertake an extraordinary task. Therefore the Ari sends him on a quest to find the *Shekhinah* in the logical place where she could be found—the Wailing Wall, the remnant of her former home. Rabbi Abraham encounters her there both as a grieving old woman and as a radiant bride, and afterward he is a new man, who through this visionary experience has rediscovered his lost anima and reintegrated his feminine side. That is why he is able to live for another twenty-two years, one year for each letter of the Hebrew alphabet, representing a whole new cycle of his life.

There is much to learn from this tale about how to read rabbinic tales to discover the psychic truths at the core of them. First, however, it is necessary to learn how to interpret their symbolic language. Identifying the *Shekhinah* with the anima is the first step toward translating this language into an archetypal framework.

The next step is to recognize that the quest of Rabbi Abraham is primarily an inner one. After all, as the Ari makes very clear to him, he must save himself. All the actions he undertakes, from wearing sackcloth and mourning to walking to Jerusalem, are mystical techniques intended to put him in a proper state of mind to receive the vision at the Wailing Wall. In this sense Rabbi Abraham might be seen as not only preparing himself for the vision, but of inducing it as well. Or the Ari can be seen as having planted the seed of the vision when he sent him on the quest. This quest and its corresponding vision, although expressed in terms of religious symbolism, is essentially an exploration of the world within.

Indeed, the folk structure that best expresses the essence of transition is that of the quest, representing the inner journey that must be taken before the transition can be completed. It is no accident that as many as half of all fairy tales are quest tales, where the quest represents just such a psychic transition. This is true, in particular, of Jewish fairy tales, since the motif of exile is one of the dominant themes of Judaism, echoed in the biblical accounts of the expulsion from the Garden of Eden and the Exodus from Egypt, as well as in the Babylonian exile that followed the destruction of the Temple, and the expulsion from Spain in 1492.

The most popular theme in all of Jewish folklore is the quest. There are a multitude of Jewish fairy tale quests for lost queens or princesses, an apple from the Tree of Life or a city of immortals, while holy quests for the palaces of heaven, the city of Jerusalem, the Bride of God, or the golden dove of the Messiah are among the most prominent themes of Jewish mystical lore. Of all the Jewish quest tales, the most significant is almost certainly Rabbi Nachman of Bratslav's "The Lost Princess,"[2] which concerns a quest to find a princess whom the disciples of Rabbi Nachman readily identify as the *Shekhinah*. More than any other tale, "The Lost Princess" presents the myth of the *Shekhinah* in fairy-tale terms that make it universally recognizable.

Rabbi Nachman of Bratslav holds a unique place in Jewish lore. The great-grandson of the Baal Shem Tov, he is widely acclaimed as the greatest Jewish storyteller of all time. "The Lost Princess" was the first tale he told to his hasidim when he began to tell stories. In all, he told thirteen primary tales and a few dozen other scattered tales.

On the surface "The Lost Princess" appears to be a conventional fairy tale, and as such it is a compelling one. But it was actually intended to serve as an allegory of a primary Jewish myth, that of the exile of the *Shekhinah*. It was Rabbi Nachman's method to disguise his mythic, kabbalistic tales in the form of intricate fairy tales, with many tales within tales, about kings and queens, princes and princesses. He hinted that he did this in order to conceal the mysteries revealed in these tales. His hasidim knew how to explore these mysteries by examining their symbolism and translating it to the appropriate mystical doctrine.

This, in brief, is the tale of "The Lost Princess":

There once was a king who had six sons and one daughter. His daughter was especially dear to him, but one day he became angry with her and said, "Go to the Devil!" and the next day she was gone.

The heartbroken king then sent his most loyal minister on a quest to find her, giving him all that he might need to accomplish the quest, including a servant. The minister searched everywhere in the world but failed to find the princess. At last he came to a remote palace where he discovered her, and he managed to talk to her. She told him that she was being held captive in the palace of the Evil One, who took her when the king sent her to him, and that in order to set her free, the minister must long for her release for a year, and at the end of that year, fast for one day, neither eating nor drinking, and then she would be able to return to her father, the king.

The minister remained there for a year, longing for her freedom, but on the last day, when he was supposed to be fasting, he saw an apple on a tree that was so appealing that he picked and ate it. After this he fell asleep and slept for seventy years. When at last he awoke, his servant told him of his long sleep. Then, heartbroken, he returned to the lost princess, who told him to repeat the year of longing, but this time he was permitted to eat—but not to drink—on the last day. He repeated the year-long vigil, but on the last day he saw that the waters of a familiar spring had turned red, and he could not resist tasting them. They turned out to be a delicious wine, and he drank his fill and once again fell asleep.

This time, while he was sleeping, the princess left the palace of the Evil One and rode past him in a carriage. She got out of the carriage and tried to wake him, but when she could not, she wept into her scarf and left it with him. When he finally awoke seventy years later, his loyal servant told him all that had taken place and showed him the scarf. He held it up to the sun and discovered that the tears of the lost princess had written a message on the scarf, in which she told him that henceforth she could be found in a palace of pearls on a golden mountain.

So it was that the heartbroken minister set out on a second quest, which turned out to be far more arduous than the first, because no one he met had ever heard of a palace of pearls on a golden mountain. He searched for many years, and his quest brought him at last to a great desert where he encountered three giants—one in charge of the animals, one in charge of the birds, and one in charge of the winds—all of whom were brothers. Each of the giants carried a giant tree as a staff. These giants called together the animals, the birds, and the winds, but none had heard of the palace of pearls. At last a late wind arrived, and when rebuked by the giant for being late, it explained that it had been carrying a princess to that very palace of pearls.

The giant then gave the minister an enchanted bag with an endless supply of gold and ordered the wind to bring him to the foot of the golden mountain. There the story ends, with Rabbi Nachman's assurance that eventually the minister did free the princess, although he does not reveal how this took place.

This appears in all respects to be a characteristic fairy tale, with a king, a lost princess, a quest, three giants, and an enchanted palace. As such, it can be interpreted from a Jungian perspective as a universal fairy tale, where the quest for the lost princess can readily be recognized as an inner journey. This is also the essential Jewish meaning of the tale, when the symbols in it are translated into their Jewish equivalents.

Such an interpretation can be found in the Bratslaver commentaries on "The Lost Princess," for this tale and the others that Rabbi Nachman told were examined by his hasidim with the kind of intense scrutiny reserved for the sacred texts. It was an article of faith with them that his stories could best be understood allegorically, and indeed "The Lost Princess" lends itself to such an interpretation. The key is the king who has six sons and one daughter. The king is easily recognizable as God, who is traditionally represented as a king in a multitude of rabbinic parables. The six sons and one daughter can be readily identified as the six days of the week and the Sabbath. And the identification of the Sabbath with a princess naturally evokes the Sabbath Queen, which is one of the primary identities of the *Shekhinah*.

The apple that the minister picks recalls the forbidden fruit of the Garden of Eden, and in eating it on the final fast day, he repeats the sin of the Fall and must wait for another generation, symbolized by the seventy years he sleeps. Indeed, the stages of the story can be seen to represent the biblical chronology. The princess is linked to the seven days of Creation. The episode of the Garden of Eden is echoed by the eating of the apple. The episode of the water turning into wine can be linked with the story of the Flood and the sin of Noah in becoming drunk. Also, the three giants that the minister encounters in the desert can be identified as the three towering patriarchs, Abraham, Isaac, and Jacob, while the trees they use as staffs can be identified with the Torah, as in the passage, *It [the Torah] is a Tree of Life to those who cling to it* (Prov. 3:18). So too does the minister's search for the palace of pearls repeat the Israelites' search of the Holy Land. As for the scarf with the words written by the tears of the lost princess, it represents the sacred writings of the Torah. These symbolic parallels to the biblical chronology demonstrate that "The Lost Princess" can also be understood as reflecting the collective Jewish experience, reliving the archetypal experiences represented in these key biblical episodes. That such a collective interpretation of the text was intended is found in the Haggadah for Passover, where it is stated that "in every generation each person must regard himself as if he himself went forth out of Egypt."

So too can this seminal story be understood on the level of personal inner experience. Once the link has been perceived between the lost princess and the *Shekhinah*, the allegorical meaning of Rabbi Nachman's tale reveals itself as a fairy-tale retelling of the myth of the exile of the *Shekhinah*. The king's angry words, which result in the disappearance of the princess, are equivalent to the destruction of the Temple in Jerusalem and the subsequent exile of both the *Shekhinah* and the Children of Israel. At the same time, they are equivalent to the expulsion from the Garden of Eden, the wandering in the wilderness, and other variations on the myth of exile, which is another of the primary Jewish myths.

Thus the figure of the lost princess in Rabbi Nachman's tale can be recognized as an anima figure. As such, she represents, in personal terms, a crucial missing element in the psychic equation, which the minister seeks to restore in his quest. In collective terms the exile of the *Shekhinah* can be seen as a psychic dislocation of the Jewish nation brought about by their exile from the Promised Land.

Rabbi Nathan of Nemirov, Rabbi Nachman's scribe, confirms the identification of the lost princess with the *Shekhinah* in the introduction to *Sippure Ma'asiyot*, Rabbi Nachman's primary volume of his tales:[3]

> Behold, the story of the princess who is lost is the mystery of the *Shekhinah* in exile. . . . And this story is about every man in every time, for this entire story occurs to every man individually, for everyone of Israel must occupy himself with this *tikkun* (act of redemption or restoration), namely to raise up the *Shekhinah* from her exile, to raise her up from the dust, and to liberate the Holy Kingdom from among the idolaters and the Other Side among whom she has been caught. . . . Thus one finds that everyone in Israel is occupied with the search for the lost princess, to take her back to her father, for Israel as a whole has the character of the minister who searches for her.

The significance of Rabbi Nathan's comment that "everyone in Israel is occupied with the search for the lost princess" should not be missed. Here is the clearest statement indicating that the process of searching for the lost princess, who is identified with the *Shekhinah* and thus with the anima, is an inner one. We must marvel at the psychological insight of Rabbi Nachman and Rabbi Nathan. It is clear from Rabbi Nathan's statement that Rabbi Nachman's tale is presumed to be allegorical. Thus the recognition of a complex symbol system is not only linked to a mystical theology but to an inner quest that "everyone of Israel is occupied with."

There are three strong possibilities for the identity of the loyal minister: The minister can be identified with the *tzaddik*, the righteous one, who must search and find the lost princess and bring her back to the king or, symbolically, to God. Or the minister can be identified with the nation of Israel whose task it is to search for the lost princess, or the *Shekhinah*, in her exile. Or the minister can be identified with the Messiah, and here the linkage seems quite natural, for kabbalistic myth holds that the exile of the

Shekhinah will not end until the Temple is rebuilt, which is not destined to take place until the advent of the Messiah. And the reason "The Lost Princess" is left unfinished is because the Messiah has not yet come.

All three of these interpretations of the role of the minister seem quite accurate, and each permits the tale to be seen from another important perspective. When the minister is seen as the nation of Israel, the responsibility for finding the lost princess rests on every Jew, and the importance of this doctrine to each individual is emphasized. When the minister is viewed as a *tzaddik*, the key role of the *tzaddik* in bringing about the reunion of *Shekhinah* and Messiah is underscored. And by identifying the minister with the Messiah we can recognize that Rabbi Nachman has combined two primary Jewish myths, that of the *Shekhinah* and that of the Messiah, into one mythic fairy tale, thus demonstrating their interdependence. Nor is it necessary to narrow these interpretations to one. One of the beautiful things about the process of commentary in Jewish texts is that multiple readings are not only permitted, but encouraged. Therefore we can easily accept the legitimacy of all three interpretations.

As for the Jungian symbolism of the coming of the Messiah, it can be identified with the individual's process of psychic growth—the individuation process. Just as individuation is an ongoing process, so too is the waiting for the Messiah, as is indicated in the twelfth of the Thirteen Principles of Maimonides, from his *Commentary on the Mishnah:* "I firmly believe in the coming of the Messiah, and although he may tarry, I daily wait for his coming." Thus the messianic era is the culmination of the series of transitions that constitute the history of the Jewish people and represents a time when the journeys of the individual and the collective will each be a journey to wholeness. We note also that both the *Shekhinah* and the Messiah are in exile, and therefore they have to be found and brought into consciousness. At the same time, the arrival of the messianic era will be the equivalent of a return to the Garden of Eden since it involves a return to a prelapsarian condition. Therefore, arriving at the messianic era represents a full return to the beginning, the meaning of the Hebrew term *teshuvah*, which means both "return" and "repentance." Such a return can also be viewed as a return to the primordial state we experienced at the beginning of our lives, which is represented by the Garden of Eden.

For the most part, the myths concerning the *Shekhinah* and the Messiah are separate, but they converge at the same conclusion, which is the End of Days. For one of the consequences of the coming of the Messiah will be a miraculous re-creation of the Temple, exactly as it was. Therefore the coming of the Messiah is essential to ending the exile of the *Shekhinah*, and the two myths are eternally bound together.

There is another hasidic tale that draws on the themes of the *Shekhinah* and the Messiah. This is "The Sabbath Guests," a tale of Rabbi Eizik of Kallo, a famous Hungarian hasidic master.

Two traveling hasidim arrived in the city of Kallo on the eve of the Sabbath and sought out the hospitality of the Rabbi of Kallo, about whom they had heard so much. Tales were told of his miracles throughout Hungary, and the visiting hasidim greatly anticipated spending the Sabbath in his company.

Soon everyone had gathered together to celebrate the Sabbath, and all looked toward the *tzaddik* of Kallo for the signal to welcome the Sabbath Queen. But the *tzaddik* did not stir. Not a single muscle moved. Every eye remained upon him, yet he seemed detached, in deep concentration.

The visiting hasidim were startled at such behavior, for no one ever delayed the beginning of the Sabbath for even an instant. Could it be that the rabbi had lost track of time?

All at once there was a knocking at the door, and when it was opened a couple came in. The young man was dressed in a white robe, as was worn in the city of Safed. The young woman, who was also wearing white, was hauntingly beautiful, with very dark eyes, her head covered with a white scarf. The *tzaddik* rose, at the same time signaling for the Sabbath to begin. The Hasidim began singing *Lekha Dodi*, the song that welcomes the Sabbath Queen, as the Rabbi of Kallo went to meet his guests. He treated them with every kindness, paying as much attention to the woman as to the man. This was too much for the visiting hasidim, but they were guests, and there was nothing they could do.

After the meal the Rabbi of Kallo rose and said, "This couple has come here to be wed this day. And I have agreed to marry them." Now these words were a deep shock to the visiting hasidim, for weddings are forbidden on the Sabbath. And they began reciting psalms to themselves, to protect themselves from the desecration of the Sabbath. At that moment the Rabbi of Kallo turned to the two hasidim and addressed them. He said, "Of course, the consent of everyone present is necessary, if the wedding is to be performed. Please tell us if we may have your consent?" And there was almost a pleading tone in his voice.

Now it is one thing to witness such a desecration, and quite another to perform one. But the two hasidim did not dare turn the *tzaddik* down. Instead they each dropped their eyes and continued reciting psalms, and a great fear was in their hearts.

At last, when they raised their eyes, they saw that the couple was gone. The Rabbi of Kallo was slumped in his chair. For a long time there was silence. At last the rabbi said, "Do you know who they were?" Each of the visiting hasidim shook his head to say no. And the rabbi said, "He was the Messiah. She was the Sabbath Queen. For so many years of exile they have sought each other, and now they were together at last, and they wanted to be wed. And, as everyone knows, on the day of their wedding our exile will come to an end. But that is possible only if everyone gives his full assent. Unfortunately, you did not, and the wedding could not take place."[4]

In this tale of Rabbi Eizik of Kallo, the Messiah and the *Shekhinah* arrive unexpectedly at his house on the Sabbath as a couple who wish to wed. The Rabbi of Kallo recognizes who they are, but the visiting hasidim do not, and because of their blindness, the opportunity to bring the messianic era is lost. Just as Rabbi Nachman's tale of "The Lost Princess" links the myths of the *Shekhinah* and the Messiah, so does this tale identify the pair as a bride and groom, suggesting that their union would herald the End of Days, the rabbinic vision of the messianic era. In a sense, this tale of Rabbi Eizik makes the convergence of the two myths of the *Shekhinah* and the Messiah complete, as symbolized by their desire for union. Such mythic fusion is common and often results in the creation of a new myth.

From a Jungian perspective, this tale seems to advocate the fusion of the male and female "inner beings," as represented by the *Shekhinah* and the Messiah. Such a union can be viewed as the full integration of the male and female archetypal figures and a symbol of psychic wholeness. Unfortunately, the tale tells us, the marriage has not taken place because you, the visitor to the realm of the unconscious, haven't given your approval for it. Thus the conclusion of the story can be interpreted as if it were a dream, reporting the present state of psychic balance. From this perspective the story reports a lost opportunity for psychic unity, while from the traditional perspective it is a tale of why the Messiah has not yet come. Such stories explain how there are opportunities in every generation for the Messiah to come, if something does not go wrong. And there are a many such tales, for the longing for the Messiah is very great.

That the quest of uniting the *Shekhinah* and Messiah is primarily an inner one is well illustrated by the concept of *tikkun,* meaning "redemption" or "restoration." This is the very term that Rabbi Nathan, Rabbi Nachman's scribe, links to the exile of the *Shekhinah* when he says that "everyone of Israel must occupy himself with this *tikkun.*" Here *tikkun* is directly understood as an internal process of healing and repair, and it is understood that it takes place on a personal level and a collective one at the same time. That is why it is known as *tikkun olam,* repair of the world.

The concept of *tikkun* is itself the subject of a vivid 16th century myth, which was the last major myth to be added to Jewish tradition. This myth, created by the same Rabbi Isaac Luria who sent Rabbi Abraham on his fateful quest, represents the core of the Ari's teachings and his greatest gift to Jewish tradition. It illustrates the Jewish vision of the very process of restoration and transformation. According to this cosmological myth, God sent forth vessels bearing a primordial light at the beginning of time. Had these vessels arrived intact, the world would have remained in its prelapsarian condition. But somehow—no one knows why—the vessels shattered and scattered their sparks throughout the world, especially on the Holy Land. This is the first stage of the Ari's cosmology, known as "The Shattering of the Vessels." It is the symbolic equivalent of other cosmic catastrophes such as the expulsion from Eden, the destruction of the Temple in

Jerusalem, and the expulsion of the Jews from Spain in 1492, which took place just forty-two years before the Ari was born.

The second phase—and it is the existence of this second phase that makes the myth so remarkable—is called "Gathering the Sparks." Here the object is to collect the fallen sparks and raise them up. This is the very definition of the process of *tikkun*, of healing a world that has become unraveled. The process of raising up the scattered sparks involves the first explanation and justification of the ritual requirements specified in the Torah, known as the *mitzvot*. Each time one of the *mitzvot* is fulfilled, according to the Ari, scattered sparks are raised up and redeemed. Ultimately, when enough sparks have been gathered, the broken vessels will be restored, and this is the symbolic equivalent of the messianic era. Thus the myth of the Ari states unambiguously that a person's deeds serve directly to transform and restore the world. And at the same time, of course, this process of transformation occurs within the individual as well. Thus the Ari's myth is a healing one, focused on the processes of breaking apart and restoring to wholeness.

Perhaps the most remarkable aspect of the Ari's myth is how it, too, combines two primary Jewish myths, that of Creation and that of the messianic era, into one. Rather than present a view of original sin, as is found in Catholicism, the imperfections in the world are made the direct responsibility of God, removing much or all of the blame from the human realm. So too is the role of the Jews defined: to gather the scattered holy sparks and raise them up. This memorable myth spread rapidly throughout the Jewish world and brought kabbalistic principles to the Jewish masses for the first time. Today it remains one of the most haunting and relevant of Jewish myths.

From a Jungian perspective, the shattering of the vessels might be identified in individual terms as the equivalent of a breakdown. It represents a breaking through of the unconscious at a time of psychic transition. On the collective level, the shattering of the vessels represents a time of upheaval, such as that resulting in the destruction of the Temple in Jerusalem, or the expulsion from Spain in 1492—or any of the dozens of crises in Jewish history. The gathering of the sparks represents the process of restoration both on the individual and collective levels that ultimately achieves the kind of psychic balance known as individuation. And we note that the developmental sequence of the Ari's myth requires the shattering to take place before the restoration can be achieved, indicating that the shattering is an essential, as well as inevitable, phase of this process.

In both teachings and tales, the primary role of the master or *tzaddik* is to guide his disciples on the path of the Torah. The myth of the Ari does this, explaining that following this path will result in personal and cosmic restoration. And in the tale of Rabbi Abraham, the matter is framed in terms of Yom Kippur and the long-established tradition that a person's future is decided on that day, while the quest on which the Ari sends him grows out of the myth of the exile of the *Shekhinah*. As a result, Rabbi Abraham survives a difficult and crucial transition in his life and emerges not only renewed but, in a very real sense, reborn.

Thus it can be seen that the roles of the *tzaddik* and the therapist are parallel. Just as the *tzaddik* brings his disciples to recognize their personal connection to Jewish myth, as in the story of Rabbi Abraham's vision at the Wailing Wall, the therapist helps an individual recognize that others go through a similar process and that the stages of personal experience that lead to individuation take place in a personal, as well as universal, sphere.

In the tale of Rabbi Abraham, the transition he confronts is identified as a matter of life and death, and this is often the case. By putting the transition in these terms, we can easily recognize its importance. In most of these tales the key events take place during times of transition, involve major life events such as birth, marriage, and death, and are often linked to one of the holy days. That is when Jews are most subject to Divine judgment.

Judaism, of course, offers a multitude of rituals and ceremonies to ease and define life transitions. The ceremony of the *brit* (circumcision) adds an eight-day-old boy to the community of Israel; *bar* and *bat mitzvah* serve as initiations into adult life; an elaborate wedding service, followed by seven days of celebrating the *Sheva Berakhot* (seven blessings), leaves a couple feeling very married; and the extensive rituals linked to death, beginning with those of *shivah* (seven days of mourning), *shloshim* (thirty days of mourning), and continuing with the reciting of the Kaddish for an eleven-month period, have the effect of providing consolation to the ones who are grieving and a meaningful structure at a time of chaos in their lives.

At the same time, Jewish tales portray a transition provoked by a time of danger, of either inner or outer origin, in which the conventional ritual structure is not enough and the presence of some kind of guide is required in order to survive. The figure who then miraculously appears is usually identified with one of the patriarchs or prophets, especially Elijah, who often appears in a time of dire need. Furthermore, the kind of survival indicated in these tales often requires radical transformation of the self in order to achieve the psychic balance found in individuation.

A good example of such a tale is "A Kiss from the Master," collected in Israel by the Israel Folktale Archives:[5]

> During the days when the shrine of Rabbi Shimon bar Yohai was still open, the wise men of Safed would enter it on Lag ba-Omer. Once a rich man who was visiting in Safed on the eve of Lag ba-Omer was invited by his host to visit Rabbi Shimon's grave in Meron. When he arrived, he saw that the sages were sitting inside the shrine, rejoicing. They invited the rich man to join them, and they gave him an honorable place among them.
>
> Then, one at a time, they read passages from the Zohar, as was their

custom. But when the guest received the book, he could not read the Aramaic in which it was written, and he was deeply ashamed.

After they had finished reading, everyone but the rich man returned to their tents. But he remained in the shrine, weeping bitterly for his lack of knowledge of the Torah, until at last he fell asleep. And no sooner did he sleep than he dreamed that Rabbi Shimon bar Yohai appeared to him and comforted him, and before departing he kissed him on the mouth. And that is when the rich man woke up.

From the moment he opened his eyes, the rich man felt as if a new spirit were within him. He picked up the book of the Zohar and opened it to the first page. There he found, much to his amazement, that he could now read the letters. Not only that, but the true meaning of every letter rose up in his vision, for the spirit of Rabbi Shimon had fused with his soul. In this way his eyes were opened to the hidden meanings of the Torah and its mysteries were revealed to him.

Later the others returned to the shrine, and they began to discuss a difficult passage in the Zohar that none of them could comprehend. Then the rich man spoke and explained that passage to them as if it were elementary, and their eyes were opened to its true meaning. Even more, they were amazed at his wisdom, for they knew he could not even read the language and yet what he said could only come from a master of the Torah.

Then the sages demanded that the rich man explain how this transformation had taken place. And the rich man revealed his dream about Shimon bar Yohai. And when the sages heard this dream, they understood that a miracle had occurred and that the rich man had been possessed by an *ibur*, the spirit of a great sage who fuses his soul to the soul of another and in this way gives it guidance. So too did they know that this sage could be none other than Shimon bar Yohai, since that was the very place where he was buried.

After that the rich man found that all he had to do to call forth the soul of Rabbi Shimon was to open the book of the Zohar. Then he would be able to understand the mysteries of the Zohar as if they were the *aleph bet*. And in the days that followed, the sages invited him to remain in Safed and to bring his family to join him. This he did, and before long they made him the head of the kabbalists of Safed, for they knew that he spoke with the wisdom of Shimon bar Yohai.

What this tale suggests is that the spirit of Rabbi Shimon bar Yohai returned in the form of an *ibbur*, literally an impregnation, a positive kind of possession in which the soul of a great sage who has died binds his spirit to one of the living in order to increase that person's wisdom and faith. This is in contrast to possession by a dybbuk, where a malevolent spirit takes possession of one of the living. Here the spirit of Shimon bar Yohai comes in a dream to a man uneducated in the Torah. The spirit kisses him, and afterward the man discovers that he has become a master of the Torah, possessed with the spirit of Shimon Bar Yohai.

It is characteristic of these tales that possession by an *ibbur* is not permanent but is triggered by something, such as the study of a particular text or the wearing of *tefillin*, the phylacteries worn by men during the morning prayers. There is a story, for example, about the *tefillin* of Rabbi Hayim ben Attar, who was known as the Or ha-Hayim.[6] These were purchased after his death by a wealthy man, who discovered that the spirit of the Or ha-Hayim would emerge whenever he wore them, giving him a spiritual awareness far beyond anything he had previously experienced. In both of these tales, that of Shimon bar Yohai and that of the Or ha-Hayim, the *ibbur* represents the inner being that emerges to guide a person through a difficult time of transition. The fact that the presence of the *ibbur* must be triggered in some way indicates that the presence of this inner being only emerges when it is required by internal or external circumstances.

One of the most tantalizing indications of the presence of an *ibbur* concerns Rabbi Abraham Isaac Kook. It was well known among the followers of Rav Kook that a great change had come over him when he came to the Holy Land. So great was the transformation that even his handwriting changed, as if he had become a different person. And, indeed, Rav Kook was once heard to say: "I am the soul of Reb Nachman." Rav Kook's statement is a mysterious one, which suggests a direct connection between the souls of the two great rabbis. Above all, it demonstrates how greatly Rav Kook admired Reb Nachman and how strongly he identified with him. Among the followers of Rav Kook, this statement was understood to mean that the soul of Reb Nachman had come to Rav Kook as an *ibbur* and the two souls had fused. This, then, explains the changes that came over Rav Kook when he arrived in the Holy Land and links him to Rabbi Nachman, whose love for the Holy Land was legendary. Furthermore, Rabbi Nachman regarded his journey to the Holy Land as the completion of a quest started by his great-grandfather, the Baal Shem Tov, the founder of hasidism. So here we have a quest started in one generation by the Baal Shem Tov, continued in another by Rabbi Nachman, and extended into yet another generation by Rav Kook.

The concept of the *ibbur* has broad psychological implications. A person possessed by an *ibbur* has become transformed—the new soul has fused with the old. The result is a soul guided by the spirit of a sage, which brings both wisdom and strength to a wavering soul facing a virtual abyss that has to be crossed. From a Jungian perspective, the man has activated the archetype of the Wise Old Man in himself. As a result of this transformation, he can now read in a language that was foreign to him. This means that he can now communicate with that part of himself whose previous messages were not received. Furthermore, his ability to comprehend the true meaning of these messages is greatly enhanced.

The Zohar itself, the book that opened to this man because of the possession of the *ibbur*, is the key text of Kabbalah. It contains many tales about Rabbi Shimon bar Yohai, a great talmudic sage of the 2nd century, who was the reputed author of the Zohar until Gershom Scholem and other scholars demonstrated that the primary author was Moses de Leon, who lived in Spain in the 13th century. Anyone who has spent any time with the Zohar will confirm the great difficulty of its text. Furthermore, the text is above all a symbolic one, drawing on a rich kabbalistic mythology, and in the process transforming the meaning of many concepts from the way in which they were understood in earlier sacred texts.

Following the earlier discussion about the need to learn to read the symbolic language of these tales, this one embodies a solution, addressing the very issue of learning to read a foreign language by finding the solution in a dream, a message from the unconscious to the conscious. The dream is the key vehicle in Jewish tales for messages to be delivered from the Divine realm to our own. So too does the dream of the man in the shrine bring with it the power of the Wise Old Man who lies dormant until activated, exactly as does the *ibbur*. Because the new soul is so closely identified with Rabbi Shimon bar Yohai, the man who receives it has no difficulty acknowledging its inherent wisdom. Thus he is open to the wisdom ultimately emanating from his unconscious self. In a nutshell, the message of the tale and the dream can be summed up as follows: The knowledge and wisdom you seek can be found within.

Here is another tale, this a hasidic one, in which a dream guides a man to a patriarchal figure, who provides salvation. This tale is "The Cave of Mattathias" and it was also collected orally in Israel, demonstrating the continued vitality of the oral tradition. It is a tale about a hasid of the Rabbi of Riminov, as follows: [7]

> In a village near the city of Riminov there was a hasid whose custom it was to bring newly made oil to Rabbi Menachem Mendel of Riminov, and the rabbi would light the first candle of Hanukkah in his presence.
>
> One year the winter was hard, the land covered with snow, and everyone was locked in their homes. But when the eve of Hanukkah arrived, the hasid was still planning to deliver the oil. His family pleaded with him not to go, but he was determined, and in the end he set out across the deep snow.
>
> That morning he entered the forest that separated his village from Riminov, and the moment he did it began to snow. The snow fell so fast it soon covered every landmark, and when at last it stopped, the hasid found that he was lost. The whole world was covered with snow.
>
> Now the hasid began to regret not listening to his family. Surely the rabbi would have forgiven his absence. Meanwhile, it had become so cold that he began to fear he might freeze. He realized that if he were to die there in the forest, he might not even be taken to a Jewish grave. That is when he remembered the oil he was carrying. In order to save his life, he would have to use it. There was no other choice.
>
> As fast as his numb fingers could move, he tore some of the lining out of his coat and fashioned it into a wick, and he put that wick in the snow. Then

he poured oil on it and prayed with great intensity. Finally, he lit the first candle of Hanukkah, and the flame seemed to light up the whole forest. And all the wolves moving through the forest saw that light and ran back to their hiding places.

After this the exhausted hasid lay down on the snow and fell asleep. He dreamed he was walking in a warm land, and before him he saw a great mountain, and next to that mountain stood a date tree. At the foot of the mountain was the opening of a cave. In the dream the hasid entered the cave and found a candle burning there. He picked up that candle, and it lit the way for him until he came to a large cavern, where an old man with a very long beard was seated. There was a sword on his thigh, and his hands were busy making wicks. All of that cavern was piled high with bales of wicks. The old man looked up when the hasid entered and said: "Blessed be you in the Name of God."

The hasid returned the old man's blessing and asked him who he was. He answered: "I am Mattathias, father of the Maccabees. During my lifetime I lit a big torch. I hoped that all of Israel would join me, but only a few obeyed my call. Now heaven has sent me to watch for the little candles in the houses of Israel to come together to form a very big flame. And that flame will announce the Redemption and the End of Days.

"Meanwhile, I prepare the wicks for the day when everyone will contribute his candle to this great flame. And now, there is something that you must do for me—when you reach the Rabbi of Riminov, tell him that the wicks are ready, and he should do whatever he can to light the flame that we have awaited so long."

Amazed at all he had heard, the hasid promised to give the message to the rabbi. As he turned to leave the cave, he awoke and found himself standing in front of the rabbi's house. Just then the rabbi himself opened the door, and his face was glowing. He said: "The power of lighting the Hanukkah candles is very great. Whoever dedicates his soul to this deed brings the time of Redemption that much closer."

Like the tale of the master's kiss, this one uses a dream as a vehicle to encounter the Wise Old Man, who is identified here as Mattathias. The message from Mattathias is that the messianic era is almost upon them, hinting that the Rabbi of Riminov can have an important role to play in this event. But the real importance of this dream is the way it provides salvation to the hasid trapped in the snow. By creating the conditions to save himself, using the oil for the Hanukkah candles, he saves himself from freezing and is able to sleep, and thus to dream. The dream first transports him from a cold place to a warm one, and then brings him face-to-face with Mattathias. This dream meeting is a fateful one for the hasid, for when he awakes he finds himself at the rabbi's door. A miracle has once more taken place, as it did to Rabbi Abraham when he had a vision of the *Shekhinah*, and as it did to the rich man who was kissed by Shimon bar Yohai.

This miracle indicates that the abyss has been crossed and the transition completed.

From these last two tales, and from a multitude of others, we can recognize that there is a pattern to the role of the Wise Old Man. This figure is inevitably identified with one of the great Jewish patriarchs or sages, whose arrival at a time of danger heralds a miraculous event. In every case we can recognize in this pattern the presence of the archetype of the Old Man who, like the *ibbur*, brings wisdom and the strength to survive a difficult transition.

Yet, for those who fail to recognize its importance, this encounter with the Wise Old Man can be disastrous. "The Cottage of Candles,"[8] a remarkable Jewish folktale from Afghanistan, presents a vivid demonstration of such an encounter:

There once was a Jew who went out into the world to seek justice. Somewhere, he was certain, true justice must exist, but he had never found it. He looked in the streets and the markets of cities but could not find it. He traveled to villages and he explored distant fields and farms, but still justice eluded him. At last he came to an immense forest, and he entered it, for he was certain that justice must exist somewhere.

He wandered there for many years and he saw many things—the hovels of the poorest peasants, the hideaways of thieves, and the huts of witches in the darkest part of the forest. And he stopped in each of these, despite the danger, and sought clues. But no one was able to help him in his quest.

One day, just as dusk was falling, he arrived at a small clay hut that looked as if it were about to collapse. Now there was something strange about this hut, for many flickering flames could be seen through the window. The man who sought justice wondered greatly about this and knocked on the door. There was no answer. He pushed the door open and entered.

As soon as he stepped inside, the man saw that the cottage was much larger on the inside than it had appeared to be from the outside. In it he saw hundreds—or was it thousands—of shelves, and on each of the shelves were a multitude of oil candles, burning brightly.

Stepping closer, he saw that some of the flames burned with a very pure fire, while others were dull, and still others were sputtering, about to go out. So too did he now notice that some of the wicks were in golden vessels, while others were in silver or marble ones, and many burned in simple vessels of clay or tin. These plain vessels had thin wicks, which burned quickly, while those made of gold or silver had wicks that lasted much longer.

While he stood there, marveling at that forest of candles, an old man in a white robe came out of one of the corners and said: "*Shalom aleikhem*, my son. What are you looking for?"

"*Aleikhem shalom*," the man answered. "I have traveled everywhere, searching for justice, but never have I seen anything like this. What are all these candles for?"

The old man spoke softly. "Know that each of these candles is the candle of a person's soul, as it is said, *The soul of man is the candle of God* (Prov. 20:27). As long as his candle burns, a man remains alive. But when the flame goes out, his soul takes leave of this world."

Then the man who sought justice turned to the old man and asked, "Can I see the candle of my soul?"

The old man nodded and led him into the depths of that cottage, which the man now saw was much larger on the inside than it appeared to be on the outside. At last they came to a low shelf, and the old man showed him a line of clay vessels on it. He pointed out one that had very little oil left. The wick was smoking and had tilted to one side. "That is the candle of your soul," said the old man.

Then a great fear fell upon the man and he started to shiver. Could it be that the end of his life was so near and he did not know it?

Then the man noticed that next to his candle there was another, filled with oil. Its wick was straight, burning with a clear, pure light.

"And this one, to whom does it belong?" asked the man, trembling. "That is a secret," answered the old man. "I can only reveal each man's candle to himself alone."

Soon after that the old man vanished from sight, and the cottage seemed empty except for the candles burning on every shelf.

While the man stood there, he heard a sputtering on another shelf, and looking up, he saw a wisp of smoke rising in the air. Somewhere a soul had just left the world.

The man's eyes returned to his own tin. He saw that only a few drops of oil remained, and that the flame would soon burn out. At that instant he saw the candle of his neighbor, burning brightly, so full of oil.

Suddenly an evil thought entered his mind. He looked around and saw that the old man had disappeared. He looked closely in the corners of the cottage, but there was no sign of him there. Then the man reached out and took hold of the candle next to his, and raised it above his own. Suddenly the old man appeared out of nowhere and gripped the man's arm with a grip like iron. It hurt so much that he closed his eyes.

And when at last he opened his eyes, the man saw that everything had disappeared: the old man, the cottage, the shelves, and all the candles. He found himself standing alone in the forest, and he heard the trees whispering his fate.

This tale is an example of a Divine test, such as that of the Garden of Eden, or that of the binding of Isaac, or that of Job. The man seeking justice attempts to fulfill the biblical injunction *Justice, justice, shalt thou pursue* (Deut. 16:20) by setting out on a quest to find justice. At last he arrives at the cottage of candles, where the old man permits him to view the candle of his soul. The identity of the old man remains a mystery, although his supernatural aspect is quite clear. As the Keeper of the Soul-

Candles he functions as an Elijah-type figure who is hidden in the forest. Above all, he is the incarnation of the archetype of the Wise Old Man.

The test that takes place in the cottage surely does so at the behest of God, so it remains a Divine one. One way of reading the tale is to see that in arriving at this cottage, the man is on the verge of completing his quest to find justice, but he is first tested to see if he himself is just. Instead of proving worthy, he attempts to steal from another's life to lengthen his own. But he is caught and made to face the consequences of his action. In this sense he does find justice at last, for justice is meted out.[9]

It is apparent from the story that the man who is seeking justice is at the very end of his life, as indicated by the fact that his soul-candle is about to burn out. If he were able to pass the test in the cottage of candles, he would have received his just reward. But he fails the test at the very end, demonstrating that he is not a true seeker after justice, since he does not abide by it himself. Thus he falls prey to the powers of the *Yetzer Hara*, the Evil Inclination, which must be overcome in order to achieve justice, which is represented in this story as a kind of inner harmony and acceptance of one's fate.

Thus we have seen how archetypal figures, such as the anima or the Wise Old Man, appear in Jewish lore and are transformed into mythic figures such as the *Shekhinah* or a patriarch. Indeed, all of the tales discussed here draw on the collective Jewish myth. Just as individuals go through a series of transitions in their lives, so have the Jewish people gone through a series of collective experiences, not only those recounted in the Scriptures, but the collective experience of the people in every generation. Therefore these tales can be understood in terms of both the collective Jewish meaning and the individual's psychic experience. So too is there a deeper collective level where these tales can be recognized in purely archetypal terms. These three levels of meaning exist simultaneously in all of these tales and provide them with a profound depth of meaning.

What is found, then, in these rabbinic tales, is the projection of unbridled imaginations set in a mythical world reflecting the conditions of their inner lives, drawing on a complex system of symbols that have a remarkable parallel to the Jungian constellation. That the symbols used by the rabbis have an archetypal character is confirmed by the tales of Rabbi Nachman of Bratslav. The traditional Bratslaver commentary on these tales clearly demonstrates they were understood to have a direct correlation to key mystical figures such as the *Shekhinah* and the Messiah and to many other mystical concepts. A study of how this mystical system was understood and what purposes it was intended to serve reveals that it was a method of spiritual purification, drawing on many mystical techniques, including prayer, fasting, ritual immersion, and, as discussed, allegorical readings of sacred texts. Dreams were recognized as Divine messages as well, and attempts were made to interpret them, since it is written that "a dream that is not interpreted is like a letter that is not read."[10]

Certain key Jewish myths, such as that of the *Shekhinah* and that of the Messiah, have a direct correlation to recognizable archetypal patterns and figures, and when considered from this perspective they readily open themselves to interpretation. The Jewish tales that draw on these myths can be seen to mirror a complex psychic process involving the interaction of a constellation of archetypes. Such an analysis reveals the central role of psychological processes, especially those concerned with patterns of change, in Jewish mystical teachings and tales.

In conclusion, there is a recurrent pattern in Jewish tales of a person in midlife reaching a crisis that is resolved by the intervention of some celestial or saintly being. In Jungian terms, these beings (anima/*Shekhinah*, Wise Old Man/Elijah) are inner beings, introjections of the person's own soul/self who emerge to help the person through the crisis and assist in a transition to a higher state of personal psychic development, that of individuation.

II
The Quest for Jerusalem

Wherever I go, I am going toward Jerusalem.

Rabbi Nachman of Bratslav

In the tale of "A Vision at the Wailing Wall" with which we began, the Ari sends Rabbi Beruchim on a double quest: to go to Jerusalem and to find God's Bride, the *Shekhinah*, at the Western Wall. Only after he completes the first quest is he able to complete the second; they are inextricably linked. In this way Jerusalem itself became identified with the *Shekhinah*, and there are many other legends that link the two together.

Once the Garden of Eden was cut off for all time (except in legends), Jerusalem became the focus of Jewish longing as the city in which God's presence is manifest. Therefore, every journey to Jerusalem becomes a quest, and there are a great many legends in which such journeys are regarded as holy quests. Ultimately, Jerusalem became the archetype of the holy city, so much so that it was said to be the mirror image of the heavenly Jerusalem.

During all of their many exiles, Jews longed to travel to the holy city of Jerusalem. This is not only a journey to the heart of the Holy Land, but also a quest for the *Shekhinah*, who is so closely linked to the *Kotel*—the Wailing Wall—all that remains of the Temple once said to have been the *Shekhinah's* home. This kind of intense longing is imprinted on all of Jewish literature, from the Bible to the folktales collected orally in Eastern Europe and Israel in this century. Sometimes these quests to Jerusalem were miraculous, as in this tale about the talmudic sage Haninah ben Dosa from Ecclesiastes Rabbah. Note the role of a stone in this story. As everyone knows, the beautiful, glowing stones out of which the buildings of Jerusalem have been constructed are world famous, and it's not surprising to see how they have worked themselves into the folklore of Jerusalem.

Long ago, in the hills of the Galilee, far from the city of Jerusalem, there lived a rabbi named Haninah ben Dosa. This rabbi was so poor that he and his wife had little to eat except for the carobs and olives that grew wild there. Yet he was still happy, for his love of God was very great.

One year, before Shavuot, Rabbi Haninah saw his neighbors preparing to go up to Jerusalem. Every year they made a pilgrimage there to celebrate the holiday. Everyone took the finest fruits of the harvest, or the finest sheep or goat from his herd, and brought it as a gift for the Temple. Rabbi Haninah also wanted to bring a gift, but he was so poor that he had nothing to offer.

But Rabbi Haninah could not go to Jerusalem empty-handed. He went into his house and looked all around it, but he could not find a worthy gift. So he took a walk, trying to think of what he might do. All at once, he noticed a large, beautiful stone lying by the side of the road. He cried out: "I can take this stone as a gift for Jerusalem. But first I must work on it, so that it will be a worthy gift."

So Rabbi Haninah began to work on that stone. He chiseled and fashioned it. Then he carved in beautiful designs. Finally he polished the stone until it shone brightly in the sun.

Rabbi Haninah stepped back and looked at his finished stone, and he saw that it was indeed a worthy gift. Then he decided it was time to set out for Jerusalem. So he put his arms around that stone and tried to lift it—but the stone did not budge. Rabbi Haninah realized that he would not be able to move it without help.

Just then, four farmers came walking down the road. Rabbi Haninah asked if they would help him carry the stone to Jerusalem. But they wanted to be paid for their work, and all Rabbi Haninah had was four pennies. So the men continued on their way.

Rabbi Haninah became very sad, for he realized that he could not afford to pay anyone to help him take that gift to Jerusalem. And when God saw how sad he was, he sent four angels down to earth to help him. The angels disguised themselves as men, and soon Rabbi Haninah saw them coming down the road.

Once again Rabbi Haninah asked for help, and the angels agreed to assist him, as long as he also lent a hand. Of course, Rabbi Haninah agreed to this. And the instant he put his hand on the stone, it flew up in the air, and Rabbi Haninah found himself flying across the heavens toward Jerusalem, along with the angels. And as they approached the holy city, it first appeared as a jewel glowing in the distance. Rabbi Haninah said to himself: "Now I know why Jerusalem is called the jewel in God's crown."

Soon Rabbi Haninah found himself standing near the entrance of the Temple in Jerusalem, and the stone was there beside him. Rabbi Haninah looked around for the four men, but they were nowhere to be seen. Just then a group of weary pilgrims arrived, and when they saw the stone that Rabbi Haninah had carved, they said: "Look at that beautiful stone! Let us rest here." Rabbi Haninah was filled with joy, for a miracle had brought his gift to Jerusalem, and now it would serve as a place for weary travelers to sit and rest.

That stone remained there as long as the Temple was still standing. But when the Temple was torn down, the stone disappeared. Some say it was used in rebuilding the walls of Jerusalem. Others say that the same angels who brought it to Jerusalem later brought it into heaven, to the Temple in the heavenly Jerusalem, where Rabbi Haninah now makes his home.[11]

Rabbi Haninah's flight with the angels, bearing the stone to Jerusalem, turns our attention to the heavens and the heavenly Jerusalem, where Rabbi Haninah now makes his home. The concept of a heavenly Jerusalem is a powerful mythic motif that immortalizes the holiness of Jerusalem, since the city below is said to be a mirror image of the city above. King David is said to have visited this heavenly city in his dreams. There King David explored the celestial Temple and came to envision the holy Temple that his son, Solomon, later built in Jerusalem. Jewish tradition holds that even though the earthly Temple has been torn down, the heavenly Temple continues to exist.

The tradition that King David's plans for the Temple were drawn from the heavenly Jerusalem is based on I Chronicles 28:11–12:

> Then David gave Solomon, his son, the pattern of the porch [of the Temple], and of the houses thereof, and of the upper room thereof, and of the inner changes there. . . . And the pattern of all he had by the spirit.

By using a kind of midrashic logic in interpreting this passage, the phrase "*And the pattern of all he had by the spirit*" seemed to imply the existence of a heavenly Jerusalem. In this way, the concept of the heavenly Jerusalem came into being. This heavenly Jerusalem also represented the archetype of Jerusalem, the embodiment of a dream of Jerusalem as it has grown over the centuries by those longing to return there. From a Jungian perspective, the heavenly Jerusalem represents the holy city within, the home of the psyche and the soul.

We can also trace the evolution of a heavenly Jerusalem from two other primary biblical passages. The first is Jacob's statement, after waking from the dream in which he saw the heavenly ladder: *This is none other than the House of God, and this is the gate of heaven* (Gen. 28:17). The identification of the celestial ladder as *the gate of heaven* gave birth to meditation about the nature of the heavenly realm, and that, in turn, gave birth to speculation about the existence of a heavenly city, which from the first was linked to Jerusalem because of its unique, holy status.

The second biblical verse to effect the evolution of the concept of a heavenly Jerusalem is Isaiah's vision: *I beheld my Lord seated on a high and lofty throne; and the skirts of his robe filled the temple. Seraphs stood in attendance around him* (Isa. 6:1). Here the notion of a heavenly temple is presented directly for the first time, and of course the existence of such a temple gave birth, in turn, to the notion of a heavenly city. An almost identical vision is reported by the prophet Micah: *I saw the Lord seated upon His throne, with all the angels of heaven standing to the right and left of him* (I Kings 22:19).

As time passed, additional details about the heavenly Temple were added. The angel Michael was said to serve as the high priest in the heavenly Temple, and it was said that the same sacrifices were performed there, and the same hymns were sung as in the earthly Temple. Since the earthly Temple was built in the earthly Jerusalem, the heavenly Temple must exist in a celestial Jerusalem.

The account of Rabbi Haninah's quest to Jerusalem is found in the Talmud, as is this legend about King David, which demonstrates the intense sanctity of Jerusalem and, especially, of the site of the Temple there:

It was King David who first dreamed of building the Temple in Jerusalem. At night, in his dreams, he would climb Jacob's ladder until he reached the heavenly Jerusalem. For there is a Jerusalem in heaven that is the mirror image of the Jerusalem on earth.

King David was fascinated with the heavenly Temple, which was built at the beginning of time. He would study it from every angle. So too did he explore every chamber of that Temple. And when he awoke from these dreams, he would write down the description of the heavenly Temple, for it was his plan to build one exactly like it in the city of Jerusalem.

From these dreams King David also learned that the earthly Temple must be built above an ancient stone, known as the Foundation Stone, which God had set into the earth at the time of creation. But where was this Foundation Stone to be found? King David commanded that shafts be dug to a depth of fifteen hundred cubits. And lo, they struck a stone in one of those shafts. As soon as he learned of it, King David went there with Ahitophel, his counselor, and with other members of the court. They descended into the pit, and there, at the bottom, they saw the immense stone, shining like the darkest emerald.

All those who saw it were amazed, and they knew that it must, indeed, be that fabled stone which served as the world's foundation. Yet all at once King David was possessed by a great curiosity to see what lay beneath it. King David ordered it to be raised, but a voice came forth from the stone, saying: "Be warned that I must not be lifted, for I serve to hold back the waters of the Abyss."

All of them stood in awe of that voice, but King David's curiosity was still not sated. He decided to ignore the warning, and once more he ordered the stone to be raised. None of his advisors dared say anything, for they feared his wrath. After a great effort, a corner of the Foundation Stone was lifted up, and King David bent down and peered into the Abyss beneath it. There he heard something like the sound of rushing waters, and he suddenly realized that by lifting the stone he had set free the waters of the Deep. Once again the world was in danger of being deluged, as in the time of Noah.

King David trembled with fear, and he asked the others what they might do to cause the waters to fall back, but no one spoke. Then King David said: "Perhaps if I wrote the Name of God on a potsherd, and cast it into the depths, we might still be saved. But does anyone know if this is permitted?" Still the others said nothing, and King David grew angry and said: "If any one of you knows this and still refuses to answer, then your soul will bear the curse of the end of existence!" Then Ahitophel spoke: "Surely the Name can be used to bring peace to the whole world." So David picked up a potsherd and scratched the four-letter Name of God into it, and cast it into the bottomless pit. All at once the roar of the waters grew fainter, and they knew that they had been saved by the power of the Name.

In the days to come King David repented many times for his sin, and he gave thanks to God for sparing the world from another flood. And his son, Solomon, had the Holy of Holies of the Temple built exactly above the Foundation Stone, for both the stone and the Temple bore the seal of God's blessing.[12]

In this story from the Talmud, King David sets out to dig the foundations of the Temple and strikes the Foundation Stone of the earth upon which God built the rest of this world. This confirms that Jerusalem is the very center of the world, as it was portrayed in ancient maps.

At the same time, this tale is a Divine test, not unlike the tests of Adam and Eve, of Abraham in the *Akedah*—the binding of Isaac—and of Job. Even though a voice from the stone warns him not to lift it, King David, not unlike Pandora, lifts the Foundation Stone and sets free the powers of chaos, the waters of the Abyss, which threaten to inundate the earth as in the time of Noah. In a desperate moment David writes the Tetragrammaton, the secret Name of God, on a sherd and throws it into the abyss, and the power of God's Name causes the waters to retreat. (Note the echo to nuclear war in this episode. David learns that the Foundation Stone must not be tampered with, as we have learned of the dangers posed by tampering with the atom.)

Indeed, as the legend of the Foundation Stone suggests, Jerusalem is at the center of Jewish life and lore. There are countless tales linked to Jerusalem, to the Wailing Wall (the *Kotel*) where visitors leave messages in the cracks in the wall for God to read, to the many synagogues, tombs, and other holy sites, and even to the caves and springs of Jerusalem. These stories are found in every phase of Jewish life, starting with the Bible, and including rabbinic literature, Jewish folklore, Jewish mystical texts, hasidic tales, and the oral tales collected in recent years.

It was not King David's fate to live to see the building of the Temple, although the dream to build it was his. It was Solomon's accomplishment to complete the Temple. There are numerous tales about the building of the Temple, such as one in the Talmud about how King Solomon captured Ashmodai, the king of demons, and kept him imprisoned until the Temple was complete.[13] So too is there an early tale in *The Testament of Solomon* about a vampire demon that victimized the son of the chief builder in order to distract his father and prevent him from completing the building of the Temple.[14]

There is also a lovely folktale about the building of the walls of the Temple that was collected by Zev Vilnay, the great expert on the folk traditions of Jerusalem, from a young man he met near the wall. This tale explains how the western wall escaped destruction when the rest of the Temple was torn down.

When the time came for King Solomon to build the Temple, he called everyone together—the rich and the poor, the princes and the priests—and he said: "People of Israel, let us build a splendid Temple in Jerusalem in honor of God. And since the Temple will be the holy place of all the people, all of the people should share in building it. Therefore you will cast lots to decide which wall you will build."

So King Solomon prepared four lots. On one he wrote North, on another South, on the third East, and on the last West. Then he had each group choose one of them. In this way, it was decided that the princes would build the northern wall as well as the pillars and the stairs of the Temple. And the priests would build the southern wall and tend the Ark and weave its curtain. As for the wealthy merchants, they were to build the eastern wall as well as supply the oil that would burn for the Eternal Light. The job of building the western wall, as well as weaving the Temple's curtains, fell to the poor people, who also were to pray for the Temple's completion. Then the building began.

The merchants took the golden jewelry of their wives and sold it to pay workers to build the wall for them, and soon it was finished. Likewise the princes and the priests found ways to have their walls built for them. But the poor people had to build the wall themselves, so it took them much longer.

Every day the poor came to the site of the Temple, and they worked with their own hands to build the western wall. And all the time they worked on it, their hearts were filled with joy, for their love of God was very great.

At last the Temple was finished, as beautiful as the Temple on high. Nothing in the world could compare with it, for it was the jewel in the crown of Jerusalem. And after that, whenever the poor people went to the Temple, fathers would say to their sons, "Do you see that stone in the wall? I put it there with my own hands." And mothers would say to their daughters, "Do you see that beautiful curtain in the Temple? I wove that curtain myself."

Many years later, when the Temple was destroyed, only the Western Wall was saved, for the angels spread their wings over it. For that wall, built by the poor, was the most precious of all in the eyes of God.

Even today the Western Wall is still standing. Now it is sometimes known as the Wailing Wall, for every morning drops of dew can be seen on its stones, and it is said among the people that the wall was crying at night for the Temple that was torn down.

And, as everyone who has been there can testify, God's presence can still be felt in that place.[15]

There are many accounts of miracles and visions associated with the Temple, for both in its presence and its absence, the Temple in Jerusalem has always been central to the holiness of the city. One of the most famous visions, as recounted in the Talmud, was that of the high priest who was said to have seen God on Yom Kippur, inside the Holy of Holies:

Once, when Rabbi Ishmael ben Elisha, the High Priest, went into the Holy of Holies of the Temple, he looked up and saw Akatriel Yah, the Lord of Hosts, seated on a high and exalted throne. And the Lord spoke to him and said: "Ishmael, My son, bless me." And Rabbi Ishmael raised his hands in a blessing and said: "May it be Your will that Your mercy overcomes Your justice, and may Your children be blessed with Your compassion." And when Rabbi Ishmael raised his eyes, the Lord inclined His head toward him.[16]

The Temple was twice destroyed: once in 586 B.C.E. by the Babylonians, who were led by Nebuchadnezzar and carried the Israelites into captivity, and again in 70 C.E. by the Romans. In Jewish folklore these two catastrophes blur into one, especially since both were said to have taken place on the 9th of Av. All that remains is the *Kotel,* the Western Wall, the last retaining wall of the Temple. There are many heart-wrenching midrashim about the destruction of the Temple, especially in Lamentations Rabbah. One of the most moving is found in the Talmud and concerns the High Priest:

The Temple in Jerusalem had been set aflame, and the moment of destruction had arrived. The High Priest went up to the roof, the keys of the Temple in his hand. There he called out: "Master of the Universe! The time has come to return these keys to You." Then he threw the keys high into the air, and at that instant a hand reached down from above and caught them and brought them back into heaven.[17]

The destruction of the second Temple was the beginning of a very long exile from Jerusalem, which did not end until Jerusalem was captured by the Israeli forces in the 1967 war. Throughout most of Jewish history, the Jewish people have been trying to get back to Jerusalem. That's why "Next year in Jerusalem!" is said at the end of the Seder and on Yom Kippur, and those who were able to fulfill this injunction were traditionally considered among the blessed.

This longing for Jerusalem found expression in a multitude of tales about quests to the Holy City. In addition to the account of quest found in "A Vision at the Wailing Wall," there is another story about the Ari and a mystical journey to Jerusalem:

> It is told that one day Rabbi Isaac Luria of Safed, known as the Ari, was meditating in a field with his disciples. Suddenly he turned to them and declared that they must set out for Jerusalem at once. The disciples were taken aback, but half of them had such perfect faith in the Ari that they stood up, ready to depart. But the others grew afraid. After all, they had not told their families, nor had they made any preparations for the journey. They begged the Ari to give them enough time to do these things before they departed. And the Ari looked at them, broken-hearted, and said: "I heard a *bat kol*, a heavenly voice, proclaim that if we undertake a journey to Jerusalem at once, without the slightest hesitation, the footsteps of the Messiah will soon be heard. But just as you raised your objections, I heard the voice say that the chance to bring the Messiah had been lost." [18]

Even though the Ari lived in the holy city of Safed, it is clear from this tale that in his eyes Jerusalem was an even holier city and that undertaking a quest to Jerusalem, at that moment, without hesitation, would have initiated the messianic era. Note that this tale implicitly links Jerusalem with the coming of the Messiah, and many tales about Jerusalem have such messianic overtones. The primary link of the Messiah to Jerusalem concerns the rebuilding of the Temple, which, it is said, will take place in the messianic era.

An incident a few years ago served as a reminder of the messianic link to Jerusalem. It was reported widely that three of the most prominent rabbis in Mea Sha'arim in Jerusalem had dreamed, on the same night, that the Messiah was about to come. This incident sent a messianic shudder through all the hasidim and many other observant Jews, who had already identified the Russian war in Afghanistan as the War of Gog and Magog that would precede the coming of the Messiah. This messianic fervor was only calmed when two of the three rabbis announced that they had not had any messianic dreams after all.

The heavenly Jerusalem is the subject of many fine tales, including the following hasidic tale told about the Kotzker Rebbe. Here we have another kind of quest to Jerusalem—a heavenly journey to the celestial Jerusalem. The story is called "The Ocean of Tears" and was transmitted by Rabbi Shlomo Carlebach:

> For Rabbi Menachem Mendel of Kotzk, known as the Kotzker Rebbe, truth was the most important thing. So dedicated to truth was he that he spent the last twenty years of his life in his study, which he seldom left and where he

only rarely received visitors. One of these guests was his closest friend, Reb Yitzhak of Vorki. So close were they that Reb Yitzhak named his younger son (later his successor as Rebbe in Vorki) Menachem Mendel, after his friend. Father and son were very close and were always seen together. And if Reb Yitzhak had to leave his son to go on a journey, they would write to each other every day. Then it happened that Reb Yitzhak died, and his son Mendele could not be consoled, but he still expected to hear from his father in some way. However, no message came, not even in a dream. So a month after his father's death, Mendele went to visit the Kotzker Rebbe to ask why no word had come from his father.

The Rabbi of Kotzk said: "Mendele, I share your grief over the death of your father, for he was my closest friend. And I, too, expected him to contact me from the world to come, and I was surprised that he did not. And since he was not coming to me, I decided to go to him.

"Therefore I pronounced a holy name and my soul flew up to heaven. I ascended all the way to the Jerusalem on high. For just as there is a city of Jerusalem in the Holy Land, so too is there one in heaven. Now I knew that all of his days your father longed to be in Jerusalem, and I was certain that I would find him there.

"Before long I found myself standing before the celestial Temple, suspended in the heavens above. For although the Temple on earth was torn down long ago, the celestial Temple still exists. There I saw angels entering and departing in great numbers, and I went to them and asked if they had seen Reb Yitzhak. And they said yes, he had been there, but he had left.

"So I left there and flew through all the palaces of heaven. For all of the great prophets and sages have their own palaces in the world to come, where they continue to teach the Torah. I went to the palace of Rashi, the great commentator. And there I was told that yes, your father had been there, but he had left.

"Then I rose up through the palaces of Maimonides, of Rabbi Akiba, and even those of Moses and Abraham. And everywhere I went I asked if they had seen Reb Yitzhak, and they always told me that yes, he had been there, but he had left.

"Finally I called upon the angel Gabriel, and from him I learned that if I wanted to find your father, I would have to search for him in a dark forest at the ends of the earth. So I girded my strength and entered that endless forest. And all the while I wondered what your father was seeking in that dark place.

"For what felt like a lifetime, I made my way through that forest. Then, when I reached the end of it, I saw the strangest sight—a mighty ocean, with waves that rose up very high, and as they rose and fell they made a sobbing sound. And there, by the shore, I saw Reb Yitzhak, leaning on a staff. And I said: 'Yitzhak, it is me, Mendel. I have found you at last!'

"And your father said: 'Mendel, come here! I have something to show you.' And when I stood beside him, he pointed to the ocean and said: 'Do you know what ocean this is?' I turned to that strange ocean, and saw how high the waves rose up, and heard its moaning and sighing. And I said: 'No, never have I seen such an ocean. What ocean is it?'

"And Reb Yitzhak said: 'Know that this is the Ocean of Tears—of all the tears shed by Israel. And the waves of this ocean cry out to God, and that is why there is the sound of sobbing. I could have spent eternity in the heavenly Jerusalem, but I have vowed never to leave this place until God dries all the tears. I have been praying day and night. Will you pray with me?'

"Of course, I said yes. So your father and I prayed together. Never have I prayed so hard. Tears fell from our eyes into the ocean of tears. And then a miracle took place, for each time one of our tears fell into the ocean, the waters went down a little further, until, at last, the ocean was dry.

"Then, all at once, a great rainbow filled the heavens, the most beautiful rainbow I had ever seen. The sight of that rainbow filled me with hope, for I was certain it was the same rainbow that Noah had seen.

"Then I knew it was time to take my leave of your father, and return to this world. We embraced, and he asked me to assure you that you would be hearing from him very soon."

Now when young Mendele heard these words, he wept tears of joy. And that night he dreamed that he and his father were standing together inside the celestial Temple in the heavenly Jerusalem, surrounded by joyful sages and angels. And a wonderful light shone from his father's face.[19]

Another account of a holy quest to Jerusalem was collected by the Israel Folktale Archives, founded 40 years ago by Professor Dov Noy of Hebrew University, which today has collected 20,000 oral tales from every Jewish ethnic community in Israel. This tale, from Poland, like so many tales concerning the Messiah, explains why the Messiah has not yet come:

Eighty years ago, in a Polish *yeshivah*, there were two students who were filled with a longing for redemption. Both of them were eager to travel to the Holy Land, and they especially wanted to see King David's tomb. They dreamed about it day and night, and at last they decided to set out on the journey, even though they didn't have any money. On the way they met with many obstacles, but at last they arrived at the Holy City of Jerusalem. They were thrilled to have arrived there safe and sound, but they did not know how to find King David's tomb. While they were wondering where it was, Elijah the Prophet appeared before them in the form of an old man and showed them the way. And when they reached the foot of Mount Zion, Elijah said:

"Now my sons, ascend Mount Zion until you reach the entrance of King David's tomb, and enter there and go down the steps, until you reach the bottom of the tomb. There you will be blinded by visions of gold, silver, and diamonds. These are only illusions, set to tempt you from your purpose. Ignore them and search for the jug of water at the head of King David. That jug contains water from the Garden of Eden. Pour the water from that jug over the hands of King David as he stretches his hands toward you. Pour the water three times over each hand, and then King David will rise up and the footsteps of the Messiah will be heard in the world. For King David is not dead; he lives and exists. He is only asleep and dreaming, and he will arise when we are worthy of it. By your virtue and merit, he will arise and redeem us. Amen, and may this come to pass."

When Elijah finished these words, he disappeared. The young men then ascended Mount Zion and went down into the depths of King David's tomb. Everything was just as Elijah had said it would be. They saw King David stretched out on a couch, with a jug of water at his head. And when they reached King David, he stretched out his hands to them. But just then the young men were blinded by all the riches they saw in that tomb, and they forgot to pour water onto the king's outstretched hands. In anguish his hands fell back, and immediately the king's image disappeared.

The young men were startled when they realized that they had let the opportunity for redemption slip through their fingers, and now it was too late.[20]

This is one of many tales about King David being alive. All of them grow out of the famous song, *"Dovid Melekh Yisrael, hai hai vikayom"*—David, King of Israel, lives and exists. And in a sense it is true. King David's presence in Jerusalem is so vivid that it seems impossible to believe that he is not alive. For among those awaiting the days of the redemption, when the footsteps of the Messiah will be heard, it is equally impossible not to believe that someone righteous enough will merely have to pour water from the Garden of Eden over King David's hands and he will wake up.

PART IV

Modern Jewish Literature
and the Ancient Models

Rabbi Nachman of Bratslav

Forerunner of Modern Jewish Literature

The emergence, in the present era, of a flourishing modern Jewish literature was made possible by the evolution from a sacred written tradition to a consciously literary, secular one. A key figure in this transition was
the hasidic master Rabbi Nachman of Bratslav (1772–1811). From his mother's side, Rabbi Nachman was the great-grandson of the Baal Shem Tov,
founder of hasidism. From his father's side, Nachman was a descendent of
the famous Rabbi Judah Loew of Prague, known as the Maharal, to whom
legend attributes the creation of the Golem, a man made out of clay. Thus
from his birth the greatest expectations were held for Rabbi Nachman, and
in light of these it is not surprising that he believed from a young age that
his destiny was a great one, perhaps even messianic in nature.

In the 17th century there had been a great messianic uproar centered
around Shabbatai Zevi, who ultimately proved to be a false messiah by
converting, under duress, to Islam. But before that happened, hundreds of
thousands of euphoric Jews made preparations to sell their possessions and
follow him to the Land of Israel. Unlike Shabbatai Zevi, Rabbi Nachman
never openly declared a messianic role for himself,[1] nor did he succeed in
acquiring more than a small circle of hasidim who accepted him as a *tzaddik*, much less a messianic figure. Yet since his death Rabbi Nachman's
importance has continued to grow so that he now stands as one of the most
highly regarded figures of hasidism after the Baal Shem Tov.

Rabbi Nachman's teachings are profound and prolific, but the primary
reason for his importance in the eyes of the world can be found in the tales
that he told, for in the last years of his life Rabbi Nachman chose to clothe
his teachings in the garb of fairy tales about unhappy kings, lost princesses,

and loyal ministers. Despite their apparent simplicity, however, these tales are actually complex and mysterious allegories. Thus Nachman was the first rebbe to make the telling of tales the primary method of conveying his teachings. While previous hasidic masters, including the Baal Shem Tov, had been the subject of a rich body of miracle tales, and some masters, such as the Baal Shem Tov and Rabbi Levi Yitzhak of Berditchev, told occasional brief parables, none had made a practice of telling tales as a primary method of instruction. But this is precisely what Rabbi Nachman did in the last four years of his life, and these tales have achieved international renown and now exist in English in several translations.[2]

The reasons that led Rabbi Nachman to begin retelling tales are veiled in mystery, but some surmises can be made. During most of his life Rabbi Nachman alternated between periods in which he felt a mythic sense of destiny and all-pervasive meaning and periods of deep despair and the sense that he knew nothing. Eventually, he came to regard these periods of despair as inevitable and even incorporated them into his vision, teaching that a descent must precede every ascent. With such teachings Nachman came to function almost as a therapist to his disciples, leading them through the depths as well as to the heights. Even after the death of his young son, Shlomo Ephraim, and the abandonment of any messianic aspirations he may have held either for himself or his son, Nachman did not retreat into silence, but discovered a new form of expression for his messianic impulses—the tales he began to tell in his final years. It is in these tales that Rabbi Nachman finally embraced his true destiny.

Since Jewish folklore had flourished as an oral tradition among the common folk (if not among the rabbis) from at least the early Middle Ages, it was not an illogical mode of expression for Rabbi Nachman. However, it must be remembered that this folklore had never achieved anything like the status of the various sacred literatures, and not until the late Middle Ages was any effort made to record these tales. Eventually some of them were preserved in collections that became widely known, such as *The Ma'aseh Book* and *Tze'enah U-Re'enah.*

It is apparent, however, that despite the low status of folklore, and its universal as opposed to specifically Jewish character, Rabbi Nachman felt drawn to this mode of expression in a powerful way. One clue for this attraction can be found in the dreams of Rabbi Nachman that have been preserved. The most striking quality is their similarity to his tales, as in the following excerpt:

> As I ascended the mountain, I saw a golden tree with branches of gold. From the branches hung all sorts of vessels that were like those depicted in the book. Inside those vessels were other vessels that were made out of these vessels and the letters in them. I wanted to take these vessels from there, but I couldn't because the thicket did not permit me to go through.[3]

Often these dreams also seem like condensed versions of one of Nachman's epic tales, such as "The Master of Prayer"[4] or "The Seven Beggars,"[5]
as the following dream, recorded in its entirety, demonstrates:

> In my dream I woke up in a forest. The forest was boundless; I wanted to
> return. Someone came to me and said: "This forest is so long it is infinite.
> All the instruments and the vessels of this world are made from this forest."
> He showed me a way out of the forest, which brought me to a river. I wanted
> to reach the end of the river. A man came to me and said: "This river is
> endless. All the people of this world drink from this river." Then he showed
> me a mill that stood at the side of the river, and someone came to me and
> said: "All the food for all the people in the world is ground in this mill."
> Then I reentered the forest, and there I saw a smith working, and they told
> me: "This smith makes the vessels for the whole world."[6]

Such dreams raise the possibility that Rabbi Nachman based his tales on
his dreams, elaborating on them in the retelling. However, it is not possible
to confirm this hypothesis, since none of the surviving dreams contains
material that was directly incorporated into the tales.

Most of all, the essential qualities of the enchanted world of fairy tales,
with its solutions that inevitably draw on the magical and the ability of the
good to prevail despite the odds, were all enormously appealing to Rabbi
Nachman and reflect his own world vision, in which the power of faith can
surmount any obstacle.

The tale "The Lost Princess," for example, has as its primary motif a
theme that commonly reappears in world folklore as a quest in which a
prince sets out to rescue a princess who has fallen under an evil spell.[7] For
the uninitiated, this tale is simply one more variant on a common theme.
But among Rabbi Nachman's hasidim it was understood that this and all of
Rabbi Nachman's tales contain meanings hidden from all but those who
knew how to seek them out. Thus among the Bratslav hasidim, Rabbi Nachman's tales are regarded as sacred texts and are subjected to the same thorough exegesis as are the sacred Scriptures.[8]

In *Sichos ha-Ran* Rabbi Nachman is quoted by Rabbi Nathan, his scribe,
as saying: "Even a *tzaddik* who searches after lost things is himself sometimes lost, as it is written: *They shall search and be lost* (Ps. 83:18)."[9] This
statement reveals the personal dimension of "The Lost Princess"—that
Rabbi Nachman identified with the loyal minister who devotes his life to
the quest of finding the lost princess. Rabbi Nachman's statement about the
lost *tzaddik* is also a comment on the inevitable obstacles that must be
overcome for a successful ascent.

It is also apparent that Rabbi Nachman made use of common folk motifs
in his tales in part because he recognized the biblical archetypes glimmer-
ing beneath the surface of the traditional fairy tale and had found a way to

relate these folk motifs to his hasidim by forcing them to consider them from the traditional Jewish perspective. He perceived that in this way his teaching would be revealed to them but would remain concealed from others, who would be misled by the simple surface of the tales.

Even more obviously intended to serve as a commentary on *Ma'aseh Bereshit*, the Work of Creation—that is, the process by which the world came into being—is Rabbi Nachman's famous last tale, "The Seven Beggars."[10] This story has an unusual structure in which seven beggars come to two orphan children who are to be wed, each telling a tale and giving the children a blessing. The number of beggars, as well as the nature of their stories, suggests the seven days of Creation. As in the biblical myth of Creation, the seventh day and the seventh beggar are singled out for particular emphasis. The seventh day, of course, represents the Sabbath, while the seventh beggar may be seen as the representative of the messianic era, if not of the Messiah himself. The tales of the first six beggars are told, but that of the seventh beggar remains mysteriously untold, with the final observation by Rabbi Nathan: "Nor will we be worthy to hear it until the Messiah comes in his mercy, may he come speedily in our days, Amen."

It also seems likely that Rabbi Nachman intended each of the beggars to represent one of the biblical patriarchs. Thus the blind beggar represents Isaac, who was blind; the deaf beggar represents Abraham, who was deaf to the noise of the world, so intently was he concentrated on the Covenant between God and himself; the beggar who stuttered represents Moses, who describes himself in the Torah as *slow of speech, and of a slow tongue* (Ex. 4:10); the beggar with the crooked neck represents Aaron, brother of Moses and the first high priest of Israel—as the high priest his duty is to unite Israel and God, and his affliction focuses on the neck, which links the head (God) to the rest of the body (Israel); the hunchbacked beggar represents Jacob, whose hunchback symbolizes the power of "the small which contains the great," just as Jacob is identified in the *Aggadah* as the pillar that supports the entire world; the beggar with no hands represents Joseph, a master of the spiritual powers sometimes associated with the hands (keeping in mind that each beggar explains that he does not in fact suffer from his deformity, quite the opposite); and the seventh beggar, who has no feet, can be seen as the representative of the Messiah, who has not yet come—when he is about to arrive we will enter the era of the "footsteps of the Messiah."

The clearest indication of the concern of this tale with *Ma'aseh Bereshit* comes in the tale of the blind beggar. He recounts a meeting of those whose memories reached back to the early phases of Creation. One remembers "the moment when they plucked the apple from the branch"; the second recalls "the moment that the candle burned"; the third the precise "moment when the fruit was formed"; the fourth "the moment that they extracted the seed to plant the fruit"; the fifth "the wise men who discovered the seed"; the sixth "the taste of the fruit before it entered the fruit"; and the seventh "the appearance of the fruit before it attached itself to the fruit." The beggar who is telling the story has a memory that reaches back even further, to "the time before there was anything—that is the Void." In this sequence Rabbi Nachman suggests the nine stages of emanation of the kabbalistic *Sefirot* that brought the world into being. The tenth stage, which precedes all of the others, goes unremarked because it is that of *Ein Sof*, that aspect of God that remains hidden and unknown from every man. These stages of emanation are the kabbalistic equivalent of the seven days of Creation, although they are far more abstract and obscure. The fact that this tale within a tale is the first to be told emphasizes its role as an allegory about Creation and of the importance of understanding of the mysteries of Creation, which are particularly difficult to comprehend.

Further kabbalistic allegories are to be found in the tales "The Portrait,"[11] "The Royal Messenger,"[12] "The Letter,"[13] and "The Tale of the Menorah."[14] In "The Portrait" a king collects portraits of all the great kings, and seeks the portrait of a king who represents God. The central symbol of "The Portrait" is clearly intended to designate the *Pargod*, the curtain referred to in kabbalistic literature behind which the Holy One sits on His Throne of Glory. This symbol thus personifies the hidden aspects of God, known as *Ein Sof*. In the early *Hekhalot* texts, recounting journeys to Paradise, and in the later kabbalistic texts, the *Pargod* is described in great detail. The side facing God is, of course, hidden, but all souls are said to be woven into the other side, facing the angels, which has been described as a kind of archetypal screen on which flickers all of past and future destiny.

The primary purpose of the *Pargod* is to serve as a reminder that complete knowledge of the Divinity is beyond the capacity of humans; they may travel so far, all the way into Paradise, but they can never probe the mystery of God Himself. Not even the angels are permitted to know that aspect of God; only the *Shekhinah*, the Divine Presence and Bride of God, and the supreme angel, Metatron, are permitted behind the *Pargod*.

Rabbi Nachman's ability to integrate kabbalistic concepts into the straightforward and essentially simple fairy-tale narrative was possible because he seemed instinctively to comprehend the personal psychic dimensions of both. He seems to have recognized how each has its source in the inner world and its own laws, which are quite independent of those of the "real" world. Furthermore he seems to have understood, as have psychologists since Jung, the nature of the psychological process of projection. Certainly for this kind of literature to succeed, it is necessary for the author to somehow descend into his unconscious and to report back the mythic and archetypal drama as it is reflected there. Nachman perceived, for example, that the exile of the *Shekhinah* concerned him in the most personal way possible. The *Shekhinah* was not only lost to Israel as a whole, but also to him individually, and it was possible and necessary to set off on the quest to restore the *Shekhinah* to her former position of glory. The quest described in "The Lost Princess," then, is not just a fairy-tale quest or an allegory of the exile of the *Shekhinah* (although it is both), but it must be understood as a mirror of a crucial drama of the psyche. The ability of Rabbi Nachman to personalize these mythic elements of Judaism by transmuting them into the universal language of fairy tales was a bold act with profound implications.

This suggests the process by which the myth of the *Shekhinah* evolved in the first place and one possible approach of the modern reader to a literature making use of such symbolic figures. Starting with a psychic truth, such as the existence of the anima, the Jewish myth projects the presence of such a figure who is concerned with the people as a whole, just as a man's own anima is concerned with his spiritual and emotional life. The modern reader might then be well advised to attempt to relate to his or her own psychic reality the mythological projections that were the starting points of this mythology in the first place. This is not an intellectual process, but a spiritual and emotional one. What it requires, above all, is that the reader be open to the psychic truths that serve as the foundation for the entire aggadic tradition. Then the mythology that finds its first expression in the Bible and is cultivated throughout all subsequent Jewish literature will once again exercise its compelling power, making possible a personal contact not only to the tradition itself, but also to all the generations that have received and transmitted it until this time.

This link between kabbalistic thinking and the theory of archetypal symbolism as proposed by Jung[15] is strongly prefigured in Rabbi Nachman's tale "The Portrait." The concept of the archetype is itself clearly defined in this tale:[16]

> Now there is a country that contains within it all countries. And in that country there is a city that contains all the cities of that country that contains all countries. And in that city there is a house that contains all houses of that city that contains all the cities of that country that contains all countries. And in that house is a man who bears all this within him.

In "The Portrait" the king represents, of course, the Holy One who "is hidden from men. He sits behind a curtain and is far from the people of his land." This king's distance, which has the effect of causing distortions of the truth among his people, is a source of mystery and confusion. No one possesses the portrait of this king because it is impossible to obtain. Yet, paradoxically, at the end of the tale "the face of the king was revealed, and the wise men saw him." This does not mean to imply that the most hidden and recondite secrets of the Divinity will be revealed to those who steep themselves in the mysteries of the Kabbalah, but rather that immersion in these mysteries makes possible a knowledge about the Divinity previously impossible among men.

The key revelation is that the king "cannot bear the lies of the kingdom." God is pained by falsehood and imperfection in the world, although, ironically, it exists because of His distance from His Creation. This paradox, which cannot be resolved simply, is at the core of Rabbi Nachman's complex vision of existence, and of the eternal kabbalistic vision itself, in which the further the distance from *Ein Sof*, the hidden aspect of God, the further the distance from the source of Truth itself, and the greater the distortions that come into being.

At the end of Rabbi Nachman's tale "The Spider and the Fly"[17] is another passage that defines, for all practical purposes, the inexhaustible aspect of the concept of archetype (symbolized by the image worn by the maiden) and the fact that it is essentially independent of the vessel through which it expresses itself:

> He saw that among the myriads of prisoners he had taken there was a beautiful maiden. The maiden possessed every loveliness that was to be found on earth, the beauty of the form that was felt as sweet water under the fingers, the beauty of the eyes that was as a caress of the hands, and the beauty that is heard like the sound of bells touched by the wind. But when the king looked upon her, he saw that her beauty was not her own, but that it came forth like a perfume out of the tiny image that she wore upon herself. And it was this image that contained all forms of beauty, and because it was upon her, it seemed that all those forms of beauty were her own.

The tale "The Royal Messenger"[18] is focused on the question of the existence of God: "The king had sent a letter to a wise but skeptical man, who, in his faraway province, refused to accept it." The quest to the end of the world to discover if the king actually exists represents the extensive kabbalistic quest for knowledge of the Divinity. Despite evidence of the greatness of the king, the skeptical man remains unsatisfied that proof of the king's existence has been given.

This tale is enhanced by comparison with Nachman's tale "The Letter,"[19] an allegory about a prince who receives a letter and recognizes the handwriting of his father, the king:

> Once there was a prince who was separated from his father, the king, in his youth, and lived in a land far from his homeland. There he greatly yearned to be reunited with his father, so far away. But because of the great distance that separated them, this was not possible at that time. So it was that many years passed without any messages between the prince and his father. Then one day, to the prince's great joy, he received a letter from the king. This letter had traveled to him over a great distance, and the messenger had overcome many obstacles to see that it reached the prince's hand. The prince read the letter as if in a dream, so vividly did it evoke his father's presence. And when he had finished reading it, his heart was filled with longing to see his father again. And he thought to himself: "If I could only see my father now. If I could only touch his hand!" And while he harbored these longings,

a thought crossed his mind: "Do I not have my father's letter? And was this letter not written in his very own hand? And is not the handwriting not unlike the very hand that penned it?" And with this thought he held the letter close to him and said over and over to himself: "The handwriting of the king—the hand of the king."

Also related is "The Portrait," previously discussed, about the king who lives behind a curtain and thus cannot be seen. In "The Letter" and "The Portrait" the nonappearance of the king is not a source for skepticism about his existence, but in "The Royal Messenger" the difficulty of accepting the paradox of a God who must remain hidden, and thus ultimately unknown, is presented in its most powerful form, with the skeptic receiving the final word.

Both "The Royal Messenger" and "The Letter" have a remarkable parallel to Franz Kafka's famous parable "An Imperial Message,"[20] which they preceded by more than a hundred years. In Kafka's parable an emperor gives his deathbed message to his faithful messenger to deliver "to you, the humble subject, the significant shadow cowering in the remotest distance before the Imperial sun; the Emperor from his deathbed has sent a message to you alone." Due to insurmountable obstacles, it becomes impossible for this message to be delivered, so that the reader remains uncertain as to whether the message actually has been sent; whether, indeed, the Emperor and the messenger even exist; or whether the "humble subject" has merely daydreamed the whole incident.

In Kafka's parable, as well as those of Rabbi Nachman, one likely meaning is that which proposes that the emperor or king is intended to represent God. The letter sent may be identified as the Torah, containing all truth, or as the very existence of the world around us. In Kafka's parable the "humble subject" in a remote corner of the kingdom deeply believes in the existence of the letter, and that the Emperor sent it to him as his dying act, and that but for the obstacles, "If he [the messenger] could reach the open fields how fast he would fly, and soon doubtless you would hear the welcome hammering of his fists on your door." In Nachman's "The Royal Messenger," on the other hand, the letter arrives, but the recipient pays no attention to its contents, instead concerning himself solely with the question of the existence of the author of the letter. We suspect that Kafka's peasant would not have been assailed by these doubts! But the most fortunate of all is the prince in "The Letter," who recognizes the handwriting of his father, that is, the *tzaddik* who recognizes the Creator through His Creation. Thus in these three parables the essence of the worldviews ranges from the total belief in the existence of but inability to receive the message sent by God to man ("An Imperial Message"), to doubt in the existence of the Creator, despite evidence to the contrary ("The Royal Messenger"). These parables can be seen to represent, respectively, the views of the believers ("The Letter"), the religious existentialists ("An Imperial Message"), and the atheists ("The Royal Messenger").

In general, Rabbi Nachman's view is closest to that held by the prince in "The Letter"—he has recognized the Creator and His Creation. It is natural, then, that the key figure reappearing in Rabbi Nachman's tales is the *tzaddik*, the spiritual guide that every rebbe sought to be to his hasidim. Certainly the central figure of the Master of Prayer in the story of the same title is clearly intended to be such a *tzaddik*. It is the clarity of vision of the Master of Prayer that enables the initial confusion of the world in this tale to be eventually overcome. Likewise, the tale "Harvest of Madness"[21] emphasizes the necessity that the *tzaddik* retain his clarity of vision even if he seems to be mad in the eyes of the world. Here the king and his counselor are the only ones spared the general madness brought on by a tainted harvest. This tale is identical in theme to a Sufi folktale collected by Idries Shah in *Tales of the Dervishes*.[22] The only difference is that in the Sufi tale the madness is carried by water, rather than wheat. The Sufi tale, which Shah calls "When the Waters Were Changed," concerns a warning given that on a certain date all the waters in the world that had not been specially preserved would disappear, to be renewed with different water, which would drive men mad. Only one man listens to this warning and stores water for himself. And when the waters stop flowing and then begin to flow again, he finds that men have begun to think in an entirely different way and have lost their memories of what has happened. They regard this last sane man as mad, and the resulting isolation leads him, eventually, to drink from the new water, despite the consequences, because he cannot bear the loneliness of being different from everyone else. After he does drink of their water he becomes like everyone else, and they regard him as a madman who has been restored to his sanity.

Another tale dealing with madness and sanity is "The Prince Who Thought He Was a Rooster."[23] Here a prince who has been given up as mad is finally restored to sanity by the action of the wise man who pretends to share his madness and, gaining his confidence in this way, eventually influences him to function again as a human being. In his own comment on this tale Rabbi Nachman makes it clear that the story is intended as an allegory of the role of the *tzaddik*, who must be prepared to descend to the level of those he hopes to influence: "In this way must the genuine teacher go down to the level of his people if he wishes to raise them up to their proper place."

A further kabbalistic allegory is found in Rabbi Nachman's "The Tale of the Menorah,"[24] which illustrates the central kabbalistic concept of *tikkun*, of redemption and restoration. In Rabbi Nachman's tale the son constructs his menorah out of the defects of those who observe it. We may assume that the craftsman is familiar with those before whom he demonstrates his skills. The primary purpose of the menorah in this tale is to make these others aware of their own defects, since this awareness is the first and most essential step before the act of *tikkun* can take place. In this way the menorah serves symbolically as the *tzaddik* should serve his hasidim—making them aware of their defects so that they can begin the process of *tikkun*. This reading of the tale can be summarized in the talmudic phrase "Anyone who finds a flaw finds his own flaw."[25]

Rabbi Zalman Schachter, however, suggests another way of approaching this tale. His view can be summed up in what might be called "The Tale of the Opal": An opal's most distinguishing feature is the fire in its center, but this fire is also its flaw. When seen from one angle, the fire resembles nothing more than a crack, but from another perspective it is the most beautiful part of the opal. Thus what appears to be the defect in the menorah is what makes it unique and more beautiful. Rabbi Schachter feels that this interpretation, which emphasizes Rabbi Nachman's belief in the essential polarity of existence, preserves the complexity of his vision.

The craftsman who creates the menorah may also be seen to represent God, while the menorah is God's Creation, the world. In such a reading the seven branches of the menorah may be seen as the seven days of Creation described in Genesis 1:1–24. In this case the light of the flames on the menorah can be identified with the primordial light that came into existence on the first day, when God said *Let there be light, and there was light* (Gen. 1:3).[26] If this tale is read as an allegory of the Creation of the world, Rabbi Nachman may be seen to be saying that the defects are the defects of this world and that God created the world out of the defects in it. Nor does this conflict with the traditional view of Creation, since *God formed man out of the dust of the earth* (Gen. 2:6).

It is interesting to note that Rabbi Nachman, as well as being a forerunner of the modern Jewish literary tradition, was also one of the very last great figures in the oral tradition. For him the *ma'aseh* could only be told orally, but fortunately these tales have been preserved because he was blessed with a highly responsible *sofer*, or scribe, Rabbi Nathan (Nussan) of Nemirov. It is as if Rabbi Nachman's soul had its source in the oral tradition, while Rabbi Nathan's derived from the written, for their mutual effort was required in order to bring Rabbi Nachman's tales back from the highest heavens, where his hasidim believed he received them.

That Rabbi Nachman was willing to permit his tales to undergo the folk process in which the tale is never told twice in exactly the same fashion is apparent by his decision, on occasion, to tell the tales on a Friday night. During the Sabbath, of course, the ban against writing was in effect, and it was therefore necessary for Rabbi Nachman's hasidim to retell the tale among themselves many times in order not to lose any of it, until the Sabbath came to an end. Only then could Nathan write down the tale, already likely to have undergone the process of recasting that naturally occurs with every retelling.

That the Bratslav hasidim believed that Rabbi Nachman had the stature of the ancient patriarchs and prophets, and that his storytelling was a continuation of an unbroken tradition, is demonstrated in this remarkable prayer, which they invoked before the telling of tales:

> Master of the Universe, Thou workest wonders in every generation through the true *tzaddikim* of every generation, as our fathers have related to us, all the great deeds and wonders and great miracles that Thou hast performed in each generation through Thy true *tzaddikim* from the beginning of time unto this day. In this generation too there are *tzaddikim* and true wonder-workers. Therefore may Thou in Thine abundant mercy grant and help me and strengthen and animate me so that I may be worthy to tell the tales of the true *tzaddikim*, of all that happened to them in their days, both to them and their children, and all the great and awe-inspiring wonders and signs that they performed both in secret and in public, and all the holiness and revelation of God that they effected in the world; all this may I merit to hear well with my ears and heart, and meditate and always retell them.[27]

Before his death Rabbi Nachman directed his hasidim to burn a box of his writings. Rabbi Nachman's first disciple, Shimon, carried out this order right after Rabbi Nachman's death, as Rabbi Nathan describes with obvious distress:

> Before Rabbi Nachman departed from this world, he left instructions to burn all his writings which, secreted in a special box, no one had been permitted to read. Immediately after his soul left him and his clothes were being removed, Rabbi Shimon hastened to open the box, took out all the hidden manuscripts, carried them to the stove, built a fire, and consigned them to the flames. I followed after him, in order to sniff the sacred fumes of the awesome Torah whose enjoyment was denied to our generation.[28]

On his deathbed, Rabbi Nachman is said to have directed his hasidim not to appoint a successor, for he would always be their rebbe.[29] The Bratslav hasidim have scrupulously observed this request, and although hasidim traditionally appoint a new rebbe upon the death of the old one, they have never named a successor to Rabbi Nachman. For this reason they are sometimes called "the dead hasidim." They regard Rabbi Nachman's teachings, and especially his tales, as sacred texts, as precious as the Torah or the Talmud. And every year, on the *yahrzeit* of Rabbi Nachman's death, his hasidim read his tales out loud in an extended ceremony.

The unusual circumstances relating to Rabbi Nachman's death led to a powerful folk belief about Rabbi Nachman's spirit. The Bratslavers believe that Rabbi Nachman's spirit chose to remain in this world, abandoning its heavenly reward, in order to guard over and guide his followers.

The most famous tale concerning Rabbi Nachman's spirit concerns the fate of his chair. One of Rabbi Nachman's hasidim carved a beautiful chair for him, which he loved. During the Second World War the Bratslavers in Eastern Europe decided to escape to Jerusalem, but they knew they could never smuggle the chair past the Nazis. Nor could they leave it behind. So they decided to cut it into small pieces, and each Bratslaver was given one piece, and they made a vow to meet in Jerusalem and reassemble the chair. And, despite the terrible dangers of that time, every Bratslaver carrying a piece of that chair arrived safely in Jerusalem. Of course, they attributed this miracle to Rabbi Nachman. After that, the chair was reassembled so perfectly that there is no indication it was ever cut apart. It can be found in the Bratslaver synagogue in Jerusalem, located in Mea Sha'arim.[30]

All in all there are an astonishing number of accounts of those who have experienced Rabbi Nachman's benevolent presence, reports not unlike those about Elijah the Prophet that are so common in Jewish folklore. Some of these reports come from non-Bratslaver sources, such as the Israeli writer Yehuda Yaari, who said that while he was working on a retelling of Rabbi Nachman's tales in modern Hebrew, he wrote them down from memory. And he swore that as he wrote, he heard Rabbi Nachman's voice reciting the tales, and like Rabbi Nachman's scribe before him, he wrote down what he heard.

One of the best-known tales about an encounter with Rabbi Nachman's spirit was told by Rabbi Yisrael Odesser.[31] When Reb Yisrael was a young man, he mistakenly ate on the 17th of Tammuz, a fast day, and he became so downcast over this that he considered suicide. But before taking such a terrible step, he decided to use the method of divination known as *Sheilat Sefer*, opening a book at random to see if he could find a reason to live.[32] He closed his eyes and took down a book from the shelf. When he opened it, a letter fell out. When he read the letter he found that it had been sent by Rabbi Nachman to him—from the beyond. In the letter Rabbi Nachman said: "It was very hard for me to descend to you. My precious student, be strong and courageous. My fire will burn until the Messiah comes. As a sign that this letter is true, on the 17th of Tammuz they will say that you are not fasting." The letter was signed with a strange code: *Na-Nach-Nachma-Nachman mi-Uman*—Nachman of Uman, referring to the city in which Rabbi Nachman was buried. During the 1990s this code phrase began to appear, first in the Galilee and then throughout Israel, written in large letters on the roofs of houses and on walls in many public place. It speaks to the ongoing faith in Rabbi Nachman and his wandering spirit among the Bratslaver hasidim, who continue to be guided by their Rebbe even after his death.[33]

After Rabbi Nachman's death the impact of his tales rapidly emerged from the limited circle of Bratslaver hasidim to the world at large. This was in part because of the universal appeal of the tales and in part because Nachman himself came to be recognized as the most charismatic hasidic figure since the Baal Shem Tov; the fact that he was the Baal Shem's great grandson only emphasized this link.[34] Because Rabbi Nachman had chosen to tell his tales in Yiddish (although Nathan, his scribe, later translated them into Hebrew, and the traditional text includes both languages), he had significant influence on the modern Yiddish literary tradition, for with the model of Nachman's broad acceptance in Yiddish literature, Yiddish writers, especially Mendele Mokher-Seforim, Sholom Aleichem, and I. L. Peretz, had the confidence to write their stories in their native tongue. And because their stories were published in the widely circulated Yiddish newspapers of Eastern Europe and Russia, they soon possessed an enviable following among Yiddish-speaking Jews.

The wide currency of Rabbi Nachman's tales also proved influential in other direct and indirect ways. Rabbi Nachman's style was the direct model for Yiddish writers such as Der Nister and Dovid Ignatow.[35] But more important, the break Rabbi Nachman had made with the past by the mere telling of his allegorical fairy tales created an atmosphere in which it was possible to approach the sacred literatures from a consciously literary perspective. It is hard to imagine the career of I. L. Peretz, for example, without the existence of Rabbi Nachman as his predecessor. Peretz was aware, of course, that Rabbi Nachman had been the first to utilize folklore in a literary creation. Peretz himself made good use of the folktales that his friend S. Ansky, author of *The Dybbuk*, gathered in his capacity as one of the first collectors of Jewish folklore.

Above all, it was Rabbi Nachman's ability to sustain a mythological vision of existence "at the meeting place between the truth of the soul and the truth of the cosmos," as Arthur Green states in his exemplary biography of Nachman, *Tormented Master*,[36] that has served to inspire subsequent Jewish authors. For Rabbi Nachman had an intuitive ability to enter into the world of the sacred and to discover the secret by which a mythic kingdom could be made to flourish. That secret he has succeeded in transmitting to his successors, who have acknowledged his role as progenitor and have sought, in turn, to keep the Jewish literary tradition alive.

S. Y. Agnon, I. L. Peretz, and I. B. Singer

Modern Masters of the *Aggadah*

I

All of the categories of sacred and secular literatures have been drawn upon by modern Jewish authors. The two primary literary traditions that have utilized these traditional sources are associated with the primary Jewish languages, Hebrew and Yiddish.[1] Each of these literatures is characterized by two distinct literary approaches: the realistic and the parabolic. The realistic approach, exemplified by writers such as Mendele Mokher-Seforim and Abraham Reisen among Yiddish writers, was largely divorced from the models of traditional Jewish literature.[2] Rather, these writers looked primarily to the trends of the current European literatures and let these serve as their primary models.

The allegorical writers, on the other hand, saw themselves as being directly in the aggadic tradition. Drawing on the various categories of sacred literature, including the rabbinic, folk, and hasidic, these writers, S. Y. Agnon, I. L. Peretz, and I. B. Singer, in particular, sought their models from the past. Of course, they were also familiar with various 20th-century literatures and drew on these sources as well. This conjunction of the ancient and modern proved a fertile meeting ground in which these two rich literatures, the Hebrew and the Yiddish, could each take root. Once again, the tradition demonstrated its flexibility by incorporating the past into the present and the present into the past.

While Hebrew and Yiddish literature each represents a separate literary tradition with its own history and primary figures, there were, in fact, considerable links between the two. Of primary importance was the fact that

many of the Yiddish writers first wrote in Hebrew, and several of the Hebrew writers began in Yiddish. This is true of major figures in both fiction
and poetry, such as I. L. Peretz, whose Hebrew contribution is highly valued, although he is primarily recognized as one of the preeminent Yiddish
writers. S. Y. Agnon, on the other hand, wrote some of his first stories in
Yiddish, and Zalman Shneur made equally valuable contributions in both
languages.

It happened that both the Hebrew and Yiddish literary traditions were
dominated at an early stage by a great master—Agnon[3] in Hebrew literature, and Peretz in Yiddish. Shmuel Yosef Agnon is often included in the
elite circle of great modern authors that includes Franz Kafka, Jorge Luis
Borges, Italo Calvino, and Bruno Schultz. Like the work of these seminal
figures, Agnon's Hebrew writings are visionary and often surreal, even as
they are presented in the stately persona of a modern scribe whose every
word is steeped in tradition. Indeed, Agnon's persona as a writer was as well
cultivated as that of Borges, and like Borges, many of his greatest stories are
written in the first person.

More so, perhaps, than any other modern Jewish writer, Agnon sought
to create a literature that was theologically compatible in all ways with the
ancient tradition. The persona that Agnon projected was that of a devout,
observant Jew steeped solely in the sacred writings, whose technique it was
to borrow and build upon the biblical and aggadic traditions in much the
same way that Israel has built new cities over ancient ones. Because of his
exquisite use of Hebrew and the traditional lore in which he was immersed,
Agnon was able to create a body of texts closer to the spirit of the original,
in terms of style and language, than those created by anyone else in this
century, for they are, in fact, cut from the same cloth.

At the same time, Agnon was also able to write in a visionary, surreal
style, not unlike that of Franz Kafka. Agnon insisted, however, that even
these surreal writings were a logical extension of the traditional sources, and
he strongly resisted the notion that more recent writers had influenced his
style. In particular, he stoutly denied that Kafka's writings had a seminal
influence on his own and went so far as to claim that he had not even read
the works of Kafka.[4]

Agnon wrote both novels and stories and edited two classic anthologies
of rabbinic texts, *Days of Awe* and *Present at Sinai*, both of which have
been translated into English. Among the novels that have been translated
are *The Bridal Canopy*, *A Guest for the Night*, *A Simple Story*, and the
posthumously published *Shira*. In addition, two novellas, *Betrothed* and *Eno
and Enam*, were published as *Two Tales*, and another novella, *In the Heart
of the Seas*, has also been translated. This list of translated works may give
the impression that Agnon was primarily a novelist, but, as with Kafka,
Agnon's true genius lies in his short stories. While only two collections of
Agnon's stories are available in English, *Twenty-one Stories* and *A Book
That Was Lost and Other Stories*, they are sufficient to demonstrate Agnon's

mastery of the form, even in translation, for Agnon's writings, which draw on every stratum of Hebrew literature, are exceptionally difficult to translate. It is not hard to imagine that had Agnon lived a few centuries earlier, and not been exposed to the temptation of writing fiction, he would have been one of the great rabbinic commentators. At the same time a deep skepticism, bordering on religious doubt, is also an essential element in his writings.

Just as Agnon straddles two worlds, one ancient, one modern, in his writings, so he did in his life, where he led the life of an Orthodox Jew while retaining close ties to the less observant literary and scholarly communities, where his closest friends included Gershom Scholem and Martin Buber. Indeed, Buber and Scholem strongly influenced Agnon to move from Berlin to make his home in Jerusalem.

Among Agnon's greatest literary influences was Rabbi Nachman of Bratslav, whose complex fairy tales are interpreted by the Bratslaver hasidim as if they were Torah. Rabbi Nachman pointed the way for Agnon to write sacred tales in a secular world. Also, in Agnon's world, as in Rabbi Nachman's, every act is a symbolic one. In "Agunot," [5] which is generally regarded as Agnon's signature tale, a girl who is betrothed is seduced by the singing of an artist as he builds an ark for a new sanctuary. Although he is expected to dedicate himself to God, he directs his song instead to the impressionable girl. Later, discovering he has gone, she strikes the ark in one fatal moment, and as a result of this symbolic striking out at God, her life and those of many others are turned upside down.

Agnon's clear and intentional use of traditional sources conveys a vision of circular history. His stories fulfill the Passover injunction to relive the Exodus, not merely recall it. In "On One Stone," [6] a writer who is clearly Agnon himself plans to write a story about the stone that opened up for the legendary kabbalist Rabbi Adam Baal Shem, so that he could deposit his manuscript there for safekeeping. At one point the writer has a vision in which he peers into the stone and sees the writing on every page. He goes off to write the story in a forest, where no one will disturb him. Just as he is about to finish it, he sees an old man who is lost and hurries to assist him, leaving the pages behind. Then, just before the Sabbath, he returns to recover his manuscript, only to see it, too, swallowed up by a stone. Yet even in this miraculous recurrence there is an irony, for in this way the writer has lost his story. And it is this balance of reverence and irony that best characterizes Agnon's writings.

This brief story about a story reveals a great deal about Agnon's relationship to the rabbinic sources he drew upon. All of Jewish literature is like an archeological dig, with the writings of each generation built on those of the previous ones, and Agnon was the greatest literary archeologist of all, whose writings transform the ancient Jewish literary tradition into a living, secular one. At the same time, his best works transcend these sources, creating universal fictions that bear the imprint of a literary master.

Agnon's use of sources is well illustrated in his "Fable of the Goat,"[7] which is based on a folktale about a goat that discovers an enchanted cave offering passage directly to and from the Holy Land. The delicious taste of the goat's milk in this tale derives from the fact that it has been grazing in the Holy Land. And when the father, in his mistaken grief, has the goat slaughtered when it returns without his son, he also destroys his link to the Holy Land, and causes the secret location of the enchanted cave to be lost.

The aggadic prototype for this fable is likely to be found in the legends concerning the Cave of Machpelah,[8] in which the bodies of Adam and Eve were said to be buried—perfectly preserved—along with those of the Patriarchs, and which was filled with the aroma of the Garden of Eden, suggesting that the cave was located in the vicinity of the Garden. This belief is directly stated in the Zohar. A parallel motif is also found in the hasidic legend about the journey of the Baal Shem Tov to the Holy Land.[9] Here robbers offer to show the Baal Shem Tov a short way to the Land of Israel through caves and underground passages. But when the Baal Shem Tov entered the cave he saw there *the flaming sword which turned every way* (Gen. 3:24), meaning that the way was closed to him. Also standing behind this fable of Agnon's is the messianic tradition that when the End of Days arrives, "the righteous who were buried abroad . . . will roll through underground caves until they reach the Land of Israel. And when they reach the Land of Israel He will put the spirit of life into them and they will stand up."[10]

The Israel Folktales Archives in Haifa has collected a dozen or more variants of this folktale, some about a goat, some a cow. One of these is remarkably close to Agnon's version of the tale, suggesting that he himself may have heard the tale and retold it in a way that is quite close to the original, except for elements of style and interpretation, which, of course, are central in Agnon's writing. A translation of this orally collected folktale follows: [11]

> In Yemen, in a village near Tzena, lived a very poor Jew who scarcely earned enough for himself and his family. Every day he went out to the fields with the few poor goats he had. In the evening he milked them and sold their milk cheaply. Only very poor people would buy the milk from him, for most Jews had their own goats and cows that were taken to graze by Arab shepherds, but our poor Jew would himself go to the fields for his goats to graze and he went to a great deal of trouble to find them grazing land. When he returned in the evening, before nightfall, to his home, he was tired, worn out, and broken.
>
> One day the poor man got sick. He did not go out to the grazing land and asked his two sons, aged fourteen and ten, to go in his stead. The two rose in the morning and went to look for grazing land. But they did not find any, for they took the wrong road.
>
> Suddenly one of the goats left the herd and the elder son followed it to bring it back. The goat started to run; the son ran also. The goat fled and the

son followed. He called to his younger brother: "Return home meanwhile with the other goats and I'll follow with the stubborn one."

So the younger brother returned with the goats and the elder continued to chase the fleeing goat. Time passed, and the elder brother failed to return home. His family began to worry, and as more time passed, their worry increased. The next day they began to pray for his well-being and even fasted. But he did not return home.

The goatherd's son continued to pursue the goat until, toward evening, he followed it to a wonderful site where he saw oranges radiating like the sun, apple trees illuminating like the moon, pears full of juice, olive groves, and vineyards. Among the various trees ran streams of pure clear water to refresh the soul and delight the eye.

The goat splashed about in the clear water and drank of it, then rubbed itself against the tree trunks. The son, intoxicated by the sight before his eyes, which seemed to him to resemble the Garden of Eden, could not leave the place. He ate of the fruit trees and his desire was great to stay there and continue to enjoy the goodness and beauty of the place.

The goatherd's son took a piece of paper and wrote, "Dear Father, I am in an enchanted place containing all the delights and beauties of the world, a veritable Garden of Eden. Please, Father! Leave your impoverished home and come here to enjoy all the goodness of the site. And you will never again suffer poverty and deprivation for God showed me the way and the goat led me here."

When he finished writing, he took the note and put it in the goat's ear and the goat returned to the poor goatherd's home.

The goat returned to the goatherd's home alive and well. When it arrived, the entire household hastened to greet it, but their pain was great when they saw that the goat had returned without the son and without any sign of what had come to pass with them.

The household believed that the son had been killed and would not return home. They immediately began to weep and eulogize the loss of their poor boy. When they got up from the days of mourning the bereaved father took the goat and out of deep sorrow and pain at the death of the son, slaughtered it, for he could not bear to look at the cause of his son's death. Morning and evening the goat reminded him of his beloved son and the cause of his death.

After the father slaughtered the goat, he suddenly found the note in its ear. He quickly read it and immediately regretted his rash behavior. What a pity that the goat could not show him where his son was, the site of happiness and plenty, of rest and tranquillity.

The poor father remained wretched until the end of his days and never again heard anything about his elder son. And the son continued to enjoy the delights of the place, which was like the Garden of Eden, and waited anxiously for his father and family to come. He never understood what prevented his father and family from joining him.

Assuming that some version of this well-known folktale was familiar to Agnon, it is interesting to note which version of the story he is drawn to retell. In the folktale, the young man is led by a goat to what appears to be "a veritable Garden of Eden," while Agnon, still alluding to reference to the Garden of Eden, directly identifies the place the young man comes to as the Land of Israel, specifically, the holy city of Safed. In doing so he transforms the meaning of the tale, which becomes instead an allegory of the process of separation between the older and younger generations that Agnon, who emigrated to Palestine from Poland, was intimately familiar with. The cave, which does not appear in this version of the folktale (but does in most other versions), becomes, in Agnon's rendering, a magical link between the old country and the Land of Israel, which both parents and their children longed for. The existence of such an enchanted cave is explained by the messianic tradition that there are hidden caves throughout the whole world, which the bones of the dead will roll through at the time of the Messiah, until they reach the Mount of Olives, where they will be resurrected. As for the reason for the continued separation of the young man and his family, this was brought about by the killing of the goat, which therefore could not lead the father to his son. In this way Agnon has made the story much more poignant to his Hebrew readers, themselves immigrants likely separated from many in their families who remained behind.

Agnon builds his stories out of biblical, rabbinic, and folk sources. In "The Fable of the Goat," the father discovers his error in slaughtering the goat and cries out, "My son, my son, where are you? My son, would that I might die in your stead, my son, my son!" These moving lines are taken directly from the words of King David on hearing of the death of his son, Absalom (2 Sam. 19:1). For the Hebrew reader familiar with the biblical text, there can be no doubt about the origin of this speech, and the emotional context of the original is easily transferred to the modern tale, enriching it in many respects.

Thus while Agnon has undoubtedly been true to the source, he has also subtly introduced new elements that have enhanced and enlarged the scope of the meaning of the original, while preserving its original intent. This approach is characteristic of a substantial part of Agnon's work, because it was his intent both to enhance and transmit the sources he was drawn to. In many other cases, however, Agnon's reworking of the original text is much more extensive. Yet even in these cases it is possible to recognize in his narratives the imprint of the tradition that stands behind them and on which his stories and novels have been built.

While Agnon was something of a self-contained phenomenon, the last in the long line of scribes, the opposite is true of Peretz, whose work became the primary model for much of Yiddish literature. Drawn to the rabbinic, the folk, and the hasidic models, Peretz was almost always true to the spirit of his sources, but not in a literal way. He would reinterpret and embellish, filling each of his stories with his generous spirit. This voice of the storyteller is always present in his tales and gives them an exceptional vitality. Peretz saw his role as that of a transmitter of Jewish tradition and also served as a mentor to a great many younger writers. Indeed, his stories, a great many of them drawing on traditional folk and hasidic sources, are an exceptional body of Jewish tales.

One of the most remarkable aspects of Peretz's career was his use of the folklore brought to him at the end of folktale expeditions by his friend S. Ansky, the author of *The Dybbuk*. Peretz would debrief Ansky of his tales and then make direct use of them. In one instance, Ansky marveled at how Peretz transformed one of the tales he had brought him only a month earlier, relating it to Ansky as a polished tale, whereas the original had been a rough gem. Another primary source for Peretz was the hasidic tale. Steeped in hasidic lore, Peretz in many cases combined and linked various tales and wove them into a seamless fabric.

An example of Peretz's use of sources can be seen by comparing his version of "The Story of the He-Goat Who Couldn't Say No"[12] with the hasidic tale of the Kotzker Rebbe, Rabbi Menachem Mendel of Kotzk, on which it is based. The Peretz story is about a he-goat who lived in the ruin of a synagogue and nibbled the grass there, in the very spots where the ark of the Torah had been and where Jewish blood had been shed. Due to some strange quality of that grass, it made the goat's horns grow so long they reached the sky. At midnight the goat used to raise its horns to the heavens and ask if it was time for the Messiah to come. The moon repeated its question to the stars, until the question reached the highest heavens, causing God to sigh. Then it happened that a Jew asked the goat if it could take a bit of its horn for a snuff box, and the goat couldn't say no. The word got around, and everyone wanted such a fine snuff box, and in this way the goat had no horns left to reach into heaven.

Here follows the original version of the tale, "The Sacred Goat," which is told about the Kotzker Rebbe:[13]

> Rabbi Yitzhak of Vorki was one of the very few who were admitted to Rabbi Mendel during the period when he kept away from the world. Once he visited Kotzk after a long absence, knocked, entered Rabbi Mendel's room, and said in greeting, "Peace be with you, rabbi."
>
> "Why do you say rabbi to me?" grumbled the rabbi of Kotzk. "I am no rabbi! Don't you recognize me! I'm the goat! I'm the sacred goat. Don't you remember the story?
>
> "An old Jew once lost his snuffbox made of horn, on his way to the house of study. He wailed, 'Just as if the dreadful exile weren't enough, this must happen to me! Oh me, oh my, I've lost my snuffbox made of horn!' And then he came upon the sacred goat. The sacred goat was pacing the earth, and the tips of his black horns touched the stars. When he heard the old Jew lamenting, he leaned down to him, and said 'Cut a piece from my horns, whatever you need to make a new snuffbox.' The old Jew did this, made a

new snuffbox, and filled it with tobacco. Then he went to the house of study
and offered everyone a pinch. They snuffed and snuffed, and everyone who
snuffed it cried, 'Oh, what a wonderful box! Wherever did you get it?' So the
old man told them about the sacred goat. And then, one after the other, they
went out on the street and looked for the sacred goat. The sacred goat was
pacing the earth and the tips of his black horns touched the stars. One after
another they went up to him and begged permission to cut off a bit of his
horns. Time after time the sacred goat leaned down to grant the request. Box
after box was made and filled with tobacco. The fame of the boxes spread far
and wide. At every step he took, the sacred goat met someone who asked for
a piece of his horns.

"Now the sacred goat still paces the earth—but he has no horns."

As can be seen by comparing this tale with that of Peretz, he has been
essentially faithful to the narrative. What he has added to the tale, above
all, is a sense of identification with the ram, which broadens our understanding of the extent of its sacrifice. Peretz invents the story of the origin
of the ram's horns (it grazed in the ruin of a synagogue). Providing such
origins is, of course, an essential element in the aggadic tradition. This
source of nourishment for the goat, who grazes, in particular, at two spots—
that of the Tabernacle and where Jewish blood had been shed—explains
the miraculous growth of its horns. In this way Peretz makes the goat a
symbol of Jewish tradition, which makes contact with God possible. The
enchanted goat described here is a figure directly out of mythology, whose
essence is Jewish because of the link its horns create between earth and
heaven, a kind of Jacob's ladder.

On the other hand, Peretz omits from his version the connection between the Kotzker Rebbe and the goat. The Kotzker Rebbe asserts that he
is the goat. But by the end of the tale it is apparent that by this he means
that he, like the goat who lost its horns, has been worn away by the demands made of him. Peretz also transforms the tale into a messianic one,
having the goat hook "the points of his horn around the moon, to hold her"
and ask: "Isn't it time yet for the Messiah to come?" This sets off a cosmic
echo, in which the ram's question reaches all the way to God's Throne of
Glory. This ability of the ram to have its question—which is also mankind's
question—reach into the highest heavens, Peretz implies, might have ultimately succeeded in bringing the Messiah. But when the ram's horns are
cut off, due to the goat's compassion and men's selfishness, the coming of
the Messiah is delayed—who knows for how long?

Peretz played a pivotal role in bringing modern Jewish readers and writers to regard the old tradition as a treasure house of riches that could be
drawn upon. And because he himself was a pure vessel, he succeeded in
transmitting, as well, an essential reverence for Jewish tradition.[14]

Through most of the history of Yiddish literature the dominant figures
were Mendele Mokher-Seforim, Sholom Aleichem, I. L. Peretz, Der Nister,

and, before his accusations of apostasy, Sholem Asch. However, all of these figures have been eclipsed by the major role Isaac Bashevis Singer came to play. Singer's receipt of the Nobel Prize in 1979 was confirmation not only of his world stature but also of the validity of the modern Yiddish tradition. Singer was one of the last of the dying tradition of Yiddish literature and possibly its greatest exemplar. Like Peretz and Sholom Aleichem, Singer published his stories and novels in the *Forward*. And like the earlier Yiddish masters, Singer mined the aggadic tradition for much of his subject matter. But unlike most of them he was a writer who was as fascinated with the passions of the flesh as he was with the mysteries of existence.

Singer was born into a rabbinic family in Leoncin, a village in Poland, in 1904 and grew up in Warsaw, where he began his writing career in 1925. It is important to emphasize the crucial role played by his older brother, Israel Joshua Singer, author of *Yoshe Kalb* and *The Brothers Ashkenazi*, in the career of his younger brother.

Singer's emigration to the United States in 1935 and the subsequent destruction of the Polish Jewish communities by the Nazis in World War II created a situation in which he had to turn, of necessity, to his memory and imagination for subject matter. So great was his success that for many readers Singer's descriptions of life in prewar Poland form the basis for their conception of this period. To his detractors, Singer's character portraits, with their emphasis on the grotesque and the tension between the sacred and the sexual, are overworked and exaggerated. But Singer has always emphasized the primary role of the imagination in his stories and novels. It is a tribute to the power of his imagined worlds that this dispute has long continued to smolder.

Spurred by the acclaim received by his first story to be translated into English (by Saul Bellow), "Gimpel the Fool," [15] and by his natural attraction to the short-story form, Singer continued to work in this genre, and the regular appearance of many of his stories in *The New Yorker* and other magazines broadened his audience immeasurably, as, of course, did the receipt of the Nobel Prize in 1978.

Singer's first novels to be translated and published in English were *The Family Moskat*, a realistic family chronicle, and *Satan in Goray*, a novel about the hysteria in 17th-century Poland brought on by the hopes raised by the false messiah, Shabbatai Zevi. These books were well received, but it was not until the publication of Singer's first book of short stories, *Gimpel the Fool*, in 1957, that his writings began to attract worldwide attention. For although Singer is a highly accomplished writer in every style and format he has tried, his greatest successes have come in the realm of the short story, where he must be numbered among the masters in world literature.

Singer is, above all, a storyteller. Indeed, on many occasions Singer stated that he considered this ability to be the most important a writer can possess. Even the demons and imps who frequently narrate his stories demonstrate the same keen, if somewhat ironic, intelligence as their creator, and like him they carefully observe every situation and attempt to penetrate every mystery. Singer is a master of irony and satire, modes that are rarely encountered in the traditional literature. While some Yiddish readers have regarded Singer's use of irony and satire in conjunction with sacred sources as a betrayal, others accept it as an evolution in style, where the essence of his sources remains essentially intact.

Such a use of irony characterizes Singer's story "Sabbath in Gehenna."[16] The myths of *Gehenna*,[17] Jewish hell, are introduced in the Talmud as the inverse of everything Paradise represents. The concept of *"Gehenna"* is based on the biblical Valley of Gehinnom and biblical passages about the punishment of sinners, such as that found in Psalm 11:6: *Upon the wicked He will cause to rain coals; fire and brimstone and burning wind shall be the portion of their cup.* In many rabbinic sources *Gehenna* is described as the place where the souls of sinners are subjected to a painful process of purification that lasts for up to twelve months before they are permitted to ascend to the heavenly abode. This parallel between Paradise and *Gehenna* is made explicit in the following talmudic passage:[18]

> Each person has two portions, one in the Garden of Eden and the other in *Gehenna*. If a person is worthy and righteous, he takes his share and that of his fellow in the Garden; while if he has incurred guilt and is wicked, he takes his share and that of his fellow in *Gehenna*.

The nature of *Gehenna* and the punishments of the wicked are portrayed in detail in a variety of talmudic passages, such as this one:[19]

> The Holy One, blessed be He, punishes the wicked in *Gehenna* for twelve months. First he forces them to enter the cold, then to enter a fire, and then to enter the snow, where they say "Woe, woe."

These punishments and others are embellished in subsequent texts, such as the Midrash Rabbah and the Zohar. It is in the Zohar (2:251a) that we find the issue of Sabbath in *Gehenna* dealt with directly:[20]

> Every Sabbath eve, when the day becomes sanctified, heralds go out to all those compartments of *Gehenna* announcing, "Cease punishing the sinners, for the Holy King approaches and the Day is about to be sanctified. He protects all!" Instantly all punishment ceases, and the guilty have a respite. But the fire of *Gehenna* does not let off from those who never observed the Sabbath. Since they did not observe the Sabbath before, they will have no respite forever. An angel whose name is Santriel, which means God is my Guardsman, goes and fetches the body of the sinner. He brings it to *Gehenna* before the eyes of the guilty, and they see how it has bred worms. They know the soul of such a sinner has no respite from the fire of *Gehenna*. And all those guilty who are there surround that body and proclaim over it that "this person is guilty, for he would not regard the honor of his Master, he denied the Holy One, blessed be He, and denied the Torah. Woe to him! It would have been

better for him never to be created and not to be subjected to this punishment and this disgrace!"

Rabbi Yehuda said: "After the Sabbath goes out the angel comes and takes that body back to its grave, and both the body and the soul are punished, each in its own way."

And all this takes place while the body is still well preserved. But once the body is decayed, it no longer suffers all these punishments. The guilty ones are punished in their bodies and their souls, each with a suitable punishment, so long as the body in the grave is intact. But when the body breaks down the punishment of the soul ceases. He who must leave *Gehenna* leaves, and he who must find rest has rest. He who must become ashes and dust under the feet of the pious turns to ashes and dust—to each one is done what is suitable for him.

While Singer's satiric view of *Gehenna* implies a lack of belief in it, there is indeed traditional basis for this view, which can also be found reflected in the following story about *Gehenna* that was attributed to Miriam, the sister of Reb Shmelke of Nicholsberg, whom it concerns:

The holy Reb Shmelke lived next door to a *mitnagdid*, a fierce opponent of the hasidim, who understood the letter of the Law in the most literal way. Therefore he performed *Havdalah*, the ceremony ending the Sabbath, as soon as three stars appeared in the sky. Reb Shelmke, on the other hand, kept the Sabbath candles burning far into the night. And long after he had finished saying *Havdalah*, the neighbor would peer outside his window and see that the Sabbath candles were still burning next door. And that bothered him to no end.

This neighbor took it on himself to save Reb Shmelke from this sin. So as soon as three stars would appear in the sky, he would open his window and shout: "Three stars! Time for *Havdalah!*" These shouts would disturb Reb Shmelke's reveries. Nonetheless, Reb Shmelke restrained himself, and never said anything about it to his neighbor. Instead, he continued to savor the Sabbath for many hours after his neighbor had reminded him that the Sabbath was over.

Seeing that he had failed to convince Reb Shmelke to change his ways, the neighbor decided on a more drastic approach. As soon as the three stars appeared, he went outside, picked up some pebbles, and threw them through Reb Shemlke's window. One of those pebbles struck Reb Shmelke, tearing him from the arms of the Sabbath Queen. Reb Shmelke felt the pain of his loss, but he knew as well that his neighbor had made a terrible mistake. And before many months had passed, the neighbor became sick and died.

Some months after that, when Reb Shmelke was sitting at the Sabbath table, about the time the first three stars appeared, he suddenly smiled mysteriously. And he mumbled the words "From below they look above, from above, below." None of his hasidim understood what he meant, but they had to wait until the end of the Sabbath to ask him. Then Reb Shmelke said: "The soul of our neighbor was sent to *Gehenna* for his sins, where he is punished all week long but spared on the Sabbath. But as soon as three stars appear, the angels drag him back to *Gehenna*. And all the way there he shouts, 'But Reb Shmelke is still celebrating the Sabbath!' " [21]

This story, which takes the form of a joke, reveals that the dark humor of the Jews even found a way to make fun of the fate of those who were being punished in *Gehenna*. This humor does not necessarily, though, imply that they no longer believe in it. Singer's satire, on the other hand, has a mocking edge, especially as he roasts his fellow Yiddish writers, and suggests more doubt than belief.

As a former *yeshivah* student in Warsaw, I. B. Singer became acquainted with the full range of traditional sources, including the Torah, the Talmud, and the Midrash, and he also explored the esoteric world of the Kabbalah and its primary text, the Zohar. Blending details about *Gehenna* drawn from these sources, Singer presents a critical view of hell that is a distorted extension of the hellish present. Despite his use of authentic sources, the primary difference between these and Singer's story is substantial because Singer chooses to regard the whole in a satirical light, and identifies the sufferers as Yiddish writers who have all been condemned to *Gehenna* for their sins. Taking a slanted look at both traditional sources and the present by bringing his ironic vision to them is quite characteristic of Singer and probably accounts for much of his literary success as well as for the animosity felt for him by the traditionalists.[22] The object of the story, then, is to satirize the Yiddish writing community as much as it is to use the traditional sources for *Gehenna*. The irony is particularly pointed when the Yiddish writers decide, even in *Gehenna*, that the thing to do is to start a newspaper, and Singer creates a great deal of comedy out of this situation.

Many readers have wondered to what extent Singer based his stories with supernatural themes on existing Jewish folktales. A close examination of these stories reveals that while Singer does occasionally base a story on an existing folk narrative, in general he creates the plots of these tales himself, but populates his stories with authentic figures out of Jewish folklore. Singer's use of these figures is entirely within their roles in Jewish folklore, while operating within plots of Singer's own creation.

To readers unfamiliar with the rich body of Jewish legends and folklore, the stories and novels of I. B. Singer have a fantastic, startling quality that is almost surreal. But to the reader familiar with these sources, Singer's writings are immediately recognizable as a fusion of the ancient and modern Jewish literary traditions with Singer's distinctive vision. Thus Singer's best writings must be acknowledged not only as literary masterpieces but also as a valuable storehouse of the folklore and superstitions of the Jewish community that was current during his childhood, which they accurately reflect.[23]

Modern Jewish Literature and the Ancient Models

The vision first formulated in the Bible and sustained and developed throughout the subsequent phases of Jewish literature has continued uninterrupted into this century in the writings of Jewish authors of many nationalities.[1] These include Nobel Prize winners such as the Hebrew author S. Y. Agnon and the Yiddish author Isaac Bashevis Singer, as well as major figures such as the Yiddish writers Mendele Moyker-Sform, I. L. Peretz, Sholom Aleichem, S. Ansky, David Pinski, Der Nister, Sholem Asch, and Itzik Manger; the Hebrew writers Hayim Nachman Bialik, M. J. Berditchevsky, Haim Hazaz, Yehuda Yaari, M. J. Feierberg, Aharon Appelfeld, Pinhas Sadeh, David Shahar and David Grossman; the Russian writer Isaac Babel; the German writers Martin Buber, Franz Kafka, Else Lasker-Schuler, Franz Werfel, Stefan Zweig, and Jakov Lind; the French writers Andre Schwarz-Bart, Edmond Jabes, Albert Memmi, Romain Gary, and Elie Wiesel; the Portugese writer Moacyr Scliar; the Spanish writers Isaac Goldemberg, Mario Satz, and Ilan Stavans; the Hungarian writers Lajos Szabolsci, Arnold Kiss, and Peter Ujvari; the Czech writers Jiří Langer and Ladislav Grosman; the Polish author Bruno Schultz; the Judezmo writers Kamelia Shahar and Alfredo Sarrana; and the English-language writers Israel Zangwill, Bernard Malamud, Cynthia Ozick, Hugh Nissenson, Meyer Levin, Dan Jacobson, Leslie A. Fiedler, Steve Stern, Tova Reich, Ellen Galford, and Francine Prose.

Before proceeding further, it would be useful to consider why these authors have sought inspiration in the ancient Jewish literary tradition and how in the process they have contributed to that same tradition and kept it alive.

Among the literary schools of modernism, two dominant models have arisen. One is primarily concerned with the external landscape, and the other is concerned with exploration of the inner, or spiritual, world. Realism is the dominant style to emerge from those authors for whom the outer world has remained the central subject, while those whose primary impulse is to map out the inner life have utilized the symbolism associated with dreams, mythology, legends, and various kinds of religious texts, and their primary literary mode has been an allegorical one. To a large extent the Jewish writers who have sought inspiration in the ancient sources manifest an impulse toward self-exploration and therefore often utilize the allegorical or parabolic mode.[2]

The key figure in redirecting the modern gaze from the world outside to that within is Franz Kafka. Kafka's stories have the impact of myths, and there are many modern readers carrying his dark myths around in their heads. Kafka's novel, *The Trial*, and many of his stories, especially "In the Penal Colony," are widely acknowledged as a prophecy of the coming war and Holocaust in Europe. Among his other accomplishments, Kafka single-handedly resurrected a lost literary form, the parable. His book *Parables and Paradoxes* includes such classics as "Before the Law," excerpted from *The Trial*, about a man from the country who seeks entrance through the gates of the Law—whether heavenly or temporal is not clear—only to be repeatedly denied. There also are brief tales that reimagine the biblical accounts of the Garden of Eden, the Tower of Babel, Abraham, Mount Sinai, and the building of the Temple in Jerusalem. These parables are remarkably similar to the kind of rabbinic commentary on the Bible found in the Midrash, and as such they constitute an early and very influential example of modern midrash.

Of course, this movement toward the use of parable has not been limited to Jewish authors by any means; it crosses the entire spectrum of modern masters such as Jorge Luis Borges, Gabriel Garcia Marquez, and Italo Calvino. But while Borges draws his inspiration from a multitude of traditions, S. Y. Agnon was able to focus all his energies into sustaining and rejuvenating a literary tradition that reaches back almost three thousand years. Very few modern authors have had the opportunity to work within such a tradition, and virtually all of the modern Jewish authors under discussion feel enhanced by their heritage and the opportunity to receive and transmit it. In contrast, many modern authors feel outside of all tradition and as a result have evolved bleak and narrow world visions, such as that of Samuel Beckett.

Naturally, there is a wide variety of styles and techniques that are used by these modern Jewish authors. Each conceives of his relationship to the ancient tradition in his or her own terms and may vary his or her approach from story to story. But the essential fact is that these writers do not regard their tradition as a burden, but as a blessing.

The advantages of working within a tradition have been amply demonstrated in the past, notably by Dante and Milton. While it is true that the modern environment does not offer the broadly based support that medieval Christian culture provided Dante, the Jewish literary tradition, which has remained unbroken, has left a remarkably deep imprint on a substantial number of modern Jewish authors. At the same time these authors have opened themselves to the various types of modern literature that have emerged in this century, and have utilized these various approaches in exploring and mining the ancient tradition. The result is that this ancient, essentially mythological literature, the *Aggadah*, emerging out of a legalistic element, the *Halakhah*, has lent itself perfectly to an infinite variety of mythic transformations.

To fully appreciate the creative process of the modern author in retelling the ancient tale, it is necessary to observe the elements of each version that coincide and those that diverge. The parts that are traditional serve as the frame on which the modern author weaves his retelling, and the parts that are original constitute the new directions the tale takes.[3] In some cases this modern material is so similar to the ancient sources as to be almost indistinguishable, while there are also stories in which the influence of the sources is far more remote and sometimes disguised. Many tales about the Baal Shem Tov, founder of hasidism, recounted by Israel Zangwill, S. Ansky, M. J. Berditchevsky, and Meyer Levin, for example, are based directly on the tales published by the Baal Shem Tov's hasidim in volumes such as *Shivhei ha-Besht*, although they have been retold in well-crafted narratives, combining those tales that can readily be linked. Martin Buber's versions of these same legends, however, in the volume *The Legend of the Baal Shem*, take greater liberties. In this case, and that of Buber's *The Tales of Rabbi Nachman*, Buber's primary impulse was clearly a literary one. Even when he veers away from the original, he remains a master of style and expression. Buber's later versions of these same stories in *Tales of the Hasidim*, on the other hand, are much closer to the original sources. In both cases, however, the early and the later, Buber sought out tales that confirmed his pure vision of Hasidism and avoided those that did not. Those he chose he then revised to conform to his own literary views, and all of these bear Buber's distinct imprint.[4]

While the sources for all of these tales of the Baal Shem are usually not difficult to locate, there are also stories such as Cynthia Ozick's "The Pagan Rabbi,"[5] which is based in a subtle, allusive way on the prototype of the talmudic heretic Elisha ben Abuyah, known as Aher. Likewise, Primo Levi's "Lilith in the Lager"[6] transports the legend of Lilith out of its familiar context and transfers it to a concentration camp, which soon comes to seem like an appropriate place, after all, for demons to be loose. So too does Mario Satz, in "The Number of the Name,"[7] link the number tattooed on a concentration camp inmate and the esoteric four-letter Name of God, known as the Tetragrammaton, subjects which on the surface seem impossibly disparate. These stories of Ozick, Levi, and Satz utilize the ancient sources in unexpected but effective ways.

The central paradox of this type of modern Jewish literature is that it is essentially a secular literature that makes extensive use of symbols drawn from a sacred tradition. This raises a key question about the intentions of the authors who choose to draw upon this rich tradition—are their objectives directed primarily toward the sacred or toward the secular? This question is complicated by the awareness that had some authors working in this genre—especially S. Y. Agnon—lived a thousand years ago, much of what they wrote would undoubtedly have been accepted into the sacred tradition. That Agnon's writings are not regarded as sacred does not necessarily reflect his most secret desires about how they should be perceived. On the other hand, it is likely that had Dante lived today he would have found it virtually impossible to create a masterpiece such as *The Divine Comedy*. Missing today is the wide acceptance of Christian principles that served as the foundation on which Dante built his literary cathedral.

The fact remains that circumstances have made it necessary for Jewish authors drawn to the ancient tradition to recognize that their writings are by necessity a blend of the sacred and secular. If we perceive the sacred element as representative of an authentic religious impulse, drawing on a powerful, numinous symbolism, we should be able to accept that the primary motivation for both ancient and modern authors to write has not changed very much over the centuries. What has changed is our perspective toward the literature that is a product of such experience. Essentially, the claim that this literature derives from a sacred source, or was handed down as part of the oral tradition, has been rejected. Nevertheless, the primary impulse behind these writings has remained the same, and for this reason the most reasonable way to regard them is as a continuation of the Jewish literary tradition, making that tradition broad enough to incorporate both the sacred and the secular.

The methods by which modern Jewish authors are inspired by and make use of traditional sources are diverse. In terms of the amount of ancient material incorporated into the modern work, this ranges from mere allusions and echoes of the source material to the actual incorporation of the source into an expanded retelling. This retelling itself may range from the reverent to the ironic, and may in some cases be literal and in others a radical reworking. The following examples should clarify these possibilities and indicate the degree to which the source material serves as a starting point for the modern author.

A good example of a modern tale that is built almost entirely on its sources is David Shahar's "On the Life and Death of Abbaye."[8] Abbaye was a prominent talmudic sage, and in the manner of the Talmud, scattered references to his life are to be found throughout the text, among his hundreds of legal comments and decisions. Shahar first located these texts, and then wove them together to form a consistent vision of Abbaye that at the same time incorporates virtually all of the sources. His virtuosity in smoothly juggling the various texts results in a highly coherent tale. This is far more of an accomplishment, however, than may at first appear to be the case. Abbaye was an eccentric among the sages; he believed so fully in the world of spirits and demons that he was afraid to be left alone in the privy and had a lamb accompany him there as a child. Shahar is taken with his personality, and because of Shahar's skill in weaving transitions between legends, he is able to accomplish what are the novelist's finest skills—bringing a character to life and at the same time imprinting on the narrative his own vision of Abbaye.

To assist this process of fleshing out Abbaye's character, Shahar does not hesitate to incorporate his own experiences, such as that of observing a great juggler, into the narrative. This is the natural impulse of the storyteller to add a part of his own experience to the story. At the same time, Shahar draws on the traditional belief that demons are born from every issue of semen that goes to waste.[9] To protect himself in that house of demons, the privy, Abbaye composed a prayer. And Shahar makes use of this information to suggest, according to the way he has linked together the legends, that in this act we gain insight into the role of religion in Abbaye's life, where the Lord offered him protection in this world, protection being something he valued above all else.[10]

Sometimes a modern Jewish author bases a fictional character on an ancient model. Such seems to be the case with Cynthia Ozick's "The Pagan Rabbi," where the character of Isaac Kornfeld, the "pagan rabbi" of the title, may well have been based on that of the ancient talmudic sage Elisha ben Abuyah, who became an apostate, and was thereafter referred to as Aher, the Other. This story pursues the mystery of Isaac's suicide into a realm where the myth and metaphysics merge into a transcendental reality.

Isaac, like Elisha, was famous for his brilliance and imagination: "His imagination was so remarkable he could concoct holiness out of the fine line of a serif." And like Elisha, Isaac read not only sacred Jewish texts, but other works as well: "No sooner did I catch his joy in Saadia Gaon than he had already sprung ahead to Yehudah Halevi. One day he was weeping with Dostoyevski and the next leaping in the air of Thomas Mann. He introduced me to Hegel and Nietzsche while our fathers wailed." In a famous episode, Greek books fell from beneath Elisha's robe: "It is told of Aher that when he used to rise from the schoolhouse, many heretical books used to fall from his lap."[11] Elisha's attraction to Greek thought in contrast to the rabbis' intense rejection of it was legendary: "Greek song did not cease from his mouth."[12] In Isaac Kornfeld's notebook, there is found "Greek writing that had the shape of verse."

The paradox about Elisha ben Abuyah is that his commentaries were so apt that they were retained in the Talmud even after he became an apostate. Likewise, Isaac Kornfeld published two books of *responsa* that were widely recognized for their brilliance and made him famous in the world of Jewish scholars. Elisha's apostasy was, it is widely believed, in becoming a Gnostic, while Isaac Kornfeld's was in becoming a pagan, writing in his notebook: "Great Pan lives." Elisha saw the angel Metatron seated in Paradise and proclaimed: "There are two powers in heaven!"[13] and like Elisha's, Isaac's world view is distinctly dualistic: there are two kinds of souls, the free and the indwelling. Objects in nature are possessed of free souls, while humans are cursed with the indwelling kind.[14] Like Elisha, Isaac comes to his view reluctantly, over a period of time, accepting it finally in the spirit of a searcher who will not allow himself to be deceived, no matter how unsatisfactory the conclusion he has reached is to him: "His intention was not to accumulate mystery but to dispel it."

Isaac's paganism is very much associated with Greek religion and is parallel to Elisha's attraction to Greek thought. And like Elisha's, Isaac's conclusions brought him isolation and alienation, from which there was no turning back. Elisha told Rabbi Meir, "I have already heard from behind the *Pargod*: '*Return ye backsliding children*' (*Jer.* 3:14)—all except Aher."[15]

After coupling with the dryad, Isaac loses his soul: "Your body is now an empty packet, that is why it is light." The tragedy of both figures is brought home in Elisha's implicit regret, and in Isaac's discovery from the nymph that "you, poor man, do not know your own soul." Both are at heart reverent, observant Jews who have somehow been led astray from their true nature. Isaac's soul takes the form of "an ugly old man . . . with a matted beard and great fierce eyebrows," who "reads as he goes." Isaac's inner conflict is thus represented in the epigram to the story from *Pirke Avot*:[16] "He who is walking along and studying, but breaks off to remark, 'How lovely is that tree!' or 'How beautiful is that fallow field!'—Scripture regards such a one as having hurt his own being." Isaac's soul, the old man, "reads the Law and breathes the dust and doesn't see the flowers," while Isaac's body cannot put the beauty of the flowers out of his sight. In this way the age-old conflict between body and soul is represented, as unresolved as ever, leading Isaac Kornfeld, inevitably, to his destruction. As a suicide, Isaac had to be buried outside the fence, and Aher, it was believed, was denied the world to come until after the death of Rabbi Meir, who said: "It is better that he should be judged and that he should enter the world to come. When I die I shall cause smoke to rise from his grave." And when Rabbi Meir died, smoke rose up from Aher's grave.[17]

A different kind of allusion to rabbinic literature is found in the writings of Itzik Manger. Manger was first and foremost a poet; he wove aggadic themes into ballad-like poems that later became the words to many popular Yiddish songs. But Manger also wrote a novel, *The Book of Paradise*, that is a comic masterpiece. Originally intended to be the first of three novels, it had the misfortune to be published just as the Germans invaded Warsaw, and the storehouse in which the copies were kept was burned. Only a few copies survived. After the war Manger found he was no longer able to evoke a comic mood, and he abandoned the other two planned volumes. But the existing volume is a classic satire, drawing on a famous midrash about the infant in the womb:[18]

When the destined time for a child to be conceived arrives, God says to the Lailah, the Angel of Conception: "Know that this night a woman shall conceive. Bring forth a sperm." This the angel does, and the Lord then decrees if the child will be strong or weak, male or female, wicked or righteous, rich or poor, beautiful or homely, tall or short. God then makes a sign to the angel in charge of the spirits to bring a certain spirit hidden in the Garden of Eden, whose name is given. This angel brings forth this spirit before God, and at that moment God says: "Enter into this sperm." The spirit, however, always pleads with the Holy One, blessed be He, not to be forced to enter the impure world of being, for it is holy and pure. But God explains that He created the spirit only for this purpose and compels it to enter the sperm against its will. The angel then causes it to enter the womb of its mother.

During pregnancy, two angels watch over the embryo. A light shines upon the head of the child, by which it sees from one end of the world to the other. During the day the angel shows the child the rewards of the Garden of Eden, where the righteous sit in glory with crowns upon their heads, while at night the punishments of *Gehenna* are revealed to him, where wicked angels beat sinners with fiery staves.

At the end of the nine months, when it is time for the child to be born, the same angel comes back and tells the child to come forth into the world. And the child always begs to remain in the place where he has become accustomed to dwell. The angel then tells the child that he was formed against his will and that he will go forth into the world against his will. The angel then lightly strikes the child above the lip with its finger, causing the child to forget whatever it has seen. Then the angel extinguishes the light shining at his head and brings the child forth into the world. And as it is brought forth, it cries.

This legend has been taken as an explanation for the presence of the indentation above the lip. Manger humorously changes this to a tug on the nose, providing a mocking explanation for the large noses associated with Jews. Manger's midrashic satire recounts that Shmuel-abba, an angel, has descended to this world, reborn as an infant. But rather than lose his memory, the independent Shmuel-abba puts a piece of clay on his nose, and then gets the angel bringing him to the world drunk on Messiah wine (which, according to a midrash, has been saved from before the Creation for the coming of the Messiah). The drunken angel only twists the clay, and Shmuel-abba is born remembering everything, which he begins at once to tell. This serves as the framework for a satire about the patriarchs, told in a mock midrashic fashion. In this tale Isaac, who was known to have a weakness for venison, now lives in Paradise, where every day he takes a piece of chalk and, although he is blind, still marks off the finest part of the Messiah Ox—the ox that will not be slaughtered and eaten until the Messiah comes, according to another midrash.

Far more allusive in his use of sources is Hugh Nissenson in his story "Forcing the End."[19] Setting his story in modern Israel, Nissenson retells the talmudic episode of the escape of Rabbi Yohanan ben Zakkai from Jerusalem during the Roman siege. Although there was a famine, the Zealots, who controlled the city, refused to let any living person leave. Therefore Yohanan ben Zakkai pretended that he had died, and he was carried outside of the city in a coffin by his disciples, with whom he later established a major *yeshivah* at Yavneh. The story is told in the Talmud as follows:[20]

Abba Sikra, the head of the Zealots of Jerusalem, was the son of Rabban Yohanan ben Zakkai's sister. Yohanan sent for him, saying, "Come to me in secret." When he came, Yohanan said to him, "How long will you act in this way and kill the world with hunger?" Abba Sikra said to him, "What shall I do? If I say anything to the other Zealots, they will kill me." Then Yohanan said to him, "Find a way for me to escape from the city; perhaps there will be some succor." Abba Sikra said to him, "Pretend to be ill, and let all the world come to ask about you. And take something putrid and put it next to you, and they will say that you died, and let only your disciples come in to you, and let no one else come in, lest they notice that you are light of weight, for they know a living person is lighter than a dead one."

So he did. Rabbi Eliezer walked on one side of the "body" of Yohanan and Rabbi Yehoshua on the other side. When they came to the gate, the guards wanted to stick their lances into Yohanan. But Abba Sikra said to them, "The Romans will say, 'They pierced their master!'" They wanted to push him. But Abba Sikra said to them, "They will say, 'They pushed their master!'" Then they opened the gate for him and he was taken out.

When Yohanan reached Vespasian, he said: "Peace be unto you, O king." But Vespasian said to him, "You have incurred two death sentences. One, because I am not king and you have called me king; and the other, because if I am king, why did you not come to me before this?" Yohanan said to him, "As for your saying that you are not king, you are about to become king, for were you not king, Jerusalem would not be delivered into your hands. And as for your saying that if you are king why did I not come to you before this, the Zealots who are among us did not let me come."

In the meantime a messenger came from Rome and said to Vespasian: "Rise, for Caesar has died and the notables of Rome have decided to elect you as king."

Then Vespasian said to him, "I am going away and shall send another to take my place. However, ask something of me and I shall give it to you." He said to him, "Give me Yavneh and its sages, the dynasty of Rabban Gamliel, and a physician to heal Rabbi Tzaddok."

In "Forcing the End" Nissenson sets this talmudic tale in a different period, with another rabbi—Rabbi Jacobi. This creates a strong sense of continuity between the generations. So too does it increase our understanding of the talmudic episode, to which the reader can now return with a new perspective, drawn from the present. Nissenson emphasizes this continuity in this exchange:

> And twisting the tuft of hair below his mouth, Jacobi says, "You're looking at the Holy City through my eyes."
> "The past?"
> He shrugs. "The future, too. What's the difference? They're one and the same."

This time it is Rabbi Jacobi who feels he must escape from Jerusalem in order to establish a *yeshivah* at Yavneh. And like his predecessor, Yohanan ben Zakkai, he has himself smuggled out of the city in a coffin. The reader, noting these parallels, cannot help being caught up, as well, in the realistic details of present-day Israel. And it is these that have the final word in this retelling, in which having escaped in a coffin, Rabbi Jacobi is soon discovered to have been murdered in Yavne. Thus are the parallels and differences between the two times clearly drawn. In this case, it is safe to say, the reader unfamiliar with the talmudic episode will miss much of the point of Nissenson's story, although the tale itself is a riveting one.

Another tale that exists in two time periods simultaneously is Aharon Appelfeld's "In the Wilderness."[21] Appelfeld tells the story of victims of the Holocaust traveling from one city to another, while describing their journey in terms of the Israelites wandering in the wilderness as described in the Book of Exodus and the subsequent midrashim. Clearly Appelfeld intends to demonstrate that the experience of the Jews during the Second World War, while unique, was at the same time prefigured by the biblical episode that is of such central importance.

The survivors in Appelfeld's story encounter a landscape parallel in many ways to that of the Israelites in the Egyptian wilderness. In a central episode the survivors reach a wide lake, which clearly represents the Red Sea in the biblical tale. Here there is no parting of the waters, as happened in Exodus, but instead there is a miracle of sorts, as the water sinks into the earth, making passage possible: "Marvelous blossoms suddenly speckled the landscape. . . . The lake came into its own. Birds hovered overhead. . . . Itzik climbed down and said, 'The water is sinking.'"

The accessibility of food in the midrashim about the crossing at the sea—"The sea yielded to the Israelites what each desired. If a child cried out as it lay in the arms of its mother, she needed but stretch out her hand and pluck an apple or pomegranate and quiet it"[22]—is transferred in Appelfeld's story into an abundance of fish that suddenly become available as the waters sink: "Startled fish were seen in their last attempt to dart away from the shallow water. Itzik would grab a handful and say, 'There are lots of little fish.'"

So too is there a parallel in Appelfeld's tale about the central episode of the Song of the Sea. In the midrashic version the singing is an incredible paean of unity among the people, an assertion of determination to continue, in which "even the embryos in their mother's wombs opened their mouths and uttered song before God."[23] This assertion of tribal unity appears as well in "In the Wilderness": "Bodies were throbbing, mouths let out cries, questions which merged into a chorus of incantations rejoicing at every discovery."

So too does Appelfeld emphasize this mythological link to the biblical episode by including a story about the Angel of Death, told by one of the survivors:

> The fire was blazing on; the *shohet* made an offering and told us a story about his father who had struggled with the angel of death for many years, until his struggle had become well-known. At times he had played sly tricks on the angel, and at times the angel of death had played tricks on him. They had waged war on one another for forty years and at the age of ninety-five the angel had got the better of him.

There are also nightmarish tortures the refugees experience in a wasteland like that described in Exodus. At one point, the horse sinks into the mud as if it were quicksand.

As for the pillar of flame that guided the Israelites in the wilderness, Appelfeld's survivors identify it with the horse that is finally lost to them for good: "Only now did we know that a living pillar had walked before us, protecting us all the way." And, as in the Egyptian wilderness, it is a place transformed into a mythical landscape: "Every object was luminous as though seen for the first time."

Here the role of Moses is played by a *shohet*,[24] a ritual slaughterer, who, like Moses, "feared we would turn to idolatry, since there was one who said: a stone." So too do the people in Appelfeld's story lose patience with the *shohet*, as did the Israelites with Moses: ". . . the *shohet* had misled us. He promised us miracles from God in the wilderness and what did He show us?" And in the end of his tale Appelfeld echoes the death of Moses, who climbed Mount Nebo at the end of his life and whose body was never found, since, according to the *Aggadah*, he received "the Kiss of the *Shekhinah*"[25] and was taken wholly into the Divine Presence: "Towards morning the *shohet* kissed our foreheads and said he was requested to leave early. We ran behind but couldn't catch up with him."

Quite often a modern author chooses to continue a story that somehow appears unfinished. A good example of a tale of this kind is Stefan Zweig's "Legend of the Third Dove,"[26] from his book *Jewish Legends*. This is the last dove that Noah released, which signaled that the waters had significantly subsided so that the land had reappeared. Zweig tells the tale of "the journey and the fate of the third dove." In the process he makes use of another tradition, that of the wanderer who has no home, which first appears in the biblical tale of Cain, and later in the rabbinic embellishments of the wanderings of Serah bat Asher, as well as in the Christian legend of the Wandering Jew. Here it is this third dove, the symbol of peace, who can find no rest:

> It whirred up and flew over our world, in order to find peace, but no matter where it flew, everywhere there were these streaks of lightning, this thundering of men; everywhere there was war. . . . As yet the dove has not found rest, nor mankind peace, and sooner than that it may not return home, it may not rest for all time.

The reader will marvel at how well this allegory builds on its three primary sources: the biblical narrative, the motif of the eternal wanderer, and the tradition that the dove is a symbol of peace. Zweig's narrative also forges links between the biblical motif of the Flood as a symbol of destruction, stating that "a Flood had again come." Thus it indicates that the Flood can serve as a metaphor for the kind of chaos that still threatens the world. Stories of this quality can only be regarded as the logical culmination of the literary tradition begun in the Bible and evidence that this tradition is still alive and flourishing.

It is also possible for a story to be based on a traditional concept rather than a legend. Here primary kabbalistic concepts such as that of the *Pargod*, the curtain that hangs before the Throne of Glory,[27] or of *tzimtzum*, the contraction of God that made possible the Creation of the world, serve as the starting points for tales such as Rabbi Nachman's "The Portrait," M. J. Berditchevsky's "Illusion," David Shahar's "The Death of the Little God," and "The Disappearance" by Edmond Jabès.

In the case of Rabbi Nachman's tale, as well as others of his such as "A Letter" and "The Royal Messenger," God is represented by a king and the *Pargod* by the curtain that conceals him. "The Portrait" serves to make the same point as does the kabbalistic concept of the *Pargod*—that is, that God's true nature is irrevocably hidden from the knowledge of men. There is a long tradition, of course, of allegories in which God is represented as a king. Another example is "Illusion" by M. J. Berditchevsky. The title of Berditchevsky's story in the original Hebrew is "*Ahizat Einayim*," literally, "Seizing the Eyes," which translates with some difficulty as "illusion," "delusion," "mirage," "chimera," or perhaps "sleight of hand." However, the closest meaning is a term used in Hindu teachings, *maya*. The classic legend defining *maya* tells of a Hindu prophet who approaches one of the gods, Arjuna, and asks to be taught the secrets of *maya*. The god agrees but asks that the prophet first bring him a glass of water from a house at some distance from them in the desert. The prophet hurries off to the house. When he arrives there it is almost evening. The people take him in, share their dinner, and convince him to stay for the night. He remains that night, nor does he leave the next day. He becomes enamored of the daughter of his hosts, and in the end he stays and marries her. They are married for twelve years and have three children. One day a tidal wave passes through the desert and uproots their house, carrying off the man's wife and in-laws. He fights the waves with two children in one arm and one in the other. A wave tears away the single child, and as he reaches for it with both arms he loses hold of the other two children and is carried downstream a great distance before the world grows dark. At last he wakes up to find himself covered by a shadow. It is the god Arjuna, leaning over him. The god is saying: "I have been waiting at least five minutes—have you brought my water yet?" [28]

This story serves to define the term *maya* as the illusion of life in this world, which seems so real to us, yet is in fact only an illusion created by the gods. The concept of *ahizat einayim* differs slightly from *maya* in that the moral is not the meaninglessness of existence, but a reminder that all existence emanates from God and ultimately has no existence apart from the Divinity.

Berditchevsky's tale is clearly an allegory in which the king represents God, and the cities the king builds and destroys, "in order to build better and more beautiful ones," are actually illusions. The effort to get past the gate in order to discover the truth, only to find another gate behind it, reminiscent of Kafka's "Before the Law," is a metaphor intended to show that ultimate truth is beyond the understanding of men. Finally those seeking entrance to the palace are reminded of this fact by a man who tells them: "There is no palace here, no grand ballrooms, no walls or gates, no building, no doors; all of it is one enormous illusion." Then the man is identified as the Baal Shem Tov, and in fact the allegory of the king and his kingdom is a teaching of the Baal Shem Tov. The Baal Shem Tov's parable about God follows: [29]

A mighty king built a great palace with many chambers, one within the other. Many walls were round about it, each surrounded by the other. Only one gate was open, and opposite it were many doors. He who entered saw many beautiful pictures and costly vessels. The king dwelt in the innermost chamber, far removed from him who entered. When they had finished building the palace, the princes of the realm and the great men of the land were invited to come to the king. But when they came to the palace gate, they found it barred and the doors locked. They now asked one another in surprise, "How shall we enter, seeing that such a multitude of walls separate us?" They looked at the gate and pondered. They saw nothing but wall upon wall. Thus they stood a long time, until finally the king's son came and spoke to them: "Know ye not that my father is exceedingly wise and practiced and skilled in the art of conjuring up false images? Behold, the entire palace is unreal. There is no wall here, no gate, and no door—it is all an illusion. It bears the semblance of reality to him who looks upon it. But in very truth, the space here is empty—it stretches unconfined in all directions."

David Shahar's use of the kabbalistic notion of *tzimtzum* in "The Death of the Little God"[30] is truly astonishing. In the first place, *tzimtzum* is one of the most esoteric concepts of Kabbalah, which was formulated to explain how God could be ever-present and still leave a place for the existence of the universe. According to this concept, God first contracted Himself in order to make room for the world, a notion not very far off from the astronomical theory that the universe was once contracted all at one point and then proceeded to expand and will someday revert to the process of contraction. Shahar makes an inspired connection between the kabbalistic concept and the present-day theological position that God is dead. For God to die, in Shahar's tale, is for Him to contract and shrink away, as He does for the man who is obsessed with the notion that God is growing smaller, and whose death comes after a dream in which he discusses with his father, who is no longer living, the imminent death of God:

> His father sat on the table, crossed his arms over his chest, which was covered only by the thin vest, and said, "Now tell me what's going on in the world."
>
> "The world is growing bigger, Father, and God is growing smaller. . . . God is growing smaller, Father, and now, already, compared to an ant, God looks like a flea compared to an elephant. He is still alive, wriggling and writhing under the weight of the world He created, but it is only a matter of time before His death agonies cease."
>
> "And how long will it take before He disappears?" asked his father, his face becoming serious.
>
> "Two or three weeks, perhaps less."
>
> "Then this is the end."
>
> "Yes, this is the end."

The impact of this story comes largely because the reader cannot help but be fascinated at the man's belief that God is growing literally smaller, which becomes ludicrous when presented in this concrete fashion, while it is far more acceptable in the abstract concept of *tzimtzum*. At the same time, the modern reader cannot help but recognize the echo of the death-of-God debate in this story and marvel at how well it is able to create a new perspective on that issue as well. Above all, the story is the moving narrative of an isolated man whose fear took the form of a kabbalistic concept made concrete and whose accidental death shortly after the dream of the imminent death of God seems to be a confirmation of his obsession, ironic as that may seem.

Edmond Jabès, on the other hand, echoes the original kabbalistic usage of the term *tzimtzum* in his brief narrative "The Disappearance."[31] In addition, Jabès hints at a parallel between *tzimtzum* and human introspection when he describes the process as "God, within himself," who "comes to terms with the Face." In many ways the writing of Jabès is in a direct line with the Talmud, and at the same time obviously is a new departure in which his fragmented style creates the impression that his words are an echo and response to a dialogue that has already lasted four thousand years.[32]

A wide range of potential approaches to the same subject is found in three stories about the Fall from grace. One of these, "Paradise"[33] by Franz Kafka, makes the remarkable assertion that the expulsion from Eden was a blessing in disguise, since otherwise it would have been necessary to destroy the Garden. Thus Kafka postulates the continued existence of the Garden, even into our own age, as an ideal of perfection that can only serve to inspire. In "The Eden Angel"[34] Nachman Rapp retells the story of the Fall and expulsion from Eden very much in the biblical mold. However, he adds to the narrative an angel sympathetic to Adam and Eve who shares in their temptation and expulsion, losing, in the process, his angelic nature to become human instead. As for Rabbi Harold S. Kushner's "The Tree of Id,"[35] it proposes that the narrative of the Fall be viewed primarily in psychological terms and identifies the Tree of Life with the source of instinctive behavior.

Each of these narratives uses the myth of the Fall as its starting point, but each leads to a different conclusion, draws a different lesson, and thus reflects the original narrative from a different perspective. Part of the power in these tales comes from the fact that they compel readers to reconsider the old narrative at the same time they are presented with the new. The tension of the divergences between the old and new, along with the delight the new vision brings to the old, provide a considerable satisfaction in themselves. Of further edification is the recognition that each of these tales is also a modern form of midrashic interpretation of the original narrative of the Fall. Together these stories expand the boundaries of meaning of the original myth and make that meaning far more personal and pertinent. Finally, they serve as proof of the profundity of the original and of the attention it continues to attract.

One of the most popular biblical episodes that has been the subject of numerous retellings is that of the *Akedah*, the binding of Isaac by Abraham. In "Abraham"[36] Franz Kafka imagines an Abraham "who was prepared to satisfy the demand for a sacrifice immediately, with the promptness of a waiter, but was unable to bring it off because he could not get away, being indispensable." Jakov Lind's "The Near Murder"[37] retells the story of the *Akedah* from a modern, almost psychiatric perspective in which a father hears a voice command him to kill his only son, and he attempts to obey. This dimension of the tale, always present in the biblical narrative but in a more latent fashion, is truly horrifying when made overt and refashions the reader's view of the *Akedah* for all time. Rabbi Michael Strassfeld's "Isaac"[38] is powerfully identified with its subject and implies an unsuspected link between Abraham and the ram, which, after it is considered, provides a valuable new perspective on the ancient tale. "The Tale of the Ram"[39] by Rabbi Tsvi Blanchard also suggests a new perspective from which to regard the *Akedah*—as an act less significant in itself than for the fact that it took place at the very moment that the ram, which had been created before the rest of the world, chose to gore the Messiah, delaying the time of his arrival. "Rivka on Mount Moriah"[40] by Laya Firestone has Rivka (Rebecca), Isaac's wife, return to the place of the *Akedah* before giving birth to Jacob and Esau, implying that the struggle of the twins in the womb, which is amply described in the midrashic literature, was the turning point in her life, as the binding was in the life of Isaac.

The *Akedah* has long remained one of the most central and perplexing episodes in the Bible, and the range of these interpretations strongly suggests that it has lost none of its power, nor is its essential meaning any more apparent at this time than when it was first written down. And each of these stories, in its own way, refutes the simplistic interpretation that the *Akedah* should merely be regarded as a test by God of Abraham, or as an event intended to demark the elimination of human sacrifice by the Jews. For these authors, certainly, the original tale has retained its mystery, which grows with each subsequent interpretation rather than being diminished.

The choice of the authors who have utilized traditional sources in the ways outlined here must be recognized, above all, as an act of affirmation. At every stage in the evolution of Jewish literature there have been those prepared and even anxious to declare that the Book was closed and that all that came afterward lacked significance. These modern Jewish authors, on the contrary, insist that the tradition is still alive and that the ancient tale may still be retold in new ways. Their desire is clearly, as Edmond Jabes puts it, "to be in the book . . . to be part of it. To be responsible for a word or a sentence, a stanza or chapter."[41]

As these examples demonstrate, many modern Jewish authors have sought out their own roles and relationships with their tradition, while retaining the right to embellish as they see fit. These embellishments are the lifeblood of this particular type of literature, for it is understood that once a tale is frozen in one form, it becomes an object for analysis, not a living force; much of the power of the retelling comes from the new perspectives brought to the old tale, so that it can be relived in another generation.

Notes

Chapter 1
Reimagining the Bible

1. *Pirke de Rabbi Eliezer*, chap. 46.

2. The Talmud was codified around the 5th century C.E., but many of the legends in it go back at least to the beginning of the rabbinic era, around the 1st century, and many are almost certainly older than that.

3. From Gen. Rabbah 56. Also Targum Jonathan on Gen. 22:19. Also *Pirke de Rabbi Eliezer*, chap. 31. Also *Hadar Zekenin* 10b in *Beit ha-Midrash*, edited by A. Jellinek (Jerusalem, 1967, V:157). Also Commentary on *Sefer Yetzirah*, p. 125.

4. *Pirke de Rabbi Eliezer*, chap. 31.

5. It seems likely that the Christian account of the death of Jesus and his resurrection on the third day are being echoed in the three years that Isaac was said to have spent in Paradise, before his soul returned and he was reborn. This indicates that there was Christian influence on Jewish legends, as well as the enormous impact of Jewish legends on the formation of the Christian legendary tradition. See *The Last Trial* by Sholem Spiegel for a thorough discussion of the Binding of Isaac.

6. The term *"Aggadah"* has both a specific and a more general meaning. In the narrow sense the term refers to the body of legends that appear within the Talmud itself. (These legends constitute about a quarter of the Talmud, and most were collected in the 16th-century anthology *Ein Yakov*.) In a broader sense, *aggadah* can refer to any postbiblical Jewish legend and is frequently used in contrast to the term *"Halakhah,"* meaning the law. This implies that there are two kinds of major realms of traditional study, that of defining and expounding on the law (*Halakhah*) and all of the remaining material, which may be grouped under the category of *Aggadah* and consists primarily of legends. The term *"Midrash"* (from the root *darash*, meaning both "to search out" and "to expound") likewise has a double

usage. In the narrow sense it refers to all post-talmudic legends up to the kabbalistic period, which begins in the 13th century. But in the broader sense it is interchangeable with the term *aggadah* to denote a Jewish legend (a midrash) or the body of Jewish legends (the Midrash).

7. The term "Torah" refers to both the Five Books of Moses and also, in a broader sense, to the whole of Jewish law and lore.

8. The primary sources for the Enoch legend are the three Books of Enoch. *The Book of Enoch (1 Enoch)* and *The Slavonic Book Enoch (2 Enoch)* are included in *The Apocrypha and Pseudepigrapha of the Old Testament*, vol. 2, edited by R. H. Charles. The most recent translations of these books can be found in *Old Testament Pseudepigrapha*, edited by James Charlesworth. Enoch's transformation into Metatron is described in *3 Enoch*.

9. On Shavuot, many Sephardic communities read a *ketubah* (Jewish wedding contract) for the marriage of God and Israel, which was written by Israel Najara in the 16th century in Safed. See p. 87 for a partial translation of the text.

10. M. Avot. 5:22.

11. From "Myth in Judaism," in *On Judaism* by Martin Buber, p. 106.

12. S. S. Rab. on Song of Songs 1:2.

13. The Talmud consists of two interrelated texts. The older is the Mishnah, which was composed around 220 C.E., and the second is known as the Gemara, which took shape in approximately 500 C.E. and is a commentary on the Mishnah. Traditionally, the pages of the Talmud reflect this relationship: the text of the Mishnah appears in bold type in the middle of the page, surrounded by the Gemara in smaller type, while both are surrounded by, in even smaller type, traditional commentaries by Rashi, the Tosafists, Hananel ben Hashiel (died 1055), and others. The Mishnah is actually far more complex than a commentary or interpretation of the Bible, in the way that we understand the term "interpretation." When we attempt to interpret a text, our goal is to understand what the author was trying to say at the time he said it. The Mishnah, on the other hand, finds an appropriate passage on which to base its innovations and then elaborates extensive rules and regulations that often come to seem remote from their source. An entire legal world can spring up from a brief, seemingly simple biblical law. The complex system of *eruvim*, for example, which permits establishing fictitious boundaries, involves the symbolic mingling (*eruv*—a mixture) of time and space and allows a Jew to engage in otherwise forbidden practices such as cooking on a holiday for the upcoming Sabbath or carrying things within a city on the Sabbath. While its origin is the biblical injunction to sanctify the Sabbath, its application goes far beyond this basic commandment and takes on a life of its own.

14. B. Hag. 3. B. Avod. Zar. 18a adds: "He who says that the Torah is not from heaven will have no portion in the World to Come."

15. For an example of a literary secret confession, see "Everything and Nothing" by Jorge Luis Borges. Here Borges suggests that the secret of Shakespeare's ability to create convincing characters along the entire social spectrum came from his own lack of identity and that Shakespeare hid a secret confession of this in *Othello*, when Othello says, "I am not what I am." See *Labyrinths*, by Jorge Luis Borges, pp. 248–249.

16. B. Men. 29b, drawing on B. Shab. 88b–89a. The crowns of the letters are the *taggin*, three small marks written on top of the letters *shin, ayin, tet, nun, zayin, gimmel*, and *tzaddik* in the form of a crown.

17. *Drashot Beit ha-Levi.* This midrash goes on to say that Moses originally wrote everything down on the first tablets of the Law, but after the sin of the golden calf and the breaking of the first set of the tablets, God told Moses not to write everything on the second set of tablets.

18. Even during the talmudic era, this constituted a great amount of learning to master, as this passage demonstrates: "Our rabbis were taught, 'Eighty disciples did Hillel have; thirty of them were worthy that the *Shekhinah* should rest upon them, as it did upon Moses, our teacher; thirty of them were worthy that the sun should be stopped for their sake, as it did before Joshua; and twenty were ordinary. The superior among them was Yonatan ben Uziel; the inferior among them was Rabbi Yohanan ben Zakkai. It was related of Rabbi Yohanan ben Zakkai that he did not leave unstudied the Bible, the Mishnah, the Gemara, the *Halakhot*, the *Aggadot*, subtle points in the interpretation of the biblical laws, the special points in rabbinic enactment, the restrictive and nonrestrictive rules, rules of analogy, astronomy, geometry, the whisper of angels, the whisper of evil spirits, and the whisper of palm trees, foxes, fables, major affairs and minor affairs. And since the most inferior of all was so great, how much the more was the most superior of all? It was said of Yonatan ben Uziel that when he studied the Law every bird that flew overhead was instantly consumed in flames' " (B. Suk. 28).

19. The first four volumes of *The Legends of the Jews* contain Ginzberg's compilation and retelling of the aggadic sources, the fifth and sixth volumes contain valuable notes, and the seventh volume is an extensive index. A single-volume condensation of the first four volumes, *Legends of the Bible,* is available.

Chapter 2
The Aggadic Tradition

1. See R. H. Charles, *The Apocrypha and Pseudepigrapha of the Old Testament,* and James H. Charlesworth, *Old Testament Pseudepigrapha.*

2. Ezekiel's vision of a *Merkavah,* a divine chariot, and a central talmudic passage (B. Hag. 14b) about four sages who entered Paradise and only one, Rabbi Akiba, who emerged in peace, serve as the models for the *Hekhalot* texts of *Merkavah* mysticism, a particular category of texts dating from the 1st to the 8th centuries that describe journeys into Paradise.

3. "Rabbi Yohanan was sitting and lecturing: 'In the future the Holy One, blessed be He, will bring jewels and pearls the size of thirty cubits square, twenty ells in height and ten in width, and will place them at the gates of Jerusalem.' And one disciple sneered at him: 'We do not even find a jewel as large as the egg of a turtle dove and you say we shall find jewels of such sizes?' Thereafter it happened that the same disciple was on a boat on the high sea, and he saw angels who sawed jewels and pearls the size of thirty ells square, boring holes in them twenty ells in height and ten in width. He asked them, 'For whom is this?' And they answered: 'The Holy One, blessed be He, will place them at the gates of Jerusalem.' When he returned he said to Rabbi Yohanan: 'Lecture, Rabbi, for all you said is true, as I have seen it for myself!' " (B. Bab. Bat. 74).

4. In the case of *Pirke de Rabbi Eliezer,* for example, it has been variously dated as originating between the 8th and 12th centuries C.E., but it is generally recognized that much of its material is based on earlier sources. Today most estimates tend toward the earlier date.

5. B. Sot. 6b for the legend about Luz as a city of immortals. B. Suk. 53a for the legend about the appointment with death. The likely reason that Luz was identified as a city of immortals is that Luz also refers to the one bone, at the bottom of the spine, that is the last to decompose.

6. Gen. Rab. 69:8.

7. See "Dovid ha-Melech's Matoneh" in *Dos Buch fun Nissyonot* (Yiddish), edited by Israel Osman (Los Angeles, 1926). See also "The Cave of King David" in *Gabriel's Palace: Jewish Mystical Tales*, ed. Howard Schwartz, pp. 139–141. The modern Hebrew author Yakov HaCohen has written a play based on this legend, *The City of Luz*. See also "The City of Luz" in *Elijah's Violin & Other Jewish Fairy Tales*, pp. 279–293.

8. B. Hag. 12a.

9. Gen. Rab. 24:2.

10. Gen. Rab. 3:6, 11:2; Rashi on Genesis 1:4.

11. *Degel Mahaneh Ephraim*, Bereshit 3c.

12. *The Holy Scriptures*, Jewish Publicity Society.

13. King James version.

14. *The Anchor Bible*, Doubleday.

15. *Midrash Tanhuma*, Kedoshim 9.

16. Gen. Rab. 31:11.

17. B. Bab. Bat. 16b.

18. For a more detailed retelling of the legend of the *Tzohar*, see "The Tzohar" in *Gabriel's Palace: Jewish Mystical Tales*, edited by Howard Schwartz, pp. 59–62, and the accompanying note on pp. 287–288.

19. The sources of this myth include B. Hag. 12a, Gen. Rab. 3:4, Mid. Teh. 104:4; Gen. Rab. 3:6; Ex. Rab. 35:1; Gen. Rab. 42:3; and Zohar I:31b–32a.

20. The midrashim trace Cain's seemingly innate evil character to his conception, which the rabbis attributed to the serpent, who is said to have fathered Cain with Eve, while Adam was the father of Abel. Thus, all generations have descended from the seed of Cain or of Abel and his brothers, such as Shem (see 1 Chron. 1:1). The seed of Cain was believed to have manifested itself in the persons of Ishmael and Esau, while Isaac and Jacob were descended from the seed of Shem (*Pirke de Rabbi Eliezer*, chap. 21).

21. In the midrash it is stated that Cain and Abel each were born with twin sisters, who served as their wives, plus one other sister, born with Abel as his twin. "Rabbi Joshua ben Karchan said: 'Only two (Adam and Eve) entered the bed, and seven left it, including Cain and his twin sister, and Abel and his two twin sisters' " (Gen. Rab. 22:2).

22. The nature of the conflict is thus portrayed in Genesis Rabbah: "About what did they quarrel? 'Come,' they said, 'let us divide the world.' One took the land and the other the movables. The former said, 'The land you stand on is mine,' while the latter retorted: 'What you are wearing is mine.' One said, 'Strip'; the other retorted, 'Fly.' Out of this quarrel Cain rose up against his brother Abel and slew him (Gen. 4:8) . . . Judah Berebbi said: 'Their quarrel was about the first Eve (Lilith).' Said Rabbi Aibu: 'The first Eve had returned to dust. Then about what was their quarrel?' Said Rabbi Huna: 'An additional twin was born with Abel, and each claimed her. The one claimed: 'I will have her, because I am the firstborn' while the other maintained: 'I must have her because she was born with me' " (Gen. Rab. 22:7).

23. There was general agreement that Cain killed Abel with a stone although Rabbi Shimon said that he killed him with a staff (Gen. Rab. 22:8).

24. Since no one had previously died, there was no precedent for burial. Furthermore, the ground was reluctant to accept Abel's body. In some versions it is said that a sparrow, burying its mate, demonstrated the principle of burial, and in others it is said that Abel's body remained unburied until after the death of Adam. It was possible to bury Adam because, according to another midrash, the dust from which he had been formed had been gathered from the four corners of the earth (*Pirke de Rabbi Eliezer*, chap. 21).

25. A late midrashic collection, *Sefer ha-Zikhronot* (Hebrew) by Jerahmeel ben Solomon, compiled by Eleazar ben Asher ha-Levi, translated by Moses Gaster as *The Chronicles of Jerahmeel* (London: 1899), states in 24:2: "Cain was the first to surround a city with a wall, for he was afraid of his enemies."

26. A sixth account appears in *Pirke de Rabbi Eliezer* (chap. 21): " 'Master of the Universe!' Cain pleaded, '*My sin is too great to be borne* (Gen. 4:13), for it has no atonement!' This confession was accounted to him as repentance. 'Moreover,' he continued, 'one will arise and slay me by pronouncing Thy Great Name against me!' What did the Holy One, blessed He, do? He took one of the twenty-two letters of the Torah, and set it upon Cain's arm like a tattoo that he should not he killed." Another version has it that the letter was affixed to his forehead. The unexpected notion that Cain's reply to God in Genesis 4:13 was reckoned as repentance can be found in *Pesikta Rabbati* (50:5), as follows: "Adam met Cain and asked: 'My son, how is it that your case turned out this way?' Cain replied: 'I resolved repentance and was delivered.' When Adam heard this, he began to strike his own face, saying, 'Is such the great power of repentance *(teshuvah)?* I did not know!' "

27. *Midrash Tanhuma-Yelammedenu*, Ber. 1:11.

28. Ibid.

29. Note how the continuity of the existence of the Angel of Death is provided for by Lamech taking over that role after Cain, although this legend does not suggest how long Lamech was condemned to this incarnation, or who succeeded him in the role.

30. It is interesting to note that one interpretation the rabbis did not propose is that Cain's curse to be "*a fugitive and a wanderer*" was intended to last for all time. While the seed of Cain were seen as a plague to future generations, the Midrash does not carry Cain beyond the generation of the Flood. But this motif of the eternal wanderer that is suggested by the biblical curse of Cain is fully developed in the Christian legend of the Wandering Jew, and it seems possible that the legend of Cain served as a prototype to that of the Wandering Jew. According to this legend, as Jesus was carrying the cross on the way to Golgotha, he stumbled and came to rest against the house of a Jew, Ahasuerus, who emerged from it and ordered Jesus to leave, perhaps out of fear of being implicated as a sympathizer. Jesus replied by saying that he would leave, but that the man would wander until he came back, that is, until the Second Coming. This initiated the legend of the Wandering Jew, who subsequently appeared in tales told in every generation and in many places. Like Cain, he was a man marked for his sin; in this case the sign that marked him was his inability to die. His role came to be that of one who witnessed all that came to pass, and also that of a man obsessed with the search for his death. The contemporary story, "The Wandering Jew," by David Slabotsky, relates how he finally succeeded in this quest. See *GNC*, pp. 533–534.

31. In *Sefer ha-Zikhronot* 24:3, reference is made to "Lamech, who slew Cain in the seventh generation, after Cain had confessed his sin, repented, and his punishment had been suspended until the seventh generation." This late version combines Cain's repentance with the legend of the slaying of Cain at the hands of Lamech.

32. Lev. 24:16–17.

33. *Sefer ha-Yashar (va-Yigash)* 109b–110a.

34. *Sefer ha-Yashar (va-Yigash)* A variant is found in *Midrash ha-Gadol, Vayigash* 45:26, where Serah waited until Jacob was praying, and then hinted the news by asking, "Is Joseph in Egypt?"

35. Ex. Rab. 5:13.

36. B. Sot. 13a, Ex. Rab. 20:19, Deut. Rab. 11:7 (where Serah is identified by the name Segulah) and *Mekilta de Rabbi Ishmael, Beshallah* 24a–24b. See also Zohar II:46a.

37. *Pesikta de Rab Kahana* 11:13. The rabbi was probably Rabbi Yohanan ben Nappaha.

38. The legend that Serah was one of those who entered heaven alive is found in *Yalkut Shimoni* II, remez and *Derekh Eretz Zuta* 1:18. The legend that Serah lives in a heavenly palace is found in the Zohar III:167b. Others who entered Paradise alive include Enoch, Elijah, the Messiah, and Eliezer, servant of Abraham.

39. See Harold Heifetz, ed., *Zen and Hasidism*.

40. *In Praise of the Baal Shem Tov*, translated and edited by Dan Ben-Amos and Jerome R. Mintz.

41. *Shivhei ha-Ram*, edited by Rabbi Nathan of Nemirov (Ostrog: 1816).

Chapter 3
Tools of Interpretation

1. B. Yeb. 13.

2. B. Ber. 55a.

3. Gen. Rab. 1:15.

4. B. Bat. Metz. 59b.

5. B. Eruv. 21b.

6. Perhaps because of the early splits with the Samaritans, who insisted that only the Pentateuch was sacred, and not the rest of the Bible, and with the Karaites, who denied the validity of the Talmud, the rabbis took care to create a system of interpretation that avoided the kinds of conflict associated with various fundamental sects, which permit only the narrowest, most literal reading of the Scriptures.

7. The seven rules of Hillel can be found in *Avot de-Rabbi Natan* 37, as well as in Sifra introd. 1:7 and B. San. 7b. The thirteen principles of Rabbi Ishmael are found in Sifra, introd. 5. In B. Git. 67a there are references to rules formulated by Rabbi Ishmael's rival, Rabbi Akiba. A discussion of these principles of Hillel and Rabbi Ishmael and those of Rabbi Eliezer ben Jose, including translations of the rules, can be found in *Introduction to the Talmud and Midrash*, by H. L. Strack and G. Stemberger, pp. 19–34.

8. Targum Pseudo-Jonathan on Gen. 11:4.

9. *Wisdom of Solomon* 10:10.

10. Philo, *On the Migration of Abraham*, chap. 11.

11. B. San. 69b.

12. B. San. 91a–b.

13. M. Yad. 3.5.

14. The marriage between God and Israel that Rabbi Akiba discerned in the Song of Songs is a theme later found in the Zohar (Prologue 8a). Describing the forthcoming wedding, on Shavuot, the day of the Giving of the Torah, Rabbi Shimon bar Yohai is quoted as saying: "O my sons, happy is your portion, for on the morrow the bride will not enter the bridal canopy except in your company; for all those who help to prepare her adornments tonight will be recorded in the book of remembrance, and the Holy One, blessed be He, will bless them with seventy blessings and crown them with crowns of the celestial word." Also, in many Sephardic congregations, prior to the Torah reading on the first day of Shavuot, a *ketubah* (marriage contract) is read, betrothing God and Israel. The most widely used text of such a *ketubah* is that of the Safed mystic and poet Israel Najara (c. 1550–1625 C.E.). For a partial translation of this text, see chapter "The Mythology of Judaism," pp. 85–99.

15. S. S. Rab. 1:8.

16. *Pardes* was originally a Persian word meaning an enclosed area. In the Bible it is used to mean "orchard" (see Song of Songs 4:13). In rabbinic Hebrew it takes on the additional meaning of "Paradise," after the Greek *paradeisos*, which is used in the Septuagint to translate *Gan Eden* (the Garden of Eden).

17. The method of interpretation known as *Pardes* was most likely invented, or at least codified, by Moshe de Leon, author of the Zohar, according to the widely accepted findings of Gershom Scholem. According to Scholem, Moshe de Leon was also the author of a text, since lost, entitled *Sefer Pardes*. Scholem speculates that this text was a theoretical treatise of *Pardes* as a method of explication, a concept that in any case dates from the same period, the 13th century. See *Major Trends in Jewish Mysticism*, p. 400, note 15.

18. For a discussion of this legend, see chapter "Tales of the Great Jewish Mystics," pp. 124–128.

19. Professor Marc Bregman of Hebrew Union College has suggested the theoretical possibility of a fifth level of *Pardes*, which he has named *nitzraf*, suggesting purification through unification—in which all four other levels of interpretation might be forged into one, permitting the text to be perceived simultaneously in all its levels of meaning as a total unity and wholeness, not unlike that which is the goal of Gestalt psychology.

Chapter 4
On Jewish Fairy Tales

1. See *Elijah's Violin & Other Jewish Fairy Tales* (hereafter *EV*), selected and retold by Howard Schwartz (New York: Harper & Row, 1983), for the folk and fairy tales discussed in this chapter.

2. For a Jewish variant of Cinderella, see "The Exiled Princess" in *EV*, pp. 263–269. For the earliest Jewish version of Rapunzel, see "The Princess in the Tower" in *EV*, pp. 47–52. For variants of "The Golden Bird," see "The Golden Feather" in *EV*, pp. 137–147, and "The Golden Bird" in *EV*, pp. 247–253. For a variant of "Sleeping Beauty," see "The Wonder Child" in *The Wonder Child & Other Jewish Fairy Tales*, edited by Howard Schwartz and Barbara Rush, pp. 1–8. For a version of "Snow White," see "Romana" in *Miriam's Tambourine*, ed. by Howard Schwartz, pp. 67–78.

3. B. San. 95a.
4. B. Git. 68b.
5. Ibid.
6. Y. Hag. 77d–78a.
7. B. San. 95a.
8. B. Git. 68b.
9. Ibid.
10. Y. Hag. 77d–78a.
11. B. Git. 68b.
12. *Maaseh ha-Nemalah* in *Beit ha-midrash*, edited by A. Jellinek (Jerusalem: 1938).
13. B. Shab. 30a.
14. B. Sot. 2a.
15. B. Suk. 53a.
16. B. Sot. 46b.
17. See *Dos Bukh fun Nisyoynes*, edited by Israel Osman (Los Angeles: 1926). Also see "The City of Luz" in *EV*, pp. 279–293.
17. Oxford Bodleiana Or 134, published in *Sefer ha-Ma'asiyot* in *The Exempla of the Rabbis*, edited by Moses Gaster (New York: 1968). A later version is found in the *Maaseh Buch* (Basel: 1601).
19. *Oseh Pele*, compiled by Y. S. Farhi (Leghorn: 1902).
20. *Ma'aseh Yerushalmi*, edited by Yehuda L. Zlotnik (Jerusalem: 1946).
21. Deut. Rab. 11:10. "Thereupon God kissed Moses and took away his soul with a kiss of the mouth, and God, if one might say so, wept."
22. "Partnership with Asmodeus" is found in *Shiv'im Sippurim ve-Sippur mi-Pi Yehudey Luv*, edited by Dov Noy (Jerusalem: 1967). IFA 3523, told by David Hadad. "The Magic Flute of Asmodeus" is found in *Min ha-Mabua*, edited by Eliezer Marcus (Haifa: 1966). IFA 6053, collected by Rivka Ashkenazi from her father, Sasson Ashkenazi.
23. *Eretz ha-Hayim*, collected by Hayim Liebersohn (Przemysl, Poland: 1926). A variant can be found in *Shivhei ha-Ari*, edited by Shlomo Meinsterl (Jerusalem: 1905).
24. *Sefer Sippure: Kedushim*, edited by Gedalyah Nigal (Jerusalem: 1977), first published in Warsaw in 1866.
25. *Eretz ha-Hayim*, collected by Hayim Liebersohn (Przemysl, Poland: 1926).
26. *Sippure: Ma'asiyot* by Rabbi Nachman of Bratslav, edited by Rabbi Nathan Sternhartz of Nemirov.
27. Ibid.
28. Ibid.
29. Ibid.
30. *Genesis Apocryphon*, columns xix–xxii. From Geza Vermes, *The Dead Sea Scrolls*, 2nd ed., pp. 215–224.
31. *Yiddishe Folklor*, edited by Yehuda L. Cahan (Vilna: 1938).
32. *Yiddishe Folkmayses*, edited by Yehuda L. Cahan (Vilna: 1931).
33. *Judeo-Spanish Ballads from New York*, edited by Samuel G. Armistead and Joseph H. Silverman (Berkeley: 1981).
34. *Aggadta di B'nai Moshe* from *Beit ha-Midrash*, edited by Adolf Jellinek (Jerusalem: 1938).
35. IFA 6414, collected by Yakov Laseri from his father, Machlouf Laseri.

36. *Hodesh Hodesh ve-Sippuro: 1968–1969*, edited by Edna Hechal (Haifa: 1969). Collected by Ilana Zohar from her mother, Flora Cohen.

Chapter 5
Mermaid and Siren: The Polar Roles of Lilith and Eve

1. *Ohel Elimelech*, edited by A. S. B. Michelson (Parmishla: 1870). A variant is found in *Sefer Or Yesharim*, story no. 199, edited by Moshe Hayim Kleinmann of Brisk (Warsaw: 1884).

2. In B. Ned. 11a it is stated that "from a negative rule you can learn a positive one"; thus by knowing what is prohibited you can derive what is permitted.

3. *Yalkut Shimoni* (Gen) 44, compiled by Shimon Ashkenazi. (Frankfurt a.M.: 1687).

4. B. Kid. 80a.

5. Ibid.

6. The legend does not explain how Lilith learned the secret of the pronunciation of the Name, but perhaps it was not secret in the Garden of Eden.

7. *The Testament of Solomon*, chap. 17. It is believed that Lilith's role as a seducer of men was based on the Babylonian night demon Lilitu, a succubus who seduces men in their sleep, while Lilith's role as a child slayer closely resembles the Babylonian demon Lamashtu. It is interesting to note that the roles of Lilitu and Lamashtu became blurred together, just as Lilith takes on the roles of both seducer and child slayer.

8. *Alte Yidishe Zagen Oder Sipurim*, edited by Ayzik-Meyer Dik, pp. 32–39 (Vilna: 1876).

9. *Kav ha-Yashar* by Tzvi Hirsh Kaidanover (Frankfurt: 1903).

10. *Lilith: the First Eve, Historical and Psychological Aspects of the Dark Feminine*, by Siegmund Hurwitz (Einsiedeln, Switzerland: 1992).

11. *The Uses of Enchantment: The Meaning and Importance of Fairy Tales* by Bruno Bettelheim (New York: 1976).

12. Gen. Rab. 19:3. See also Rashi on Gen. 3:4.

13. *Pirke de Rabbi Eliezer*, chap. 13.

14. *Pirke de Rabbi Eliezer*, chap. 21.

15. Foreword, by Dov Noy, in *The Book of Jewish Women's Tales* edited by Barbara Rush, pp. xiii–xxiii.

16. IFA 4563, collected by Zalman Barhav from Yakov Chaprak. From *Shishim Sippure Am*, edited by Zalman Bararav (Haifa: 1964).

17. "The Story of Lilith and Eve" from *The Stove and Other Stories* by Jakov Lind (New York: 1986), pp. 59–61.

Chapter 6
Jewish Tales of the Supernatural

1. The story of the demon in the tree is from a 16th-century Yiddish manuscript in Cambridge (Trinity College) Hebrew mss. 136 #5. Note that most of the tales referred to in this chapter can be found in *Lilith's Cave: Jewish Tales of the Supernatural*, originally published by Harper & Row in 1987 and reprinted by Oxford University Press. (Abbreviated after this as *LC*.) A version of this chapter appears as the Introduction to that book.

2. Y. San. 7:13. See "Rabbi Joshua and the Witch," p. 35, in *Miriam's Tambourine: Jewish Folktales from Around the World*, selected and retold by Howard Schwartz. (Abbreviated after this as *MT*).

3. See "The Rabbi and the Witch" in *LC*, pp. 62–63, and the accompanying note.

4. B. San. 67b. The passage reads in full as follows:

> Abaye said: "The laws regarding sorcerers indicate that certain actions are punished by stoning, others are exempt from punishment, yet forbidden, while still others are entirely permitted. Thus if one actually performs magic, he is stoned; if he merely creates an illusion, he is exempt, yet it is forbidden. What is entirely permitted? Such as was performed by Rabbi Hanina and Rabbi Oshaia, who spent every Sabbath eve studying the Laws of Creation, by means of which they created a calf and ate it.

Note that this creation of a calf is not only parallel to the creation of Adam by God, but also of the later creation of the Golem, a man of clay, by Rabbi Judah Loew.

5. See *Shabbatai Sevi: The Mystical Messiah*, by Gershom Scholem.

6. Forty years after it was founded by Professor Dov Noy of Hebrew University, the Israel Folktale Archives (IFA), located in Haifa, has collected more than twenty thousand tales from every Jewish ethnic group in Israel and has published more than sixty volumes of these tales.

7. "The Chronicle of Ephraim" is found in *Sippure Kedoshim* (Leipzig: 1866). The story of Moses in the pit is found in *Sefer ha-Zikhronot* (Hebrew) by Jerahmeel ben Solomon, compiled by Eleazar ben Asher ha-Levi, translated by Moses Gaster as *The Chronicles of Jerahmeel* (London: 1899), 46:9–10.

8. According to a startling legend found in the Zohar (III:69a), after the destruction of the Temple and the exile of the *Shekhinah*, the Bride of God, Lilith offered herself to God in place of his bride. And so fallen was the state of existence that God accepted Lilith as His consort.

9. For *The Testament of Solomon*, see *The Old Testament Pseudepigrapha*, edited by James H. Charlesworth, vol. 1, pp. 935–988. For *The Book of Tobit*, see *The Apocrypha: An American Translation* by Edgar J. Goodspeed, pp. 107–130.

10. B. Git. 68b.

11. Although the majority of tales portray the marriage of humans and demons, a few variants describe marriages between humans and ghosts (such a tale is recounted by Zipporah Greenfield of Yemen) or even humans and the dead (see "The Finger" in *LC*, pp. 51–54).

12. *Midrash Tanhuma* (Hebrew) 1:20, edited by Solomon Buber (Vilna: 1891). See Gershom Scholem, *Jewish Gnosticism, Merkabah Mysticism and Talmudic Tradition*, pp. 72–74.

13. *Ma'aseh Yerushalmi* (Hebrew), edited by Yehuda L. Zlotnik (Jerusalem: 1946). See "The Demon Princess" in Howard Schwartz, *Elijah's Violin & Other Jewish Fairy Tales* (hereafter *EV*) for a retelling of this tale.

14. *Maaseh Nissim* (Yiddish), compiled by Jeptha Yozpa ben Naftali (Amsterdam: 1696).

15. For an extended discussion of the midwife tale type, see "Is There a Jewish Folk Religion?" by Dov Noy in *Studies in Jewish Folklore*, edited by Frank Talmage, pp. 273–286.

16. Note that the aunt's name, Shifra, is the same as that of the midwife in Exodus 1:15.

17. Why is it that older written versions of this story all concern a man and the prevalent oral versions all concern a woman? One possible reason is that the version about the midwife serves as an ideal story to be told by women to other women, especially girls, as a means of teaching a strong feminine role model. It seems likely that the medieval written version reentered the oral tradition and was transformed in the process into a woman's tale.

18. Even though this tale strongly appears to have been shaped by actual events, the pattern it follows is familiar in world folklore and is identified in *The Types of the Folktale* by Antti Aarne and Stith Thompson as type 926A, where a demon takes on the appearance of a man or woman. Interestingly, it is most often a shepherd in these tales that recognizes the demon for what it is, just as happens in this story. The most likely explanation is that the mystifying events surrounding the wife's madness were best explained within the existing framework of this tale type.

19. *Shivhei ha-Ari*, compiled by Shlomo Meinsterl (Jerusalem: 1905).

20. *Maaseh Buch* (Yiddish) #152, compiled by Jacob ben Abraham of Mezhirech (Basel: 1601).

21. Both of these texts emerged in the 16th century, showing that accounts of dybbuks were told in both Palestine and Eastern Europe at around the same time, probably due to travelers who brought such tales back and forth. Indeed, travelers from the Holy Land who sought funds in Europe were particularly welcomed because of their ability to regale their hosts with tales.

22. "The Lost Princess" in *Sippurei Ma'asiyot* (Hebrew) by Rabbi Nachman of Bratslav, edited by Rabbi Nathan Sternhart of Nemirov (Ostrog: 1816). For a retelling of this tale, see "The Lost Princess" in *EV*, pp. 210–218.

23. Ansky's *The Dybbuk* was first produced in Yiddish by the Vilna troupe in 1920.

24. The earliest accounts of such possessions by demons (rather than dybbuks) appear much earlier, however, and are recorded both in the history of Josephus and in the Talmud. The account of Josephus, in the *Antiquities* (8:2.5), is probably the earliest Jewish report of possession and exorcism to be found, and the method of exorcism is attributed to none other than King Solomon himself: "He put to the nose of the possessed man a ring that had under its seal one of the roots prescribed by Solomon, and then, as the man smelled it, drew out the demons through his nostrils, and, when the man at once fell down, adjured the demon never to come back to him, speaking Solomon's name and reciting the incantations that he had composed." In the Talmud (B. Meil. 17b) we find the legend of Ben Temalion, a demon who agrees to assist Rabbi Shimon bar Yohai by entering the body of the emperor's daughter in a ploy to save the Jews.

25. First Samuel 28:15. For a modern variant of this tale, see "Partnership with Asmodeus" in *EV*, pp. 102–106.

26. B. Ber 18a. A variant legend found in *Sefer Hasidim* (#266) tells of the spirit of a man reluctant to join the other spirits because he had been buried in a shroud with a torn sleeve. See note 28 for a full citation of *Sefer Hasidim*.

27. B. Bab. Mez. 83b–85a.

28. *Sefer Hasidim* (attributed to Rabbi Judah the Pious). Parma edition, Hebrew manuscript De Rossi 33, published by Yehuda Wistynezki (Berlin: 1891).

29. *Sefer Hasidim* #711.

30. Another one of the rare Jewish vampire tales is found in *Sefer Hasidim* #1465. Here the vampire is Astryiah, an old woman who uses her hair to suck the blood from her victims. Another brief tale in *Sefer Hasidim* describes how to be certain that a witch does not come back from the dead to haunt her enemies. This is reminiscent of the method of killing vampires with a stake in the heart:

> Even after a witch dies, she is dangerous. Once a witch was captured and when they were about to put her to death she said: "Even after my death you will not be safe from me." And they said to her: "Tell us, how can we be safe from you after you die?" She said, "Take a stick and push it through my cheek so that it enters the earth, and then I will not be able to do any more damage."

Why the witch revealed this secret is not reported, but these tales are clear evidence of the fear of vampires and witches among the people and of the countermeasures they were prepared to take. Another example of witch lore found in the *Sefer Hasidim* (#1465–1467) holds that the mouth of a witch must be stopped up with dirt when she is buried: otherwise she will resume her destructive activities.

31. Y. San. 6.9 and Y. Hag. 2.2. See "The Witches of Ashkelon" in *EV*, pp. 25–28.

32. B. Git. 45a.

33. For the tale about the knife, see "The Knife" in *LC*, p. 88. The tale of the black cat is found in *Sefer Hasidim* #1466.

34. The tale about the witch is found in *Shivhei ha-Besht* (Hebrew) #98, edited by Samuel A. Horodezky (Berlin: 1922). See "The Boy Israel and the Witch" in *EV* pp. 203–209. The tale about the wizard is included in *LC*. See "A Combat in Magic," pp. 181–198, and the accompanying note. Jewish lore about witches has survived even into the present. One famous example is the witch of the Israeli city of Dovev, who has been sighted frequently and described as having "evil eyes and talon-like fingernails" (*The Jerusalem Post*, April 26, 1986).

35. *Ma'aseh Buch* #158–183.

36. See "The Magic Mirror of Rabbi Adam" in *EV*, pp. 187–195, and "The Magic Lamp of Rabbi Adam" in *MT*, pp. 230–237.

37. *Niflaot Maharal* (Hebrew) by Yudel Rosenberg, first published in 1909.

38. See "The Tales About Rabbi Adam Baal Shem and Their Different Versions as Formulated in Shivhei ha-Besht" (Hebrew) in *Zion* 28, 1963. For the version of this tale about Rabbi Adam, see "The Enchanted Palace" in *MT*, pp. 245–249.

39. *Shivhei ha-Besht* #7.

40. This motif is parallel to that in a tale about Rabbi Samuel the Pious found in the *Ma'aseh Book* #174.

Chapter 7
The Mythology of Judaism

1. *Midrash Ribesh Tov* (Hebrew), edited by Lipot Abraham (Kecskemet: 1927). According to the Zohar (II:8a–9a and III:196b), the Messiah dwells in a special palace known as the Bird's Next.

2. *Ketubah le-Shavuot* from the *Sephardi Machzor*, the Sephardic prayerbook for Shavuot, written by Israel Najara in the 16th century.

3. *Pirke de Rabbi Eliezer* 46: "Rabbi Joshua ben Korchah said: 'Forty days was Moses on the mountain, reading the Written Law by day, and studying the Oral Law by night.'"

4. B. Pes. 6b and Sifre Numbers, sec. 64.

5. *Divre Shlomo* by Rabbi Shlomo be-Babbi Yitzhak ha-Levi, Venice: 1596, 68b.

6. Tosefta B. Sotah 17a.

7. *Mekilta de-Rabbi Ishmael,* ed. Horovitz (Frankfort: 1931), *Massekhta de-Pisha* 14:51–52.

8. Zohar II:134a.

9. Zohar II:176b.

10. See Marc Bregman, "Past and Present in Midrashic Literature" in *Hebrew Annual Review,* vol. 2, 1978, pp. 45–59.

11. Zohar I:202b–203a.

12. See, for example, Zev Vilnay, *Legends of Jerusalem,* pp. 165–166.

13. *Gates to the New City: A Treasury of Modern Jewish Tales,* edited by Howard Schwartz, pp. 439–444. Penina Villenchik is a pseudonym for Penina Adelman, author of *Miriam's Well.*

14. B. Betz. 16a.

15. Zohar II:133b–134a. For more on the role of allegory in the Zohar, see *Parables in Midrash* by David Stern, pp. 227–233.

16. B. Shab. 119a and B. Baba Kama 32b. Another early echo of the ritual of *Kabbalat Shabbat* is also found in these passages, where it is said that Rabbi Yannai attired himself on the eve of the Sabbath and said, "Come, O bride, come, O bride." It is interesting to note that in the Laws of *Shabbat* in *Mishneh Torah,* Maimonides changed this passage to read "Comes, let us go out to greet the Sabbath King," *Mishneh Torah,* chap. 30.

17. Walter F. Otto, *Die Gestalt und das Sein; Abhandlungen über den Mythos und seine Bedeutung für die Menschheit* (Düsseldorf-Koln: 1955), pp. 73–78.

Chapter 8
Tales of the Great Jewish Mystics

1. For examples of Sufi and Zen tales, see *Tales of the Dervishes,* edited by Idries Shah, and *Zen Flesh, Zen Bones,* edited by Paul Reps. For accounts of Christian mystical experience, see *The Lives of the Saints* by Alban Butler. The mystical tales referred to throughout this essay can be found in *Gabriel's Palace: Jewish Mystical Tales,* edited by Howard Schwartz, published by Oxford University Press, 1993, hereafter referred to as *GP.*

2. This legend is found in two versions in the Talmud. B. Hag. 14b uses the phrasing "Rabbi Akiba entered and departed in peace," and B. Hag. 15b and Tosefta Hag. 23 have "Rabbi Akiba ascended in peace and descended in peace."

3. In addition to these primary biblical roots of Kabbalah, other biblical episodes play an important role in the evolution of a Jewish mystical consciousness, including the visions of Isaiah and Daniel and the Giving of the Torah.

4. The term "kabbalistic" has both a broad and a narrow definition. The definition offered on p. 101 is the broad one. The narrow definition refers specifically to the period between the appearance of the Zohar in the 13th century and the failure of the messianic movement of Shabbatai Zevi in the 17th century.

5. In fact, de Leon gave several accounts of how the Zohar was found: in a cave in Palestine, and later sent to Spain by Nachmanides; or by an Arab boy digging for treasure; or that it was discovered among the plunder of a library. All later evidence, including testimony by de Leon's wife after his death, indicates that it was indeed a work of pseudepigraphy, of de Leon's Creation, or that it was the Creation of the circle of mystics to which Moshe de Leon belonged. For more on the theory of group creation of the Zohar, see *Studies in the Zohar* by Yehuda Liebes, chap. 2, "How the Zohar Was Written," pp. 85–138.

6. See *Shabbatai Zevi: The Mystical Messiah* by Gershom Scholem.

7. Two novels have been written about the Maid of Ludomir. One is *Ha-Betulah mi-Ludomir* by Yohanan Twersky (Tel Aviv: 1949), and the other is *They Called Her Rebbe* by Gershon Winkler (New York: 1992). The other woman recognized as a rabbi is Asenath bat Samuel Barazani of Kurdistan. See "Asenath's Dove" in *GP*, pp. 148–149.

8. See, for example, "The Three Tasks of Elijah" in *Miriam's Tambourine: Jewish Folktales from Around the World*, edited by Howard Schwartz, pp. 56–63. See also *Tales of Elijah the Prophet*, by Peninnah Schram (Northvale, N.J.: 1991).

9. B. Shab. 33b.

10. Eccles. Rab. 10:10. Because of the ambiguity of the text, it is not completely clear if it is Rabbi Shimon bar Yohai himself (or his spirit) who comes to the disciple, or simply that the disciple remembers the lesson. But since Bar Yohai clearly states in the dream that he will come to the disciple, it is reasonable to assume that this is what takes place. This interpretation is confirmed by the oral variant "A Kiss from the Master." See *GP*, pp. 79–80.

11. The concept of the *ibbur* is suggested in the Zohar II:100b: "The Supernal Holy King does not permit anything to perish, not even the breath of the mouth, which emerges into the world as a new creation." Possession by an *ibur* should be distinguished from *gilgul*, the transmigration of souls. In the latter, the soul of a person who has died is reincarnated in the body of a person born later. In the case of an *ibur*, the soul of a sage who has died fuses with the soul of one who is living, and this kind of metempsychosis is usually temporary rather than permanent.

12. *Shivhei ha-Ari*, edited by Shlomo Meinsterl (Jerusalem: 1905). See *Sippurei Dybbuk*, edited by Gedalya Nigal (Jerusalem: 1983), for a comprehensive collection of accounts of possession by dybbuks.

13. IFA 612, collected by S. Arnest.

14. *Ateret Tiferet* (Bilgorai: 1910). A variant can be found in *Sefer ha-Ma'asyiot*, edited by Mordecai ben Yehezkel (Tel Aviv: 1937), who attributes it to oral tradition. There are many other variants of this tale, including *Sihot Tzaddikim* (Warsaw: 1921) and *Esser Kedoshot* (Piatrakov: 1906).

15. *Shivhei ha-Ari*, p. 26, and *Shivhei ha-Rabbi Hayim Vital*, p. 28a.

16. The traditional belief is that there is one *tzaddik*, or righteous one, who is the greatest in that generation, and if the conditions are right, he could serve as the Messiah. See *The Zaddik* by Samuel H. Dresner (New York: 1974).

17. See Arthur Green's biography of Rabbi Nachman, *Tormented Master* (New York: 1982).

18. *Shivhei-ha Ari*, p. 37b.

19. *Devet Bran*, by Jiří Langer (Prague: 1937). See "A Vision" in *GP*, pp. 264–265.

20. See Heinreich Zimmer, *Myths and Symbols in Indian Art and Civilization*, pp. 32–33.

21. Gen. Rab. 77:2 and *Midrash Tanhuma, Vayishlach* 1.

22. B. Git. 68b. See "The Beggar King" in *EV*, pp. 59–66. (Hereafter *EV*).

23. For examples of Rabbi Adam's use of illusion, see "The Enchanted Journey" and "The King's Dream" in *EV*, pp. 181–186 and 197–202, respectively.

24. *Ma'aysiot ve-Shichot Tzaddikim* (Warsaw: 1881). See "The Underground Forest" in *GP*, pp. 214–218.

25. *Devarim Arevim* (Munkacs: 1863). See "The Young Magician" in *GP*, pp. 224–225.

26. Collected by Rabbi Zalman Schachter-Shalomi from Reb Avraham Paris. See "The Tale of the Kugel" in *GP*, pp. 268–271.

27. *Midrash Ribesh Tov* (Kecskemet: 1927). See "The Ladder of Prayers" in *GP*, p. 191.

28. Collected by Max Grunwald from an unknown soldier from the Balkans. From *Sippurei-am, Romanssot, ve'Orebot-hayim shel Yehudei Sefard* by Max Grunwald, edited by Dov Noy (Jerusalem: 1982). See "Rabbi Shimon's Escape" in *GP*, pp. 126–127.

29. Zohar I:216b–217a. See "The Book of Flying Letters" in *GP*, pp. 77–78.

30. Collected by Howard Schwartz from Yehuda Yaari. See *GP*, pp. 156–157.

31. *Shivhei he-Besht* (Berlin: 1922). See "The Circle of Fire," pp. 202–203.

32. *Mei Be'er Yeshashya* (Solvaki: 1888). See "The Prayer Leader" in *GP*, pp. 254–255.

33. *Shivhei he-Besht* by Rabbi Dov Ben Samuel, edited by Samuel A. Horodezky (Berlin: 1922). See "Unlocking the Gates of Heaven" in *GP*, pp. 205–207.

34. See Chapter 3, footnotes 16–17, for a discussion of the system of interpretation known by the acronym *PaRDes*.

35. The myth of the Ari offers, for the first time in Jewish history, a rationale and purpose for the *mitzvot*. Prior to the Ari, observing the *mitzvot* was simply a requirement of God which could not be questioned or explained. But the Ari's myth suggests that by performing these ritual acts Jews are raising up the fallen sparks, and thus contributing to the repair of the world.

36. IFA 477, collected by S. Arenst from a new immigrant from Morocco.

37. *Toledot Hakhmei Yerushalayim* by Aryeh Leib Frumkin (Vilna: 1874). See "Redemption of the Lost Souls" in *GP*, pp. 115–116.

38. *Iggeret Sod ha-Ge'ullah* by Abraham ben Eliezer ha-Levi (Jerusalem: 1519). See "The Tzaddik of the Forest" in *GP*, pp. 109–112.

39. *Mei Be'er Yeshashya* (Solvaki: 1888). See "The Prayer Leader" in *GP*, pp. 254–255.

40. Y. Hag. 77a and B. Hag. 14b. See "Mysteries of the Chariot" in *GP*, pp. 50–51.

41. From *Pesikta Rabbati* 26:7. This legend grows out of the *drash* of Jeremiah's lamentation over the destruction of the Temple in Jerusalem and the Babylonian exile. Mother Zion is the personification of Zion, who is grieving and in need of comfort. At the same time, Mother Zion is an early incarnation of the *Shekhinah*, whose home was the Temple in Jerusalem. The image of Mother Zion was probably inspired by Is. 66:8: *For as soon as Zion travailed, she brought fourth her children.*

42. *Shivhei ha-Ari*, edited by Shlomo Meinsterl (Jerusalem: 1905). See "A Vision at the Wailing Wall" in *GP*, pp. 87–89.

43. *Sippure Hasidim*, edited by Shlomo Yosef Zevin (Tel Aviv: 1964). See "A Vision of the Bride" in *GP*, pp. 245–250.

44. *Tortenetek a "Kalloi Cadit"—roi* (Hungarian) by Albert Neumann (Nyiregyhaza, Hungary: 1935). See "The Sabbath Guests" in *GP*, pp. 250–251.

45. Some traditions view both Messiah ben Joseph and Messiah ben David as human figures. The separate traditions of an earthly and a heavenly Messiah are sometimes resolved by identifying the heavenly Messiah as the celestial soul of the earthly Messiah, whose fusion with his earthly soul will transform the human Messiah and unleash his destiny. This is the position taken by Jacob Immanuel Schochet and other Lubavitch hasidim. For more on the complex traditions linked to the Messiah, see *The Messiah Texts*, edited by Raphael Patai (Detroit: 1979).

46. *Iggeret Sod ha-Ge'ullah* by Abraham ben Eliezer ha-Levi (Jerusalem: 1519). See "The Chains of the Messiah" in *GP*, pp. 106–109.

47. *Shivhei ha-Ari*, edited by Shlomo Meinsterl (Jerusalem: 1905). See "The Journey to Jerusalem" in *GP*, p. 86.

48. *Tortenetek a "Kalloi Cadik"—roi* Hungarian by Albert Neumann (Nyiregyhaza, Hungary: 1935). See "The Sabbath Guests" in *GP*, pp. 250–251.

49. IFA 6928, collected in Israel by Uri Resler from his uncle.

50. For additional information about these prayers of unification see *The Hebrew Goddess* by Raphael Patai, third edition, chap. 8 (New York: 1991).

51. *Sippurei Hasidim*, edited by Shlomo Yosef Zevin (Tel Aviv: 1964). See "A Vision of the Bride" in *GP*, pp. 245–250.

52. *Em la-Binah*, edited by Yekutiel Aryeh Kamelhar (Lemberg: 1909). See "A Bowl of Soup" in *GP*, p. 222.

53. It is sometimes difficult to distinguish between the kind of astral projection practiced in these tales and sympathetic magic. The former requires some form of soul travel, while the latter draws upon the powers of magic to make an action that is performed in one place have effect in another. "A Bowl of Soup" is an example of a tale in which it is particularly difficult to make this distinction.

54. *Sippurei Ya'akov*, edited by Rabbi Yakov Sofer (Dobromill: 1864). See "Rabbi Naftali's Trance" in *GP*, pp. 152–154.

55. *Hayey Moharan*, no. 88, by Reb Nathan of Nemirov (Jerusalem: 1982). While traveling to Uman from Bratslav, Rabbi Nachman told a story to his scribe, Reb Nathan of Nemirov, about the Baal Shem Tov going to a city where souls had been waiting for three hundred years to ascend on high (*Hayey Moharan*, no. 87). This tale about his great-grandfather, the Baal Shem Tov, probably explains Reb Nachman's desire to be buried in Uman, where over twenty thousand Jews were killed by Cossacks on June 19, 1768. Reb Nachman explicitly referred to this on the day before he died, saying: " 'Do you remember the story I told you?' 'Which one?' Reb Nathan asked. 'The story of the Baal Shem Tov which I told you on the way to Uman.' 'Yes,' said Reb Nathan. Reb Nachman said: 'For a long time now they have had their eyes on me, to get me here. There are not just thousands of souls here, but hundreds upon hundreds upon hundreds of thousands' " (*Hayey Moharan*, no. 88).

Rabbi Nachman is said to have seen a dead soul for the first time when he was a child. He prayed to see such a soul, and one did indeed seek him out, terrifying him. Later he was said to have seen many such souls of the dead, and at the end of his life he became the Master of the Field, sought out by thousands of souls for the *tikkun*, or repair, he could do for their souls (*Hayey Moharan*, no. 7). The phrase "Master of the Field" comes from one of Reb Nachman's teachings (*Hayey Moharan*, no. 48) in which he spoke of a field where souls grow, and how they require a master of the field to repair them.

56. *Shivhei ha-Ari*, edited by Shlomo Meinsterl (Jerusalem: 1905). See "The Field of Souls" in *GP*, pp. 204–206.

57. Collected by Howard Schwartz from Yehuda Yaari. See "The Boy Who Blew the Shofar" in *GP*, pp. 127–130.

58. There are a variety of kabbalistic techniques in which the letters of the words of the Torah are manipulated. The most popular technique is *gematria*, where the numerical total of a word is believed to link it to any other words with that same total, making it possible to insert the alternate word in the same context as a means of revealing secrets concealed in the Torah. The use of *gematria* was especially popular in trying to determine when the coming of the Messiah was to take place. See *The Spice of Torah—Gematria*, by Gutman G. Locks (New York: 1985), which lists all the words of the Torah according to their numerical value.

59. *Sippurei Hasidim*, edited by Shlomo Yosef Zevin (Tel Aviv: 1964). See "The Flaming Letters" in *GP*, pp. 247–248.

60. "Figure/ground" refers to texts or illustrations that can be reversed depending on one's visual perception. The figure is the central perception, while the ground is the background. When these are reversed, the figure becomes the ground, and vice versa. A good example of this is the diagram found in many psychology textbooks of an illustration of a young woman. Hidden in her hair is an illustration of an old woman, which at first is difficult to perceive, but once it has been seen, it becomes difficult to see the original young woman.

61. An example of combining the letters from different names of God is found in Hayim Vital's diary of his visions, *Sefer Hezyonot* V:32. Here Vital describes prostrating himself on the grave of the talmudic sage Abbaye and attempting a unification in which he combined the letters of the Tetragrammaton with those of the name Adonai. In this case the attempt failed, as his thoughts became confused and he was unable to combine the letters.

62. There are several rabbinic depictions of the abode of the souls of the unborn. B. Hag. 12b describes it as the seventh heaven, while B. Yeb. 62a and B. San. 98a speak of the *Guf*, where the souls of future generations are stored, noting that the Messiah will not come until the *Guf* is emptied: "The Messiah will not come until all the souls in the heavenly chamber of souls (*Guf*) have entered bodies and have been born into this world." The film *The Seventh Sign* is based on the premise that the *Guf* is empty and that the first child without a soul is about to be born. Other sources identify the *Guf* with the *Pargod*, the curtain that separates God from the angels, on which all souls are portrayed. Still others speak of a Quarry of Souls.

63. B. Tamid 32b. See "The Gates of Eden" in *GP*, p. 62.

64. *Gan ha-Hasidut*, edited by Eliezer Steinmann. See "A Crown of Shoes" in *GP*, pp. 195–195.

65. *Shivhei he-Besht* by Rabbi Dov Ben Samuel, edited by Samuel A. Horodezky (Berlin: 1922). See "The Tree of Life" in *GP*, pp. 192–193.

66. *Midrash Asseret Harugei Malkhut* in *Otzar ha-Midrashim*. See "The Tzohar" in *GP*, pp. 59–62. For additional sources to this legend, see *GP*, note 16, pp. 287–288.

67. *The Legend of the Ten Martyrs.* Versions of this legend are found in *Hekhalot Rabbati* and in *Midrash Eleh Ezkerah* in A. Jellinek, *Beit ha-Midrash* (Jerusalem: 1967). See "Rabbi Ishmael's Ascent" in *GP*, pp. 52–53. See note 101, p. 222.

68. *Sefer ha-Ma'aysiot*, edited by Mordecai ben Yehezkel (Tel Aviv: 1937). See "Gabriel's Palace" in *GP*, pp. 121–123.

69. *Sipurei Tzaddikim* (Cracow: 1886). See "The Evil Angel" in *GP*, pp. 143–145.

70. *Shivhei ha-Ari*, edited by Shlomo Meinstrel (Jerusalem: 1905). Also, *Maggid Mesharim*, by Joseph Karo (Amsterdam: 1704). See "The Angel of the Mishnah" in *GP*, pp. 112–113. See also *Joseph Karo: Lawyer and Mystic* by R. J. Zwi Werblowsky (Philadelphia: 1977). Here the point is made that there are significant links between Kabbalah and *Halakhah*, the body of Jewish law. Indeed, most of the great kabbalists, including Joseph Karo and the Ari, were also masters of the *Halakhah*.

71. A number of rabbinic legends strongly suggest the concept of the archetype. One common legend lists a number of things that God created before the Creation of the world: "Seven things were created before the world was created. They are: The Torah, *Gehenna*, the Garden of Eden, the Throne of Glory, the Temple, Repentance, and the Name of the Messiah" (*Pirke de Rabbi Eliezer*, no. 3). In Num. Rab. 15:10, God shows a heavenly model of a candlestick to Moses so that he will know how to fulfill the injunction, *And thou shalt make a candlestick of pure gold* (Ex. 25:31).

72. *Sippurei Ma'asiyot* by Rabbi Nachman of Bratslav, edited by Rabbi Nathan of Nemirov (Warsaw: 1881). See "The Lost Princess" in *EV*, p. 210.

73. B. Hag. 15a. The passage goes on to say: "He created mountains and hills. He created seas and rivers. . . . He created the righteous and the wicked. He created the Garden of Eden and *Gehenna*."

74. *Admorei Chernobyl*, edited by Yisrael Yakov Klapholtz (B'nai Brak: 1971). See "The Blind Angel" in *GP*, pp. 259–261.

75. *Sefer ha-Razim* was an early work of Jewish mystical literature, consisting of magic spells, witchcraft, incantations, and supernatural remedies. It took its name from the legendary Book of Raziel, which the angel Raziel was said to have delivered to Adam, and which later was said to have reached virtually all of the patriarchal figures until it was lost when the Temple in Jerusalem was destroyed. See *Sefer ha-Razim*, edited by M. Margoliot (Jerusalem: 1966).

76. IFA 10200, collected by Edna Balay from Raphael Balay, in *Tova Ba'al Tova* by Rafael Babay, edited by Batya Mazoz (Jerusalem: 1980). See "The Voice in the Tree" in *GP*, pp. 177–178.

77. *Sipurei Tzaddikim* (Cracow: 1886). See "The Sabbath Fish" in *GP*, pp. 233–234.

78. For the legend of Joseph della Reina, see "The Chains of the Messiah," in *GP*, pp. 106–109. This is the classic tale of attempting to force the coming of the Messiah.

79. *Emet ha-Melekh*, edited by Naphtali Hirsh ben Eliezer (Amsterdam: 1653). See "A Stone in the Wall" in *GP*, p. 97.

80. *Devět Bran* (zech) by Jiři Langer (Prague: 1937). See "A Wandering Soul" in *GP*, pp. 266–267.

81. IFA 7830, collected by Zevulon Qort from Ben Zion Asherov. See "The Cottage of Candles" in *GP*, pp. 124–126.

82. *Sihot Moharan* in *Hayey Moharan* by Rabbi Nathan of Nemirov (Lemberg: 1874). See "The Souls of Trees" in *GP*, p. 236.

83. Ibid.

84. IFA 487, collected by S. Arnest from Reb Zaidel Buch. See "Divining from the Zohar" in *GP*, p. 237.

85. The Legend of the Ten Martyrs. Versions of this legend are found in *Hekhalot Rabbati* and in *Midrash Eleh Ezkerah* in A. Jellinek, *Beit ha-Midrash* (Jerusalem: 1967). See "Rabbi Ishmael's Ascent" in *GP*, pp. 52–53.

86. *Shivhei ha-Ari*, edited by Shlomo Meinsterl (Jerusalem: 1905). See "A Vision at the Wailing Wall" in *GP*, pp. 87–89.

87. *Sippurei Hasidim*, edited by Shlomo Yosef Zevin (Tel Aviv: 1964). See "A Vision of the Bride" in *GP*, pp. 245–250.

88. B. Ber. 7a. See "The Vision of the High Priest" in *GP*, p. 55.

89. *Sipurei Tzaddikim* (Cracow: 1886). See "The Enchanted Island" in *GP*, pp. 199–201.

90. Such multiple interpretations of the same passage are common under the system of interpretation known by the acronym *PaRDeS*.

91. There is a scholarly controversy over the meaning of the term *Pardes* in its original context, concerning whether it had already acquired a mystical meaning. Gershom Scholem held that it did have such a meaning, whereas Ephraim Urbach and David Halperin concluded that in the original legend it had only a literal meaning of "garden/orchard/park," as it does in most other places in rabbinic literature. But it took on a metaphorical/mystical meaning of Paradise when it was inserted into its literary context in the Talmud. For further discussion of this issue, see David Halperin's *The Merkavah in Rabbinic Literature*, pp. 86ff. See note 2 for the sources of these variant readings. See also Marc Bregmen's Introduction and Commentary in *The Four Who Entered Paradise* by Howard Schwartz.

There is also considerable scholarly controversy over the meaning of the accounts of ascents in the *Hekhalot* texts and other apocalypses. The most basic debate is whether or not the ancient rabbis engaged in mystical practices, as Gershom Scholem held that they did (*Major Trends in Jewish Mysticism* and *Jewish Gnosticism, Merkavah Mysticism, and Talmudic Tradition*). Scholem's view was criticized by Ephraim E. Urbach in "The Traditions about Merkabah Mysticism in the Tannaitic Period" in *Studies in Mysticism and Religion Presented to Gershom G. Scholem* (Jerusalem: 1967, pp. 1–28) [Hebrew]. Following this point of view, Martha Himmelfarb argues in *Ascent to Heaven in Jewish and Christian Apocalypses* that the ascents and other mystical accounts are nothing more than a literary fiction (pp. 95–113). A related viewpoint is that of David J. Halperin in "Heavenly Ascension in Ancient Judaism: The Nature of the Experience," *Society of Biblical Literature Seminar Papers*, 1987, pp. 218–232. See also Halperin's *The Merkabah in Rabbinic Literature* and *Faces of the Chariot: Early Jewish Responses to Ezekiel's Vision*. More recently, Alon Goshen Gottstein has suggested in "Four Entered Paradise Revisited" (*Harvard Theological Review* 88, 1995, pp. 69–133) that although the legend of the four who entered *Pardes* is not an account of an actual mystical experience, it is a polemical document that reflects a rabbinic debate about the appropriate role of mysticism in Judaism.

92. B. Hag. 15a.

93. Thus *Pardes* may be understood as a metaphor inside a metaphor. The orchard represents Paradise, which in turn represents mystical contemplation. This

becomes clearer when cast in terms of the system of interpretation known as *PaRDeS*, where the orchard represents the literal interpretation, Paradise the allegorical one, and the mystical meaning takes the form of mystical contemplation.

94. B. Hag. 13a.

95. Mishnah Hag. 2:1.

96. B. Hag. 15a

97. Ibid.

98. Ibid.

99. The upper waters and lower waters are personified in the midrash as male and female, respectively. *Midrash Konen* 25 describes the male and female waters as locked in a passionate embrace and that God had to tear them apart in order to separate them. Ben Zoma was especially interested in the division of the upper and lower waters. In Gen. Rab. 4:6 he disputed the verse *And God made the firmament* (Gen. 1:7), saying: "He made—how remarkable! Surely it came into existence at God's word, as it is written, *By the word of the Lord were the heavens made, and all the host of them by the breath of his mouth*" (Ps. 33:6).

100. Rabbi Azriel of Gerona's *Commentary on Talmudic Aggadot*, p. 40. Note that by an enigmatic kabbalistic reversal, "descending to the *Merkavah*" means the opposite, to ascend on high. This statement about Ben Azzai appears in several variations, including Lev. Rab. 16:4: "Ben Azzai was sitting and expounding Torah, and a flame was burning around him. They said to him: 'Are you perhaps engaged in the study of the *Merkavah*?' He replied: 'No, I am but finding in the Torah parallels to the prophets and in the Prophets parallels to the *Aggadah*. And the words of the Torah are joyful even as they were on the day they were being given at Sinai, and they were originally given in fire, as it is said, *And the mountain burned with fire*'" (Deut. 4:11). For a further discussion of these passages about Ben Azzai, see *Kabbalah: New Perspectives* by Moshe Idel, p. 318, note 99 (New Haven and London: 1988).

101. There are several versions of *The Legend of the Ten Martyrs*. The earliest of these is found in *Hekhalot Rabbati*, one of the most important of the *Hekhalot* texts of *Merkavah* mysticism. The best-known version is that found in *Midrash Eleh Ezkerah*. See the note to "Rabbi Ishmael's Ascent" in *GP*, p. 52. For a further discussion of the background of this legend, see *Rabbinic Fantasies*, edited by David Stern and Mark Jay Mirsky (Philadelphia: 1990), pp. 143–146.

102. Lev. Rab. 16:4.

103. B. Hag. 15a and Gen. Rab. 2:40.

104. The midrashic commentaries explain that there were upper waters that were male and lower waters that were female. They greatly resisted being torn apart, when God said: *Let there be a firmament in the midst of the waters, and let it divide the waters from the waters* (Gen. 1:6), and they still long for each other. See *Midrash Konen* 25; Gen. Rab. 34–35; *Seder Rabba di-Bereshit* 314; *Midash Aseret ha-Dibrot* 63; *Midrash Tehillim* 414; *Pirke de Rabbi Eliezer*, chap. 5.

105. *Hekhalot Zutarti*. See Peter Schäfer, *The Hidden and Manifest God: Some Major Themes in Early Jewish Mysticism* (Albany, N.Y.: 1992), pp. 56–75.

106. *Sefer ha-Hezyonot* by Rabbi Hayim Vital (Jerusalem: 1914). See "The Handwriting of the Messiah" in *GP*, pp. 103–104.

107. *Sipurei Tzaddikim* (Cracow: 1886). See "The Sword of the Messiah" in *GP*, pp. 234–236.

108. *Hag La'am*, edited by Eliezer Marcus (Jerusalem: 1990). See "The Cave of Mattathias" in *GP*, pp. 261–262.

109. See "The Tzohar" in *GP*, pp. 59–62. For the extensive sources of this legend, see *GP*, note 16, pp. 287–288.

Chapter 9
The Quest for the Lost Princess: Transition and Change in Jewish Lore

1. *Shivhei ha-Ari*, edited by Shlomo Meinsterl (Jerusalem: 1905).

2. *Sippure Ma'asiyot* by Rabbi Nachman of Bratslav, edited by Rabbi Nathan Sternhartz of Nemirov (Warsaw: 1881).

3. Ibid. Parables of the Torah as a princess secluded in a palace are found in Zohar II:94b and *Seder ha-Yom* (Slavita: 1793). These parables are the likely inspiration for Rabbi Nachman's tale, where the princess is identified not with the Torah but with the *Shekhinah*. See *Beyond Appearances*, ed. by Aryeh Wineman, pp. 18–23.

4. *Tortenetek a "Kalloi Cadik"—rol* (Hungarian) by Albert Neumann (Nyiregyhaza, Hungary: 1935).

5. IFA 612, collected by S. Arnest.

6. *Sefer Sgulat Moshe*. Also found in *Toldot Rabbenu Hayim ben Attar*, edited by Reuven Margarliot (Lemberg: 1904) and many other sources.

7. *Hag La'am*, edited by Eliezer Marcus (Jerusalem: 1990). Told by Shimon Toder. The original legend about Hanukkah is found in B. Shab. 21b.

8. IFA 7830, collected by Zevulon Qort from Ben Zion Asherov.

9. It is interesting to note that the man's quest in "The Cottage of Candles" is in many ways parallel to that of the man from the country in Kafka's famous parable "Before the Law," found in his novel *The Trial*, who comes seeking justice at the gates of the Law. And in both tales the man fails to find the justice he is seeking.

10. B. Ber. 55b.

11. B. Ta'anit 25a.

12. B. Sukkah 52a–b and Y. Sanh. 29b. Additional legends about the *Even Shetiyah* (Foundation Stone) are found in the M. Yoma 5.2, in B. Yoma 54a–b, and in Zohar II:222a–b.

13. B. Gittin 68b.

14. *The Testament of Solomon* (Greek), edited by F. F. Fleck, in *Wissenschaftliche Reise durch das südliche Deutschland, Italien, Sicilien und Frankreich*, volume 2, pp. 113–140 (Leipzig: 1837). See also the translation by D. C. Duling in *Old Testament Pseudepigrapha*, ed. by James H. Charlesworth, vol 1., pp. 960–987.

15. From Zev Vilnay, *Aggadot Eretz Yisrael*, 4th edition (no. 193) (Jerusalem: 1953). Collected by Zev Vilnay from a Jewish youth in Jerusalem in 1922.

16. B. Ber. 7a.

17. The earliest source seems to be Apocalypse of Baruch, 7–8 and 80. The legend is also found in Y. Shekalim 50a and B., Ta'anit 29a, and *Pesikta Rabbati* 26:6.

18. *Shivhei ha-Ari* 9b–10a, edited by Shlomo Meinsterl (Jerusalem: 1905). An oral variant is IFA 16159, collected by Shimon Shababo from Orna Fadida of Israel.

19. Collected by Howard Schwartz from Rabbi Shlomo Carlebach. For a variant of this tale, see S. Y. Zevin, *A Treasury of Chassidic Tales on the Festivals*, vol. 2, pp. 461–462 (Brooklyn: 1982).

20. IFA 966, collected by Nehama Zion from Miriam Tschernobilski of Poland. See *Folktales of Israel*, edited by Dov Noy (Chicago: 1963), pp. 7–9. The ritual

pouring water over King David's hands recalls the ritual of washing of the hands at the start of the Sabbath meal.

Chapter 10
Rabbi Nachman of Bratslav: Forerunner of Modern Jewish Literature

1. Although Rabbi Nachman did not publicly declare such a messianic role for himself, it appears that he may have viewed himself as the possible *tzaddik ha-dor* or potential Messiah ben Joseph of his generation, who would prepare the way for the coming of Messiah ben David. See Arthur Green's biography of Nachman, *Tormented Master*, for a full discussion of Nachman's messianic aspirations. For more on the messianic tradition, see *The Messiah Texts* by Raphael Patai. For more on Shabbatai Zevi, see Gershom Scholem's *Shabbatai Sevi: The Mystical Messiah.*

2. These are *Rabbi Nachman's Stories*, translated and with commentaries by Rabbi Aryeh Kaplan; *Classic Hasidic Tales* by Meyer Levin (which also includes versions of the tales of the Baal Shem Tov); *The Tales of Rabbi Nachman* by Martin Buber; *Beggars and Prayers* by Adin Steinsaltz; *Nachman of Bratslav: The Tales* by Arnold J. Band; and *The Thirteen Stories of Rebbe Nachman of Breslov*, translated by Ester Koenig, edited by Mordechai Kramer. Other Nachman tales can be found in *Yenne Velt: The Great Works of Jewish Fantasy and the Occult* and in the four collections of Jewish folklore edited by Howard Schwartz: *Elijah's Violin & Other Jewish Fairy Tales, Miriam's Tambourine: Jewish Folktales from Around the World, Lilith's Cave: Jewish Tales of the Supernatural,* and *Gabriel's Palace: Jewish Mystical Tales.* See the Bibliography for additional details of publication.

3. From *Fragments of a Future Scroll* by Zalman Schachter, p. 99. This book contains an extensive translation of Nachman's dreams, pp. 95–100. Additional dreams are reported in Arthur Green's *Tormented Master*, pp. 165–166. See also "The 'Dream-Talks' of Nahman of Bratslav," in *Rabbinic Fantasies: Imaginative Narratives from Classical Hebrew Literature*, edited by David Stern and Mark Jay Mirsky, pp. 333–347, translated by Arthur Green.

4. *Sippure Ma'asiyot* by Rabbi Nachman of Bratslav, edited by Rabbi Nathan Sternhartz of Nemirov (Warsaw: 1881).

5. Ibid.

6. *Fragments of a Future Scroll*, pp. 99–100.

7. Compare the following passage from an Italian folktale, "The Enchanted Palace," whose theme and setting are in many ways identical to that of "The Lost Princess," with a similar passage from that tale:

"The queen arrived. With cries, embraces, slaps in the face, kisses and shakes, she did her best to awaken Fiordiando. But realizing she would not succeed, she began weeping so violently that instead of tears a few drops of blood trickled down her cheeks. She wiped the blood off with her handkerchief, which she placed over Fiordiando's face. Then she got back into her carriage and sped straight to Peterborough" (*Italian Folktales*, selected and retold by Italo Calvino, p. 235).

"And after the troops had passed, a carriage came by, and in the carriage sat the daughter of the king. She stopped near him, and left the carriage, and sat down next to him, and recognized him. And although she shook him very strongly, he did not wake up, and she began to lament. . . . Not long afterward he woke up and asked his servant: 'Where am I?' And the servant told all that had happened. . . . Then the minister saw the kerchief and asked: 'From where did this come?' And the servant told him that the lost princess had written on it with her tears, and he read all that she had written" ("The Lost Princess," retold by Meyer Levin, *Classic Hasidic Tales,* pp. 190–197).

8. Bratslaver hasidim can be found in present-day Jerusalem and in B'nai Brak, outside Tel Aviv. There are also Bratslaver groups to be found in the Galilee in Israel and in New York City. The Bratslavers in Me'ah She'arim are led by Chaim Kramer, who has overseen the extensive translation and publication of many of Rabbi Nachman's texts and himself wrote an epic biography of Rabbi Nathan, *Through Fire and Water: The Life of Reb Noson of Breslov.*

9. *Sihot ha-Ran* 180.

10. *Sippurei Ma'asiyot* by Rabbi Nachman of Bratslav, edited by Rabbi Nathan Sternhartz of Nemirov (Warsaw: 1881).

11. Ibid.

12. *Sippurei Ma'asiyot Hadashim* (Warsaw: 1909). The stories in this collection are attributed to Rabbi Nachman, although some doubt has been raised about their authenticity.

13. Ibid.

14. *Ma'asiyot U'Meshalim* in *Kochavay Or* (Jerusalem: 1896).

15. See Jung, *The Archetypes and the Collective Unconscious,* vol. 9 of *The Collected Works of C. G. Jung.*

16. *Sippurei Ma'asiyot* by Rabbi Nachman of Bratslav, edited by Rabbi Nathan Sternhartz of Nemirov (Warsaw: 1881).

17. Ibid.

18. *Sippurei Ma'aysiot Hadashim* (Warsaw: 1909).

19. Ibid.

20. Franz Kafka, *Collected Stories,* pp. 4–5.

21. *Sippurei Ma'aysiot Hadashim* (Warsaw: 1909). For a Sufi variant of this tale, see "The Tale of the Sands" in *Tales of the Dervishes,* edited by Idries Shah, pp. 23–24.

22. New York: Dutton, 1967, p. 21.

23. *Ma'asiyot U'Meshalim* in *Kochavay Or* (Jerusalem: 1896).

24. *Sippurei Ma'aysiot Hadashim* (Warsaw: 1909).

25. B. Kid. 70a.

26. Reference to the origin of this primordial light is found in Gen. Rab. 3:4: "Rabbi Shimon ben Jehozadak asked Rabbi Samuel ben Nachman: 'As I have heard that you are a master of *Aggadah,* tell me from what the primordial light was created?' He replied: 'The Holy One, blessed be He, wrapped Himself therein as in a robe and radiated with the luster of His majesty from one end of the world to the other.'" This metaphor is developed further in *Pirke de Rabbi Eliezer* 3: "Whence were the heavens created? From the light of the garment with which He was robed. He took this light and stretched it as it is written, *Who converts thyself with light as with a garment, who stretched out the heavens like a curtain* (Ps. 104:2).

27. "The Poetry of Hassidism" by Koppel S. Pinson, *The Menorah Journal,* Autumn 1941, p. 304.

28. *Yemey Maharnat* by Rabbi Nathan of Nemirov (Lemberg: 1876). The parallel of this episode with one involving Franz Kafka is remarkable and noteworthy.

On his deathbed Kafka directed his friend and mentor Max Brod to burn all his unpublished writings—novels, stories, journals, diaries, and letters. Brod gave his word, then promptly published all of this material, which resulted in Kafka's being acclaimed as one of the seminal figures of 20th-century literature. Had Brod followed Kafka's expressed wish, as did Rabbi Shimon, Kafka might be known as an obscure Czech writer who published only a handful of stories in his lifetime and left no other legacy. One of the first articles to bring attention to the parallels between Kafka and Rabbi Nachman was "Franz Kafka and Rabbi Nachman" by Rabbi Jack Riemer, *Jewish Frontier*, Fall 1961, pp. 16–20.

29. There is some dispute over what Rabbi Nachman said or didn't say on his deathbed. In *Yemey Maharnat* 43b Rabbi Nathan recounts that those standing around Rabbi Nachman's deathbed thought that he had died. Rabbi Nathan began to cry out, "Rebbe! Rebbe! To whom have you left us?" Rabbi Nachman then lifted up his head with an expression that said, "I am not leaving you, God forbid!" So it appears that the Bratslaver belief that Rabbi Nachman would always be their rebbe is based on Rabbi Nathan's interpretation of an expression on Rabbi Nachman's face before he died.

30. Told by Yehuda Yaari to Howard Schwartz.

31. *Mikhtav mi-Rebbe Nachman* by Rabbi Yisrael Ber Odesser (Jerusalem: 1984).

32. Rabbi Nachman himself made use of this method of divination, known as *Sheilat Sefer*. See the stories "The Souls of Trees" and "Divining from the Zohar" in *Gabriel's Palace: Jewish Mystical Tales*, edited by Howard Schwartz, pp. 236–237.

33. Since the death of Rabbi Menachem Mendel of Lubavitch, the Lubavitcher Rebbe, who died without a successor, there have been indications that the Lubavitch hasidim intend to be guided by their departed rebbe without appointing a successor, precisely as did the Bratslaver hasidim.

34. All his life Rabbi Nachman was obsessed with the Baal Shem Tov, and as a child he spent many hours praying on the grave of the Baal Shem in Medzhibozh. See Arthur Green, *Tormented Master*, p. 28.

35. A long, Nachman-like tale by Der Nister called "A Tale of Kings" can be found in *Yenne Velt: The Great Works of Jewish Fantasy and the Occult*, edited and translated by Joachim Neugroschel.

36. Arthur Green, *Tormented Master*, p. 347.

Chapter 11
S. Y. Agnon, I. L. Peretz, and I. B. Singer: Modern Masters of the Aggadah

1. The stories discussed in this chapter can be found in *Gates to the New City: A Treasury of Modern Jewish Tales* (hereafter GNC), edited by Howard Schwartz. The majority of these stories derive from the modern Hebrew and Yiddish literary traditions. There is no other fully developed modern tradition, although there are to be found individuals writing in at least a dozen languages who have utilized traditional sources and found inspiration in them.

2. While this is true regarding their literary form, it should be noted that Mendele's style was filled with folk sayings, proverbs, talmudic phrases, etc. In this respect Agnon has always been viewed as an heir of Mendele.

3. Agnon's preeminence was, however, not apparent from the first. For a time M. J. Berditchevsky was regarded as the leading figure, and Agnon was considered an interesting, if somewhat esoteric, writer of hasidic tales.

4. Agnon always insisted that he had never read Kafka, but no one believed him, as Kafka's influence is unmistakable, especially in Agnon's *The Book of Deeds*, where many of the stories, such as "To the Doctor" (with its strong echo of Kafka's "A Country Doctor"), are dreamlike and surreal. The Israeli writer Yehuda Yaari, a close friend of Agnon's, reported that he was once sitting in Agnon's living room when he noticed Kafka's collected writings on one bookshelf. Yaari asked Agnon why he claimed that he had never read Kafka, when there was clear evidence that he had. "Ah," Agnon is said to have replied, "those are my wife's books." It seems that Agnon preferred not to admit being influenced by a contemporary writer because it interfered with the image of a "simple" writer steeped in tradition. Yet the truth is that he was a deeply complex writer, fully cognizant of modernism and very much a part of it.

5. *Twenty-One Stories* by S. Y. Agnon (New York: 1970), pp. 30–44.

6. *A Book that was Lost and Other Stories* by S. Y. Agnon (New York: 1995), pp. 136–138.

7. *Twenty-One Stories* by S. Y. Agnon (New York: 1970), pp. 26–29.

8. B. Bab. Bat. 57b–58a and *Pirke de Rabbi Eliezer*, chap. 36.

9. Zohar I:57b and *Shivhei ha-Besht* 11, by Rabbi Dov Baer ben Samuel, edited by Samuel A. Horodezky (Berlin: 1922).

10. *Midrash Tanhuma*, ed. Buber, 1:214.

11. "A Story with a Goat" from *The Holy Amulet: Twelve Jewish-Yemenite Folktales*, collected by Rachel Seri, edited and annotated by Aliza Shenhar, no. 11, pp. 44–47. Translated from the Hebrew by Evelyn Abel. For other IFA variants of this folktale, see "The Cave to the Holy Land" and "The Cave of Temptations" in *Gabriel's Palace: Jewish Mystical Tales*, edited by Howard Schwartz, pp. 164–168.

12. For more on Peretz and Ansky, see "How I. L. Peretz Wrote His Tales" by A. Mukdoni in *In This World and the Next* by I. L. Peretz, pp. 352–359. For "The Story of the He-Goat Who Couldn't Say No" see *The Book of Fire* by I. L. Peretz (New York and London: 1959), pp. 72–75.

13. "The Sacred Goat" from Martin Buber, *Tales of the Hasidim: The Later Masters*, pp. 288–289.

14. On the other hand, Peretz found less to utilize of the halakhic tradition and was a leader of the Haskalah. This splitting of the halakhic and aggadic is a development of this century, but it may not necessarily be a negative one, for it permits the *Aggadah* to retain its power even among those who do not accept the rule of the *Halakhah*.

15. *Gimpel the Fool* by Isaac Bashevis Singer (New York: 1957), pp. 3–21.

16. GNC, pp. 185–189.

17. For more on *Gehenna* see *Hell in Jewish Literature* by Samuel J. Fox.

18. B. Hag. 15a.

19. Y. San. 29b.

20. Zohar II:221a. This passage links the decay of the body with the cessation of the suffering of the soul after twelve months. As such, it explains why Jewish hell differs from the Christian one, where punishment is eternal.

21. *Sipure Beit Din shel Ma'alah*, edited by Yisroel Yakov Klapholtz (B'nai Brak: 1978). This story is attributed to Miriam of Mohilev, the sister of Reb Shmelke, who is said to have told it to Reb Abraham Yehoshua Heschel, the Apter Rebbe.

22. The source of Singer's isolation from the Yiddish writing community derives from the hostile reception he received at the time of his arrival in the United States when, as the younger brother of Israel Joshua Singer, who had already established

himself as a major Yiddish novelist, Singer found that he had immediate access to the crucial Yiddish newspaper, the *Jewish Daily Forward* and its editor, Abraham Cahan. Virtually simultaneous with his arrival, the *Forward* began to serialize a novel of his, a fact that quickly brought him into opposition with a large number of jealous Yiddish writers who had already been in this country many years without having so much as their picture appear in that newspaper. As he relates in the third volume of his autobiography, *Lost in America*, Singer was then broke and desperate for the fifty dollars he received for each installment, although he regarded then and still regards this novel as a complete failure (and leaves it unnamed and, of course, untranslated). This fact, coupled with his early prominence, led to his immediate isolation within the community of Yiddish writers. It is worth observing that the effects of Singer's initial isolation and rejection by the Yiddish writers was profound. After Singer's emergence as an international success, he was in a position to direct his attention to the rich Yiddish literary tradition, but invariably he chose not to. Instead, he always singled out non-Yiddish authors such as Tolstoy and Balzac as his primary influences, while perpetuating the illusion that his writings were unique in Yiddish, when in fact they are deeply influenced by the tradition of Mendele Mokher-Seforim, I. L. Peretz, and, of course, his brother, I. J. Singer. Unfortunately, Singer's claim to uniqueness has gone essentially unquestioned, and the result has been little impetus to explore and translate many other important Yiddish figures, such as Der Nister, Dovid Ignatow, and Y. Y. Trunk, who subsequently have fallen into obscurity because of the inaccessibility of the Yiddish language to most readers. In this way an entire literary tradition has suffered grave damage because of a jealousy-engendered literary quarrel.

23. See *In My Father's Court* by I. B. Singer for an account of the traditions he was exposed to as the son of a prominent Warsaw rabbi.

Chapter 12
Modern Jewish Literature and the Ancient Models

1. The stories discussed in this chapter can be found in *Gates to the New City: A Treasury of Modern Jewish Tales* (hereafter GNC), edited by Howard Schwartz (New York: 1983).

2. For a further discussion of the use and interpretation of allegory, see the chapter, "Tools of Interpretation," pp. 34–37.

3. See *Modern Midrash: The Retelling of Traditional Jewish Narratives by Twentieth Century Hebrew Writers* by David C. Jacobson (New York: 1987).

4. Hayim Nachman Bialik took these same kinds of liberties in editing, with N. Ravnitsky, *Sefer ha-Aggadah*, translated into English by William Brande.

5. *The Pagan Rabbi and Other Stories* by Cynthia Ozick (New York: 1971), pp. 1–37.

6. GNC, pp. 512–516.

7. Ibid., pp. 400–403.

8. Ibid., pp. 263–268.

9. *Midrash Tanhuma*, ed. Buber, on Bereshit, sect. 27.

10. The following are just a few of the many passage where Abbaye begins with "the matriarch said to me": B. Shab. 133b, B. Ket. 50a, B. M.K. 12a, B. M.K. 18b, and B. Yeb. 25a. On Abbaye's rejoicing, see B. Ber. 30b. The statement about Abbaye's juggling appears in B. Suk. 53a. The episode of the boys pointing to the roof

appears in B. Ber. 48a. The lamb that accompanied Abbaye to the outhouse is mentioned in B. Ber. 48a: "The mother of Abbaye trained a lamb for him to go with him into the privy." The prayer in the privy is based on B. Ber. 60b: "On entering a privy one should say: 'Be honored, ye honored and holy ones that minister to the Most High. Give honor to the God of Israel. Wait for me till I enter and do my needs, and return to you.'" This is based on the belief that in the privy a man is abandoned by the angels and thus open to the approach of demons. That certain privies are the homes of demons derives from B. Ber. 62a: "There was a certain privy in Tiberias which if two persons entered together, even by day, they came to harm." The exorcism against demons appears in B. Shab. 67a. The window through which Rava's wife placed her hand on his head is mentioned in B. Ber. 62a. The two previous husbands of Abbaye's wife are mentioned in B. Yeb. 64b. The old man who consoled Abbaye about his passion for women is mentioned in B. Suk. 62a: "A certain old man came up to him and taught him: 'The greater the man, the greater his *Yetzer Hara* (Evil Inclination).'" Tradition identifies the anonymous man with Elijah. The legend of the rocks of the Tigris kissing each other after the death of Abbaye appears in B.M.K. 25b. The attack on Abbaye's wife Homa is reported in B. Ket. 65a. This is based on the belief that when a wife outlives three husbands there is the presumption that she was somehow responsible for their deaths (B. Yeb. 64b). (This note was prepared with the assistance of Jeremy Garber.)

11. B. Hag. 15b.

12. Ibid.

13. B. Hag. 15a.

14. In contrast, the Zohar speaks of three aspects of the soul, *nefesh* (life), *ruah* (spirit), and *neshamah* (soul), with two additional higher levels, *haayah* and *yehidah*, which only the elect can obtain. In addition, the human soul has sparks of other souls in it.

15. B. Hag. 15a.

16. *Pirke Avot* 3:7.

17. B. Hag. 15b.

18. From *Midrash Tanhuma*, Pekude 3. Also found in *Sefer ha-Zikhronot (The Chronicles of Jerahmeel)* 9:1–8.

19. From *In the Reign of Peace* by Hugh Nissenson (New York: 1972), pp. 107–117.

20. B. Git. 56a–b.

21. GNC, pp. 160–164.

22. Ex. Rab. 21:10.

23. *Mekilta de Rabbi Ishmael* on Ex. 15:1.

24. The unlikely association of Moses with a *shohet* is explained by the tradition that it was Moses who was taught the correct procedure of slaughtering animals by God and in turn transmitted it orally to the people. Also, while the Jews were journeying in the desert, they were permitted to eat only of the meat of the sacrifices that were brought into the Tabernacle (B. Men. 29a).

25. B. Sot. 13b.

26. *Jewish Legends* by Stefan Zweig (New York: 1987), pp. 167–171.

27. For a further discussion of the *Pargod*, see the chapter "Tales of the Great Jewish Mystics," p. 121.

28. Heinrich Zimmer, *Myths and Symbols in Indian Art and Civilization*, pp. 32–33.

29. *Keter Shem Tov*, edited by Rabbi Aharon b'Reb Zvi HaCohen Apta (Zolkova: 1794).

30. GNC, pp. 383–390.

31. From *The Book of Questions: Yael, Elya, Aely* by Edmond Jabès (Middletown, Conn.: 1983), pp. 143–144.

32. The theme of *tzimtzum* also plays a prominent part in Jay Neugeboren's novel *The Stolen Jew*.

33. From *Parables and Paradoxes* by Franz Kafka (New York: 1961), pp. 29–33.

34. GNC, pp. 122–126.

35. Ibid., p. 127.

36. From *Parables and Paradoxes* by Franz Kafka (New York: 1961), pp. 41–45.

37. *The Stove and Other Stories* by Jakov Lind (New York: 1986), pp. 45–47.

38. GNC, p. 150.

39. Ibid., p. 152.

40. Ibid., pp. 152–154.

41. *The Book of Questions* by Edmond Jabès (Hanover and London: 1991), pp. 31.

Glossary

All the following terms are in Hebrew unless otherwise noted.

Aggadah (pl. **Aggadot**) the body of Jewish legends; specifically those found in the Talmud and Midrash.

Ahizat Einayim lit. "seizing the eyes." A term meaning illusion, delusion, mirage, chimera, or sleight of hand.

Akedah the binding of Isaac by Abraham on Mount Moriah.

Aravot the highest realm of heaven.

Bar Mitzvah a ceremony recognizing the transition into adulthood of a thirteen-year-old Jewish boy.

Beit Din a rabbinic court convened to decide matters of the Law.

Beit ha-Midrash a house of study.

Bereshit lit. "in the beginning." The first word of the Torah.

Bet the second letter of the Hebrew alphabet and the first letter of the first word of the Torah, *Bereshit.*

Birkat ha-Mazon the blessing after meals.

Brit lit "covenant." The circumcision given to every male Jewish child on the eighth day after birth. The complete term is *brit milah,* or "covenant of the circumcision."

Devekut cleaving to God, often of a mystical nature.

Drash an interpretation of a passage of the Bible.

Dybbuk the soul of one who has died that enters the body of one who is living and remains until exorcised.

Ein Sof lit. "endless" or "infinite." The highest, unknowable aspect of the Divinity.

Ein Yakov   a collection of the *Aggadah* of the Talmud, compiled in the 16th century by Rabbi Jacob ibn Chabib.

Gehenna   the place where the souls of the wicked are punished and purified; the Jewish equivalent of hell.

Gematria   a technique used by Jewish mystics to discern secret meanings in the Torah. In this system each Hebrew letter has a numerical value, and the commentator seeks out words or word combinations that have the same total, which are then regarded as linked.

Gilgul   the transmigration of souls. The kabbalistic equivalent of the belief in reincarnation.

Guf   the treasury of souls in Paradise.

Haggadah   the text used for the Passover seder.

Hagiyah   a tractate of the Talmud that contains many episodes of a mystical nature.

Halakhah   the code of Jewish religious law, which also includes ethical, civil, and criminal matters.

Hanukkah   festival celebrated for eight days to commemorate the successful struggle of the Jews against the Greeks, led by Judah Maccabee, and the rededication of the Holy Temple in Jerusalem.

Hasid (pl. **Hasidim**) lit. "a pious one."   A follower of Hasidism, a Jewish sect founded by the Baal Shem Tov. Hasidim are usually associated with a religious leader, known as a "rebbe," as disciples.

Haskalah lit. "enlightenment."   A movement that originated in central Europe in the 18th century; it encouraged Jews to broaden their knowledge of the world through secular studies.

Havdalah lit. "to distinguish" or "to separate."   The ceremony performed at the end of the Sabbath, denoting the separation of the Sabbath from the rest of the week that follows.

Hekhalot lit. "palaces."   Refers to the visions of the Jewish mystics of the palaces of heaven. The texts describing these visionary journeys into Paradise are known as "*Hekhalot* texts."

Ibbur   the spirit of a dead sage that fuses with a living person and strengthens his faith and wisdom. A positive kind of possession, the opposite of possession by a *dybbuk*.

Kabbalah lit. "to receive."   The term designating the texts of Jewish mysticism. A kabbalist is one who devotes himself to the study of those texts.

Kaddish   an ancient prayer, written in Aramaic, sanctifying the name of God, which is recited by mourners as a prayer for the dead. A son is required to say it for his parents three times a day for eleven months following their deaths.

Kavanah lit. "intention."   The spirit or intensity that is brought to prayer and other rituals, without which prayer is an empty form.

Kfitzat ha-Derekh lit. "leaping the way."   A kind of enchanted travel, often associated with the tales of the Baal Shem Tov, in which his wagon traveled great distances in a short time, without the wheels ever touching the ground.

Kotel Western Wall. Also known as the Wailing Wall.

Lag ba-Omer festival that falls between Passover and Shavuot.

Lamed-Vav Tzaddikim the thirty-six just men who, according to legend, exist in every generation. By their merit the world is sustained.

Lekhah Dodi a famous hymn of the 16th century that welcomes the Sabbath Queen every Friday evening at the beginning of the Sabbath.

Ma'aseh (pl. Ma'asiyot) a tale or story, often a folktale.

Ma'aseh Bereshit lit. "the work of the creation." The mystical doctrine of the mysteries of creation.

Ma'aseh Merkavah lit. "the work of the chariot." The mystical doctrine associated with the vision of Ezekiel.

Maggid (pl. Maggidim) a preacher who confined his talks to easily understood homiletics, such as the *Maggid* of Dubno. Also, a spirit invoked by the study of a sacred text.

Malkhut lit. "kingdom." The tenth *Sefirah*, identified as Kingdom, which is linked to the *Shekhinah*.

Matzah the traditional unleavened bread for Passover.

Mezzuzah (pl. Mezzuzot) lit. "doorpost." A small case containing a piece of parchment on which is written the prayer that begins "*Shema Yisrael*." This case is affixed to the right doorpost of a Jew's home in accordance with the biblical injunction.

Middot lit. "rules." The Middot is one of the tractates of the Mishnah, the division Kodashim, which deals primarily with the laws pertaining to the Temple.

Midrash a method of exegesis of the biblical text. Also refers to post-talmudic Jewish legends as a whole. A *midrash* (lowercased, with the plural *midrashim*) is an individual rabbinic legend.

Mikveh the ritual bath in which women immerse themselves after menstruation has ended. It is also used occasionally by men for purposes of ritual purification.

Mohel one who performs the ritual circumcision of the *brit*.

Neshamah Yeterah the extra soul that is said to be received on the Sabbath, which departs after the ceremony of *Havdalah* is performed.

Notarikon a system of interpretation in which every letter of a word is taken as an initial or abbreviation of a word, used primarily as a kabbalistic technique.

Olam Haba the world to come. Often used as a synonym for heaven.

Pardes, PaRDeS lit. "orchard;" often linked to Paradise. Refers to the enticing but dangerous realms of mystical speculation and contemplation symbolized by heavenly ascent. Also, an acronym for a system of textural exegesis based on four levels of interpretation: *peshat* (literal), *remez* (symbolic), *drash* (allegorical), and *sod* (mystical).

Pargod lit. "curtain." In Jewish mysticism it refers to the curtain that is said to hang before the Throne of Glory in Paradise, which separates God from the angels.

Peshat a literal kind of textural exegesis. Also the first level of interpretation in the system known as *PaRDeS*.

Remez lit. "a hint." The second level of interpretation in the system known by the acronym *PaRDeS*. It implies the perception that the meaning has moved from the literal to the symbolic.

Responsa the replies of the rabbis to questions that relate to Jewish Law.

Ruah ha-Kodesh the Holy Spirit.

Sefirah (pl. **Sefirot**) kabbalistic concept of emanations, ten in all, through which the world came into being.

Shalom Aleikhem lit. "peace be to you." The traditional Jewish greeting. The traditional reply is *"Aleikhem Shalom,"* "to you, peace."

Sheilat Halom a method of divination in which a question is asked before going to sleep, in hopes that the answer will be given in a dream.

Sheilat Sefer a method of divination in which the Bible or another sacred text is opened at random and a passage is pointed to, which is understood to be the reply to the question.

Shekhinah lit. "to dwell." The Divine Presence, usually identified as a feminine aspect of the Divinity, which evolved into an independent mythic figure in the kabbalistic period. Also identified as the Bride of God and the Sabbath Queen.

Sheva Berakhot the seven benedictions of marriage. Also refers to a week-long series of ceremonies after a wedding, in which the celebration continues.

Shivah the seven-day period of mourning observed by close relatives of a person who has died.

Shloshim the thirty-day period of mourning after a person dies.

Shohet a ritual slaughterer.

Sitra Ahra the side of evil in kabbalistic terminology.

Smikhah rabbinic ordination, traditionally given to a student who has demonstrated his mastery of Jewish law.

Sod the fourth level of the four-level system of biblical interpretation known as *PaRDeS*. It refers to secret or mystical interpretations.

Sofer a scribe. One who writes holy texts and also records, as they are spoken, the teachings and tales of hasidic rabbis.

Tammuz the fourth month of the Jewish religious calendar.

Targum (pl. **Targumim**) lit "translation" in Aramaic. The translation of the Bible into Aramaic.

Temurah a kabbalistic technique in which one letter is substituted for another.

Tetragrammaton the four-letter ineffable Name of God: YHVH. The true pronunciation is believed to have been lost, and the knowledge of it is believed to confer great power. According to one tradition, only one great sage in each generation knows the true pronunciation of the Tetragrammaton.

Tikkun lit. "repair."   Restoration and redemption.

Tzaddik   an unusually righteous and spiritually pure person. Hasidim believe their rebbes to be *tzaddikim.*

Tzaddik ha-Dor   the leading *tzaddik* of his generation.

Tzeruf   a kabbalistic technique in which a word is rearranged into another—i.e., an anagram.

Tzimtzum   the kabbalistic concept of the contraction of God that took place at the time of the creation to make space for the world to exist.

Yahrzeit   Yiddish term meaning the anniversary of the death of a close relative.

Yeshivah   school for talmudic and rabbinic studies.

Yetzer Hara   the Evil Inclination.

Yetzer Tov   the Good Inclination.

Bibliography

The following is a selected bibliography of books and articles in English and in English translation relevant to the subjects of these essays.

Aarne, Antti, and Stith Thompson, eds. *The Types of the Folktale.* Helsinki: 1961.

Abelson, J. *The Immanence of God in Rabbinical Literature.* New York: 1969.

Abelson, J. *Jewish Mysticism.* London: 1913.

Abelson, J. *Jewish Mysticism: An Introduction to the Kabbalah.* New York: 1981.

Aberbach, Moses, and Bernard Grossfeld, eds. *Targum Onkelos for Genesis.* New York: 1981.

Abramovitsh, S. Y. (Mendele Moyker-Sforim). *Tales of Mendele the Book Peddler.* New York: 1966.

Abrahams, Israel. *Jewish Life in the Middle Ages.* New York: 1975.

Abramowicz, Dina, ed. *Yiddish Literature in English Translation 1945–1967.* New York: 1967.

Achtemeier, Paul J., general ed. *Harper's Bible Dictionary.* San Francisco: 1985.

Adelman, Penina, V. *Miriam's Well: Rituals for Jewish Women Around the Year.* Fresh Meadows, New York: 1986.

Adler, Morris. *The World of the Talmud.* New York: 1963.

Afterman, Allen. *Kabbalah and Consciousness.* Riverdale-on-Hudson, N.Y.: 1992.

Agnon, S. Y. *A Book That Was Lost and Other Stories.* New York: 1995.

Agnon, S. Y. *The Bridal Canopy.* New York: 1937.

Agnon, S. Y., ed. *Days of Awe.* New York: 1948.

Agnon, S. Y. *A Guest for the Night.* New York: 1968.

Agnon, S. Y. *In the Heart of the Seas.* New York: 1947.

Agnon, S. Y., ed. *Present At Sinai: The Giving of the Law.* New York: 1994.

Agnon, S. Y. *Twenty-one Stories.* New York: 1970.

Agnon, S. Y. *Two Tales: Betrothed and Edo and Enam.* New York: 1966.

Albright, William Foxwell. *Archaeology and the Religion of Israel*. Baltimore: 1942.

Albright, William Foxwell. *From the Stone Age to Christianity*. New York: 1957.

Albright, William Foxwell. *Yahweh and the Gods of Canaan*. New York: 1968.

Aleichem, Sholom. *Adventures of Mottel the Cantor's Son*. New York: 1961.

Aleichem, Sholom. *The Best of Sholem Aleichem*. Washington, D.C.: 1979.

Aleichem, Sholom. *Collected Stories of Sholem Aleichem*. New York: 1965. Two volumes.

Aleichem, Sholom. *The Great Fair: Scenes from My Childhood*. New York: 1955.

Aleichem, Sholom. *Hanukah Money*. New York: 1978.

Aleichem, Sholom. *Inside Kasrilevke*. New York: 1948.

Aleichem, Sholom. *Marienbad*. New York: 1982.

Aleichem, Sholom. *The Old Country*. New York: 1953.

Aleichem, Sholom. *Old Country Tales*. New York: 1966.

Aleichem, Sholom. *Selected Stories*. New York: 1956.

Aleichem, Sholom. *Some Laughter, Some Tears*. New York: 1969.

Aleichem, Sholom. *Stories and Satires*. London: 1959.

Aleichem, Sholom. *Tovye's Daughter*. New York: 1965.

Aleichem, Sholom. *Wandering Star*. New York: 1952.

Alon, Gedaliah. *The Jews in their Land in the Talmudic Age*, translated by Gershon Levi. Jerusalem: 1980.

Alter, Michael J., ed. *What is the Purpose of Creation?: A Jewish Anthology*. Northvale, N.J.: 1991.

Alter, Robert. *After the Tradition: Essays on Modern Jewish Writing*. New York: 1971.

Alter, Robert. *The Art of Biblical Narrative*. New York: 1981.

Alter, Robert. *Defenses of the Imagination: Jewish Writers and Modern Historical Crises*. Philadelphia: 1977.

Alter, Robert, tr. *Genesis: Translation and Commentary*. New York: 1996.

Alter, Robert. *Modern Hebrew Literature*. New York: 1966.

Alter, Robert and Frank Kermode. *The Literary Guide to the Bible*. Cambridge, Mass.: 1987.

Ansky, S. *The Dybbuk and Other Writings*, edited by David G. Roskies. New York: 1992.

Antonelli, Judith S. *In the Image of God: A Feminist Commentary on the Torah*. Northvale, N.J.: 1995.

Appelfeld, Aharon. *The Age of Wonders*. Boston: 1981.

Appelfeld, Aharon. *Badenheim 1939*. Boston: 1980.

Appelfeld, Aharon, ed. *From the World of Rabbi Nahman of Bratslav*. Jerusalem: 1973.

Appelfeld, Aharon. *The Healer*. New York: 1990.

Appelfeld, Aharon. *In the Wilderness*. Jerusalem: 1965.

Appelfeld, Aharon. *The Retreat*. New York: 1984.

Appelfeld, Aharon. *To the Land of the Cattails*. New York: 1986.

Appelfeld, Aharon. *Unto the Soul*. New York: 1994.

Ari, Mark. *The Shoemaker's Tale*. Boston: 1993.

Ariel, David S. *The Mystic Quest: An Introduction to Jewish Mysticism*. Northvale, N.J.: 1988.

Armstead, Samuel G. and Joseph H. Silverman, eds., *Judeo-Spanish Ballads from New York*. Berkeley: 1981.

Armstrong, Karen. A *History of God: The 4,000-Year Quest of Judaism, Christianity and Islam*. New York: 1993.

Aron, Milton. *Ideas and Ideals of the Hasidim*. New York: 1980.

Aryeh, Isaiah, and Joshua Dvorkes, eds. *The Baal Shem Tov on Pirkey Avoth*. Jerusalem: 1974.

Asch, Sholem. *Children of Abraham*. New York: 1942.

Asch, Sholem. *In the Beginning*. New York: 1966.

Asch, Sholem. *Kiddush Ha'sbem: An Epic of 1648 and Sabbatai Zevi*. Philadelphia: 1926.

Asch, Sholem. *Mottke the Thief*. Westport, Conn.: 1970.

Asch, Sholem. *A Passage in the Night*. New York: 1953.

Asch, Sholem. *The Prophet*. New York: 1955.

Asch, Sholem. *Sabbatai Zevi: A Tragedy in Three Acts and Six Scenes*. Philadelphia: 1930.

Asch, Sholem. *Salvation*. New York: 1933.

Asch, Sholem. *Tales of My People*. New York: 1948.

Asch, Sholem. *Three Cities: A Trilogy*. New York: 1933.

Aschikenasy, Nehama. *Eve's Journey: Feminine Images in Hebraic Literary Tradition*. Detroit: 1986.

Ausubel, Nathan, ed. *A Treasury of Jewish Folklore*. New York: 1948.

Avi-Yonah, Michael. *The Jews of Palestine: A Political History from the Bar Kokhba War to the Arab Conquest*. New York: 1976.

Babel, Isaac. *Benya Krik, the Gangster*. New York: 1948.

Babel, Isaac. *The Collected Stones*. New York: 1955.

Babel, Isaac. *You Must Know Everything*. New York: 1969.

Badanes, Jerome. *The Final Opus of Leon Solomon*. New York: 1988.

Bader, Gershom. *The Encyclopedia of Talmudic Sages*. Northvale, N. J.: 1988.

Baer, Yitzhak. *A History of the Jews in Christian Spain*. Philadelphia: 1961. Two volumes.

Bakan, David. *Sigmund Freud & the Jewish Mystical Tradition*. New York: 1965.

Band, Arnold J., tr. *Nahman of Bratslav: The Tales*. New York: 1978.

Band, Arnold J. *Nostalgia and Nightmare: A Study in the Fiction of S. Y. Agnon*. Berkeley: 1968.

Barash, Asher. *A Golden Treasury of Jewish Tales*. Tel Aviv: 1965.

Bar-Ilan, Meir. "Witches in the Bible and in the Talmud." In *Approaches to Ancient Jerusalem*, edited by Herbert W. Basser and Simcha Fishbane, Vol. 5, pp. 7–32.

Bar-Itzhak, Haya, and Aliza Shenhar. *Jewish Moroccan Folk Narratives from Israel*. Detroit: 1993.

Bar-Lev, Rabbi Yechiel. *Song of the Soul: Introduction to Kaballa*. Petach Tikva: 1994.

Barnstone, Willis. *The Other Bible: Jewish Pseudepigrapha, Christian Apocrypha, Gnostic Scriptures, Kabbalah, and Dead Sea Scrolls*. San Francisco: 1984.

Baron, Salo Wittmayer. *A Social and Religious History of the Jews*. New York: 1957. Second edition. Seventeen volumes.

Barth, Lewis M. "The Midrashic Enterprise." *Jewish Book Annual* 40 (1982–1983): 7–19.

Basser, Herbert. *In the Margins of the Midrash*. Atlanta: 1990.

Basser, Herbert W. *Midrashic Interpretations of the Song of Moses*. New York: 1984.

Batto, Bernard F. *Slaying the Dragon: Mythmaking in the Biblical Tradition*. Louisville: 1992.

Bazak, Joseph. *Judaism and Psychical Phenomena*. New York: 1967.

Bellow, Saul, ed. *Great Jewish Short Stories*. New York: 1963.

Ben-Ami, Issachar, and Joseph Dan, eds. *Studies in Aggadah and Jewish Folklore*. Jerusalem: 1983.

Ben-Amos, Dan. *Narrative Forms in the Haggadah: Structural Analysis*. Ann Arbor: 1973.

Ben-Amos, Dan. "Talmudic Tale Tales." In *Folklore Today: A Festschrift for Richard M. Dorson*, edited by L. Degh, H. Glassie, and F. J. Oinas, 25–44. Bloomington: 1976.

Ben-Amos, Dan, and Jerome Mintz, tr. *In Praise of the Baal Shem Tov: The Earliest Collection of Legends about the Founder of Hasidism (Shivhei ha-Besht)*. Bloomington: 1970.

Ben Bezalel, Rabbi Yehudah Leove. *The Book of Divine Power*. Jerusalem: 1975.

Ben Sasson, H. H., ed. *A History of the Jewish People*. Cambridge, Mass.: 1976.

Ben Shalom, Benzion. *Hebrew Literature Between the Two World Wars*. New York: 1953.

Bension, Ariel. *The Zohar in Moslem and Christian Spain*. New York: 1974.

Ben Zion, Raphael. *The Way of the Faithful: An Anthology of Jewish Mysticism*. Los Angeles: 1945.

Ben-Zvi, Itzhak. *The Exiled and the Redeemed*. Philadelphia: 1957.

Berger, Abraham. "The Literature of Jewish Folklore." *The Journal of Jewish Bibliography* 1 (1938–1939): 12–20, 40–49.

Bergman, Simcha, tr. *Likutey Moharan by Rabbi Nachman of Breslov*. Jerusalem: 1986–1990. Three volumes to date.

Berman, Samuel A., tr. *Midrash Tanhuma-Yelammedenu*. Hoboken, N.J.: 1996.

Bettan, Israel. *Studies in Jewish Preaching*. New York: 1976.

Bettelheim, Bruno. *The Uses of Enchantment: The Meaning and Importance of Fairy Tales*. New York: 1976.

Bever, Julius A. *The Literature of the Old Testament in Its Historical Development*. New York: 1922.

Biale, David. *Gershom Scholem: Kabbalah and Counter-History*. Cambridge, Mass.: 1979.

Bialik, Hayim Nachman. *Aftergrowth and Other Stories*. Philadelphia: 1939.

Bialik, Hayim Nachman. *And It Came to Pass: Legends and Stories About King David and King Solomon*. New York: 1938.

Bialik, Hayim Nahman, and Yehoshua Hana Ravnitzky, eds. *The Book of Legends (Sefer Ha-Aggadah): Legends from the Talmud and Midrash*. New York: 1992.

Bialik, Hayim Nachman. "Halakhah and Aggadah" in *Modern Jewish Thought*, edited by Nahum N. Glatzer, pp. 55–64. New York: 1977.

Bilu, Yoram. "Demonic Explanations of Illness Among Moroccan Jews." *Culture, Medicine and Psychiatry* 3 (1979): 363–380.

Bin Gorion, Micha Joseph (Berditchevsky). *Mimekor Yisrael: Classical Jewish Folktales*. Abridged and Annotated Edition. Bloomington: 1990.

Birnbaum, Philip. *A Book of Jewish Concepts*. New York: 1964.

Birnbaum, Philip. *A Treasury of Judaism*. New York: 1957.

Birnbaum, Salomo. *The Life and Sayings of the Baal Shem*. New York: 1933.

Bloch, Abraham P. *The Biblical and Historical Background of the Jewish Holy Days.* New York: 1978.

Bloch, Chayim. *The Golem: Legends of the Ghetto of Prague.* Vienna: 1925.

Bloch, Chayim. "Legends of the Ari." *Menorah Journal:* 14 (1928), 371–84, 466–77.

Block, Renee. "Methodological Note for the Study of Rabbinic Literature." in *Approaches to Ancient Judaism I,* edited by William Scott Green, 51–76. Missoula: 1978.

Block, Ariel, and Chana Bloch, tr. *The Song of Songs: A New Translation.* New York: 1995.

Blocker, Joel, ed. *Israeli Stories.* New York: 1962.

Blocker, Joel. "Midrash." In *Approaches to Ancient Judaism I,* edited by William Scott Green, 29–50. Missoula: 1978.

Blumenthal, David R. *God at the Center: Meditations on Jewish Spirituality.* Northvale, N.J.: 1994.

Blumenthal, David R. *Understanding Jewish Mysticism—The Merkabah Tradition and the Zoharic Tradition.* New York: 1978–1982. Two volumes.

Blumenthal, Nachman. "Magical Thinking Among the Jews During the Nazi Occupation." *Yad Vashem Studies on the European Jewish Catastrophe and Resistance* 5 (1963): 221–236.

Bokser, Ben Zion, tr. *Abraham Isaac Kook: The Lights of Penitence, the Moral Principles, Lights of Holiness, Essays, Letters and Poems.* New York: 1978.

Bokser, Ben Zion. *From the World of the Cabbalah.* New York: 1954.

Bokser, Ben Zion. *The Jewish Mystical Tradition.* New York: 1981

Bokser, Ben Zion. *The Talmud: Selected Writings.* New York: 1989.

Boman, Thorleif. *Hebrew Thought Compared with Greek.* New York: 1970.

Borges, Jorge Luis. *Labyrinths.* New York: 1964.

Boteach, Shmuel. *Dreams.* Brooklyn: 1991.

Boteach, Shmuel. *Wresting with the Divine: A Jewish Response to Suffering.* Northvale, N.J.: 1995.

Bowker, John. *The Targums and Rabbinic Literature.* Cambridge, England: 1969.

Box, G.H., and R. H. Charles. *The Apocalypse of Abraham.* New York: 1918.

Boyarin, Daniel. *Carnal Israel: Reading Sex in Talmudic Culture.* Berkeley: 1993.

Boyarin, Daniel. *Intertextuality and the Reading of Midrash.* Bloomington and Indianapolis: 1994.

Braude, William G., and Israel J. Kapstein, tr. *The Midrash on Psalms (Midrash Tehillim).* New Haven: 1959. Two volumes.

Braude, William G. and Israel J. Kapstein, tr. *Pesikta de-Rab Kahana: R. Kahana's Compilation of Discourses for Sabbaths and Festal Days.* Philadelphia: 1975.

Braude, William G., and Israel J. Kapstein, tr. *Pesikta Rabbati: Discourses for Feasts, Fasts and Special Sabbaths.* New Haven: 1968. Two volumes.

Braude, William G., and Israel J. Kapstein, tr. *Tanna Debe Eliyahu: The Lore of the School of Elijah.* Philadelphia: 1981.

Braun, Moshe A. *The Jewish Holy Days: Their Spiritual Significance.* Northvale, N.J.: 1996.

Bregman, Marc. "The Art of Retelling." In *Jewish Book Annual,* edited by Jacob Kabakoff, vol. 53, pp. 177–182. New York: 1995–1996.

Bregman, Marc. "Introduction" and "Thematic Commentary" in *The Four Who Entered Paradise* by Howard Schwartz, pp. xiii–xxxiii, 125–198. Northvale, N.J.: 1995.

Bregman, Marc. "Joseph Heinemann's Studies on the Aggadah." *Immanuel* 9 (1979): 58–62.

Bregman, Marc. "Past and Present in Midrashic Literature." *Hebrew Annual Review* 2 (1978): 45–59.

Brichto, H. C. *The Problem of "Curse" in the Hebrew Bible.* Philadelphia: 1963.

Brinner, William M., tr. *An Elegant Composition Concerning Relief After Adversity, by Nissim ben Jacob ibn Shahin.* New Haven: 1977.

Broch, Yitzhak I. *Shir Ha-Shirim: The Song of Songs with a Midrashic Commentary.* Jerusalem and New York: 1968.

Brod, Max. *Franz Kafka: A Biography.* New York: 1964.

Bronner, Leila Leah. *From Eve to Esther: Rabbinic Reconstructions of Biblical Women.* Louisville: 1994.

Broznick, Norman M. *Some Aspects of German Mysticism as Reflected in the Sefer Hasidim.* M.A. Thesis, Columbia University, 1947.

Buber, Martin. *Between Man and Man.* New York: 1947.

Buber, Martin. *Hasidism & Modern Man.* New York: 1958.

Buber, Martin. *The Legend of the Baal-Shem.* New York: 1969.

Buber, Martin. *On Judaism.* New York: 1972.

Buber, Martin. *On the Bible.* New York: 1982.

Buber, Martin. *The Origin and Meaning of Hasidism.* New York: 1960.

Buber, Martin. *The Prophetic Faith.* New York: 1949.

Buber, Martin. *Tales of Angels, Spirits and Demons.* New York: 1958.

Buber, Martin. *Tales of the Hasidim: Early Masters.* New York: 1947.

Buber, Martin. *Tales of the Hasidim: Later Masters.* New York: 1948.

Buber, Martin. *The Tales of Rabbi Nachman.* New York: 1956.

Buber, Martin. *The Way of Man: According to the Teaching of Hasidism.* New York: 1950.

Buchmann, Christina, and Celina Spiegel, eds. *Out of the Garden: Women Writers on the Bible.* New York: 1994.

Bukiet, Melvin Jules. *After.* New York: 1996.

Bukiet, Melvin Jules. *While the Messiah Tarries: Stories.* New York: 1995.

Burton, Richard F., tr. *The Book of a Thousand Nights and a Night (The Arabian Nights).* New York: 1934. Three volumes.

Buxbaum, Yitzhak. *Jewish Spiritual Practices.* Northvale, N.J.: 1990.

Buxbaum, Yitzhak. *The Life and Teachings of Hillel.* Northvale, N.J.: 1994.

Buxbaum, Yitzhak. *Storytelling and Spirituality.* Northvale, N.J.: 1994.

Canetti, Elias. *Kafka's Other Trial.* New York: 1969.

Caplan, Samuel, ed. *The Great Jewish Books.* New York: 1963.

Carlebach, Shlomo with Susan Yael Mesinai. *Shlomo's Stories: Selected Tales.* Northvale, N.J.: 1994.

Carmi, T., ed. *The Penguin Book of Hebrew Verse.* New York: 1981.

Chajes, Z. H. *The Student's Guide Through the Talmud.* New York: 1960.

Chapman, Abraham. *Jewish American Literature.* New York: 1974.

Charles, R. H., ed. *The Apocrypha and Pseudepigrapha of the Old Testament.* Oxford: 1913. Two volumes.

Charlesworth, James H., ed. *The Old Testament Pseudepigrapha.* New York: 1983–1985. Two volumes.

Chasidah, Yishai. *Encyclopedia of Biblical Personalities: Anthologized from the Talmud, Midrash and Rabbinic Writings.* Jerusalem: 1994.

Cheyne, T. K. *Traditions and Beliefs of Ancient Israel*. London: 1907.

Chill, Abraham. *The Minhagim: The Customs and Ceremonies of Judaism, Their Origins and Rationale*. New York: 1980.

Chill, Abraham. *The Mitzvot: The Commandments and Their Rationale*. New York: 1981.

Chitrik, Yehuda. *From My Father's Shabbos Table: A Treasury of Chabad Chassidic Stories*. Jerusalem: 1991.

Citron, Sterna. *Why the Baal Shem Tov Laughed: Fifty-two Stories about Our Great Chasidic Rabbis*. Northvale, N.J.: 1993.

Cohen, A. *Everyman's Talmud*. New York: 1975.

Cohen, A., ed. *The Soncino Books of the Bible*. Surrey, England: 1947.

Cohen, A., ed. *The Soncino Chumash: The Five Books of Moses with Haftaroth*. London: 1947.

Cohen, Arthur A. *A Hero in His Time*. New York: 1976.

Cohen, Arthur A. *In the Days of Simon Stern*. New York: 1972.

Cohen, Arthur A. *The Myth of the Judeo-Christian Tradition*. New York: 1969.

Cohen, Arthur A. *The Natural and the Supernatural Jew*. New York: 1962.

Cohen, Arthur A., and Paul Mendes-Flohr, eds. *Contemporary Jewish Religious Thought*. New York: 1987.

Cohen, Gerson D. "The Talmudic Age." In *Great Ages and Ideas of the Jewish People*, edited by Leo W. Schwartz, 141–212. New York: 1956.

Cohen, Norman J. *Self, Struggle and Change: Family Conflict Stories in Genesis and Their Healing Insights for Our Lives*. Woodstock, Vt: 1995.

Cohn-Sherbok, Dan. *Jewish Mysticism: An Anthology*. Oxford: 1995.

Cohn-Sherbok, Dan, and Lavinia Cohn-Sherbok. *Jewish & Christian Mysticism: An Introduction*. New York: 1994.

Collins, John J., and Michael Fishbane, eds. *Death, Ecstasy, and Other Worldly Journeys*. Albany: 1995.

Cole, Peter, tr. *The Selected Poems of Shmuel HaNagid*. Princeton: 1996.

Comay, Joan. *The Diaspora Story*. New York: 1980.

Conybeare, E. C., tr. "The Testament of Solomon." *Jewish Quarterly Review* 11 (1899): 1–45.

Cordovero, Moses. *The Palm Tree of Deborah*. London: 1960.

Corre, Alan. *Understanding the Talmud*. New York: 1975.

Covitz, Joel. *Visions of the Night: A Study of Jewish Dream Interpretation*. Boston: 1990.

Crews, Cynthia. "Judeo-Spanish Folktales in Macedonia." *Folklore* 43 (1932): 193–224.

Culi, Yaakov. *The Torah Anthology*. New York: 1977. Two volumes.

Dahbany-Miraglia, Dina. "Yemenite Verbal Protective Behavior." *Working Papers in Yiddish and East European Jewish Studies* (YIVO) 13 (1975): 1–12.

Daiches, Samuel. *Babylonian Oil Magic in the Talmud and in the Later Jewish Literature*. London: 1913.

Dale, Rodney, ed. *The Kabbalah Decoded*. London: 1978.

Dame, Enid. *Lilith and Her Demons*. Merrick, N.Y.: 1987.

Dan, Joseph. "The Beginnings of Jewish Mysticism in Europe." In *The World History of the Jewish People*, edited by Cecil Roth, vol. II, 282–290. New Brunswick, N.J.: 1966.

Dan, Joseph, ed. *Binah: Studies in Jewish History*. Westport, Conn.: 1989, 1994. Three volumes.

Dan, Joseph. "The Desert in Jewish Mysticism: The Kingdom of Samael." *Ariel*, (1976): 38–43.

Dan, Joseph, ed. *The Early Kabbalah*. New York: 1987.

Dan, Joseph. "An Early Source of the Yiddish Aqdemoth Story." *Hebrew University Studies in Literature* I (1973): 39–46.

Dan, Joseph. "Five Versions of the Story of the Jerusalemite." *Proceedings of the American Academy for Jewish Research* 35 (1976): 99–111.

Dan, Joseph. *Gershom Scholem and the Mystical Dimension of Jewish History*. New York: 1988.

Dan, Joseph. *Jewish Mysticism and Jewish Ethics*. Seattle and London: 1986.

Dan, Joseph. "Rabbi Judah the Pious and Casarius of Heisterbach—Common Motifs in Their Stories." *Scripta Hierosolymitana* 22 (1971): 18–27.

Dan, Joseph, ed. *Readings in Hasidism*. New York: 1979.

Dan, Joseph. *The Revelation of the Secret of the World: The Beginning of Jewish Mysticism in Late Antiquity*. Providence: 1992.

Dan, Joseph. "Samael, Lilith and the Concept of Evil in Early Kabbalah." *AJS Review*, 5 (1980): 17–40.

Dan, Joseph, ed. *Studies in Jewish Mysticism*. New York: 1981.

Dan, Joseph. *The Teachings of Hasidism*. New York: 1983.

Dan, Joseph. "Teraphim: From Popular Belief to a Folktale." *Scripta Hierosolymitana* 27 (1978): 99–106.

Dan, Joseph. *Three Types of Ancient Jewish Mysticism*. Cincinnati: 1984.

Danby, Herbert. *The Mishnah*. London: 1933.

Daube, David. "Rabbinic Methods of Interpretation and Hellenistic Rhetoric." *Hebrew Union College Annual* 22 (1949): 239–64.

Davidowicz, Lucy. *The Golden Tradition*. New York: 1968.

Davidson, Gustav. *A Dictionary of Angels*. New York: 1967.

Davidson, Israel. *Parody in Jewish Literature*. New York: 1907.

Davidson, Israel, tr. *Sepher Shaashuim: A Book of Medieval Lore*, by Joseph ben Meir Ibn Zabara. New York: 1914.

Davies, Thomas Witton. *Magic, Divination and Demonology Among the Hebrews and Their Neighbors*. New York: 1909.

De Lange, Nicholas. *Apocrypha: Jewish Literature of the Hellenistic Age*. New York: 1978.

De Lange, Nicholas R. M. *Origen and the Jews*. Cambridge: 1976.

Delumeau, Jean. *History of Paradise: The Garden of Eden in Myth and Tradition*. New York: 1995.

De Manhar, Nurho, tr. *Zohar*. San Diego: 1978.

Der Nister. *The Family Mashber*. New York: 1987.

Dobh Baer of Lubavitch. *On Ecstasy*. Chappaqua, N.Y.: 1963.

Dorfman, Yitzchak. *The Maggid of Mezritch*. Southfield, Mi.: 1989.

Dorian, Marguerite. *The Year of the Waterbearer*. New York: 1976.

Dobrinsky, Herbert C. *A Treasury of Sephardic Laws and Customs*. New York: 1986.

Drazin, Israel. *Targum Onkelos on Deuteronomy*. New York: 1981.

Dreifuss, Gustav, and Judith Riemer. *Abraham: The Man and the Symbol: A Jungian Interpretation of the Biblical Story*. Wilmette, Ill.: 1995.

Dresner, Samuel H. *Levi Yitzhak of Berditchev: Portrait of a Hasidic Master*. New York: 1974.

Dresner, Samuel H. *The Sabbath*. New York: 1963.

Dresner, Samuel H. *The Zaddik: The Doctrine of the Zaddik According to the Writings of Rabbi Yaakov Yosef of Polnoy.* New York: 1974.

Driver, S. R. *Introduction to the Literature of the Old Testament.* New York: 1895.

Einhorn, David. *The Seventh Candle and Other Folk Tales of Eastern Europe.* New York: 1968.

Elata-Alster, Gerda, and Rachel Salmon. "Vertical and Horizontal Readings of the Biblical Text." *Linguistica Biblica* 60 (1988): 31–59.

Elbaz, Andre E. *Folktales of the Canadian Sephardim.* Toronto: 1982.

Eliach, Yaffa, ed. *Hasidic Tales of the Holocaust.* New York: 1982.

Elior, Rachel. *The Paradoxical Ascent to God: The Kabbalistic Theosophy of Habad Hasidism.* Albany: 1993.

Elworthy, Frederick Thomas. *The Evil Eye.* London: 1895.

Epstein, I., ed. *The Babylonian Talmud.* London: 1935–1952. Eighteen volumes.

Epstein, Isidore. *Judaism.* New York: 1959.

Epstein, Morris. ed. and tr. *Tales of Sendebar.* Philadelphia: 1967.

Epstein, Perle. *Kabbalah: The Way of the Jewish Mystic.* New York: 1978.

Epstein, Shifra. "Recent Literature on Jewish Folklore and Ethnography." *Jewish Book Annual* 36 (1978–1979): 106–113.

Feierberg, Mordecai Ze'ev. *Whither? and Other Stories.* Philadelphia: 1978.

Feldman, Asher. *The Parables and Similes of the Rabbis.* Cambridge, England: 1927.

Fiedler, Leslie A. *The Collected Essays of Leslie Fiedler.* New York: 1971.

Fiedler, Leslie A. *A Fiedler Reader.* New York: 1977.

Fiedler, Leslie A. *The Jew in the American Novel.* New York: 1959.

Fiedler, Leslie A. *The Last Jew in America.* New York: 1966.

Fiedler, Leslie A. *No! in Thunder: Essays on Myth and Literature.* Boston: 1960.

Fiedler, Leslie A. *Nude Croquet: The Stories of Leslie A. Fiedler.* New York: 1969.

Filoramo, Giovanni. *A History of Gnosticism.* Oxford and Cambridge, Mass.: 1990.

Fiedler, Leslie A. *Pull Down Vanity and Other Stories.* Philadelphia: 1962.

Fine, Lawrence, ed. *Essential Papers on Kabbalah.* New York and London: 1995.

Fine, Lawrence. *Safed Spirituality: Rules of Mystical Piety, The Beginning of Wisdom.* New York: 1984.

Finkel, Avraham Yaakov. *The Essence of the Holy Days: Insights from the Jewish Sages.* Northvale, N.J.: 1993.

Finkel, Avraham Yaakov. *The Great Chasidic Masters.* Northvale, N.J.: 1992.

Finkel, Avraham Yaakov. *In My Flesh I See God: A Treasury of Rabbinic Insights about the Human Anatomy.* Northvale, N.J.: 1995.

Finkelstein, Louis. *Akiba: Scholar, Saint, and Martyr.* Philadelphia: 1962.

Finkelstein, Louis. *The Beliefs and Practices of Judaism.* New York: 1952.

Finkelstein, Louis, ed. *The Jewish People, Past and Present.* New York: 1952.

Finkelstein, Louis. *The Jews: Their History, Culture, and Religion.* New York: 1960. Third edition. Two volumes.

Finkelstein, Louis. "Prolegomena to an Edition of the Sifre on Deuteronomy." *Proceedings of the American Academy for Jewish Research* 3 (1931–1932): 3–42.

Fischel, Henry A. *Essays in Greco-Roman and Related Talmudic Literature.* New York: 1980.

Fischel, Henry A. *Rabbinic Literature and Greco-Roman Philosophy.* Leiden: 1973.

Fishbane, Michael. *Biblical Interpretation in Ancient Israel.* Oxford: 1985.

Fishbane, Michael. *The Garments of Torah: Essays in Biblical Hermeneutics.* Bloomington: 1989.

Fishbane, Michael A. *Judaism: Revelation and Traditions*. San Francisco: 1987.

Fishbane, Michael. *The Kiss of God: Spiritual and Mystical Death in Judaism*. Seattle: 1994.

Fishbane, Michael, ed. *The Midrashic Imagination*. Albany: 1993.

Fishbane, Michael. "Torah and Tradition." In *Tradition and Theology in the Old Testament*, edited by Douglas A. Night, 275–300. Philadelphia: 1977.

Fishbane, Simcha. "Most Women Engage in Sorcery: An Analysis of Female Sorceresses in the Babylonian Talmud." In *Approaches to Ancient Judaism*, edited by Herbert W. Basser and Simcha Fishbane, Vol. 5, pp. 143–165.

Fleer, Gedaliah. *Rabbi Nachman's Fire: An Introduction to Breslover Chassidus*. New York: 1975.

Fleer, Gedaliah. *Rabbi Nachman's Foundation*. New York: 1976.

Fleg, Edmond. *The Life of Solomon*. New York: 1930.

Fohrer, Georg. *History of Israelite Religion*. Nashville: 1972.

Fox, Samuel J. *Hell in Jewish Literature*. Wheeling, Ill.: 1972.

Fraade, Steven D. *From Tradition to Commentary: Torah and Its Interpretation in the Midrash Sifre to Deuteronomy*. Albany: 1991.

Franck, Adolphe. *The Kabbalah: The Religious Philosophy of the Hebrew*. New York: 1940.

Frazer, James G. *Folklore of the Old Testament*. London: 1918. Three volumes.

Freedman, H., and Maurice Simon, eds. *Midrash Rabbah*. London: 1939. Ten volumes.

Freedman, Shalom. *In the Service of God: Conversations with Teachers of Torah in Jerusalem*. Northvale, N. J.: 1995.

Freedman, Shalom. *Life as Creation: A Jewish Way of Thinking about the World*. Northvale, N. J.: 1993.

Freud, Sigmund. *Moses and Monotheism*. New York: 1955.

Friedenwald, Harry. "The Evil Eye." *Medical Leaves* (1939): 44–48.

Friedlander, Gerald, tr. *Pirke de Rabbi Eliezer*. New York: 1970.

Friedlander, M. *The Jewish Religion*. London: 1922.

Friedman, Irving, tr. *The Book of Creation*. New York: 1977.

Freidus, Abraham Solomon. *A Bibliography of Lilith*. New York: 1917.

Gabbai, R. Meiribn. *Sod ha-Shabbat (The Mystery of the Sabbath)*. Albany, N.Y.: 1989.

Gaer, Joseph. *The Legend of the Wandering Jew*. New York: 1961.

Gaer, Joseph. *The Lore of the Old Testament*. Boston: 1952.

Gary, Romain. *The Dance of Genghis Cohn*. New York: 1968.

Gaster, Moses. *The Chronicles of Jerahmeel*. New York: 1971.

Gaster, Moses. *The Exempla of the Rabbis*. New York: 1968.

Gaster, Moses. *Jewish Folklore in the Middle Ages*. London: 1887.

Gaster, Moses, tr. *Ma'aseh Book of Jewish Tales and Legends*. Philadelphia: 1934. Two volumes.

Gaster, Moses, ed. *Studies and Texts in Folklore, Magic, Medieval Romance, Hebrew Apocrypha and Samaritan Archeology*. London: 1896. Three volumes.

Gaster, Moses. *The Sword of Moses: An Ancient Book of Magic*. London: 1896.

Gaster, Theodor, H. "A Canaanite Magical Text." *Orientalia* 11 (1942): 41–79.

Gaster, Theodor H. *The Dead Sea Scriptures*. New York: 1976. Third edition.

Gaster, Theodor H. *Festivals of the Jewish Year*. New York: 1974.

Gaster, Theodor H. *The Holy and the Profane: Evolution of Jewish Folkways.* New York: 1955.

Gaster, Theodor H. *Myth, Legend and Custom in the Old Testament.* New York: 1969.

Gaster, Theodor H. *Passover: Its History and Traditions.* Boston: 1962.

Gaster, Theodor H. *Thespis: Ritual, Myth and Drama in the Ancient Near East.* New York: 1959.

Gerhardson, Birger. *Memory and Manuscript.* Uppsala: 1961.

Gersh, Harry. *The Sacred Books of the Jews.* New York: 1968.

Gikatilla, Joseph. *Sha'are Orah: Gates of Light.* New York: 1994.

Giller, Pinchas. *The Enlightened Will Shine: Symbolization and Theurgy in the Later Strata of the Zohar.* Albany: 1993.

Ginsburg, Christian D. *The Kabbalah: Its Doctrines, Development, and Literature.* London: 1920.

Ginsburg, Elliot K. *The Sabbath in the Classical Kabbalah.* Albany: 1989.

Ginsburg, Elliot K., tr. *Sod Ha-Shabbat: The Mystery of the Sabbath.* Albany: 1989.

Ginzberg, Louis. *The Legends of the Jews.* Philadelphia: 1909–1935. Seven volumes.

Ginzberg, Louis. *On Jewish Law and Lore.* Philadelphia: 1955.

Ginzberg, Simon. *The Life and Works of Moses Hayyim Luzzatto.* Philadelphia: 1931.

Glatzer, Nahum N. *Hammer on the Rock: A Midrash Reader.* New York: 1962.

Glatzer, Nahum N. *A Jewish Reader.* New York: 1961.

Glatzer, Nahum N. *The Judaic Tradition.* New York: 1969.

Glick, S. H., tr. *En Jacob: Aggadah of the Babylonian Talmud.* New York: 1921. Five volumes.

Goell, Yohai. *Bibliography of Modern Hebrew Literature in Translation.* Tel Aviv: 1975.

Goitein, S. F. *From the Land of Sheba: Tales of the Jews of Yemen.* New York: 1947.

Goldemberg, Isaac. *The Fragmented Life of Don Jacobo Lerner.* New York: 1978.

Goldin, Judah, tr. *The Fathers According to Rabbi Nathan.* New York: 1974.

Goldin, Judah. "From Text to Interpretation and From Experience to the Interpreted Text." *Prooftexts* 3, no. 2 (1983): 157–68.

Goldin, Judah, ed. *The Jewish Expression.* New Haven: 1976.

Goldin, Judah. *The Living Talmud.* Chicago: 1957.

Goldin, Judah. *The Song at the Sea (Mekilta de-Rabbi Ishmael).* New Haven: 1971.

Goldin, Judah. *Studies in Midrash and Related Literature.* Philadelphia: 1988.

Goldsmith, Arnold L. *The Golem Remembered: 1909–1980.* Detroit: 1981.

Goldstein, David. *Jewish Folklore and Legend.* London: 1980.

Goldman, Edward A. "Parallel Texts in the Palestinian Talmud to Genesis Rabba." Rabbinic Thesis, *Hebrew Union College Annual,* 1969.

Goldwurm, Hersh. *The Rishonim.* New York: 1982.

Goodenough, E. R. *An Introduction to Philo Judaeus.* Naperville, Ill.: 1962.

Goodenough, Erwin. *By Light, Light: The Mystic Gospel of Hellenistic Judaism.* London and New Haven: 1935.

Goodenough, Erwin R. *Jewish Symbols in the Greco-Roman Period.* New York: 1953–1968. Thirteen volumes.

Goodman, Philip, ed. *The Passover Anthology.* Philadelphia: 1961.

Goodman, Philip, ed. *The Purim Anthology.* Philadelphia: 1949.

Goodman, Philip, ed. *The Rosh Hashanah Anthology.* Philadelphia: 1970.

Goodman, Philip, ed. *Sukkot and Simbat Torah Anthology.* Philadelphia: 1973.

Goodman, Philip, ed. *The Yom Kippur Anthology.* Philadelphia: 1971.

Goodspeed, Edgar J. *The Apocrypha: An American Translation.* New York: 1959.

Gordis, Robert. *Judaism for the Modern Age.* New York: 1955.

Gore, Norman C., tr. *Tzeenah U-Reenah: A Jewish Commentary on the Book of Exodus.* New York: 1965.

Gottlieb, Freema. *The Lamp of God: A Jewish Book of Light.* Northvale, N.J.: 1989.

Gottstein, Alon Goshen. "Four Entered Paradise Revisited." *Harvard Theological Review* 88, 1995, pp. 69–133.

Gratus, Jack. *The False Messiahs.* London: 1975.

Graves, Robert, ed. *Greek Myths.* London: 1955. Two volumes.

Graves, Robert, and Raphael Patai, eds. *Hebrew Myths: The Book of Genesis.* New York: 1966.

Grayzel, Solomon. *A History of the Jews.* Philadelphia: 1963.

Green, Arthur, tr. "Bratslav Dreams." In *Fiction,* nos. 1 and 2 (1983): 185–202.

Green, Arthur. *Keter: The Crown of God in Early Jewish Mysticism.* Princeton: 1997.

Green, Arthur, ed. *Jewish Spirituality.* New York: 1986, 1994. Two volumes.

Green, Arthur, tr. *Menahem Nahum of Chernobyl: Upright Practices, The Light of the Eyes.* New York: 1982.

Green, Arthur. *Seek My Face, Speak My Name: A Contemporary Jewish Theology.* Northvale, N.J.: 1992.

Green, Arthur. *Tormented Master: A Life of Rabbi Nachman of Bratslav.* University, Alabama: 1979.

Green, Arthur and Barry Holtz, eds. *Your Word Is Fire: The Hasidic Masters on Contemplation.* New York: 1977.

Green, William Scott. "Romancing the Tome: Rabbinic Hermeneutics and the Theory of Literature." *Semeia* (1987): 147–68.

Greenbaum, Avraham, tr. *Garden of the Souls: Rebbe Nachman on Suffering.* Jerusalem: 1990.

Greenbaum, Avraham, tr. *Rabbi Nachman's Tikkun: The Comprehensive Remedy (Tikkun Haklali).* Jerusalem: 1984.

Greenbaum, Avraham. *Under the Table & How to Get Up: Jewish Pathways of Spiritual Growth.* Jerusalem: 1991.

Greenberg, Irving. *The Jewish Way: Living the Holidays.* New York: 1988.

Greenspahn, Frederick E., ed. *Essential Papers on Israel and the Ancient Near East.* New York and London: 1991.

Grimm, Jacob, and Wilhelm Grimm. *Grimm's Tales for Young and Old: The Complete Stories.* Trans. by Ralph Manheim. Garden City, N.Y.: 1983.

Grossfeld, Bernard. *A Critical Commentary on Targum Neofiti I to Genesis.* New York: 1981.

Grossman, David. *See Under: Love.* New York: 1989.

Grossman, Ladislav. *The Shop on Main Street.* Garden City, N.Y.: 1970.

Grozinger, Karl Erich. *Kafka and Kabbalah.* New York: 1994.

Grozinger, Karl Erich and Joseph Dan. *Mysticism, Magic and Kabbalah in Askenazi Judaism.* Berlin: 1995.

Gruenwald, Ithamar. *Apocalyptic and Merkavah Mysticism.* Leiden and Koln: 1980.

Grunwald, Max. *Tales, Songs & Folkways of Sephardic Jews.* Edited by Dov Noy, Jerusalem: 1982. Folklore Research Center Studies VI.

Gunkel, Hermann. *The Legends of Genesis.* New York: 1970.

Guttmann, Alexander. *Rabbinic Judaism in the Making: A Chapter in the History of the Halakhah From Ezra to Judah I.* Detroit: 1970.

Guttman, Allen. *The Jewish Writer in America: Assimilation and the Crisis of Identity.* New York: 1971.

Hadas, Moses, tr. *Fables of a Jewish Aesop.* (Fables of Rabbi Berechiah) Ha-Nakdan. New York: 1967.

Halbertal, Moshe, and Avishai Margalit. *Idolatry.* Cambridge, Mass.: 1992.

Halivni, David Weiss. *Peshat and Derash—Plain and Applied Meaning in Rabbinic Exegesis.* Oxford: 1991.

Halkin, Simon. *Modern Hebrew Literature.* New York: 1970.

Halperin, David. *Faces of the Chariot: Early Jewish Responses to Ezekiel's Vision.* Tubingen: 1988.

Halperin, David. "Heavenly Ascension in Ancient Judaism: The Nature of the Experience. *Society of Biblical Literature Seminar Papers,* 1987, pp. 218–232.

Halperin, David. *The Merkabah in Rabbinic Literature.* New Haven: 1980.

Halperin, David J. *Seeking Ezekiel: Text and Psychology.* University Park, Penn.: 1993.

Hammer, Reuven. *The Classic Midrash: Tannaitic Commentaries on the Bible.* New York: 1995.

Hammer, Reuven. *Entering Jewish Prayer: A Guide to Personal Devotion and the Worship Service.* New York: 1994.

Hammer, Reuven. *The Jerusalem Anthology: A Literary Guide.* Philadelphia and Jerusalem: 1995.

Hammer, Reuven, tr. *Sifre: A Tannaitic Commentary on the Book of Deuteronomy.* New Haven and London: 1986.

Hanauer, J. E. *Folk-lore of the Holy Land.* London: 1977.

Handelman, Susan A. *The Slayers of Moses: The Emergence of Rabbinic Interpretation in Modern Literary Theory.* Albany: 1982.

Handler, Andrew. *Ararat: A Collection of Hungarian-Jewish Short Stories.* Rutherford, N.J.: 1980.

Handler, Andrew. *Rabbi Eizik: Hasidic Stories About the Zaddik of Kallo.* Rutherford, N.J.: 1978.

Harris, Jay M. "How Do We Know This?" *Midrash and the Fragmentation of Modern Judaism.* Albany: 1994.

Harris, Maurice H. *Hebraic Literature.* New York: 1941.

Harris, Monford. "Dreams in Sefer Hasidim." *Proceedings of the American Academy for Jewish Research* 31 (1963): 51–80.

Harris, Monford. *Studies in Jewish Dream Interpretation.* Northvale, N.J.: 1994.

Harris-Wiener, Shohama and Jonathan Omer-Man, eds. *Worlds of Jewish Prayer: A Festschrift in Honor of Rabbi Zalman M. Schachter-Shalomi.* Northvale, N.J.: 1993.

Hartman, Geoffrey H., and Sanford Budick. *Midrash and Literature.* New Haven and London: 1986.

Hartman, Geoffrey H. "On the Jewish Imagination." *Prooftexts* 5 (1985): 201–20.

Hastings, James, ed. *Dictionary of the Bible.* New York: 1946.

Hazaz, Hayim. *Gates of Bronze.* Philadelphia: 1975.

Hazaz, Hayim. *Mori Sa'id.* New York: 1956.

HeChasid, Rabbi Yehuda. *Sefer Chasidim: The Book of the Pious.* Northvale, N.J. and London: 1997.

Heidel, Alexander. *The Babylonian Genesis*. Chicago: 1951.

Heidel, Alexander. *The Gilgamesh Epic and Old Testament Parallels*. Chicago: 1963.

Heifetz, Harold. *Zen and Hasidism*. Wheaton, Il.: 1978.

Heilman, Samuel C. *Synagogue Life*. Chicago: 1976.

Heinemann, Benno. *The Maggid of Dubno and His Parables*. New York: 1967.

Heinemann, Joseph. "The Proem in the Aggadic Midrashim—A Form Critical Study." *Scripta Hierosolymitana* 22 (1971): 100–22.

Heinnemann, Joseph, and Dov Noy, eds. *Studies in Aggada and Folk Literature*. Jerusalem: 1971.

Heinnemann, Joseph, and Jakob J. Petuchowski, eds. *Literature of the Synagogue*. New York: 1976.

Heinnemann, Joseph, and Shmuel Werses, eds. *Studies in Hebrew Narrative Art Throughout the Ages*. Jerusalem: 1978.

Helman, Cecil. *The Emperor's Aversion and Other Fables*. London: 1977.

Helman, Cecil. *The Exploding Newspaper*. London: 1977.

Herford, R. T. *Talmud and Apocrypha: A Comparative Study of the Ethical Teachings in the Rabbinical and Non-Rabbinical Sources*. New York: 1971.

Hertz, J. H., ed. *The Pentateuch and Haftorahs*. London: 1947.

Heschel, Abraham J. *The Circle of the Baal Shem Tov: Studies in Hasidism*. Chicago: 1985.

Heschel, Abraham Joshua. *The Earth Is the Lord's: The Inner Life of the Jew in East Europe*. New York: 1950.

Heschel, Abraham Joshua. *God in Search of Man: A Philosophy of Judaism*. New York: 1955.

Heschel, Abraham J. *Man Is Not Alone*. New York: 1976.

Heschel, Abraham J. *A Passion for Truth*. New York: 1983.

Heschel, Abraham J. *Man's Quest for God*. New York: 1981.

Heschel, Abraham Joshua. "The Mystical Element in Judaism." In *The Jews: Their History, Culture, and Religion*, edited by Louis Finkelstein, 932–953. New York: 1960, Third Edition. Two volumes.

Heschel, Abraham J. *The Prophets*. New York: 1955. Two volumes.

Heschel, Abraham Joshua. *The Sabbath: Its Meaning for Modern Man*. New York: 1951.

Higgins, Elford. *Hebrew Idolatry and Superstition: Its Place in Folklore*. London: 1893.

Hillers, Delbert R. *Covenant: The History of a Biblical Idea*. Baltimore and London: 1969.

Himmelfarb, Martha. *Ascent to Heaven in Jewish & Christian Apocalypses*. New York: 1993.

Himmelfarb, Martha. *Tours of Hell: An Apocalyptic Form in Jewish and Christian Literature*. Philadelphia: 1985.

Hirsch, W. *Rabbinic Psychology: Beliefs About the Soul in the Rabbinic Literature of the Talmudic Period*. London: 1947.

Hirschman, Jack, tr. *The Book of Noah*. Berkeley: 1975.

Hirshman, Marc. *A Rivalry of Genius: Jewish and Christian Biblical Interpretation in Late Antiquity*. Albany: 1996.

Hochman, Baruch. *The Fiction of S. Y. Agnon*. Ithaca, N.Y.: 1970.

Hoffman, Edward, ed. *Opening the Inner Gates: New Paths in Kabbalah and Psychology*. Boston and London: 1995.

Hoffman, Edward. *The Way of Splendor: Jewish Mysticism and Modern Psychology.* Northvale, N.J.: 1989.

Hoffman, Lawrence A. *Beyond the Text: A Holistic Approach to Liturgy.* Bloomington and Indianapolis: 1987.

Holden, Lynn. *Forms of Deformity.* Sheffield, England: 1991.

The Holy Scriptures According to the Masoretic Text. Philadelphia: 1955.

Horodezky, S. A. *Leaders of Hassidism.* London: 1928.

Horowitz, Carmi. *The Jewish Sermon in 14th Century Spain: The Derashot of R. Joshua ibn Shu'eib.* Cambridge, Mass.: 1989.

Howe, Irving, ed. *Jewish American Stories.* New York: 1977.

Howe, Irving, ed. *Voices from the Yiddish.* Ann Arbor: 1972.

Howe, Irving, ed. Isaac B. Singer. *Selected Short Stories.* New York: 1966.

Howe, Irving, and Eliezer Greenberg, eds. *A Treasury of Yiddish Stories.* New York: 1954.

Hsia, R. Po-chia. *The Myth of Ritual Murder: Jews and Magic in Reformation Germany.* New Haven and London: 1988.

Hundert, Gershon David, ed. *Essential Papers on Hasidism: Origins to Present.* New York and London: 1991.

Hurwitz, Siegmund. *Lilith: The First Eve, Historical and Psychological Aspects of the Dark Feminine.* Einssiedeln, Switzerland: 1992.

Hyman, Naomi M., ed. *Biblical Women in the Midrash: A Sourcebook.* Northvale, N.J. and London: 1997.

Idel, Moshe. *Golem: Jewish Magical and Mystical Traditions on the Artificial Anthropoid.* Albany: 1990.

Idel, Moshe. *Hasidism: Between Ecstasy and Magic.* Albany: 1995.

Idel, Moshe. *Kabbalah: New Perspectives.* New Haven and London: 1988.

Idel, Moshe. *Language, Torah, and Hermeneutics in Abraham Abulafia.* Albany: 1989.

Idel, Moshe. *The Mystical Experience in Abraham Abulafia.* Albany: 1988.

Idel, Moshe, and Bernard McGinn, eds. *Mystical Union in Judaism, Christianity and Islam: An Ecumenical Dialogue.* New York: 1996.

Isaacs, Abram S. *Stories from the Rabbis.* New York: 1928.

Isaacs, Ronald H. and Kerry M. Olitzky, ed. *Sacred Moments: Tales from the Jewish Life Cycle.* Northvale, N.J.: 1993.

Ish Kishor, Shulamit. *The Master of Miracle.* New York: 1971.

Jabès, Edmond. *The Book of Questions,* vol. 1. Hanover, N.H.: 1991.

Jabès, Edmond. *The Book of Questions: Yael, Elya, Aely.* Middletown, Conn.: 1983.

Jacobs, Irving. "Elements of Near-Eastern Mythology in Rabbinic Aggadah." *Journal of Jewish Studies* 28 (1977): 1–11.

Jacobs, Irving. *The Midrashic Process.* Cambridge: 1995.

Jacobs, Louis. "The Doctrine of the 'Divine Sparks' in Man in Jewish Sources." In *Studies in Rationalism, Judaism and Universalism in Memory of Leon Roth,* edited by Raphael Loewe, 87–114. New York: 1966.

Jacobs, Louis. *Hasidic Prayer.* New York: 1973.

Jacobs, Louis. *Hasidic Thought.* New York: 1976.

Jacobs, Louis. *Holy Living: Saints and Saintliness in Judaism.* Northvale, N.J.: 1990.

Jacobs, Louis. *Jewish Ethics: Philosophy and Mysticism.* New York: 1969.

Jacobs, Louis. *Jewish Mystical Testimonies.* New York: 1977.

Jacobs, Louis. *The Jewish Religion: A Companion.* New York: 1995.

Jacobs, Louis, tr. *The Palm Tree of Deborah.* New York: 1974.

Jacobs, Louis. *Principles of the Jewish Faith.* New York: 1964.

Jacobs, Louis. *Seekers of Unity: The Life and Works of Aaron of Starosselje.* New York: 1966.

Jacobson, David C. *Modern Midrash: The Retelling of Traditional Jewish Narratives by Twentieth Century Hebrew Writers.* Albany: 1987.

Janouch, Gustav. *Conversations with Kafka.* New York: 1972.

Janowitz, Naomi. *The Poetics of Ascent: Theories of Language in a Rabbinic Ascent Text.* Albany: 1989.

Jason, Heda. *Conflict and Resolution in Jewish Sacred Tales.* Thesis, Indiana University, 1968.

Jason, Heda. "Rabbi Wazana and the Demons: Analysis of a Legend." In *Folklore Today: A Festschrift for Richard M. Dorson,* edited by L. Degh, H. Glassie, and E. J. Oinas, 273–290. Bloomington, Ind.: 1976.

Jason, Heda."Types of Jewish-Oriental Oral Tales." *Fabula* 7 (1965): 115–224.

Jason, Heda. *Types of Oral Tales in Israel: Part 2.* Jerusalem: 1975.

Jastrow, Marcus. *A Dictionary of the Targumim, the Talmud Babli and Yerushalmi, and the Midrashic Literature.* Brooklyn: 1903.

Jonas, Hans. *The Gnostic Religion: The Message of the Alien God and the Birth of Christianity,* 2nd edition. Boston: 1963.

Josephus. *Jewish Antiquities.* London: 1950. Nine volumes.

Jung, Leo. *Fallen Angels in Jewish, Christian and Mohammedan Literature.* Philadelphia: 1926.

Kadushin, Max. *A Conceptual Approach to the Mekilta,* 1–30. New York: 1969.

Kahof, Abram. *Jewish Symbolic Art.* Jerusalem: 1990.

Kadushin, Max. *The Rabbinic Mind.* New York: 1972.

Kafka, Franz. *The Castle.* New York: 1930.

Kafka, Franz. *The Complete Stories.* New York: 1971.

Kafka, Franz. *Diaries 1910–1913.* New York: 1965.

Kafka, Franz. *Diaries 1914–1923.* New York: 1974.

Kafka, Franz. *Letters to Felice.* New York: 1973.

Kafka, Franz. *Letters to Friends, Family and Editors.* New York: 1977.

Kafka, Franz. *Letter to His Father.* New York: 1953.

Kafka, Franz. *Letters to Milena.* New York: 1953.

Kafka, Franz. *Letters to Ottla and the Family.* New York: 1982.

Kafka, Franz. *Parables and Paradoxes.* New York: 1961.

Kafka, Franz. *The Penal Colony.* New York: 1961.

Kafka, Franz. *Stories and Reflections.* New York: 1970.

Kafka, Franz. *The Trial.* New York: 1953.

Kafka, Franz. *Wedding Preparations in the Country and Other Stories.* London: 1978.

Kahana, S. Z. *Legends of Zion.* Ramat Hasharon, Israel: 1974.

Kahn, Sholom J., ed. *A Whole Loaf: Stories from Israel.* Tel Aviv: 1957.

Kahof, Abram. *Jewish Symbolic Art.* Jerusalem: 1990.

Kalmin, Richard. *Sages, Stories, Authors and Editors in Rabbinic Babylonia.* Atlanta: 1994.

Kamenetz, Rodger. *The Jew in the Lotus: A Poet's Rediscovery of Jewish Identity in Buddhist India.* San Francisco: 1994.

Kaplan, Aryeh, tr. *The Bahir.* New York: 1979.

Kaplan, Aryeh. *A Call to the Infinite.* New York: 1986.

Kaplan, Aryeh. *Chasidic Masters.* New York: 1984.

Kaplan, Aryeh, tr. *Gems of Rabbi Nachman.* Jerusalem: 1980.

Kaplan, Aryeh. *Innerspace.* Jerusalem: 1990.

Kaplan, Aryeh. *Jewish Meditation: A Practical Guide.* New York: 1985.

Kaplan, Aryeh. *The Light Beyond: Adventures in Hasidic Thought.* New York: 1981.

Kaplan, Aryeh. *The Living Torah: The Five Books of Moses.* New York and Jerusalem: 1981.

Kaplan, Aryeh. *Meditation and Kabbalah.* York Beach, Maine: 1982.

Kaplan, Aryeh. *Meditation and the Bible.* York Beach, Maine: 1978.

Kaplan, Aryeh, tr. *Outpouring of the Soul: Rabbi Nachman's Path in Meditation.* Jerusalem: 1980.

Kaplan, Aryeh, tr. *Rabbi Nachman's Stories (Sippurey Ma'asioth): The Stories of Rabbi Nachman of Breslov.* Jerusalem: 1983.

Kaplan, Aryeh, tr. *Rabbi Nachman's Wisdom.* New York: 1971.

Kaplan, Aryeh. *Sefer Yetzirah: The Book of Creation.* York Beach, Maine: 1990.

Kasher, Menahem M., ed. *Encyclopedia of Biblical Interpretation.* New York: 1980. Nine volumes.

Kasher, Menahem M. *The Western Wall.* New York: 1972.

Katz, David A., and Peter Lovenheim. *Reading Between the Lines: New Stories from the Bible.* Northvale, N.J.: 1996.

Katz, Steven T. *Jewish Ideas and Concepts.* New York: 1977.

Kaufman, William E. *Journeys: An Introductory Guide to Jewish Mysticism.* New York: 1980.

Kaufmann, Yehezkel. *The Religion of Israel.* New York: 1972.

Kazin, Alfred, ed. *Selected Stories of Sholom Aleichem.* New York: 1956.

Kazis, Israel J., tr. *The Book of the Gests of Alexander of Macedon.* Cambridge: 1962.

Kelly, Henry A. *The Devil, Demonology and Witchcraft.* Garden City, N.Y.: 1968.

Kepnes, Stephen. "Narrative Jewish Theology." *Judaism,* 37 (1988): 210–219.

Kirsch, James. "The Zaddik in Nachman's Dream." *Journal of Psychology and Judaism,* 3 (1979): 227–234.

Kitov, Eliyahu. *The Book of Our Heritage.* Jerusalem: 1970. Three volumes.

Klapholtz, Yisroel Yaakov. *From Our Torah Treasury.* Tel Aviv: 1972. Two volumes.

Klapholtz, Yisroel Yaakov. *Stories of Elijah the Prophet.* Bnei Brak, Israel: 1971–1973. Four volumes.

Klapholtz, Yisroel, ed. *Tales of the Baal Shem Tov.* Jerusalem: 1970–1971. Five volumes.

Klapholtz, Yisroel, ed. *Tales of the Heavenly Court.* B'nai Brak: 1982. Two volumes.

Klar, B. *The Chronicles of Ahimaaz.* New York: 1945.

Klausner, J. *The Messianic Idea in Israel: From Its Beginning to the Completion of the Mishnah.* New York: 1955.

Klein, Aron, and Jenny Machlowitz Klein, tr. *Tales in Praise of the Ari (Shivhei ha-Ari) by Shlomo Meeinsterl.* Philadelphia: 1970.

Klein, Eliahu. *Legends of the Baal Shem Tov.* Northvale, N.J.: 1995.

Klein, Isaac. *A Guide to Jewish Religious Practice.* New York: 1979.

Kluger, Rivkah Scharf. *Satan in the Old Testament.* Evanston, Ill: 1967.

Knapp, Bettina L. *Manna & Mystery: A Jungian Approach to Hebrew Myth and Legend.* Wilmette, Ill.: 1995.

Koenig, Ester, tr. *The Thirteen Stories of Rebbe Nachman of Breslev.* Jerusalem: 1978.

Koltuv, Barbara Black. *The Book of Lilith.* York Beach, Maine: 1986.

Koltuv, Barbara Black. *Solomon and Sheba: Inner Marriage and Individuation.* York Beach, Maine: 1993.

Kook, Abraham Isaac. *The Lights of Penitence, the Moral Principles, Lights of Holiness, Essays, Letters, and Poems.* New York: 1978.

Kramer, Chaim. *Crossing the Narrow Bridge: A Practical Guide to Rebbe Nachman's Teachings.* Jerusalem and New York: 1989.

Kramer, Chaim. *Through Fire and Water: The Life of Reb Noson of Breslov.* Jerusalem: 1992.

Kramer, Simon. *God and Man in the Sefer Hasidim.* New York: 1966.

Kravitz, Leonard S., and Kerry M. Olitzky. *The Journey of the Soul: Traditional Sources on Teshuvah.* Northvale, N.J.: 1995.

Kugel, James L. *In Potiphar's House: The Interpretive Life of Biblical Texts.* San Francisco: 1990.

Kugel, James L., and Rowan A. Greer. *Early Biblical Interpretation.* Philadelphia: 1986.

Kushelevsky, Rella. *Moses and the Angel of Death.* New York: 1995.

Kushner, Lawrence. *Honey From the Rock.* New York: 1977.

Kushner, Lawrence. *The River of Light.* New York: 1981.

Kushner, Lawrence S., and Kerry M. Olitzky, *Sparks Beneath the Surface: A Spiritual Commentary on the Torah.* Northvale, N.J.: 1993.

Lachs, Samuel T. "The Alphabet of Ben Sira: A Study in Folk Literature." *Gratz College Annual of Jewish Studies* (1973): 9–28.

Lachs, Samuel T. "Serpent Folklore in Rabbinic Literature." *Jewish Social Studies* 27 (1967): 168–184.

Lamm, Norman, tr. "The Letter of the Besht to R. Gershon of Kutov." *Tradition* 14, 4 (Fall 1974): 110–125.

Landis, Joseph C., tr. *The Dybbuk and Other Great Yiddish Plays.* New York: 1966.

Landman, Leo. *Messianism in the Talmudic Era.* New York: 1979.

Langer, Jiří. *Nine Gates to the Chassidic Mysteries.* New York: 1976.

Langer, Lawrence L., ed. *Art from the Ashes: A Holocaust Anthology.* New York and Oxford: 1995.

Langermann, Yitzhak Tzvi, tr. *Yemenite Midrash: Philosophical Commentary on the Torah.* San Francisco: 1996.

Langton, Edward. *Essentials of Demonology.* London: 1945.

Langton, Edward. *Good and Evil Spirits: A Study of the Jewish and Christian Doctrine, Its Origin and Development.* London: 1942.

Laurence, Richard. *The Book of Enoch the Prophet.* London: 1883.

Lauterbach, Jacob Z. "The Arrangement and the Division of the Mekilta." *Hebrew Union College Annual* (1924): 427–66.

Lauterbach, Jacob Z., tr. *Mekilta de-Rabbi Ishmael.* Philadelphia: 1935. Three volumes.

Lauterbach, Jacob Z. *Rabbinic Essays.* Cincinnati: 1957.

Lauterbach, Jacob Z. *Studies in Jewish Law, Custom and Folklore.* New York: 1968.

LeDeaut, Roger. "Apropos a Definition of Midrash." *Interpretation* 25 (1971): 259–82.

Leftwich, Joseph, ed. *Yisroel: The First Jewish Omnibus.* New York: 1952.

Lehrman, S. M. *The World of the Midrash.* New York: 1961.

Leibowitz, Nehama. *Studies in Bereshit.* Jerusalem: 1974.

Leivick, Halper. *The Golem.* In *Great Jewish Plays,* edited by Joseph Landis. New York: 1972.

Leslau, Wolf. *Falasha Anthology: The Black Jews of Ethiopia.* New York: 1951.

Levenson, Jon D. *Creation and the Persistence of Evil: The Jewish Drama of Divine Omnipotence.* Princeton: 1988.

Levenson, Jon D. *The Death and Resurrection of the Beloved Son: The Transformation of Child Sacrifice in Judaism and Christianity.* New Haven: 1993.

Levenson, Jon D. *Sinai & Zion: An Entry into the Jewish Bible.* San Francisco: 1985.

Levi, Primo. *The Truce.* London: 1965.

Levin, Meyer, ed. *Classic Hassidic Tales.* New York: 1975.

Levin, Meyer. *Compulsion.* New York: 1956.

Levin, Meyer. *The Fanatic.* New York: 1964.

Levin, Meyer. *My Father's House.* New York: 1947.

Levin, Meyer. *The Obsession.* New York: 1973.

Levin, Meyer. *The Old Bunch.* New York: 1944.

Levin, Meyer. *The Settlers.* New York: 1972.

Levin, Meyer. *The Spell of Time.* New York: 1974.

Levner, J. B. *The Legends of Israel.* London: 1946. Two volumes.

Levy, Isaac. *The Synagogue: Its History and Function.* London: 1964.

Lieberman, Saul. *Greek in Jewish Palestine.* New York: 1942.

Lieberman, Saul. *Hellenism in Jewish Palestine.* New York: 1962.

Liebes, Yehuda. *Studies in Jewish Myth and Jewish Messianism.* Albany: 1993.

Liebes, Yehuda. *Studies in the Zohar.* Albany: 1993.

Lightstone, J. N. "Form As Meaning in Halakhic Midrash. A Programmatic Statement." *Semeia* 27 (1983): 24–35.

Lind, Jakov. *Counting My Steps.* New York: 1969.

Lind, Jakov. *Ergo.* New York: 1968.

Lind, Jakov. *Landscape in Concrete.* New York: 1966.

Lind, Jakov. *Soul of Wood and Other Stories.* New York: 1964.

Lind, Jakov. *The Stove.* New York: 1983

Lind, Jakov. *The Trip to Jerusalem.* New York: 1967.

Liptzin, Sol. *The Flowering of Yiddish Literature.* New York: 1965.

Liptzin, Sol. *The History of Yiddish Literature.* New York: 1972.

Liptzin, Sol. *The Jew in American Literature.* New York: 1966.

Liptzin, Sol. *The Maturing of Yiddish Literature.* New York: 1970.

Locks, Gutman G. *The Spice of Torah — Gematria.* New York: 1985.

Loewe, Raphael. "The 'Plain' Meaning of Scripture in Early Jewish Exegesis." *Papers of the Institute of Jewish Studies* [London] 1 (1964): 140–85.

Lorand, Sandor. "Dream Interpretation in the Talmud." *The International Journal of Psychoanalysis* 38 (1957): 92–97.

Louis, S. "Palestinian Demonology." *Proceedings of the Society of Biblical Archeology* 9 (1887): 217–228.

Luzzatto, Moses Chaim. *The Path of the Just.* Jerusalem: 1966.

Luzzatto, Moses. *The Way of God.* Jerusalem: 1978.

Lysman, Eugene J., tr. *The Mishnah: Oral Teachings of Judaism.* New York: 1974.

Lyndon, Sonja, and Sylvia Paskin, eds. *The Slow Mirror and Other Stories: New Fiction by Jewish Women.* Nottingham: 1996.

Maccoby, Hyam. *The Day God Laughed.* London: 1978.

Maccoby, Haym. *Early Rabbinic Writings.* Cambridge: 1988.

Maccoby, Hyam. *Revolution in Judea: Jews and the Jewish Renaissance.* London: 1973.

Maccoby, Hyam. *The Sacred Executioner: Human Sacrifice and the Legacy of Guilt.* New York: 1982.

MacDonald, George. *Lilith.* London: 1962.

Mack, Hananel. *The Aggadic Midrash Literature.* Tel Aviv: 1989.

Madison, Charles. *Yiddish Literature: Its Scope and Major Writers.* New York: 1971.

Maimonides, Moses. *The Guide for the Perplexed.* New York: 1956.

Maitlis, Jacob. *The Ma'aseh in the Yiddish Ethical Literature.* London: 1958.

Malamud, Bernard. *The Assistant.* New York: 1957.

Malamud, Bernard. *Dubin's Lives.* New York: 1979.

Malamud, Bernard. *The Fixer.* New York: 1966.

Malamud, Bernard. *God's Grace.* New York: 1982.

Malamud, Bernard. *Idiots First.* New York: 1963.

Malamud, Bernard. *The Magic Barrel.* New York: 1958.

Malamud, Bernard. *A Malamud Reader.* New York: 1967.

Malamud, Bernard. *The Natural.* New York: 1952.

Malamud, Bernard. *A New Life.* New York: 1961.

Malamud, Bernard. *Pictures of Fidelman.* New York: 1969.

Malamud, Bernard. *Rembrandt's Hat.* New York: 1973.

Malamud, Bernard. *The Stories of Bernard Malamud.* New York: 1983.

Malamud, Bernard. *The Tenants.* New York: 1971

Malin, Irving, ed. *Contemporary American-Jewish Literature: Critical Essays.* Bloomington: 1973.

Manger, Itzik. *The Book of Paradise.* New York: 1963.

Marcus, Ivan G. "The Recensions and Structure of Sefer Hasidim." *Proceedings of the American Academy for Jewish Research,* 45 (1978): 131–153.

Marcus, Jacob R. *The Jew in the Medieval World.* Philadelphia: 1960.

Margolis, Max. L. *A History of the Jewish People.* New York: 1958.

Marmorstein, Alfred. *The Doctrine of Merits in Old Rabbinic Literature.* New York: 1968. Three volumes.

Marks, Richard. *The Image of Bar Kokhba in Traditional Jewish Literature.* University Park, Pa.: 1994.

Matt, Daniel C. *The Essential Kabbalah: The Heart of Jewish Mysticism.* San Francisco: 1995.

Matt, Daniel Chanan, ed. *Zohar: The Book of Enlightenment.* New York: 1983.

Meltzer, David, ed. *The Path of the Names, Writings by Abraham ben Samuel Abulafia.* Berkeley: 1976.

Meltzer, David. *The Secret Garden: An Anthology in the Kabbalah.* New York: 1976.

Memi, Albert. *The Pillar of Salt.* New York: 1955.

Memi, Albert. *The Scorpion.* New York: 1971.

Memi, Albert. *Strangers.* New York: 1960.

Mendele Mokher-Seforim. *Fishke the Lame.* London: 1928.

Mendele Mokher-Seforim. *The Parasite.* New York: 1956.

Mendele Mokher-Seforim. *The Travels and Adventures of Benjamin the Third.* New York: 1949.

Mendenhall, George E. *The Tenth Generation.* Baltimore: 1973.

Mendes-Flohr, Paul, ed. *Gershom Scholem: The Man and His Work.* Albany: 1994.

Mersand, Joseph. *Traditions in American Literature: A Study of Jewish Characters and Authors.* New York: 1968.

Metzger, Bruce M., ed. *The Apocrypha of the Old Testament.* New York: 1965.

Metzger, Bruce M. *An Introduction to the Apocrypha*. New York: 1977.

Michener, James A., ed. *Firstfruits: A Harvest of 25 Years of Israeli Writing*. Philadelphia: 1973.

Mielziner, Moses. *Introduction to the Talmud*. New York: 1968.

Mihaly, Eugene. *A Song to Creation*. Cincinnati: 1975.

Mihaly, Eugene. "A Rabbinic Defense of the Election of Israel—An Analysis of Sifre Deuteronomy 32, 9, Pisqa 312." *Hebrew Union College Union Annual* 35 (1964): 103–43.

Mikliszanski, J. K. *The Saga of Traditional Judaism: A Survey of Post-Biblical Literature*. Los Angeles: 1977.

Miles, Jack. *God: A Biography*. New York: 1995.

Miller, Amos W. *Understanding the Midrash*. New York: 1965.

Millgram, Abraham E. *An Anthology of Medieval Hebrew Literature*. New York and London: 1961.

Millgram, Abraham E. *Great Jewish Ideas*. New York: 1964.

Millgram, Abraham E. *Jerusalem Curiosities*. Philadelphia: 1990.

Millgram, Abraham E. *Jewish Worship*. Philadelphia: 1971.

Millgram, Abraham E. *Sabbath: The Day of Delight*. Philadelphia: 1944.

Minkin, Jacob S. *The Romance of Hasidism*. New York: 1935.

Minsky, Mark. *Blue Hill Avenue*. New York: 1972.

Minsky, Mark. *My Search for the Messiah*. New York: 1977.

Minsky, Mark. *Proceedings of the Rabble*. New York: 1971.

Minsky, Mark. *The Secret Table*. New York: 1975.

Minsky, Mark. *Thou Worm Jacob*. New York: 1967.

Mintz, Jerome R., ed. *Legends of the Hasidim: An Introduction to Hasidic Culture and Oral Tradition in the New World*. Chicago: 1968.

Miron, Dan. *A Traveler Disguised: A Study in the Rise of Modern Yiddish Fiction in the Nineteenth Century*. New York: 1973.

Mitchell, Stephen, tr. *Genesis: A New Translation of the classic Biblical Stories*. New York: 1996.

Montefiore, C. G., and H. Loewe, eds. *A Rabbinic Anthology*. New York: 1974.

Moore, George Foot. *Judaism*. Cambridge, Mass.: 1927.

Moore, George Foot. "The Sources." in Judaism in the Age of the Tannaim, 1: 125–60. Cambridge, Mass.: 1927.

Mordell, Phineas. *The Origin of Letters & Numerals According to the Sefer Yetzirah*. New York: 1975.

Morgenstern, Julian. *The Book of Genesis*. New York: 1965.

Morgenstern, Julian. *Rites of Birth, Marriage, Death and Kindred Occasions among the Semites*. New York: 1973.

Mukdoni, A. "How I. L. Peretz Wrote His Tales." *In This World and the Next* by I. L. Peretz. New York: 1958, pp. 352–359.

Muller, Ernst. *History of Jewish Mysticism*. New York: no date.

Musaph-Andriesse, R. C. *From Torah to Kabbalah: A Basic Introduction to the Writings of Judaism*. New York: 1982.

Mykoff, Moshe, ed. *The Breslov Haggadah*. Jerusalem: 1989.

Mykoff, Moshe, tr. *Once Upon a Tzaddik: Tales of Rebbe Nachman of Breslov*. Jerusalem: 1989.

Mykoff, Moshe, and Ozer Bergman, eds. *Likutey Moharan*. Jerusalem: 1886–1990. Four volumes to date.

Nachman of Breslov. *The Aleph-Bet Book: Rabbi Nachman's Aphorisms on Jewish Living (Sefer Hamiddot).* Jerusalem: 1986.

Nachman of Bratslav. *Azambra!* Jerusalem: 1984.

Nachman of Bratslav. *Mayim.* Jerusalem: 1987.

Nachman of Bratslav. *Restore My Soul! (Meshivat Nefesh).* Jerusalem: 1980.

Nachman of Bratslav. *Tsohar.* Jerusalem: 1986.

Nadich, Judah, ed. *Jewish Legends of the Second Commonwealth.* Philadelphia: 1983.

Nadich, Judah. *The Legends of the Rabbis.* Northvale, N.J. and London: 1994. Two volumes.

Nahmad, H. M. *A Portion in Paradise and Other Jewish Folktales.* New York: 1970.

Nahmad, H.M.A. "Superstitions Among Jews." *The Jewish Chronicle.* London: 19 December, 1969.

Nathan of Breslov. *Advice (Likutey Etzot).* Jerusalem: 1983.

Nathan of Breslov. *Tefillin: A Chassidic Discourse.* Jerusalem: 1989.

Nathan of Breslov. *Tzaddik (Chayey Moharan): A Portrait of Rabbi Nachman.* Jerusalem: 1987.

Neubauer, A., and A. Cowley, eds. *Catalogue of the Hebrew Manuscripts in the Bodleian Library.* Oxford: 1886–1906. Two volumes.

Neugroschel, Joachim, ed. *The Shtetl.* New York: 1979.

Neugroschel, Joachim, ed. *Yenne Velt: The Great Works of Jewish Fantasy & Occult.* New York: 1976. Two volumes.

Neuman, [Noy] D. *Motif Index of Talmudic-Midrashic Literature.* Dissertation, Indiana University, 1954. Two volumes.

Neusner, Jacob. *The Canonical History of Ideas: The Place of the So-Called Tannaite Midrashim.* Atlanta: 1990.

Neusner, Jacob. *Development of a Legend: Studies on the Traditions Concerning Yohanan ben Zakkai.* Leiden: 1970.

Neusner, Jacob. *Eliezer ben Hyrcanus.* Leiden: 1973. Two volumes.

Neusner, Jacob. *First Century Judaism in Crisis.* Nashville: 1975.

Neusner, Jacob. *The Formation of the Babylonian Talmud.* Leiden: 1970.

Neusner, Jacob. *Invitation to the Talmud.* New York: 1973.

Neusner, Jacob. *A Life of Yohanan ben Zakkai.* Leiden: 1962.

Neusner, Jacob. *Mekhilta According to Rabbi Ishmael: An Introduction to Judaism's First Scriptural Encyclopedia.* Atlanta: 1988.

Neusner, Jacob. *The Midrash: An Introduction.* Northvale, N.J.: 1990.

Neusner, Jacob. *The Oral Torah: The Sacred Books of Judaism.* San Francisco: 1986.

Neusner, Jacob. *Sifra in Perspective: The Documentary Comparison of the Midrashim of Ancient Judaism.* Atlanta: 1988.

Neusner, Jacob. *Sifre to Deuteronomy: An Introduction to the Rhetorical, Logical and Topical Program.* Atlanta: 1987.

Neusner, Jacob, tr. *The Tosefta.* New York: 1981. Six volumes.

Neusner, Jacob. *Understanding Rabbinic Judaism.* New York: 1974.

Neusner, Jacob. *Uniting the Dual Torah: Sifra and the Problem of the Mishnah.* Atlanta: 1988.

Neusner, Jacob, and William Scott Green, eds. *Origins of Judaism: Religion, History, and Literature in Late Antiquity.* New York: 1990. Twenty volumes.

Neusner, Jacob, William S. Green, and Ernest Frerichs, eds. *Judaisms and Their Messiahs at the Turn of the Christian Era.* Cambridge: 1987.

Neusner, Jacob. *What Is Midrash?* Phildelphia: 1987.

Neusner, Jacob, with William Scott Green. *Writing with Scripture: The Authority and Uses of the Hebrew Bible in Formative Judaism.* Philadelphia: 1989.

Newall, Venetia. "The Jew as a Witch Figure." In *The Witch Figure*, edited by Venetia Newall, 96–124. London: 1973.

Newman, Louis, and Samuel Spitz, eds. *The Hasidic Anthology: Tales and Teachings of the Hasidism.* New York: 1963.

Newman, Louis, and Samuel Spitz, eds. *Maggidim and Hasidim: Their Wisdom.* New York: 1962.

Newman, Louis, and Samuel Spitz, eds. *The Talmudic Anthology.* New York: 1945.

Niditch, S. "Merits, Martyrs, and 'Your Life as Booty': An Exegesis of Mekilta, Pisha." *Journal for the Study of Judaism* 13 (1982): 160–71.

Nigal, Gedalyah. *Magic, Mysticism, and Hasidism: The Supernatural in Jewish Thought.* Northvale, N.J.: 1994.

Nissenson, Hugh. *The Elephant and My Jewish Problem: Selected Stories and Journals 1957–1987.* New York: 1988.

Nissenson, Hugh. *In the Reign of Peace.* New York: 1972.

Nissenson, Hugh. *Notes From the Frontier.* New York: 1968.

Nissenson, Hugh. *A Pile of Stones.* New York: 1965.

Nissenson, Hugh. *The Tree of Life.* New York: 1983.

Noah, Mordecai Manuel, tr. *The Book of Yashar (Sefer ha-Yashar).* New York: 1972.

Noy, Dov, ed. *Folktales of Israel.* Chicago: 1963.

Noy, Dov. "The Jewish Versions of the 'Animal Languages' Folktale (AT 670): Typological-Structural Study." *Scripta Hierosolymitana* 22 (1971): 171–208.

Noy, Dov, ed. *Moroccan Jewish Folktales.* New York: 1966.

Noy, Dov, Francis Utley, and Raphael Patai, eds. *Studies in Biblical and Jewish Folklore.* Bloomington: 1959.

Nulman, Macy. *The Encyclopedia of Jewish Prayer: Ashkenazic and Sephardic Rites.* Northvale, N.J.: 1993.

Odeberg, Hugo. *3 Enoch or The Hebrew Book of Enoch.* New York: 1973.

Odeberg, Hugo. *The Aramaic Portions of Bereshit Rabba.* Lund: 1939.

Oesterley, William O. E., and George H. Box. *A Short Survey of the Literature of Rabbinical and Medieval Judaism.* London and New York: 1920.

Oesterreich, Traugott. *Possession: Demoniacal and Other, Among Primitive Races, in Antiquity, Middle Ages and Modern Times.* New York: 1930.

Opatashu, Joseph. *A Day in Regensburg.* Philadelphia: 1968.

Ozick, Cynthia. *Bloodshed and Three Novellas.* New York: 1976.

Ozick, Cynthia. *Levitation: Five Fictions.* New York: 1982.

Ozick, Cynthia. *The Messiah of Stockholm.* New York: 1987.

Ozick, Cynthia. *The Pagan Rabbi and Other Stories.* New York: 1971.

Ozick, Cynthia. *Trust.* New York: 1966.

Pascheles, Wolff. *Jewish Legends of the Middle Ages.* London: no date.

Pagels, Elaine. *The Origin of Satan.* New York: 1995.

Patai, Raphael. "Exorcism and Xenoglossia among the Safed Kabbalists," in *Journal of American Folklore* 91 (1978): 823–833.

Patai, Raphael, ed. *Gates to the New City: A Book of Jewish Legends.* Detroit: 1981.

Patai, Raphael. *The Hebrew Goddess.* Detroit: 1991. Third edition.

Patai, Raphael. *The Jewish Alchemists: A History and Source Book.* Princeton: 1994.

Patai, Raphael, ed. *The Messiah Texts.* Detroit: 1979.

Patai, Raphael. *On Jewish Folklore*. Detroit: 1983.

Patterson, David. *The Hebrew Novel in Czarist Russia*. Edinburgh: 1964.

Patterson, David, ed. *Studies in Modern Hebrew Literature Series*. New York: 1974.

Pearl, Chaim, tr. *Sefer Ha-Aggadah*. Tel Aviv: 1989.

Pearl, Chaim, tr. *Stories of the Sages*. Tel Aviv: 1991.

Pearson, Birger A. "Jewish Elements in Gnosticism and the Development of Gnostic Self-Definition." In *Jewish and Christian Self-Definition. I. The Shaping of Christianity in the Second and Third Centuries*, edited by E. P. Sanders, 151–160. 3 volumes. Philadelphia: 1980.

Penueli, Shmuel Yeshayahu, and Ukhmani Azriel, eds. *Hebrew Short Stories*. Tel Aviv: 1965. Two volumes.

Peretz, I. L. *The Book of Fire*. New York: 1959.

Peretz, I. L. *The Case Against the Wind*. New York: 1975.

Peretz, I. L. *In This World and the Next*. New York: 1975.

Peretz, I. L. *Keys to a Magic Door*. New York: 1959.

Peretz, I. L. *My Memories*. New York: 1964.

Peretz, I. L. *Selected Stories*, edited by Irving Howe and Eliezer Greenberg. New York: 1982.

Perutz, Leo. *By Night Under the Stone Bridge*. New York: 1990.

Petuchowski, Jakob J. *Ever Since Sinai: A Modern View of Torah*. New York: 1961.

Petuchowski, Jakob J. *Our Masters Taught: Rabbinic Stories and Sayings*. New York: 1982.

Pick, Bernard. *The Cabala: Its Influence on Judaism and Christianity*. La Salle, Ill.: 1974.

Pinsky, David. *King David and His Wives*. New York: 1923.

Pinsky, David. *Temptations*. New York: 1919.

Pinson, Koppel S. "The Poetry of Hassidism." *The Menoral Journal*, Autumn, 1941.

Piontac, Nechemiah, ed. *The Arizal: The Life and Times of Rabbi Yitzchak Luria*. New York: 1969.

Porter, J. R. "Witchcraft and Magic in the Old Testament, and Their Relation to Animals." In *Animals in Folklore*, edited by J. R. Porter and W. M. S. Russel, 70–85. Norwich, England: 1978.

Porton, Gary. "Defining Midrash." In *The Study of Ancient Judaism I*, edited by Jacob Neusner, 55–103. New York: 1981.

Posner, Raphael. *Jewish Liturgy*. Jerusalem: 1975.

Posy, Arnold. *Israeli Tales and Legends*. New York: 1966.

Prager, Moshe. *Rabbi Yisroel Baal-Shem-Tov*. New York: 1976.

Pritchard, J. B., ed. *Solomon and Sheba*. London: 1974.

Prose, Francine. *Judah the Pious*. New York: 1973.

Pye, Faye. "A Brief Study of an Hasidic Fairy Tale." *Harvest: Journal for Jungian Studies of the Analytical Psychology Club* 21 (London, 1975): 94–104.

Rabinowicz, H. *A Guide to Hassidism*. New York: 1960.

Rabinowicz, Harry M. *Hasidism: The Movement and Its Masters*. Northvale, N.J.: 1988.

Rabinowicz, Harry M. *The Slave Who Saved the City and Other Hasidic Tales*. New York: 1960.

Rabinowicz, Harry M. *The World of Hasidism*. New York: 1970.

Rabinowicz, Tzvi M. *The Encyclopedia of Hasidism*. Northvale, N.J.: 1996.

Rabinowitch, Wolf Zeev. *Lithuanian Hasidism*. New York: 1971.

Rader, Benzion, ed. *To Touch the Divine: A Jewish Mysticism Primer.* Brooklyn: 1989.

Rand, Baruch, and Barbara Rush. *Jews of Kurdistan.* Toledo, Ohio: 1978.

Rankin, O. S. *Israel's Wisdom Literature.* New York: 1936.

Raphael, Simcha Paull. *Jewish Views of the Afterlife.* Northvale, N.J.: 1994.

Rapp, Nachman. *Men in His Way: Biblical Stories.* Tel Aviv: 1973.

Rappoport, Angelo S. *The Folklore of the Jews.* London: 1937.

Rappoport, Angelo S. *Myth and Legend of Ancient Israel.* New York: 1966. Three volumes.

Rappoport, Samuel. *A Treasury of the Midrash.* New York: 1988.

Rawidowicz, Simon. "On Interpretation." In *Studies in Jewish Thought,* edited by Nahum Glatzer. Philadelphia: 1974.

Raz, Simcha. *This World and the World to Come: Hasidic Legends.* Jerusalem: 1993.

Reich, Tova. *The Jewish War: A Novel.* New York: 1995.

Reich, Tova. *Masters of the Return.* San Diego, New York and London: 1985.

Ribalow, Harold W., ed. *A Treasury of American Jewish Stories.* New York: 1952.

Ribalow, Menachem. *The Flowering of Modern Hebrew Literature.* New York: 1959.

Richler, Mordecai. *Solomon Gursky Was Here.* New York: 1990.

Riemer, Jack. "Franz Kafka and Rabbi Nachman." *Jewish Frontier* 28:4 (April 1961): 16–20.

Riemer, Jack, ed. *Jewish Reflections on Death.* New York: 1976.

Roback, A. A. *The Story of Yiddish Literature.* New York: 1940.

Robinson, James M. *The Nag Hammadi Library.* San Francisco: 1988. Third edition.

Rogerson, John W. *The Supernatural in the Old Testament.* London: 1976.

Rosenberg, Roy A., tr. *The Anatomy of God.* New York: 1973.

Rosenblatt, Jason P., and Joseph C. Sitterson, Jr., eds. *"Not in Heaven": Coherence and Complexity in Biblical Narrative.* Bloomington: 1991.

Roskies, David G. *A Bridge of Longing: The Lost Art of Yiddish Storytelling.* Cambridge, Mass.: 1995.

Roskies, Diane K., and David G. Roskies. *The Shtetl Book.* New York: 1975.

Rossman, Moshe. *Founder of Hasidism: A Quest for the Historical Baal Shem Tov.* Berkeley: The University of California Press, 1996.

Rossoff, Dovid. *Safed: The Mystical City.* Jerusalem: 1991.

Roth, Cecil. *The Concise Jewish Encyclopedia.* New York: 1980.

Roth, Cecil, ed. *The Dark Ages: Jews in Christian Europe 711–1096.* Volume II of *World History of the Jewish People.* New Brunswick, N.J.: 1966.

Roth, Cecil. "Folklore of the Ghetto." *Folklore* 59 (1948): 75–83.

Roth, Cecil. *The Jewish Contribution to Civilization.* London: 1956.

Roth, Cecil, and G. Wigoder, eds. *Encyclopedia Judaica.* Jerusalem: 1972. Sixteen volumes.

Rothenberg, Jerome, Harris Lenowitz, and Charles Doria, eds. *A Big Jewish Book.* Garden City, N.Y.: 1978.

Rubenstein, Richard. *The Religious Imagination: A Study in Psychoanalysis and Jewish Theology.* Indianapolis: 1968.

Rudavsky, David. *Modern Jewish Religious Movements.* New York: 1979. Third edition.

Ruderman, David B., ed. *Essential Papers on Jewish Culture in Renaissance and Baroque Italy.* New York and London: 1992.

Ruderman, David B. *Kabbalah, Magic and Science: The Cultural Universe of a Hananiah Yagel.* Philadelphia: 1990.

Ruderman, David B. tr. A *Valley of Vision: the Heavenly Journey of Abraham ben Hananiah Yagel*. Philadelphia: 1990.

Rudolph, Kurt. *Gnosis: The Nature and History of Gnosticism*. San Francisco: 1987.

Rudwin, Maximilian. *The Devil in Legend and Literature*. La Salle, Ill.: 1973.

Runes, Dagobert D., ed. *The Talmud of Jerusalem*. New York: 1956.

Rush, Barbara, ed. *The Book of Jewish Women's Tales*. Northvale, N.J.: 1995.

Rush, Barbara, and Eliezer Marcus, eds. *Seventy and One Tales*. New York: 1980.

Sabar, Yona. *The Folk Literature of the Kurdistani Jews: An Anthology*. New Haven and London: 1982.

Sadeh, Pinhas. *Life As a Parable*. London: 1966.

Safran, Alexandre. *The Kabbalah: Laws and Mysticism in the Jewish Tradition*. New York and Jerusalem: 1975.

Safran, Bezalel, ed. *Hasidism: Continuity or Innovation?* Cambridge, Mass., and London: 1988.

St. John, Seymour D. *Tales of King Solomon*. London: 1924.

Salutin, Rick. *A Man of Little Faith*. Toronto: 1988.

Samuel, Maurice. *Prince of the Ghetto: The Stories of Y. L. Peretz Retold*. New York: 1973.

Samuel, Maurice. *The World of Sholom Aleichem*. New York: 1947.

Sandmel, Samuel. *Philo of Alexandria*. New York: 1979.

Saperstein, Marc. *Decoding the Rabbis: A Thirteenth Century Commentary on the Aggadah*. Cambridge: 1980.

Saperstein, Marc, ed. *Essential Papers on Messianic Personalities in Jewish History*. New York: 1992.

Saperstein, Marc. *Jewish Preaching 1200–1800: An Anthology*. New Haven and London: 1989

Saperstein, Marc. *Your Voice Like a Ram's Horn: Themes and Texts in Traditional Jewish Preaching*. New York: 1996.

Sarachek, Joseph. *The Doctrine of the Messiah in Medieval Jewish Literature*. New York: 1932.

Sarna, Nahum M. *Exploring Exodus*. New York: 1986.

Sarason, Richard S. "Kadushin's Study of Midrash: Value-Concepts and Their Literary Embodiment." In *Understanding the Rabbinic Mind: Essays on the Rabbinic Thought of Max Kadushin*, edited by Peter Ochs, 45–72. Atlanta: 1990.

Sarason, Richard S. "Toward a New Agendum for the Study of Rabbinic Midrashic Literature." In *Studies in Aggadah, Targum and Jewish Liturgy in Memory of Joseph Heinemann*, edited by Petuchowski, Jakob J. and Ezra Fleischer, 55–73. Jerusalem: 1981.

Sarason, Richard S. *The World of the Aggadah*. Tel-Aviv: 1990.

Sarna, Nahum M. *Understanding Genesis*. New York: 1976.

Sawyer, Deborah F. *Midrash Aleph Bet*. Atlanta: 1993.

Schachter, Zalman. *Fragments of a Future Scroll*. Germantown, Penn.: 1975.

Schachter, Zalman M., and Edward Hoffman. *Sparks of Light: Counseling in the Hasidic Tradition*. Boulder: 1983.

Schachter-Shalomi, Zalman. *Paradigm Shift*. Northvale, N.J.: 1993.

Schachter-Shalomi, Zalman Meshullam. *Spiritual Intimacy: A Study of Counseling in Hasidism*. Northvale, N.J.: 1991.

Schäfer, Peter. *The Hidden and Manifest God: Some Major Themes in Early Jewish Mysticism.* Albany: 1992.

Schäfer, Peter. *The History of the Jews of Antiquity: The Jews of Palestine from Alexander the Great to the Arab Conquest.* Toronto: 1995.

Schauss, Hayyim. *The Jewish Festivals.* New York: 1962.

Schaya, Leo. *The Universal Meaning of the Kabbalah.* Baltimore: 1972.

Schechter, Solomon. *Aspects of Rabbinic Theology: Major Concepts of the Talmud.* New York: 1961.

Schechter, Solomon. *Studies in Judaism: Essays on Persons, Concepts, and Movements of Thought in Jewish Tradition.* New York: 1970.

Schimmel, Harry C. *The Oral Law: A Study of the Rabbinic Contribution to Torah She-Be-Al-Peh.* Jerusalem and New York: 1971.

Schmithals, Walter. *The Apocalyptic Movement.* Nashville: 1975.

Schochet, Elijah Judah. *Animal Life in Jewish Tradition: Attitudes and Relationships.* New York: 1984.

Schochet, Elijah Judah. *The Hasidic Movement and the Gaon of Vilna.* Northvale, N.J.: 1994.

Schochet, Jacob Immanuel. *The Great Maggid: The Life and Teachings of Rabbi Dov Ber of Mezhirech.* New York: 1974.

Schochet, Jacob Immanuel. *Mystical Concepts in Chassidism.* Brooklyn: 1979.

Schochet, Jacob Immanuel. *The Mystical Dimension.* Brooklyn, N.Y.: 1990. Three volumes.

Schochet, Jacob Immanuel. *Rabbi Israel Baal Shem Tov.* Toronto: 1961.

Scholem, Gershom G. "The Curious History of the Six-Pointed Star." *Commentary* 8 (1949): 243–251.

Scholem, Gershom. *Jewish Gnosticism, Merkabah Mysticism and Talmudic Tradition.* New York: 1960.

Scholem, Gershom. *Kabbalah.* Jerusalem and New York: 1974.

Scholem, Gershom. *Major Trends in Jewish Mysticism.* New York: 1964.

Scholem, Gershom. *The Messianic Idea in Judaism and Other Essays on Jewish Spirituality.* New York: 1971.

Scholem, Gershom. *On Jews & Judaism in Crisis: Selected Essays.* New York: 1976.

Scholem, Gershom. *On the Mystical Shape of the Godhead: Basic Concepts in the Kabbalah.* New York: 1991.

Scholem, Gershom. *On the Kabbalah and Its Symbolism.* New York: 1965.

Scholem, Gershom. *Origins of the Kabbalah.* Philadelphia: 1987.

Scholem, Gershom. *Shabbatai Sevi: The Mystical Messiah.* Princeton: 1973.

Scholem, Gershom. *Zohar: The Book of Splendor.* New York: 1963.

Schram, Peninnah, ed. *Chosen Tales: Stories Told by Jewish Storytellers.* Northvale, N.J.: 1995.

Schram, Peninnah, ed. *Jewish Stories One Generation Tells Another.* Northvale, N.J.: 1987.

Schram, Peninnah, and Steven M. Rosman, eds.. *Eight Tales for Eight Nights: Stories for Chanukah.* Northvale, N.J.: 1990.

Schram, Peninnah, ed. *Tales of Elijah the Prophet.* Northvale, N.J. 1991.

Schrire, T. *Hebrew Magic Amulets: Their Decipherment and Interpretation.* London: 1966.

Schurer, Emil. *The Literature of the Jewish People in the Time of Jesus*. New York: 1972.

Schwartz, Howard. *Adam's Soul: The Collected Tales of Howard Schwartz*. Northvale, N.J.: 1992.

Schwartz, Howard. "The Aggadic Tradition." In *Origins of Judaism*, edited by Jacob Neusner vol. 1, part 3, pp. 446–463. New York and London: 1990.

Schwartz, Howard. *The Captive Soul of the Messiah: New Tales About Reb Nachman*. New York: 1983.

Schwartz, Howard. *The Dream Assembly: Tales of Rabbi Zalman Schachter-Shalomi*. Nevada City, Calif.: 1989.

Schwartz, Howard, ed. *Elijah's Violin & Other Jewish Fairy Tales*. New York: 1983.

Schwartz, Howard. *The Four Who Entered Paradise*. Northvale, N.J.: 1996.

Schwartz, Howard, ed. *Gabriel's Palace: Jewish Mystical Tales*. New York and London: 1993.

Schwartz, Howard, ed. *Gates to the New City: A Treasury of Modern Jewish Tales*. New York: 1983.

Schwartz, Howard, ed. *Imperial Messages: One Hundred Modern Parables*. New York: 1976.

Schwartz, Howard, ed. *Lilith's Cave: Jewish Tales of the Supernatural*. San Francisco: 1988.

Schwartz, Howard, ed. *Miriam's Tambourine: Jewish Folktales from Around the World*. New York: 1986.

Schwartz, Howard. "The Mythology of Judaism." In *The Seductiveness of Jewish Myth: Challenge or Response*, edited by S. Daniel Breslauer, pp. 11–25. Albany: 1997.

Schwartz, Howard. "The Quest for the Lost Princess." In *Opening the Inner Gates: New Paths in Kabbalah and Psychology*, edited by Edward Hoffman pp. 20–46. Boston: 1995.

Schwartz, Howard. "Rabbi Nachman of Bratslav: Forerunner of Modern Jewish Literature." *Judaism*, 31 (1982): 211–224.

Schwartz, Howard. *Rooms of the Soul*. Chappaqua, N.Y.: 1984.

Schwartz, Howard and Tony Rudolf, eds. *Voices Within the Ark: The Modern Jewish Poets*. New York: 1980.

Schwartz, Howard and Barbara Rush, eds. *The Wonder Child & Other Jewish Fairy Tales*. New York: 1997.

Schwarz, Leo W., ed. *Feast of Leviathan*. New York: 1966.

Schwarz, Leo W., ed. *A Golden Treasury of Jewish Literature*. New York: 1937.

Schwarz, Leo, ed. *Great Ages and Ideas of the Jewish People*. New York: 1956.

Schwarz, Leo, ed. *The Jewish Caravan: Great Stories of Twenty-five Centuries*. New York: 1976.

Schwarz, Leo., ed. *Memoirs of My People*. Philadelphia: 1943.

Schwarz, Leo, ed. *The Menorah Treasury*. Philadelphia: 1964.

Schwarz-Bart, Andre. *The Last of the Just*. New York: 1961.

Schwarzbaum, Haim. "The Hero Predestined to Die on His Wedding Day, AT 934B:" *Folklore Research Center Studies* 4 (1974): 223–252.

Schwarzbaum, Haim. *The Mishle Shu'alim (Fox Fables) of Rabbi Berechiah Ha-Nakdan: A Study in Comparative Folklore and Fable Lore*. Kiron, Israel: 1979.

Schwarzbaum, Haim. *Studies in Jewish and World Folklore*. Berlin: 1968.

Scliar, Moacyr. *The Ballad of the False Messiah*. New York: 1987.

Scliar, Moacyr. *The Centaur in the Garden.* New York: 1984.

Scliar, Moacyr. *The Enigmatic Eye.* New York: 1989.

Scliar, Moacyr. *The Gods of Raquel.* New York: 1996.

Scliar, Moacyr. *The One-Man Army.* New York: 1985.

Scliar, Moacyr. *The Strange Nation of Rafael Mendes.* New York: 1987.

Scliar, Moacyr. *The Volunteers.* New York: 1988.

Segal, Alan. *Two Powers in Heaven: Early Rabbinic Reports About Christianity and Gnosticism.* Leiden: 1977.

Segal, S. M. *Elijah: A Study in Jewish Folklore.* New York: 1935.

Seltzer, Robert M. *Jewish People, Jewish Thought: The Jewish Experience in History,* 171–314. New York: 1980.

Sender, Yitzchak. *The Commentators' Gift of Torah: Exploring the Treasures of the Oral and Written Torah.* Spring Valley, N.Y.: 1993.

Shah, Idries. *Tales of the Dervishes: Teaching Stories of the Sufi Masters Over the Past Thousand Years.* New York: 1970.

Shahar, David. *News from Jerusalem.* Boston: 1974.

Shahar, David. *The Palace of Shattered Vessels.* New York: 1976.

Sharot, Stephen. *Messianism, Mysticism and Magic: A Sociological Analysis of Jewish Religious Movements.* Chapel Hill, N.C.: 1982.

Shashar, Michael. *Sambatyon: Essays on Jewish Holidays.* Jerusalem: 1987.

Sheinkin, David. *Path of the Kabbalah.* New York: 1986.

Shelley, Mary Wollstonecraft. *Frankenstein.* London: 1818.

Shenhar, Aliza. "Concerning the Nature of the Motif 'Death by a Kiss' (Motif A185.6.11)." *Fabula* 19 (1978): 62–73.

Sherwin, Byron L. "The Exorcist's Role in Jewish Tradition." *Occult* (October 1975).

Sherwin, Byron L. *The Golem Legend: Origins and Implications.* New York: 1985.

Sherwin, Byron L. *Mystical Theology and Social Dissent: The Life and Works of Judah Loew of Prague.* Rutherford, N.J.: 1982.

Shrut, Samuel D. "Coping with the 'Evil Eye' or Early Rabbinical Attempts at Psychotherapy." *The American Imago* 17 (1960): 201–213.

Shulman, Y. David. *The Chambers of the Palace: Teachings of Rabbi Nachman of Bratslav.* Northvale, N.J.: 1993.

Shulman, Yaacov Dovid, tr. *The Return to G-d: Based on the Works of Rabbi Nachman of Breslov and His Holy Disciples (Derech Hatshuvah).* Brooklyn: no date.

Siegel, Richard, Michael Strassfeld, and Sharon Strassfeld, eds. *The Jewish Catalog.* Philadelphia: 1973.

Silberschlag, Eisig. *From Renaissance to Renaissance.* New York: 1981. Three volumes.

Silberschlag, Eisig. *Hebrew Literature: An Evaluation.* New York: 1959.

Silk, Dennis, ed. *Retrievements: A Jewish Anthology.* Jerusalem: 1968.

Silver, Daniel J. *Maimonidian Criticism and the Maimonidian Controversy, 1180–1240.* New York: 1965.

Silver, Daniel J. *The Story of Scripture: From Oral Tradition to the Written Word.* New York: 1990.

Silverman, Dov. *Legends of Safed.* Jerusalem: 1991.

Singer, Isaac Bashevis. *Alone in the Wild Forest.* New York: 1971.

Singer, Isaac Bashevis. *The Collected Stories.* New York: 1982.

Singer, Isaac Bashevis. *A Crown of Feathers.* New York: 1970.

Singer, Isaac Bashevis. *A Day of Pleasure.* New York: 1963.
Singer, Isaac Bashevis. *Enemies: A Love Story.* New York: 1972.
Singer, Isaac Bashevis. *The Estate.* New York: 1969.
Singer, Isaac Bashevis. *The Family Moskat.* New York: 1950.
Singer, Isaac Bashevis. *A Friend of Kafka.* New York: 1962.
Singer, Isaac Bashevis. *Gimpel the Fool.* New York: 1953.
Singer, Isaac Bashevis. *The Golem.* New York: 1982.
Singer, Isaac Bashevis. *In My Father's Court.* New York: 1967.
Singer, Isaac Bashevis. *An Isaac Bashevis Singer Reader.* New York: 1953.
Singer, Isaac Bashevis. *A Little Boy in Search of God.* New York: 1976.
Singer, Isaac Bashevis. *Lost in America.* New York: 1981.
Singer, Isaac Bashevis. *The Magician of Lublin.* New York: 1960.
Singer, Isaac Bashevis. *The Manor.* New York: 1967.
Singer, Isaac Bashevis. *Meshugah.* New York: 1994.
Singer, Isaac Bashevis. *Passions.* New York: 1974.
Singer, Isaac Bashevis. *The Power of Light.* New York: 1980.
Singer, Isaac Bashevis. *Reaches of Heaven.* New York: 1980.
Singer, Isaac Bashevis. *Satan in Goray.* New York: 1979.
Singer, Isaac Bashevis. *The Seance.* London: 1970.
Singer, Isaac Bashevis. *Short Friday.* Philadelphia: 1964.
Singer, Isaac Bashevis. *Shosha.* New York: 1978.
Singer, Isaac Bashevis. *The Slave.* New York: 1962.
Singer, Isaac Bashevis. *The Spinoza of Market Street.* New York: 1963.
Singer, Isaac Bashevis. *Stories for Children.* New York: 1984.
Singer, Isadore, ed. *The Jewish Encyclopedia.* New York: 1901. Twelve volumes.
Singer, Sholom Alchanan. *Medieval Jewish Mysticism: Book of the Pious (Sefer Hasidim).* Wheeling, Ill.: 1971.
Slabotsky, David. *The Mind of Genesis.* Ottawa: 1975.
Slonimsky, Henry. "The Philosophy Implicit in the Midrash." *Hebrew Union College Annual* 27 (1956): 235–91.
Smith, Morton. "Observations on Hekhalot Rabbati." In *Biblical and Other Studies,* edited by Alexander Altmann, Cambridge, Mass.: 1963.
Smolar, Levy, Moses Aberbach, and Pinkhos Churgin. *Studies in Targum Jonathan to the Prophets.* New York: 1981.
Soloveitchik, Hayim. "Three Themes in the Sefer Hasidim." AJS *Review* I (1976): 311–357.
Sparks, H.F.D. *The Apocryphal Old Tesatment.* Oxford: 1984.
Spector, Sheila A. *Jewish Mysticism: An Annotated Bibliography on the Kabbalah in English.* New York and London: 1984.
Sperber, Daniel. *Midrash Yerushalem: A Metaphysical History of Jerusalem.* Jerusalem: 1982.
Sperling, Harry, and Maurice Simon, eds. *The Zohar.* London: 1931–1934. Five volumes.
Spicehandler, Ezra, ed. *Modern Hebrew Stories.* New York: 1971.
Spicehandler, Ezra and Curtis Aronson. *New Writing in Israel.* New York: 1976.
Spiegel, Shalom. *The Last Trial.* Philadelphia: 1967.
Spiegel, Shalom. Introduction to *Legends of the Bible* by Louis Ginzberg, edited by Judah Goldin. Philadelphia: 1956.
Spiegelman, J. Marvin. *Judaism and Jungian Psychology.* Lanham, Md.: 1993.

Stavans, Ilan. *The Left-handed Pianist.* New York: 1996.

Stavans, Ilan. *Tropical Synagogues: Short Stories by Jewish Latin American Writers.* New York and London: 1994.

Steinberg, Milton. *As a Driven Leaf.* New York: 1939.

Steinberg, Milton. *Basic Judaism.* New York: 1947.

Steinman, Eliezer. *The Garden of Hasidism.* Jerusalem: 1961.

Steinsaltz, Adin. *Beggars and Prayers.* New York: 1979.

Steinsaltz, Adin. *The Essential Talmud.* New York: 1976.

Steinsaltz, Adin. "The Imagery Concept in Jewish Thought." *Shefa Quarterly* 1:3 (April 1978): 56–62.

Steinsaltz, Adin. *In the Beginning: Discourses on Chasidic Thought.* Northvale, N.J.: 1992.

Steinsaltz, Adin. *The Thirteen Petaled Rose.* New York: 1980.

Steinschneider, Moritz. *Jewish Literature from the Eighth to the Eighteenth Century with an Introduction on Talmud & Midrash.* New York: 1965.

Stemberger, Gunter. *Jewish Contemporaries of Jesus: Pharisees, Sadducees, Essenes.* Minneapolis: 1995.

Stern, David. "Midrash." In *Contemporary Jewish Thought,* edited by Arthur A. Cohen and Paul Mendes-Flohr, 613–20. New York: 1987.

Stern, David. *Parables in Midrash: Narrative and Exegesis in Rabbinic Literature.* Cambridge, Mass., and London: 1991.

Stern, David, and Mark Jay Mirsky, eds. *Rabbinic Fantasies: Imaginative Narratives from Classical Hebrew Literature.* Philadelphia: 1990.

Stern, Steve. *Isaac and the Undertaker's Daughter.* New York: 1985.

Stern, Steve. *Lazar Malkin Enters Heaven.* New York: 1986.

Stern, Steve. *The Moon and Ruben Shein.* New York: 1984.

Stern, Steve. *A Plague of Dreamers.* New York: 1994.

Stillman, Yedida K. "The Evil Eye in Morocco." *Folklore Research Center Studies* I (1970): 81–94.

Stone, Michael. *Scriptures, Sects and Visions: A Profile of Judaism from Ezra to the Jewish Revolts.* Philadelphia: 1980.

Stone, Michael E., tr. *The Testament of Abraham: The Greek Recensions.* Minneapolis: 1992.

Strack, Hermann L. Revised by Gunter Stemberger. *Introduction to the Talmud and Midrash.* Translated by Markus Bockmuehl. Minneapolis: 1992.

Strack, Hermann L. "Midrash and Indeterminacy." *Critical Inquiry* 15 (1988): 132–61.

Strassfeld, Sharon and Michael. *The Second Jewish Catalog.* Philadelphia: 1976.

Strassfeld, Sharon and Michael. *The Third Jewish Catalog.* Philadelphia: 1980.

Sussaman, Aaron. *The Flying Ark.* St. Louis: 1980.

Talmage, Frank, ed. *Studies in Jewish Folklore.* Cambridge, Mass.: 1980.

Tammuz, Binyamin, and Leon I. Yudkin, eds. *Meetings with the Angel: Seven Stories from Israel.* London: 1973.

Tanakh: A New Translation of the Scriptures. Philadelphia: 1985.

Teubal, Savina. *Sarah the Priestess: The First Matriarch of Genesis.* Athens, Ohio: 1984.

Thieberger, Frederic. *The Great Rabbi Loew of Prague: His Life and Work and the Legend of the Golem.* London: 1955.

Thieberger, Frederic. *King Solomon.* New York: 1947.

Thompson, R. Campbell. *Semitic Magic: Its Origins and Development.* New York: 1911.

Tishby, Isaiah. "Gnostic Doctrines in Sixteenth-Century Jewish Mysticism." *Journal of Jewish Studies* 6 (1955): 146–152.

Tishby, Isaiah. *The Wisdom of the Zohar.* Three volumes. Oxford: 1989.

The Torah: The Five Books of Moses. Philadelphia: 1962.

Torrey, C. C. *The Apocryphal Literature.* New Haven: 1945.

Towner, W. S. "Halachic Literary Patterns and Types: History and Affinity with New Testament Literature." *Jewish Quarterly Review* 74 (1983): 46–60.

Towner, Wayne Sibley. *The Rabbinic Enumeration of Scriptural Examples.* Leiden: 1973.

Townsend, John T., tr. *Midrash Tanhuma.* Vol. I: *Genesis.* Hoboken, N.J.: 1989.

Trachtenberg, Joshua. *The Devil and the Jews.* New Haven: 1943.

Trachtenberg, Joshua. "The Folk Element in Judaism." *The Journal of Religion* 22 (1942): 173–186.

Trachtenberg, Joshua. *Jewish Magic and Superstition: A Study in Folk Religion.* New York: 1961.

Turner, Mark. *The Literary Mind.* New York: 1997.

Twersky, Isadore, ed. *Rabbi Moses Nahmanides (Ramban): Explorations in His Religious and Literary Virtuosity.* Cambridge, Mass.: 1983.

Twersky, Isadore, and Bernard Septimus, eds. *Jewish Thought in the Seventeenth Century.* Cambridge, Mass., and London: 1987.

Uffenheimer, Rivka Schatz. *Hasidism As Mysticism: Quietistic Elements in Eighteenth Century Thought.* Princeton: 1993.

Ujvari, Peter. *By Candlelight.* London: 1978.

Ulmer, Rivka. *The Evil Eye in the Bible and in Rabbinic Literature.* Hoboken, N.J.: 1994.

Unterman, Alan. *Dictionary of Jewish Lore & Legend.* London: 1991.

Unterman, Alan. *Jews: Their Religious Beliefs and Practices.* Boston: 1981.

Unterman, Alan, ed. *The Wisdom of the Jewish Mystics.* New York: 1976.

Unterman, Isaac. *The Talmud: An Analytical Guide to Its History and Teaching.* New York: 1952.

Urbach, Ephraim. *The Sages: Their Concepts and Beliefs.* Jerusalem: 1975. Two volumes.

Van der Horst, Pieter. "Moses' Throne Vision in Ezekiel the Dramatist." *Journal of Jewish Studies* 34:1 (Spring 1983) 21–29.

Vanderkam, James C. *The Dead Sea Scrolls Today.* Grand Rapids, Mich.: 1994.

van der Toorn, Karel, Bob Becking, and Pieter W. van der Horst. *Dictionary of Deities and Demons in the Bible.* Leiden: 1995.

Vermes, Geza. "Bible and Midrash: Early Old Testament Exegesis." In *Post Biblical Jewish Studies,* 59–91. Leiden: 1975.

Vermes, Geza. *Scripture and Tradition in Judaism.* 2nd edition. Leiden: 1973.

Vermes, G., tr. *The Dead Sea Scrolls in English.* New York: 1968.

Vilnay, Zev. *Legends of Galilee, Jordan and Sinai.* Philadelphia: 1978.

Vilnay, Zev. *Legends of Jerusalem.* Philadelphia: 1973.

Vilnay, Zev. *Legends of Judea and Samaria.* Philadelphia: 1973.

Visotzky, Burton L. *Fathers of the World: Essays in Rabbinic and Patristic Literature.* Tübingen; 1995.

Visotzky, Burton, tr. *The Midrash on Proverbs.* New Haven: 1992.

Visotzky, Burton. *Reading the Book: Making the Bible a Timeless Text.* New York: 1991.

Wacholder, Ben Zion. "The Date of the Mekilta De-Rabbi Ishmael." *Hebrew Union College Annual* 39 (1968): 117–44.

Wakeman, Mary K. *God's Battle with the Monster: A Study in Biblical Imagery.* Leiden, the Netherlands: 1973.

Waldman, Nahum M. *The Recent Study of Hebrew: A Survey of the Literature with Selected Bibliography.* Cincinnati and Winona Lake: 1989.

Wallach, Shalom Meir. *Haggadah of the Chassidic Masters.* Brooklyn: 1990.

Wallenrod, Rueben. *The Literature of Modern Israel.* New York: 1956.

Wallich, Reb Moshe. *Book of Fables: The Yiddish Fable Collection of Reb Moshe Wallich.* Detroit: 1994.

Waskow, Arthur. *Godwrestling.* New York: 1978.

Waskow, Arthur. *Seasons of Our Joy.* New York: 1982.

Waxman, Meyer. *A History of Jewish Literature from the Close of the Bible to Our Own Days.* New York: 1960. Six volumes.

Weiner, Herbert. *9 1/2 Mystics: The Kabbala Today.* New York: 1969.

Weinreich, B. S. *The Prophet Elijah in Modern Yiddish Folktales.* Master's Thesis, Columbia University, 1957.

Weinreich, Beatrice Silverman, ed. *Yiddish Folktales.* New York: 1988.

Weinreich, Max. "*Lantukh:* A Jewish Hobgoblin." *YIVO Annual of Jewish Social Science* 2–3 (1947–1948): 243–251.

Weinreich, Uriel and Beatrice. *Yiddish Language and Folklore: A Selective Bibliography for Research.* The Hague: 1959.

Weiss, Joseph. *Studies in Eastern European Jewish Mysticism.* London and New York: 1985.

Werblowsky, R. J. Zwi. *Joseph Karo: Lawyer and Mystic.* Philadelphia: 1977.

Werblowsky, R. J. Zwi. "Mystical and Magical Contemplation: The Kabbalists in Sixteenth-Century Safed." *History of Religions* 1 (1961): 9–36.

Werblowsky, R. J. Zwi and Geoffrey Wigoder, eds. *The Oxford Dictionary of the Jewish Religion.* New York: 1997.

Werblowsky, R. J. Zwi. "Some Psychological Aspects of the Kabbalah." *Harvest: Journal of the Analytical Psychology Club of London* 3 (London, 1956): 77–96.

Werblowsky, R. J. Zwi, and Geoffrey Wigoder. *The Encyclopedia of the Jewish Religion.* New York: 1965.

Wertheim, Aaron. *Law and Custom in Hasidism.* Hoboken, N.J.: 1992.

Westcott, Wm. Wynn, tr. *Sepher Yetzirah: The Book of Formation and the Thirty-Two Paths of Wisdom.* New York: 1975.

Wiener, Aharon. *The Prophet Elijah in the Development of Judaism: A Depth-Psychological Study.* London: 1978.

Wiener, Leo. *The History of Yiddish Literature in the Nineteenth Century.* New York: 1972.

Wiener, Shohama Harris, ed. *The Fifty-Eighth Century: A Jewish Renewal Sourcebook.* Northvale, N.J.: 1996.

Wiesel, Elie. *A Beggar in Jerusalem.* New York: 1970.

Wiesel, Elie. *Dawn.* New York: 1961.

Wiesel, Elie. *Four Hasidic Masters and Their Struggle Against Melancholy.* Notre Dame, Ind.: 1978.

Wiesel, Elie. *The Gates of the Forest.* New York: 1966.

Wiesel. Elie. *The Golem.* New York: 1983.

Wiesel, Elie. *Messengers of God: Biblical Portraits and Legends.* New York: 1976.

Wiesel, Elie. *Night.* New York: 1960.

Wiesel, Elie. *The Oath.* New York: 1973.

Wiesel, Elie. *Sages and Dreamers: Biblical, Talmudic, and Hasidic Portraits and Legends.* New York: 1991.

Wiesel, Elie. *Somewhere a Master: Further Hasidic Portraits and Legends.* New York: 1981.

Wiesel, Elie. *Souls on Fire: Portraits and Legends of Hasidic Masters.* New York: 1972.

Wiesel, Elie. *The Testament.* New York: 1981.

Wiesel, Elie. *The Town Beyond the Wall.* New York: 1964.

Wigoder, Geoffrey, ed. *Encyclopedic Dictionary of Judaica.* New York: 1974.

Wineman, Aryeh. *Beyond Appearances: Stories from the Kabbalistic Ethical Writings.* Philadelphia: 1988.

Wineman, Aryeh. *Mystic Tales from the Zohar.* Philadelphia and Jerusalem: 1997.

Winkler, Gershom. *Dybbuk.* New York: 1980.

Winkler, Gershom. *The Golem of Prague.* New York: 1982.

Winkler, Gershom. *They Called Her Rebbe.* New York: 1992.

Wirth-Nesher, Hana. *What Is Jewish Literature?* Philadelphia: 1994.

Wisse, Ruth, ed. *The I. L. Peretz Reader.* New York: 1990.

Wolfson, Elliot R. *Along the Path: Studies in Kabbalistic Myth, Symbolism and Hermeneutics.* Albany: 1995.

Wolfson, Elliot R. *Circle in the Square: Studies in the Use of Gender in Kabbalistic Symbolism.* Albany: 1995.

Wolfson, Elliot R. *Through a Speculum that Shines: Vision and Imagination in Medieval Jewish Mysticism.* Princeton: 1994.

Wolfson, H. A. Philo. *Foundations of Religious Philosophy in Judaism, Christianity and Islam.* Cambridge, Mass.: 1962.

Wright, Addison G. *The Literary Genre Midrash.* Staten Island, N.Y.: 1967.

Yaari, Yehuda. *The Covenant: Ten Stories.* Jerusalem: 1965.

Yassif, Eli. *Jewish Folklore: An Annotated Bibliography.* New York: 1986.

Yehoshua, A. B. *The Continuing Silence of a Poet: Collected Stories.* New York: 1991.

Zabara, Joseph ben Meir. *The Book of Delight.* Philadelphia: 1912.

Zachner, R. C., ed. *Living Faiths: Judaism or the Religion of Israel.* New York: 1959.

Zahavy, Zev, ed. *Idra Zuta Kadisha.* New York: 1977.

Zakon, Miriam Stark, tr. *Tz'enah Ur'enah: The Classic Anthology of Torah Lore and Midrashic Commentary.* 1983.

Zangwill, Israel. *Children of the Ghetto.* New York: 1899.

Zangwill, Israel. *Dreamers of the Ghetto.* London: 1898.

Zangwill, Israel. *Ghetto Tragedies.* Philadelphia: 1899.

Zangwill, Israel. *The King of Schnorrers.* New York: 1899.

Zangwill, Israel. *The Mantle of Elijah.* London: 1900.

Zangwill, Israel. *The Master.* New York: 1897.

Zangwill, Israel. *Selected Works of Israel Zangwill.* Philadelphia: 1938.

Zangwill, Israel. *The Voice of Jerusalem.* London: 1920.

Zayis, Shimon, ed. *The Holy Candelabrum: Tales of the Talmud.* Jerusalem: 1988.

Zenner, Walter P. "Saints and Piecemeal Supernaturalism Among the Jerusalem Sephardim." *Anthropological Quarterly* 38 (1965): 201–217.

Zevin, S. Y. *A Treasury of Chassidic Tales on the Festivals*. Brooklyn: 1982. Two volumes.

Zevin, S. Y. *A Treasury of Chassidic Tales on the Torah*. New York: 1980. Two volumes.

Ziff, Joel. *Mirrors in Time: A Psycho-Spiritual Journey Through the Jewish Year*. Northvale, N.J.: 1996.

Zimmels, H. J. *Magicians, Theologians and Doctors*. New York: 1952.

Zimmer, Heinrich. *Myths and Symbols in Indian Art and Civilization*. New York: 1946.

Zinberg, Israel. *A History of Jewish Literature*. New York: 1972–1978. Twelve volumes.

Zornberg, Avivah Gottlieb. *Genesis: The Beginning of Desire*. Philadelphia: 1995.

Zweig, Stefan. *Jewish Legends*. New York: 1987.

Index